MW00909176

Learning
WORDPERFECT® 6.1
for Windows®

Iris Blanc

DDC Publishing

Acknowledgments

TO MY FAMILY

Alan, Pamela, Jaime and Mom
As always, thank you for your patience, support, inspiration and love.

TO MY FRIENDS AND COLLEAGUES

Shirley Dembo, Cathy Vento, Adrienne Frosch, and Paul Bergman
Thank you for your continued encouragement and support.

TO THE STAFF AT DDC

Kathy Berkemeyer, Managing Editor
Carol Havlicek, Technical Editor
Rebecca Fiala, Editor
Rosemary O'Connell, Editor
Ellen Wollensky, Editorial Assistant

TO THE STAFF AT CHASSMAN GRAPHICS

Michael Shevlin, Design and Layout
Pamela Kersage, Design and Layout

Thank you for your professionalism and coordinating efforts in the production of this book.

First DDC, Inc. Printing
Catalog No. H9

ISBN: 1-56243-256-7
UPC 7-15829-15020-0

10   9   8   7

Printed in the United States of America

Table of Contents

Table of Contents

Log of Exercises

LESSON	EXERCISE	FILENAME	ON DISK AS*
1 Introductory Basics	1	—	—
	2	—	
2 Creating and Printing Documents	3	TRY	TRY.3S
	4	TRYAGAIN	TRYAGAIN.4S
	5	LETTER	LETTER.5S
	6	BLOCK	BLOCK.6S
	7	PERSONAL	PERSONAL.7S
	A	OPEN	OPEN.2A, OPEN.2AS
	B	REGRETS	REGRETS.2B, REGRETS.2BS
3 Opening and Editing Documents	8 (3)	TRY	TRY.8, TRY.8S
	9	GOODJOB	GOODJOB.9, GOODJOB.9S
	10 (4)	TRYAGAIN	TRYAGAIN.10, TRYAGAIN.10S
	11	DIVE	DIVE.11S
	12 (5)	LETTER	LETTER.12, LETTER.12S
	13 (6)	BLOCK	BLOCK.13, BLOCK.13S
	A (2B)	REGRETS	REGRETS.3A, REGRETS.3AS
	B (2A)	OPEN	OPEN.3B, OPEN.3BS
4 Text Alignments and Enhancements	14	EXPO/RSVP	EXPO.14, RSVP.14, EXPO.14S
	15	GLOBAL	GLOBAL.15, GLOBAL.15S
	16	RSVP	RSVP.16S
	17	FOOD	FOOD.17, FOOD.17S
	18	GLOBAL	GLOBAL.18, GLOBAL.18S
	19 (17)	FOOD	FOOD.19, FOOD.19S
	20 (17, 19)	FOOD	FOOD.20, FOOD.20S
	A	COLOR	COLOR.4A, COLOR.4AS
	B	DESIGN	DESIGN.4B, DESIGN.4BS
5 Formatting and Editing Documents	21 (11)	DIVE	DIVE.21, DIVE.21S
	22	BULLETIN	BULLETIN.22, BULLETIN.22S
	23	OCR	OCR.23, OCR.23S
	24	TIPS	TIPS.24, TIPS.24S
	25 (22)	BULLETIN	BULLETIN.25, BULLETIN.25S
	26 (24)	TIPS	TIPS.26, TIPS.26S
	27 (11, 21)	DIVE	DIVE.27, DIVE.27S
	A	BATS	BATS.5A, BATS.5AS
	B	NEWS	NEWS.5B, NEWS.5BS
6 Additional Formatting and Editing	28	PAPER	PAPER.28, PAPER.28S
	29	PICNIC	PICNIC.29, PICNIC.29S
	30 (22, 25)	BULLETIN	BULLETIN.30, BULLETIN.30S
	31 (23)	OCR	OCR.31, OCR.31S
	32	JOB	JOB.32S
	33	TOURS	TOURS.33, TOURS.33S
	34	CARS	CARS.34S
	35	CAREER	CAREER.35S
	A	BULLET	BULLET.6A, BULLET.6AS
	B	SERVICES	SERVICES.6B, SERVICES.6BS
7 Multiple-Page Documents	36	NYC	NYC.36, NYC.36S
	37	PREVIEW	PREVIEW.37, PREVIEW.37S
	38 (11, 21, 27)	DIVE	DIVE.38
		DIVING	DIVING.38S
	39	SCORPION	SCORPION.39, SCORPION.39S
	40	COMPUTER	COMPUTER.40, COMPUTER.40S
	41	VOYAGE	VOYAGE.41, VOYAGE.41S
	42	USA	USA.42, USA.42S
	43 (37)	PREVIEW	PREVIEW.43, PREVIEW.43S
	44 (42)	USA	USA.44, USA.44S
	A	CHOICES	CHOICES.7A, CHOICES.7AS
	B	NUWORLD	NUWORLD.7B, NUWORLD.7BS

*S after a filename indicates a SOLUTION file.

Log of Exercises

LESSON	EXERCISE	FILENAME	ON DISK AS*
8 Windowing; Multiple Documents; Macros	45 (11, 21, 27, 38) (15) (14)	DIVE GLOBAL EXPO	DIVE.45S GLOBAL.45S EXPO.45S
	46	GLOBAL EXPO DIVE HOTELS	HOTELS.46, HOTELS.46S EXPO.46S DIVE.46 GLOBAL.46
	47	HOTELS CAYMAN	CAYMAN.47, CAYMAN47S
	48	WILL1/WILL2 WARRANTY USELASER	LASER.48 WARRANTY.46S USELASER.48S
	49	LASTWILL	LASTWILL.49, LASTWILL.49S
	50	P C DT	—
	51	SA L M	—
	52	SETTLE	SETTLE.52S
	53	M DT SA DOCUMENT	 DOCUMENT.53, DOCUMENT.53S
	54	S R M PAUSE	 PAUSE.54, PAUSE.54S
	A	TRIN WARRENT CLIENT	 CLIENT.8A, CLIENT.8AS
	B	AD SA WORKOUT	 WORKOUT.8B, WORKOUT.8BS
9 Columns and Tables	55	COCOA	COCOA.55, COCOA.55S
	56	GOODBYE	GOODBYE.56, GOODBYE.56S
	57	AGELESS	AGELESS.57, AGELESS.57S
	58	PHONE	PHONE.58, PHONE.58S
	59	WAGES	WAGES.59, WAGES.59S
	60	CRUISE	CRUISE.60S
	61	SALARY	SALARY.61S
	62	PURCHASE	PURCHASE.62S
	63(60)	CRUISE	CRUISE.63, CRUISE.63S
	64	ROSEWOOD	ROSEWOOD.64S
	65 (61)	SALARY	SALARY.65, SALARY.65S
	66 (60, 63)	CRUISE	CRUISE.66, CRUISE.66S
	67 (60, 63, 66) (61, 65)	CRUISE SALARY	CRUISE.67, CRUISE.67S SALARY.67, SALARY.67S
	68 (64)	ROSEWOOD	ROSEWOOD.68, ROSEWOOD.68S
	A	IS	IS.9AS
	B	COURSES/ COURSES1	COURSES.9B COURSES1.9BS
10 Calculate and Sort	69	RECEIPT	RECEIPT.69, RECEIPT.69S
	70	COMPARE	COMPARE.70, COMPARE.70S
	71	ABC	ABC.71, ABC.71S
	72	PRICE	PRICE.72, PRICE.72S
	73	EXPENSES	EXPENSES.73, EXPENSES.73S
	74	SORT/SORT1/ SORT2	SORT.74, SORT1.74S SORT2.74S
	75	DEBT/DEBT1/ DEBT2	DEBT.75, DEBT1.75S DEBT2.75S
	76	JOIN/JOIN1/ JOIN2/JOIN3/JOIN4	JOIN.76, JOIN1.76S JOIN2.76S, JOIN3.76S, JOIN4.76S
	A	BRANCH	BRANCH.10A, BRANCH.10AS
	B	QTRSALES	QTRSALES.10B, QTRSALES.10BS

Log of Exercises

LESSON	EXERCISE	FILENAME	ON DISK AS*
11 Merge	77	INVITE.FRM	INVITEFR.77
	78	INVITE.DAT	INVITEDA.78
	79	INVITE.FI	INVITEFI.79S
	80	DUE.FRM	DUEFRM.80
		DUE.DAT	DUEDAT.80
	81	DUE.FI	DUEFI.81S
	82	BUY.FRM	BUYFRM.82
		BUY.DAT	BUYDAT.82
		BUY.FI	BUYFI.82S
	83	SHOW.FRM	SHOWFRM.83
		SHOW.DAT	SHOWDAT.83
		SHOW.FI	SHOWFI.83S
	84	MISTAKE.FRM	MISTAKEF.84,
		MISTAKE.DAT	MISTAKED.84
		MISTAKE.FI	MISTAKFI.84S
	A	TRAVEL.FRM	TRAVELFR.11A
		TRAVEL.DAT	TRAVELDA.11A
		TRAVEL.FI	TRAVELFI.11A, TRAVELFI.11S
	B	STOCK.FRM	STOCKFR.11B
		STOCK.DAT	STOCKDA.11B
		STOCK.FI	STOCKFI.11S
12 Graphics	85	IMAGES	IMAGES.85S
	86	TEXTBOX	TEXTBOX.86S
	87	PICTURE	PICTURE.87S
	88	GLOBELET	GLOBELET.88S
	89	CARDLET	CARDLET.89S
	90	BORDERS	BORDERS.90S
	91	EXTINCT	EXTINCT.91S
	92	RSVP2	RSVP.92, RSVP.92S
	93	DRAGON	DRAGON.93S
	94	PAPER1	PAPER.94
		PAPER2	PAPER1.94S, PAPER2.94S
	95	WISH	WISH.95S
	96	DESIGN1	DESIGN.96, DESIGN1.96
	97	INN	INN.97S
	98	FOOD1	FOOD.98, FOOD1.98S
	99 (55)	COCOA	COOCA.99, COCOA.99S
	100	MUSIC	MUSIC.OOS
	101	JOURNEY	JOURNEY.O1S
	A	CONDOR	CONDOR12.AS
	B	MAGAZINE	MAGAZINE.13S
13 Templates, Envelopes and Labels	102	ANNOUNCE	ANNOUNCE.02S
	103	VIDEO	VIDEO.03S
	104	RESPONSE	RESPONSE.04S
	105	FAX	FAX.05S
	106	CALENDAR	CALENDAR.06S
	107	RESUME	RESUME.07S
	108	ALUMNI	ALUMNI.08S
	109 (2B, 3A)	REGRETS	—
	110	LABEL	—
	A	SHOWIT	SHOWIT12.AS
	B	MYRESUME	—
14 Managing Files; Preferences	111	—	
	112	LUNCH	LUNCH112.S
	113	—	
	114	—	

Directory of Documents

INTRODUCTION

LEARNING WORDPERFECT® 6.1 FOR WINDOWS®

LEARNING WORDPERFECT 6.1 FOR WINDOWS will introduce the user to WordPerfect 6.1 for Windows word processing software on an IBM PC or compatible computer.

Each lesson in this book explains WordPerfect concepts in step-by-step instructions, provides numerous exercises to apply those concepts, and illustrates the necessary keystrokes or mouse actions to complete the applications. Lesson summary exercises are provided to challenge and reinforce the concepts learned.

After completing the 114 exercises in this book, students will be able to use the features of WordPerfect 6.1 for Windows software with ease.

FEATURES OF THIS TEXT

- Lesson Objectives
- Exercise Objectives
- WordPerfect 6.1 for Windows concepts and vocabulary
- A Log of Exercises, which lists exercise and data/solutions disk filenames in exercise order
- A Directory of Files, which lists filenames alphabetically and the exercise numbers in which they were used
- Screen Illustrations
- Exercises to apply each word processing concept.
- End-of-Lesson summary exercises to review and test your knowledge of lesson concepts
- Cautions and warnings
- Keystrokes necessary to complete each application
- Appendix of ClipArt
- Appendix of proofreaders' marks
- Index
- Comprehensive Instructor's Guide

THE DATA DISK AND SOLUTIONS DISK

A data disk is available and may be purchased from the publisher. Use the data files to complete an exercise without keyboarding lengthy text. If you do not purchase or choose not to use the data disk, you may create the exercises as directed. Each data file is named using a descriptive name and an exercise number (example: DIVE.11).

A solutions disk is also available and may be purchased from the publisher. Use the solutions files to compare your work to the solution on disk. Each solution file is named using a descriptive name, an exercise number and the letter "s" (example: DIVE.11S).

NOTE: *The data disk and solutions disk are not provided with this text. They may be purchased separately from the publisher.*

HOW TO USE THIS BOOK

Each exercise contains four parts:

■ NOTES

- Explain the WordPerfect concept being introduced.
- Graphic symbols to call your attention to

 Cautions and Warnings

 Exercise Objectives

 Tips for using a feature or completing an exercise

■ EXERCISE DIRECTIONS

- Tell you how to complete the exercise.

A disk icon appearing in the exercise directions 💾 indicates that the file noted is available on the data disk.

■ EXERCISE APPLICATION

- Applies the concept that was introduced.

■ KEYSTROKE/MOUSE PROCEDURES

- *Outline the keystrokes or mouse actions required to complete the exercise.*

- *Keystrokes and mouse actions are provided only when a new concept is introduced. Therefore, if you forget the keystrokes and/or mouse procedure for completing a task, use WordPerfect's Help feature or the book's index to locate the page where the keystroke and/or mouse procedures are provided. WordPerfect 6.1 for Windows screens and icons are provided when necessary to clarify lesson concepts.*

- *After reading the Notes section introducing the WordPerfect concept, students should then complete the exercise using the keystrokes provided.*

THE INSTRUCTOR'S GUIDE

While this text can be used as a self-paced learning book, a comprehensive instructor's guide is available. The instructor's guide contains the following:

- Lesson objectives
- Exercise objectives
- Related vocabulary
- Points to emphasize
- Exercise settings

LESSON 1

Exercises 1-2

- The Keyboard

- The Mouse

- Starting WordPerfect 6.1 for Windows

- The WordPerfect 6.1 for Windows Screen

- Selecting Menu Items

- Pull-down Menus

- QuickMenu

- The Dialog Box

- Getting Help

- Exit

EXERCISE

1-2

▪ **THE KEYBOARD** ▪ **THE MOUSE** ▪ **STARTING WORDPERFECT 6.1 FOR WINDOWS**
▪ **THE WORDPERFECT 6.1 FOR WINDOWS SCREEN** ▪ **SELECTING MENU ITEMS**
▪ **PULL-DOWN MENUS** ▪ **QUICKMENU** ▪ **THE DIALOG BOX** ▪ **GETTING HELP** ▪ **EXIT**

NOTES:

The Keyboard

▪ In addition to the **alphanumeric keys** found
on typewriters, computers contain:

Function Keys (F1 through F12) that
perform special functions and are located
across the top of an enhanced keyboard.

Modifier Keys (two each: Shift, Alt and Ctrl)
that are used with other keys to select certain
commands.

To use a modifier key (Shift, Alt or Ctrl) with
another key, hold down the modifier key while
you tap the other key.

Numeric Keys that allow you to enter
numbers quickly when the Num Lock key
(located above the 7/Home key) is pressed.
When Num Lock is OFF, the arrow keys and
other application keys found on the numbers
(Home, PgUp, End, PgDn) are activated.

Escape (Esc) Key is used to cancel some
commands.

Enter Keys (most keyboards have two) that
are used to move the insertion point to the
next line or may be used to complete a
command.

Insertion Point Movement Keys
(Arrows, Home, End, Page Up, Page Down)
that move the insertion point (the blinking
marker that indicates where the next character
to be keyed will appear) through the
text in the direction indicated by the key.

The Mouse

▪ When the **mouse** is rolled on the tabletop, a
corresponding movement of the mouse pointer
occurs on screen. The mouse pointer will not
move if the mouse is lifted up and placed back
on the tabletop.

▪ The mouse pointer changes its shape to signal
different functions:

When the mouse is pointing anywhere on the
document window screen, it looks like an
"I" (I). When the mouse is pointing to a menu
item or border area, it changes to an arrow (↖).

When the mouse is pointing between border
areas (at the top of the screen), it may change to
a "hand" (✋).

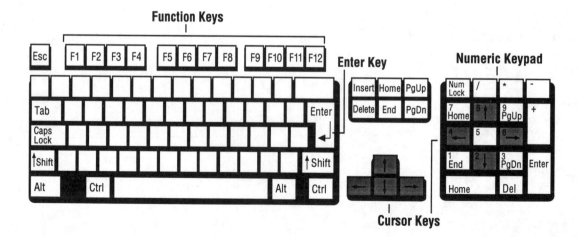

Function Keys

Enter Key

Numeric Keypad

Cursor Keys

- The following mouse terms and corresponding actions are described below and will be used throughout the book:

TERM	ACTION
Point	Roll the mouse in any direction until the pointer is on a specific item.
Click	Quickly press and release the mouse button.
	NOTE: Use the left mouse button unless otherwise instructed.
Double-Click	Press and release the mouse button twice in rapid succession.
Drag	Press and hold down the mouse button while rolling the mouse.

Starting WordPerfect for Windows

- At the Program Manager screen, a small **icon** is displayed representing WordPerfect 6.1 for Windows. Point to the icon and double-click.

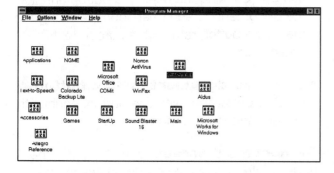

- Another set of icons should appear. These are called **program group icons**.

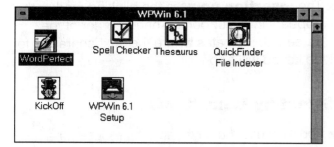

- To open WordPerfect so that a document screen appears, double-click on the WordPerfect application icon.

The WordPerfect 6.1 for Windows Screen

- When WordPerfect 6.1 for Windows is accessed, the following screen appears:

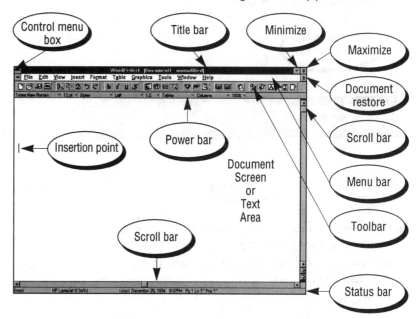

- There are many different **bars** available in WordPerfect 6.1 for Windows which display when the screen appears (unless changes were made when WordPerfect was installed). They are: title bar, menu bar, Toolbar, Power Bar, scroll bars and status bar.

- The **title bar**, located at the very top of the WordPerfect screen, indicates the name of the program, the directory and the name of the current document.

    EXAMPLE:
    WordPerfect - [C:\ngwp61\first]

- The **menu bar**, located below the title bar, contains a group of selections that lets you perform most WordPerfect tasks. Within each main menu item are numerous submenu commands.

- The **Toolbar**, located below the menu bar, contains icons (symbols or graphic images that represents a command or function) that execute functions. The Toolbar is accessible only with the mouse. Use the Toolbar as a shortcut to execute a command.

■ When you point to the bottom of a button on the Toolbar or Power Bar, a **QuickTip** displays and an explanation of that button's function is displayed on the title bar.

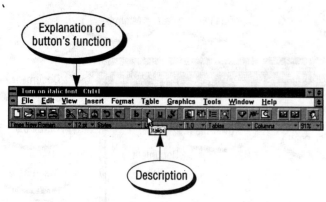

■ The **Power Bar**, located below the Toolbar, contains buttons that represent the most frequently used text editing and text layout features. The Power Bar is accessible only with the mouse.

■ The **scroll bars** appear along the right side of the screen (vertical scroll bar) and across the bottom of the screen (horizontal scroll bar). The scroll bars, accessed only with the mouse, allow you to see parts of the document that are not currently visible on the screen.

■ The **status bar**, located below the text area at the bottom of the screen, displays information about your document:

General status	Indicates whether you are working in Insert or Typeover mode. Displays information about columns, tables, macros, and other features when applicable.
Printer	Shows name and type of printer.
Select on/off	Indicates when text is selected (highlighted).
Date	Displays current system date.
Time	Displays current time.

Pg 1	Displays the page number on which you are currently working.
	Displays the vertical position of the insertion point (in inches), as measured from the top of the page.
Pos 1"	Displays the horizontal position of the insertion point (in inches), from the left edge of the page.

■ You can hide or display the Toolbar and/or Power Bar to make more room on your screen. The Toolbar may be positioned at the top, bottom, left or right of your screen.

■ Other parts of the WordPerfect 6.1 for Windows screen include:

• The **control menu box** ▭ is located at the left end of the title bar. Clicking it once gives you a pull-down menu; clicking it twice exits the window.

• The **minimize** ▾ and **maximize buttons** ▴ are located at the right end of the title bar. Clicking the minimize button shrinks the document screen to an icon. Clicking the maximize button returns the screen to its original size.

• Clicking the **document restore button** ▢, located below the minimize button, shrinks the current document window.

■ The **document screen** (or text area) is the large, white part of the screen on which you create and edit documents.

■ The **insertion point** is the blinking marker that appears in the upper left-hand corner of the screen. It indicates where the next character to be keyed will appear.

Selecting Menu Items

■ You may use the keyboard, the mouse, or a combination of both to select menu items. **Keyboard shortcut keys** may also be used to accomplish tasks.

To issue a command:

- Use the mouse to point to a menu item and click once, or

- Press Alt + underlined letter to choose a menu item and make a selection, or

- Click a button on the Toolbar or Power Bar, or

- Press keyboard shortcut keys.

■ In this text, procedures for completing a task will be illustrated with mouse actions on the left, keyboard commands on the right, and keyboard shortcut keys below the heading. If a Toolbar or Power Bar button can be used, it too will be illustrated. You may use whichever method you find most convenient.

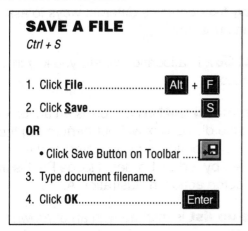

SAVE A FILE
Ctrl + S

1. Click **File** .... Alt + F
2. Click **Save** .... S
OR
   • Click Save Button on Toolbar ..... 🖫
3. Type document filename.
4. Click **OK** .... Enter

Pull-Down Menus

■ Once a main menu item is accessed, a **pull-down menu** appears listing additional options.

Note the pull-down menu that appears when Edit is accessed:

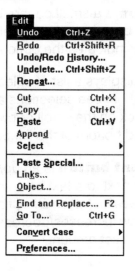

■ You will notice some options are dimmed while others appear black. **Dimmed options** are not available for selection at this time while black options are.

■ A **check mark** next to a pull-down item means that the option is currently selected.

NOTE: None of the items in the Edit pull-down menu contain check marks. To see submenu selections with check marks, select View from the main menu bar.

■ An item followed by an **arrow** opens a **cascading menu** with additional choices.

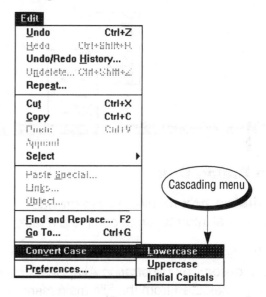

Cascading menu

■ An item followed by an **ellipsis** (...) opens a dialog box.

To access commands from the pull-down menu:

- Use the mouse to point to the item and click once, or

- Press the underlined letter, or

- Press the shortcut keys shown to the right of word commands.

QuickMenus

■ Clicking the *right* mouse button displays a **QuickMenu**, listing options that may be used to access tasks. Depending on the location of the insertion point when the right mouse button is pressed, QuickMenus display different options.

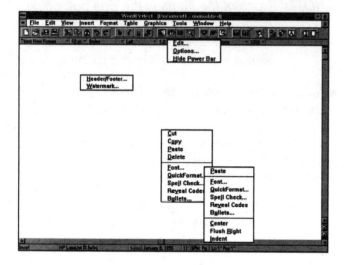

The Dialog Box

■ A **dialog box** requires you to provide additional information to complete a task.

Note the dialog boxes below and top right. The Print dialog box *(illustration A)* appears after Print is selected from the File main menu; the Font dialog box *(illustration B)* appears after Font is selected from the Format main menu.

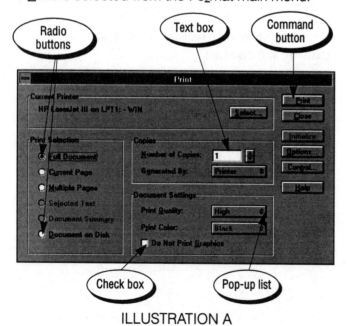

ILLUSTRATION A

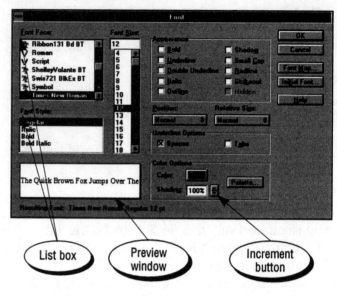

ILLUSTRATION B

■ A **dialog box** contains different ways to ask you for information:

- A **text box** is a location where you key in information.

- A **command button** performs an action or closes the dialog box without performing the action. One button is preselected and is indicated by a dark border. Notice Print is the preselected action in illustration A.

- A **pop-up list** is marked with an up/down arrow. Clicking and holding the pop-up list arrow causes a short list of options to appear. Choose one of the options on the list.

- A **radio button** is a round button which is part of a group of options. Only one option in the group may be selected at a time.

- A **check box** is a small square box where options may be selected or deselected. An "X" in the box indicates the option is selected.

- A **list box** displays a list of selections *(see illustration B)*. To see selections at the bottom of the list, click on the scroll arrows appearing at the top and bottom of the list box.

- An **increment button** is an up/down arrow button, often next to a text box, which contains a number *(see illustration B)*. Clicking the up/down arrow increases/decreases the text box entry by a set amount.

- A **preview window** shows the effect of a selected item *(illustration B)*.

To move around a dialog box:

- Use the Tab key, or

- Press Shift + Tab to move backwards.

To select an item:

- Press the underlined letter of the item, or

- Click the item, or

- Tab to the item, then press Enter.

Getting Help

- Help may be accessed by clicking on <u>H</u>elp in the main menu or pressing Alt + H. The following pull-down menu options will assist you:

```
 Help
 Contents...
 Search for Help on...
 How Do I...

 Macros...
 Coaches...
 Upgrade Expert...
 Tutorial...

 About WordPerfect...
```

- **Contents** allows you to choose from a list of items with which you might need help.

- **Search for Help on** allows you to type in a help topic. This gives you an alphabetical list of topics beginning with the letters you typed.

- **How Do I** provides help on common tasks.

- **Macros** provides macro information.

- **Coaches** walk you through procedures for specified tasks.

- **Upgrade Expert** provides help moving to WordPerfect 6.1 from a previous word processor.

- **Tutorial** provides short exercises for each basic WP task.

- **About WordPerfect** provides system status information.

Exit WordPerfect for Windows

- When you have completed the work session, you may exit the WordPerfect program. If text is on the screen, WordPerfect will ask if you wish to save your work. (Saving a file will be covered in Lesson 2.)

EXERCISE DIRECTIONS:

 In this exercise, you will select menu items and become familiar with menu options. You will also exit WordPerfect.

1. Roll the mouse on the tabletop (or the mouse pad) up, down, left, right.

2. Point to File and click once (or press Alt + F) to select this menu item.

   Note the selections on the pull-down menu.

3. Click once off the menu (or press Escape) to close the File menu.

4. Point to Edit and click once (or press Alt + E) to select this menu item.

   Note the selections on the pull-down menu.

5. Click once off the menu (or press Escape) to close the Edit menu.

6. Select View from the menu.

   Note the selections on the pull-down menu.

   If your Toolbar and/or Power Bar is not displayed:

   • Click View.

   • Click Toolbar, and/or

   • Click Power Bar

7. Close the View menu.

8. Select Format from the menu.

   Note the selections on the pull-down menu.

9. Close the Format menu.

10. Select each remaining main menu item.

    Note the pull-down selections on each menu.

    REMINDER: To close a menu, click once off the menu, click another menu item or press Escape.

11. Point to each Toolbar icon.

    Note the QuickTip and the explanation in the title bar.

12. Point to each Power Bar icon.

    Note the QuickTip and the explanation in the title bar.

13. Exit the WordPerfect program.

14. If prompted to save changes to Doc 1, click No.

EXERCISE DIRECTIONS:

 In this exercise, you will hide and display the Toolbar and Power Bar. You will also gain practice moving around dialog boxes and using Help.

1. Select <u>V</u>iew from the main menu.

2. Display the Toolbar and Power Bar. If they are already displayed, skip to step 5.

   Note the check mark next to each after they have been selected.

3. Hide the Power Bar.

4. Select <u>E</u>dit from the main menu.

   Note the gray selections.

5. Select <u>F</u>ile from the main menu.

6. Select <u>P</u>rint.

   Note the dialog box selections. Use the Tab key to move around the dialog box.

   • Double-click in <u>N</u>umber of Copies text box. Type 3.

   • Click down increment arrow twice to return setting to 1.

7. Exit the Print dialog box (click <u>C</u>lose or press Escape).

8. Press F9 to access the Font dialog box.

   Note the preview window display.

   • Click any item in the Font Face list other than the one currently highlighted.

   Note the new display in the Preview window.

9. Exit the Font box without making changes (click Cancel or press Escape).

10. Select <u>H</u>elp from the main menu.

11. Select <u>C</u>ontents.

    • Click <u>S</u>earch.

    • Type DOS.

    • Double-click DOS keyboard template.

    • Click <u>G</u>o To.

    • Click C<u>l</u>ose.

12. Exit WordPerfect (click <u>F</u>ile, click E<u>x</u>it).

13. If prompted to save Doc 1, click <u>N</u>o.

NOTE: *Mouse action procedures are indicated on the left; keyboard procedures are indicated on the right; "shortcut keys" (if any) are indicated below title. You may use either the mouse or the keystrokes or a combination of both.*

SELECT A MENU ITEM

1. Click menu item .. [Alt] + *underlined letter*

2. Click submenu item ....*underlined letter*

CLOSE A MENU

Click off the menu .... [Esc] or [Alt]

DISPLAY TOOLBAR/ POWER BAR

—*POWER BAR*—

1. Click **V**iew .... [Alt] + [V]

2. Click **P**ower Bar .... [O]

—*TOOLBAR*—

1. Click **V**iew .... [Alt] + [V]

2. Click **T**oolbar .... [T]

NOTE: *To hide Toolbar/Power Bar, repeat procedure.*

EXIT WORDPERFECT

Alt + F4

1. Click **F**ile .... [Alt] + [F]

2. Click E**x**it .... [X]

   OR

1. Click WordPerfect Control Box .... [—]

2. Click **C**lose .... [C]

   OR

   Double-click WordPerfect
   Control Box .... [—]

HELP

F1

1. Click **H**elp .... [Alt] + [H]

2. Click a help option:

   • **C**ontents .... [C]

   • **S**earch for Help On .... [S]

   • **H**ow Do I .... [H]

   • **M**acros .... [M]

   • C**o**aches .... [O]

   • **U**pgrade Expert .... [U]

   • **T**utorial .... [T]

   • **A**bout WordPerfect .... [A]

EXIT HELP

Double-click on Control Menu Box .... [—]

OR

1. Click **F**ile .... [Alt] + [F]

2. Click E**x**it .... [X]

   OR

   Click **Close** button .... [—]

LESSON 2

Exercises 3-7

- Defaults

- Creating, Closing, Saving and Exiting a New Document

- Using the Tab Key

- QuickCorrect

- Spell Check

- Insertion Point Movements

- Scrolling a Document

- Creating a Business Letter

- Previewing a Document

- The Date Feature

- Printing

- The Caps Lock Key

- Creating a Personal Business Letter

EXERCISE

▪ DEFAULTS ▪ CREATING, CLOSING, SAVING AND EXITING A NEW DOCUMENT

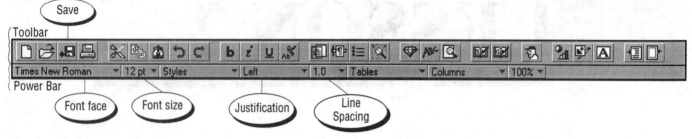

NOTES:

Defaults

▪ **Defaults** are preset conditions within the program. Settings such as margins, tabs, line spacing, type style, type size and text alignment are automatically set by the WordPerfect program. (Changing default settings will be covered in later lessons.)

Defaults may be changed at any time and as many times as desired throughout a document. Defaults may be changed to affect all documents or individual ones.

▪ **Margins** are set at 1" on the left, right, top and bottom. (WordPerfect assumes you are working on a standard 8.5" x 11" sheet of paper.) The line (Ln) and position (Pos) indicators on the status bar are defaulted to inches; when the insertion point is at the left margin, the **Pos** indicator displays 1", indicating a 1" left margin. The **Ln** indicator displays 1", indicating a 1" top margin. (Setting margins will be covered in Lesson 5.)

▪ When you begin WordPerfect, note that the Power Bar indicates some default settings. When settings are changed, the new settings will display on the Power Bar.

• **Font face** is set to Times New Roman or Courier (depending on your printer).

• **Font size** is set to 12 point (12 pt).

• **Justification** is set to Left.

• **Line spacing** is set for single (1.0).

Creating a Document

▪ The insertion point will be flashing at the beginning of the document. Text appears at this point when you start typing.

▪ As you type, the **Pos** indicator on the bottom right of the screen changes. As text advances to another line, the **Ln** indicator also changes. The **Pos** indicator shows the insertion point's horizontal position on the page, while the **Ln** indicator shows its vertical position.

▪ As you type, text automatically advances to the next line. This is called **word wrap**. You only have to use the Enter key at the end of a short line or to begin a new paragraph.

▪ Use the Backspace key to correct immediate errors to the left of the insertion point.

Closing a Document

▪ Most documents are saved on a disk for future use. However, you do not necessarily need to save all documents. If you want to discard your document, you can click the document control box at the left side of the menu bar and select Close. WordPerfect will ask if you want to save your work. Responding *No* will close your document and give you a new document window. You may also close your document by selecting Close from the File main menu. Again, WordPerfect will ask if you wish to save your work. Respond *No* to close without saving.

Saving a New Document

- Documents may be saved on a removable disk or on an internal hard drive.

- Documents that are saved must be named for identification. A **filename** may contain a maximum of eight characters, with no spaces, and may have an optional extension of one to three characters. The **file extension** may be used to further identify your document. The filename and extension are separated by a period.

    EXAMPLE: travel.box

- If you do not include a filename extension, WordPerfect automatically assigns .wpd (WordPerfect document) as the extension. Filenames are not case sensitive; they may be typed in either upper- or lowercase.

- When saving a file, you must preface the file name with the drive letter where the disk is located. A disk drive letter is usually "A" or "B"; the hard drive letter is usually "C." Thus, if you were saving a document named "TRYAGAIN" to a disk located in a disk drive, the filename would appear as:

    a:tryagain (A colon separates drives from filenames.)
    or
    b:tryagain

- If you save to the hard drive, you may indicate a specific location or **directory** on the drive where you want your document saved. Think of a hard drive as a file cabinet; think of a drawer in the file cabinet as the directory; think of a folder in the drawer as a **subdirectory**. Thus, if you were saving a document named "tryagain" to the hard drive, it would automatically be saved to the default directory/subdirectories which is c:\office\wpwin\wpdocs. The filename would appear as follows:

    c:\office\wpwin\wpdocs\tryagain.wpd

- A **colon** (:) separates drives from directories and filenames; a **backslash** (\) separates directories from subdirectories and filenames.

- To save a document for the first time, select Save from the File main menu or click the Save icon 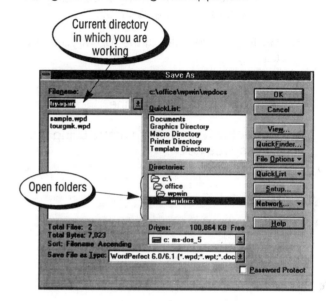 on the Toolbar.

- When you save a document for the first time, the following Save As dialog box appears:

- Note the open folders in the Directories box. These tell you that you are currently working in "wpdocs" which is a subdirectory of "wpwin" which is a subdirectory of "office," all of which are on the C drive (hard drive). Your saved file will actually reside in the subdirectory "wpdocs." To save a file in this directory/subdirectory, type the name of your file in the Filename text box.

- Once your document is named, the filename appears in the title bar.

- After saving your document for the first time, you can save the document again and continue working (update it) by selecting Save from the File main menu or clicking on the Save button on the Toolbar. The Save As dialog box does not reappear; it simply saves any changes you have made to your file. *Save often to prevent losing data.*

- Documents may also be saved by selecting Save As from the File main menu. Use this command when you want to save your document under a different filename or in a different drive/directory.

EXERCISE DIRECTIONS:

 In this exercise, you will create a document, use word wrap, correct immediate errors using the Backspace key and save the exercise.

1. Begin the exercise at the top of your screen (Ln 1").

2. Keyboard the *first* paragraph, allowing the text to wrap to the next line.

3. Correct only immediate errors using the Backspace key.

4. Close the file without saving it.

5. Begin the exercise again and complete it. Press the Enter key twice to begin a new paragraph.

6. Save the exercise; name it **TRY**.

7. Close the document window.

As you type, notice the "Pos" indicator on your status bar change as the position of your insertion point changes.

The wraparound feature allows the operator to decide on line endings, making the use of Enter unnecessary except at the end of a paragraph or short line. Each file is saved on a disk or hard drive for recall. Documents must be given a name for identification.

EXERCISE

4

▪ USING THE TAB KEY ▪ QUICKCORRECT ▪ SPELL CHECK

NOTES:

Using the Tab Key

- Tab stops are preset .5" apart. Each time the Tab key is pressed, the insertion point advances half an inch. Therefore, when the insertion point is at the left margin (1") and the Tab key is pressed once, the Pos indicator shows 1.5".

- Defaults may be changed at any time and as many times as desired throughout a document. Thus, if you wanted to tab .8" instead of .5", this could be done. (Changing defaults will be covered in a later lesson.)

QuickCorrect

- The **QuickCorrect** feature automatically replaces common spelling errors and mistyped words with the correct text as soon as you press the Spacebar.

- There are numerous words already in the QuickCorrect dictionary. However, you can enter words that you commonly misspell into the QuickCorrect dictionary by selecting QuickCorrect from the Tools main menu.

- If you find this feature annoying, you can deselect the Replace Words as You Type option.

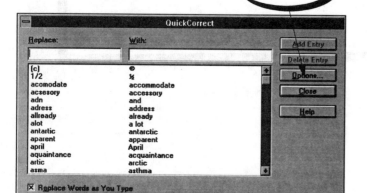

- By selecting Options from the dialog box shown below left, you can specify other types of corrections in the QuickCorrect Options dialog box which follows.

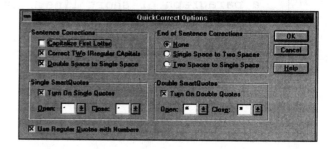

- **Capitalize First Letter** automatically capitalizes the first letter of a sentence.

- **Correct TWo IRregular CApitals** automatically converts two initial capital letters of a word to an initial capital letter and a lowercase second letter.

- **Double Space to Single Space** automatically eliminates double spaces between words in a sentence.

- **Single Space to Two Spaces** automatically converts a single space at the end of a sentence to two spaces.

- **Two Spaces to Single Space** automatically converts two spaces at the end of a sentence to a single space.

- **Turn On Single Quotes/Turn On Double Quotes** allows you to use quotation characters you select from the drop-down list.

- **Use Regular Quotes with Numbers** allows you to use a straight line quote following typed numbers instead of the single or double close quote.

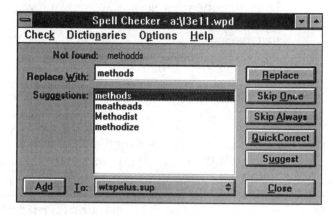

Spell Check

- The WordPerfect **Spell Check** feature checks your document for general spelling errors, double words, words containing numbers, and irregular capitalization.

- A word, a sentence, a section of a page, an entire page or an entire document may be checked for spelling errors. When a misspelled or unrecognized word is found, Spell Check offers possible alternatives so you can replace the error.

- Spell Check may be accessed by selecting Spell Check from the Tools main menu or by clicking the Speller button on the Toolbar [image]. You may also click the *right* mouse button in the document window and select Spell Check.

The following dialog box will appear:

- Words may be added to the supplementary dictionary before, after or during the Spell Check session.

- To avoid having proper names flagged as incorrect spellings during the Spell Check session, add them to the supplementary dictionary.

- Spell Check does not find errors in word usage (e.g., using *their* instead of *there*). Finding usage errors will be covered when Grammatik is introduced in Lesson 6.

- You can use QuickCorrect inside Spell Check to add a word and its replacement to the correction list. Any word added to the correction list (through the QuickCorrect option button) will be automatically corrected during the Spell Check session.

EXERCISE DIRECTIONS:

In this exercise, you will type two short paragraphs using word wrap and purposely misspell several words. After typing the word incorrectly and pressing the Spacebar, you will note the correct spelling appear for several words. You will then use Spell Check to correct the other misspellings.

1. Start with a clear screen.

2. Begin the exercise at the top of your screen (1").

3. Access the QuickCorrect feature. Be sure Replace Words as You Type has been selected.

4. Keyboard the paragraphs on the following page, exactly as shown, including the circled misspelled words. Allow the text to word wrap to the next line. Press the Enter key twice to begin a new paragraph. Press the Tab key once to indent the paragraph.

5. Spell check the document.

6. Save the exercise using the Save button on the Toolbar; name it **TRYAGAIN**.

7. Close the document window.

TAB

Press Tab .... Tab

QUICKCORRECT

Ctrl + Shift + F1

1. Click **Tools**............................ Alt + T

2. Click **QuickCorrect**..................... Q

3. Select **Replace Words as You Type** option.

   To add words to QuickCorrect dictionary:

   a. Click **Replace** text box. ...... Alt + R

   b. Type commonly misspelled word to be included.

   c. Click **With** text box............ Alt + W

   d. Type corrected version of word.

   To select QuickCorrect options:

   a. Click **Options**.................... Alt + O

   b. Click desired options.

   c. Click **OK** .... Enter

4. Click **Close**.................... Alt + C

SPELL CHECK

Ctrl + F1

   Click Speller button on Toolbar.........

OR

1. Click *right* mouse button in document window.

2. Click **Spell Check**.................... L

3. Skip to step 3.

OR

1. Click **Tools**......................... Alt + T

2. Click **Spell Check**............................... S

   To check anything other than the full document:

   a. Click **Check**.................................. K

   b. Click a spell check option:

      • **Word** .... W

      • **Sentence**................................. C

      • **Paragraph** .... A

      • **Page**................................. P

      • **Document** .... D

      • **To End of Document** .... E

      • **Selected Text**........................... S

      • **Text Entry Box**.......................... T

      • **Number of Pages**..................... N

3. Click **Start** .... S

   If an error is found, click on one or more options:

   • **Replace** .... R
   to replace word with correctly spelled word.

   • **Skip Once** .... O
   to ignore selected word and continue.

   • **Skip Always**............................ A
   to ignore all occurrences of word in document.

   • **QuickCorrect**............................ Q
   to correct a word in the QuickCorrect dictionary.

   • **Add** .... D
   to add word to WP dictionary.

   • **Suggest** .... U
   to see offered spelling suggestions.

   • **Replace With**............................... W

   • Highlight correct spelling from list of **Suggestions**................. E

   If correct spelling is not found:

   • Enter correct spelling of word.......... W
   in **Replace With** text box.

   • Click **Replace**................................ R

4. Click **Close**................................. Enter

WordPerfect is simple to use since you can begin typing as soon as you enter (teh) program.

(THe) way text will lay out or "format" on a page is set by the WordPerfect program. For example, margins are set for 1" on the left (adn) 1" on the right; line (spaceing) is set for single space; tabs are set to advance the (insersion) point 1/2 inch each time the tab key is pressed. Formats may be changed at any time and as many times (throughtout) the document.

EXERCISE

5

▪ INSERTION POINT MOVEMENTS ▪ CREATING A BUSINESS LETTER
▪ PREVIEWING A DOCUMENT ▪ SCROLLING A DOCUMENT

NOTES:

Insertion Point Movements

▪ As noted earlier, the **insertion point** is the blinking vertical bar that shows you where you are in the document.

▪ You may move the insertion point using the keyboard or the mouse:

• **Keyboard:** Press the arrow key in the direction you wish the insertion point to move. You may use the arrow keys located on the numeric keypad or (depending on your keyboard) the separate arrow keys located to the left of the keypad. You can express move the insertion point from one point on the document to another using special key combinations *(see keystrokes on page 22).*

• **Mouse:** Move the mouse pointer to where you want to place the insertion point. Then, click the *left* mouse button.

▪ The insertion point will only move through text, spaces or codes. The insertion point stops moving when the end or beginning of your document is reached.

Scrolling a Document

▪ To move the insertion point to a part of the document that does not appear on screen, you can **scroll** your document vertically by clicking with your mouse on the **scroll arrows** (up/down arrows) on the right of your document screen.

To scroll through a document quickly, you may click and drag the **scroll box** (located on the **scroll bar**) up or down. Dragging the scroll box down or clicking the scroll down arrow scrolls the page up; dragging the scroll box up or clicking the scroll up arrow scrolls the page down.

▪ To scroll one page up or down, you may click on the Page Up/Page Down arrows.

▪ While the **horizontal scroll bars** are seldom used, they horizontally scroll a document.

▪ You may choose to hide scroll bars so they do not display on the screen.

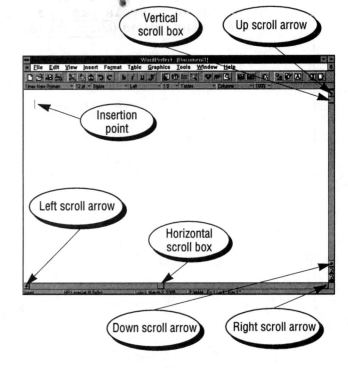

Creating a Business Letter

▪ There are a variety of letter styles for business and personal use.

▪ The parts of a business letter and the vertical spacing of letter parts are the same regardless of the style used.

- A business letter is made up of eight parts:
  1. **date** 2. **inside address** (to whom and where the letter is going) 3. **salutation**
  4. **body** 5. **closing** 6. **signature line**
  7. **title line** 8. **reference initials** (the first set of initials identifies the person who wrote the letter; the second set of initials identifies the person who typed the letter).

- Whenever you see "yo" as part of the reference initials in an exercise, substitute *your own* initials.

- Most business letters are printed on letterhead paper.

- In the inside address, there are two spaces between the state abbreviation and the zip code.

- A letter generally begins 2.5" down from the top of a page. If the letter is long, it may begin 2" from the top. If the letter is short, it may begin beyond 2.5".

- Margins and the size of the characters (type size) may also be adjusted to accommodate longer or shorter correspondence. (Changing margins and type size will be covered in a later lesson.)

- The letter style illustrated in this exercise is a **modified-block** business letter, since the date, closing, signature and title lines begin at the center point of the paper (4.5").

  NOTE: You will learn to use WordPerfect's template feature to create letters in Lesson 13.

Previewing a Document

- To see how your letter will format or appear on a page, you may preview your work by clicking the Page Zoom Full button on the Toolbar or by selecting Zoom, Full Page from the View main menu.

Since available printers and fonts vary, your line endings may differ from the examples illustrated in the exercises throughout this book.

EXERCISE DIRECTIONS:

 In this exercise, you will create a modified-block letter and practice moving the insertion point through the document. This is an essential skill when you are ready to correct errors.

1. Start with a clear screen.

2. Keyboard the letter on the right as directed.

3. Use the default margins and tabs.

4. Access the QuickCorrect feature. Be sure Replace Words as You Type has been selected.

5. With your insertion point at the top of the screen (Ln 1"), press the Enter key as many times as necessary to begin the date on line (Ln) 2.5".

6. Press the Tab key 7 times to begin the date and closing at position (Pos) 4.5" on the page.

   NOTE: It is more efficient to set one tab stop at 4.5" and press the Tab key once to type the date and closing. Setting tabs will covered in Lesson 5.

7. Press the Enter key between parts of the letter as directed in the exercise.

8. Use the Backspace key to correct an immediate error not corrected by QuickCorrect.

9. After completing the exercise, use the scroll bar to scroll your page up. Move the insertion point through the document as follows:

   • One line up/down

   • One character right/left

   • Previous word

   • End of screen

   • Beginning of line

   • End of line

10. Preview your work using the Page/Zoom Full button on the Toolbar.

11. Save the exercise using the Save button on the Toolbar; name it **LETTER**.

12. Close the document window.

PREVIEW (Full Page)

Click Page/Zoom Full button on Toolbar... [icon]

OR

1. Click **V**iew .... Alt + V

2. Click **Z**oom .... Z

3. Click **F**ull Page .... F

4. Click **OK** .... Enter

EXIT PREVIEW

Click Page/Zoom Full button on Toolbar.. [icon]

OR

1. Click **V**iew .... Alt + V

2. Click **Z**oom .... Z

3. Click **100%** 1

4. Click **OK** .... Enter

SCROLL

Click up/down left/right arrows on scroll bar until desired text is in view, or click and drag the scroll box up/down to express move the window.

EXPRESS INSERTION POINT MOVEMENT KEYSTROKES

TO MOVE:	PRESS:
One character left	◄
One character right	►
One line up	▲
One line down	▼
Previous word	Ctrl + ◄
Next word	Ctrl + ►
Top of screen	PgUp

Bottom of screen	PgDn
Beginning of document	Ctrl + Home
End of document	Ctrl + End
Beginning of line	Home
End of line	End
First line on previous page	Alt + PgUp
First line on next page	Alt + PgDn

_2.5"_ ↓

Tab → _Tab_ → _Tab_ → _Tab_ → _Tab_ → _Tab_ → _Tab_ → ④.5" ↓   October 1, 199-

↓ _4_

Ms. Renee S. Brown
54 Williams Street
Omaha, NE 68101
↓ _2_
Dear Ms. Brown:
↓ _2_
Thank you for your $ 150 contribution to the American Art Institution. This contribution automatically makes you a member in our arts program.
↓ _2_
As an active member, you can participate in our many educational activities.
↓ _2_
For example, you can take part in our monthly art lectures, our semi-annual auctions and our frequent art exhibits. Admission to all these events is free.
↓ _2_
We look forward to seeing you at our next meeting. We know you will enjoy speaking with our other members and participating in very stimulating conversation.

Tab → _Tab_ → _Tab_ → _Tab_ → _Tab_ → _Tab_ → _Tab_ →   ↓ _2_   Sincerely,

↓ _4_

Tab → _Tab_ → _Tab_ → _Tab_ → _Tab_ → _Tab_ → _Tab_ →
→   →   →   →   →   →   →   Alan Barry
President
↓ _2_

ab/yo

EXERCISE

6

▪ CREATING A BUSINESS LETTER ▪ THE DATE FEATURE ▪ PRINTING
▪ THE CAPS LOCK KEY

Print

NOTES:

Creating a Business Letter

▪ The letter style in this exercise is called **full block**. This style is very popular because all parts of the letter begin at the left margin and there is no need to Tab the date and closing. The spacing between letter parts in this style is the same as the modified-block letter.

▪ When you type the date in this exercise, you will use WordPerfect's Date feature.

The Date Feature

▪ WordPerfect's **Date Text** feature enables you to insert the current date into your document automatically. You also have the option of inserting a **Date Code** which automatically updates the date whenever you retrieve or print the document. The date is pulled from the computer's memory.

▪ You can insert date text by either selecting Date, Date Text from the Insert main menu or pressing Ctrl + D.

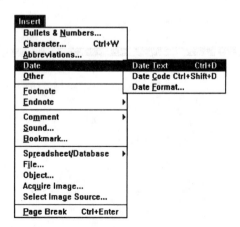

▪ The default format for a date is Month Day, Year. You can change this format, if desired, by selecting Date, Date Format from the Insert main menu, then selecting the desired format.

Document Date/Time Format		
Current Format: January 31, 1995		OK
Predefined Formats: January 31, 1995		Cancel
1/31/95		Custom...
Jan 31, 1995		
31 January 1995		Help
Tuesday, January 31, 1995		
1:15 pm		
31Jan95		
January 31, 1995 [1:15pm]		

Printing

▪ WordPerfect allows you to print part or all of a document that is in the screen window. You can print a page of the document, the full document, selected pages of a document, multiple pages, or one or more blocks of text within the document. Document summaries may also be printed. A document may also be printed from the disk without retrieving it to the screen.

REMINDER: Check to see that the printer is turned on and paper is loaded.

▪ After you access Print, a dialog box appears asking you to indicate whether you wish to print the full document (more than one page) the current page, multiple pages (which you designate), or a document on disk. You may also indicate the number of copies you desire to be printed. Printing multiple pages will be covered in Lesson 7. Note the Print dialog box below:

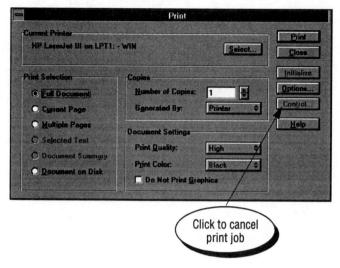

Click to cancel print job

■ You can cancel an individual print job or all print jobs while they are printing.

The Caps Lock Key

■ Pressing the Caps Lock key once will enable you to type all capital letters without pressing the Shift key. Only letters are changed by Caps Lock. Pressing the Caps Lock key again will turn caps lock OFF and ends the uppercase mode. If you forget to press the Caps Lock key to create uppercase mode, you can change lowercase text to uppercase after keyboarding. (Case conversion will be covered in a later exercise.)

EXERCISE DIRECTIONS:

 In this exercise, you will create a full-block letter using the Date Text feature and print one copy of the full document.

1. Start with a clear screen.

2. Keyboard the letter on the right. Use the default margins.

3. Access the QuickCorrect feature. Be sure Replace Words as You Type has been selected.

4. Begin the date on about line (Ln) 2.5". Use the Date Text feature to insert today's date.

5. Press the Enter key between parts of the letter as directed in the exercise.

6. Spell check your document.

7. Preview your work.

8. Click the Print button on the Toolbar and print one copy of the exercise.

9. Save the exercise; name it **BLOCK**.

10. Close the document window.

INSERT CURRENT DATE
Ctrl + D

1. Click **I**nsert .... `Alt` + `I`
2. Click **D**ate.. `D`
3. Click Date **T**ext...................................... `T`

INSERT DATE CODE
Ctrl + Shift + D

1. Click **I**nsert .... `Alt` + `I`
2. Click **D**ate.. `D`
3. Click Date **C**ode .... `C`

CHANGE DATE FORMAT

1. Click **I**nsert .... `Alt` + `I`
2. Click **D**ate.. `D`
3. Click Date **F**ormat .... `F`
4. Click desired format.
5. Click **OK** .... `Enter`

ALL CAPITALS

1. Press Caps Lock key
2. Type text.
3. Press Caps Lock key to end uppercase.

PRINT
F5 or Ctrl + P

1. Click Print button on Toolbar .... 🖨
   OR
   a. Click **F**ile....................... `Alt` + `F`
   b. Click **P**rint.............................. `P`
2. Click a Print Selection Option:
   • **F**ull Document.............................. `F`
   • C**u**rrent Page .... `U`
   • **M**ultiple Pages.............................. `M`
   • Se**l**ected Text .... `L`
   • Document Summ**a**ry .... `A`
   • **D**ocument on Disk.......................... `D`
3. Click **P**rint .... `Enter`

CANCEL PRINT JOB

1. Click Print button on Toolbar .... 🖨
   OR
   a. Click **F**ile....................... `Alt` + `F`
   b. Click **P**rint.............................. `P`
2. Click **C**ontrol .... `T`
3. Click **C**ancel Print Job...................... `C`

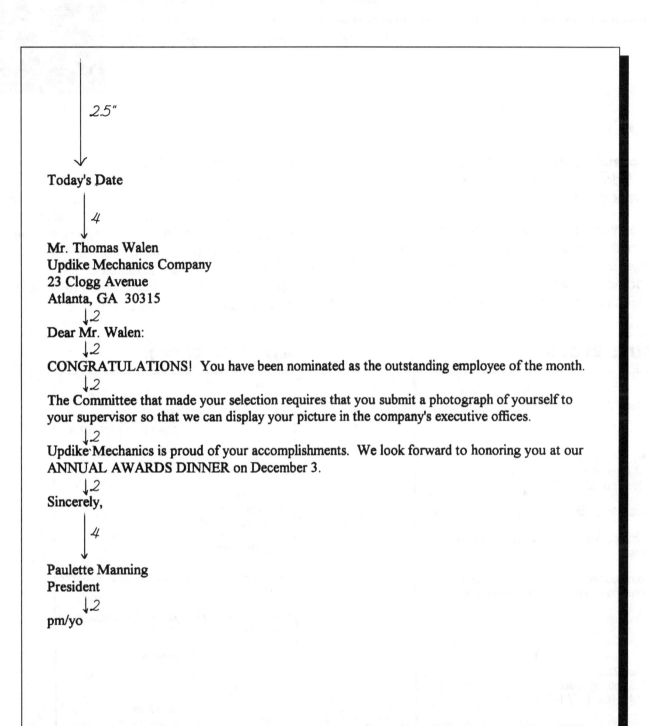

2.5"

Today's Date

↓4

Mr. Thomas Walen
Updike Mechanics Company
23 Clogg Avenue
Atlanta, GA 30315

↓2

Dear Mr. Walen:

↓2

CONGRATULATIONS! You have been nominated as the outstanding employee of the month.

↓2

The Committee that made your selection requires that you submit a photograph of yourself to your supervisor so that we can display your picture in the company's executive offices.

↓2

Updike Mechanics is proud of your accomplishments. We look forward to honoring you at our ANNUAL AWARDS DINNER on December 3.

↓2

Sincerely,

↓4

Paulette Manning
President

↓2

pm/yo

EXERCISE

7

CREATING A PERSONAL BUSINESS LETTER

NOTES:

■ A **personal business letter** is written by an individual representing him-/herself, not a business firm.

■ A personal business letter begins 2.5" down from the top of the page (same as the other letter styles) and includes the writer's return address (address, city, state and zip code) which precedes the date. However,

if personalized letterhead is used, keying the return address is unnecessary. Personal business letters may be formatted in full-block or modified-block style. Operator's initials are not included. Depending on the style used, the writer's return address will appear in a different location on the letter. A full-block format appears below left. Note that the return address is typed below the writer's name.

FULL BLOCK

```
March 7, 199-


Mr. John Smith
54 Astor Place
New York, NY 10078

Dear Mr. Smith:


xxxxxxxxxxxxxxxxxxxxxxxxxxxxxxxxxxxx
xxxxx.


xxxxxxxxxxxxxxxxxxxxxxxxxxxxxxxxxxxx
xxxxxxxxxxxxxxxxxxxxxxxxxxxxxxxxxxx.


Sincerely,


Paula Zahn
765 Nehring Street
Staten Island, NY 10324
```

MODIFIED BLOCK

```
                          657 Nehring Street
                          Staten Island, NY 10324
                          March 7, 199-


Mr. John Smith
54 Astor Place
New York, NY 10078

Dear Mr. Smith:


xxxxxxxxxxxxxxxxxxxxxxxxxxxxxxxxxxxxxxx
xxxxxx.


xxxxxxxxxxxxxx xxxxxxxxxxxxxxxxxxxxxxxx
xxxxxxxxx.

                          Sincerely,


                          Paula Zahn
```

EXERCISE DIRECTIONS:

In this exercise, you will create a modified block personal business letter using the automatic Date feature. You will then print one copy of the full document.

1. Start with a clear screen.
2. Keyboard the personal business letter below in modified block style as shown.
3. Use the default margins and tabs.
4. Access the QuickCorrect feature. Be sure Replace Words as you Type has been selected.
5. Begin the exercise on Ln 2.5".
6. Press the Tab key 7 times to begin the return address and closing at position (Pos) 4.5" on the page.

   NOTE: It is more efficient to set one tab stop at 4.5" and press the

Tab key once to type the return address and closing. After learning to set tabs in Lesson 5, you will format subsequent exercises using a single tab setting for the (inside address), date and closing of a modified block letter.

7. Press the Enter key between parts of the letter as directed in the exercise.
8. Spell check your document.
9. After completing the exercise, use the scroll bars to scroll your page up.
10. Preview your work.
11. Print one copy.
12. Save the exercise; name it **PERSONAL**.
13. Close the document window.

---

636 Jay Boulevard West
Chaska, MN 55318
[Date Code]

Ms. Anita Price, Vice President
Milton Investment Counselors
One Pratt Circle
Baltimore, MD 21202

Dear Ms. Price:

Please consider me an applicant for the position of Financial Advisor that was advertised in the Sunday edition of THE HERALD.

As my enclosed resume will show, I have been working for Sutton Investment Group for the past six years. I am particularly proud of several accomplishments:

In 1991, I helped to organize $1.5 million zero-coupon bond offering for the French Treasury.

In 1992, my group handled $120 million municipal bond offering for New York City.

In 1993, I helped to underwrite $200 million offering for a foreign company.

I am confident that my past experience will be an asset to your organization. If you would like to meet with me for an interview, I can be reached at the number indicated on my resume.

Sincerely,

Lawrence Schneider

enclosure

EXERCISE DIRECTIONS:

1. Start with a clear screen.

2. Use the default margins.

3. Access the QuickCorrect feature. Be sure Replace Words as You Type has been selected.

4. Keyboard the letter below in **modified-block** style. Create a new paragraph (press the Enter key twice) where you see a paragraph symbol (¶).

5. Use the Date Text feature to insert today's date.

6. Spell check your document.

7. Print one copy.

8. Save the exercise; name it **OPEN**.

9. Close the document window.

Today's date Mr. Martin Quincy 641 Lexington Avenue New York, NY 10022 Dear Mr. Quincy: We are pleased to announce the opening of a new subsidiary of our company. We specialize in selling, training and service of portable personal computers. ¶This may be hard to believe, but we carry portable personal computers that can do everything a conventional desktop can. Our portables can run all of the same applications as your company's conventional PCs. With the purchase of a computer, we will train two employees in your firm on how to use an application of your choice. ¶For a free demonstration, call us at 212-456-9876 any business day from 9:00 a.m. to 5:00 p.m. Sincerely, Theresa Mann President tm/yo

LESSON 2
SUMMARY EXERCISE B

EXERCISE DIRECTIONS:

1. Start with a clear screen.

2. Use the default margins.

3. Access the QuickCorrect feature. Be sure Replace Words as You Type has been selected.

4. Keyboard the letter below in full-block style. Create a new paragraph (press the Enter key twice) where you see a paragraph symbol (¶).

5. Use the Date Code feature to insert today's date.

6. Spell check your document.

7. Print one copy.

8. Save the exercise; name it **REGRETS**.

9. Close the document window.

Today's date Ms. Kristin Paulo 765 Rand Road Palatine, IL 60074 Dear Ms. Paulo: Thank you for your inquiry regarding employment with our firm. ¶We have reviewed your qualifications with several members of our firm. We regret to report that we do not have an appropriate vacancy at this time. ¶We will retain your resume in our files in the event that an opening occurs in your field. ¶Your interest in our organization is very much appreciated. We hope to be able to offer you a position at another time. Very truly yours, Carol B. Giles PERSONNEL MANAGER cbg/yo

LESSON 3

Exercises 8–13

- Opening a Document File

- Specifying a File

- Inserting/Typing Over Text

- Opening a Copy of a File (Read-Only)

- Save As

- Undo and Redo

- Open a Document after Viewing

- Inserting Text

- Printing Multiple Files

- Selecting, Deleting and Undeleting Text

- Undeleting vs. Undo

- Reveal Codes

- Show Symbols

- Deleting Codes

- Hard Space

- Convert Case

EXERCISE

▪ OPENING A DOCUMENT FILE ▪ SPECIFYING A FILE
▪ INSERTING/TYPING OVER TEXT

Open File

NOTES:

Opening a Document File

▪ Before a file can be revised or edited, it must be opened from the disk and placed on the screen.

▪ A document is revised when corrections need to be made. **Proofreaders' marks** are markings on a document that indicate errors to be corrected. These markings are often abbreviated in the form of symbols. As each proofreaders' mark is introduced in an exercise, it is explained and illustrated. A summary list of all proofreaders' symbols and their meanings appears in Appendix C. Documents containing proofreaders' symbols are often referred to as a **rough-draft** (or draft copy). After revisions are made, the completed document is referred to as a **final copy**.

Opening a Recently Saved File

▪ WordPerfect lists the last four opened documents at the bottom of the File drop-down menu. To open a recently-saved file which appears at the bottom of the File drop-down menu, click the desired file name.

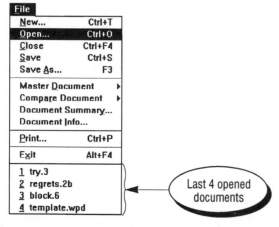

Last 4 opened documents

Opening a File Not Recently Saved

▪ After you select Open from the File main menu or click the Open button on the Toolbar, the Open File dialog box appears listing all files that have been saved:

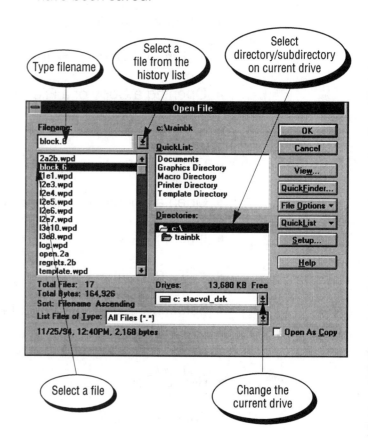

Type filename

Select a file from the history list

Select directory/subdirectory on current drive

Select a file

Change the current drive

Specifying a File

- To specify the file you want opened, type the filename in the Filename text box, or click on one of the files listed in the file list. Note that files appear in alphabetical order. If the document is not displayed, it may be residing in another drive and/or directory. To display files in another drive/directory, click on the Drives list box and/or click on another directory in the Directories list.

- You may also select a file from the history list. Clicking the list box arrow next to the filename textbox displays the last ten recently saved files.

- When you select a file to open, the date and time the file was created and the size of the file (bytes) displays in the lower left corner of the dialog box.

Inserting/Typing Over Text

- To make corrections, use the insertion point movement keys to move to the point of correction, or use the mouse to click at the point of correction.

- Text is inserted immediately before the insertion point when **Insert** mode is on. (Insert is the default keyboarding mode indicated at the bottom left of the status bar.) When you type inserted text, the existing text moves to the right. When you insert a word, you must also insert the space following the word.

- To insert a new paragraph, place the insertion point to the left of the first character of the new paragraph and press the Enter key twice.

- Another way to edit text is to type over existing text with new text. To put WordPerfect in Typeover mode, press the Insert (Ins) key once. In this mode, existing text does not move to the right; it is typed over. (After pressing the Insert key, note the bottom left of the status bar—Typeover is displayed.)

- Text is automatically adjusted after insertions have been made.

- When a file is opened and revisions are made, the revised or updated version must be resaved or "replaced." When a document is resaved, the old version is replaced with the new version. WordPerfect lets you update your document with or without confirmation.

If you select Save from the File menu or click the Save button, your document is saved without confirmation and you can continue working; if you close the file or exit, WordPerfect asks if you wish to save your changes. If no changes were made, WordPerfect just closes the file.

The proofreaders' mark for insertion is: ∧

The proofreaders' mark for a new paragraph is: ⁋

EXERCISE DIRECTIONS:

 In this exercise, you will open a previously saved document and insert new text.

1. Start with a clear screen.

2. Open **TRY**.

   OR

    Open **TRY.8** from the data disk.

3. Make the indicated insertions.

4. Use the Typeover mode to insert the word "determine" over "decide on" in the second paragraph.

5. Spell check your document.

6. Print one copy.

7. Close your file; save the changes.

   NOTE: The data disk contains the corrected version of each file (if corrections were made) and is noted by an S following the file name, for example: TRY.8S. you may compare your printout with the corrected version.

OPEN A SAVED DOCUMENT
Ctrl + O

1. Click Open button on Toolbar........... 🗁

   OR

   a. Click **File**.......................... `Alt` + `F`

   b. Click **Open**................................... `O`

2. Type document name to be opened or click document name in list.

3. Click **OK** .... `Enter`

NOTE: You can also double-click a file name in the file list to open the file without choosing OK.

INSERT TEXT

1. Using insertion point movement keys, place the insertion point one character to the left of where text is to be inserted.

   OR

   Using the mouse, place the mouse pointer one character to the left of where text is to be inserted and click once.

2. Type text.

TYPEOVER

1. Place the insertion point where text is to be overwritten.

2. Press **Insert** key.............................. `Ins`

3. Type text.

4. Press **Insert** key.............................. `Ins`
   to exit Typeover mode.

SAVE CHANGES
(without confirmation).
Ctrl + O

Click Save button on Toolbar.................

OR

1. Click **File**.............................. `Alt` + `F`

2. Click **Save** .... `S`

                    you will
As you type, notice the "Pos" indicator on your status bar change
as the position of your insertion point changes.

           the   *computer*   *determine*
The "wraparound" feature allows the operator to ~~decide on~~ line
endings, making the use of Enter unnecessary except at the end of
a paragraph or short line. ¶Each file is saved on a disk or hard
drive for recall. Documents must be given a name for
identification.   *key*   *data*
                                        or number

EXERCISE

9

▪ OPENING A DOCUMENT ▪ SAVE AS ▪ UNDO AND REDO

Undo   Redo

NOTES:

Opening a Copy of a File (Read-Only)

▪ If you wish to open a file but not make changes to it, you can click the Open As Copy option in the Open File dialog box.

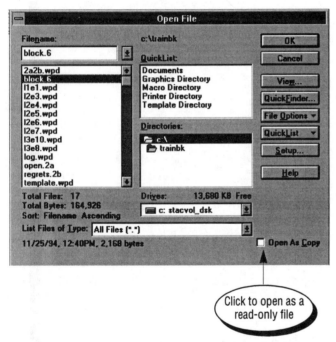

Click to open as a read-only file

This will make the document a **read-only** copy and will require you to save it with a different file name. Selecting this option prevents you from accidentally affecting the file.

• If you save, close or exit a document that you opened using the Open As Copy option, WordPerfect automatically displays the Save As dialog box (illustrated right) for you to to give the file another name, thus leaving the original document intact.

Save As

▪ If you wish to save any document under a different file name or in a different location, you may select Save As from the File menu. Enter the new filename or new location in the Save As dialog box. Remember, when any document is saved under a new filename, the original document remains intact.

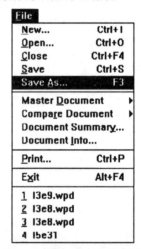

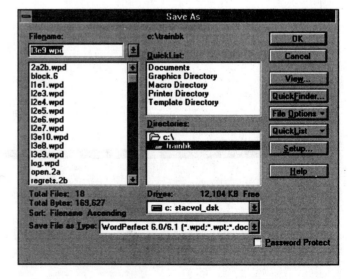

Undo and Redo

- The **Undo** feature lets you undo the last change you made to the document.

- **Redo** allows you to reverse the last undo. For example, if you insert a word then decide you don't want the word in the sentence, you can undo the change. But then, if you decide the word should be in the sentence, you can use redo to reinsert the word into the sentence.

- If you wish to undo or redo an action that occurred at the start of your document, you may use the **Undo/Redo History** feature, which allows you to reverse up to 300 actions in a document.

- Undo and Redo restores information in its original location.

- Certain actions, like saving or scrolling a document, are not affected by Undo.

 The proofreaders' mark for changing uppercase to lowercase is / or lc.

EXERCISE DIRECTIONS:

 In this exercise, you will open a document from the data disk as a read-only file. This will allow you to keep the file on disk intact. You will make insertions and print the document. You will then save it with a new file name.

1. Start with a clear screen.

2. ⌨ Keyboard the exercise as shown on the next page.

   OR

   💾 Open **GOODJOB.9** from the data disk as a read-only file (Open As <u>C</u>opy).

3. Make the indicated insertions.

   TIP: To insert "Computer Associates," place the insertion point at the end of the first line (Mr. Wallace Redfield); press the Enter key once, then type the insertion.

4. Use Typeover mode to change the uppercase letters to lowercase where you see the proofreaders' mark /.

5. Preview your document.

6. After typing the initials (ah/yo), use Undo. Retype them in all caps.

7. After typing the initials in all caps, use Undo.

8. Use Redo to return the initials to all capitals.

9. Print one copy.

10. Use Undo to return the initials to lowercase.

11. Close the file; save as **GOODJOB**.

SAVE AS
F3

1. Click **<u>F</u>ile**.......................... `Alt` + `F`
2. Click **Save <u>A</u>s** .... `A`
3. Keyboard new filename.

   AND/OR

   Keyboard new file location.
4. Click **OK** .... `Enter`

UNDO
Ctrl + Z

1. Click Undo button on Toolbar.......... `↺`

   OR

   a. Click **<u>E</u>dit** .... `E`
   b. Click **<u>U</u>ndo** .... `U`

REDO
Ctrl + Shift + R

1. Click Redo button on Toolbar........... `↻`

   OR

   a. Click **<u>E</u>dit** .... `E`
   b. Click **<u>R</u>edo** .... `R`

UNDO/REDO HISTORY

1. Click **<u>E</u>dit**.................................. `Alt` + `E`
2. Click **Undo/Redo <u>H</u>istory** .... `Alt` + `H`
3. Select an action to undo/redo.
4. Click **Undo/Redo** .... `N` or `D`
5. Click **Close** .... `C`

Today's date

Computer Associates

Mr. Wallace Redfield
23 Main Street
Staten Island, NY 10312

Dear Mr. Redfield:

You are to be commended for an outstanding job as convention chair. *As a result of your efforts,* The computer
convention held last week was the best I attended. *person*

guest *have* *in a long while*

The choices you made for lecturers were excellent. Every seminar I attended was interesting.

and informative

Congratulations on a great job.

Again,

                          Sincerely,

                          Adam Howard
                          President

insert ah/yo

EXERCISE

▪ **OPENING A DOCUMENT AFTER VIEWING** ▪ **INSERTING TEXT**
▪ **PRINTING MULTIPLE FILES**

Open File

NOTES:

- In previous exercises, you opened your document to the screen and then printed it. However, sometimes you might wish to print one or several documents without opening them first. Or, sometimes you might forget the content of a document and would like to view it before opening or printing it. Selecting File Options in the Open File dialog box lets you print one or several files and/or view the contents of your document without opening it into a document window. (Other options are available within the Open File dialog box screen and will be covered in later lessons.)

- You may also print a copy of the filenames listed in the dialog box, if you desire such a list.

- Note the Open File dialog box below.

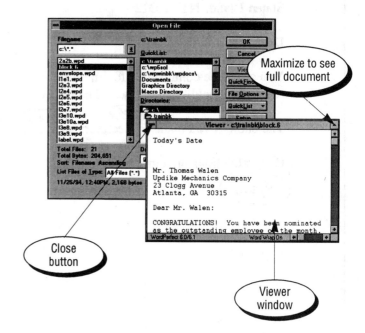

- The Viewer wraps a text of the document to fit the Viewer display window. Click the maximize button ▲ to see the full document size. To close the Viewer window, click the Close button ▭ and click Close.

EXERCISE DIRECTIONS:

 In this exercise, you will insert text from the top of the page to create a modified-block letter.

1. Start with a clear screen.
2. Select <u>O</u>pen from the <u>F</u>ile main menu.
3. View **PERSONAL, TRYAGAIN** and **TRY** files (if you created them in Lesson 2).

   OR

   View **PERSONAL.7, TRYAGAIN.4** and **TRY.3** on the data disk.
4. Open the file (your own or from the data disk) containing the text illustrated in the exercise.
5. Use the Date Text feature to insert today's date.

    After inserting the date, you will continue inserting the inside address and salutation. Text will adjust as you continue creating the letter.

6. Make the indicated insertions. Follow the formatting for a modified-block letter illustrated in Exercise 6.

    To insert the date, press the Enter key enough times to bring the Ln indicator to 2.5"; then, press the Tab key enough times to bring the Pos indicator to 4.5".

   NOTE: It is more efficient to set one tab stop at 4.5" and press the Tab key once to insert the date and closing. This method should be used after you learn to set tabs in Lesson 5.

7. Use Typeover mode to insert the word "start" over "begin" in the second paragraph.
8. Print one copy.
9. Close the file; save the changes.

   OR

    Close the file; *save as* **TRYAGAIN**.

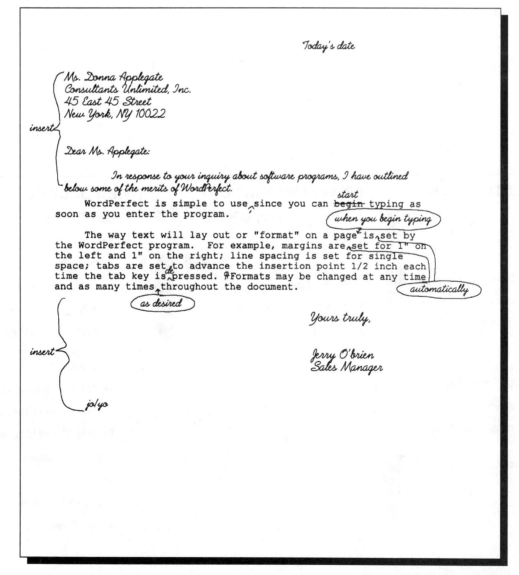

PRINT SELECTED FILES
F4

1. Click Open File icon on Toolbar........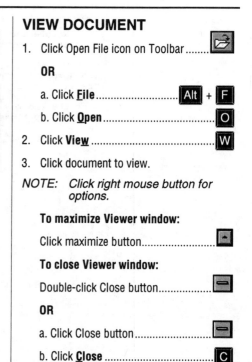

   OR

   a. Click **File**............................ Alt + F

   b. Click **Open**...................................... O

2. Click file to be printed.

   OR

   Hold down **Ctrl**
   and click multiple files to be printed.

   OR

   Drag to select consecutive files to be printed.

3. Click **File Options**............................ O
4. Click **Print** .... P
5. Lcick **Print** .... P

PRINT DIRECTORY LIST

1. Click Open File icon on Toolbar........

   OR

   a. Click **File**............................ Alt + F

   b. Click **Open**...................................... O

2. Click **File Options**............................ O
3. Click **Print List** L

VIEW DOCUMENT

1. Click Open File icon on Toolbar........

   OR

   a. Click **File**............................ Alt + F

   b. Click **Open**...................................... O

2. Click **View**...................................... W
3. Click document to view.

   NOTE: Click right mouse button for options.

   To maximize Viewer window:

   Click maximize button........................ ▲

   To close Viewer window:

   Double-click Close button................ ▬

   OR

   a. Click Close button........................ ▬

   b. Click **Close** C

NEXT EXERCISE...

EXERCISE

11

▪ OPENING A DOCUMENT ▪ SELECTING, DELETING AND UNDELETING TEXT
▪ UNDELETING VS. UNDO

NOTES:

▪ The **Delete** feature allows you to remove text, graphics or codes from a document. This exercise will focus on the methods to delete text.

▪ Procedures for deleting text vary depending on what is being deleted: a character, previous character, word, sentence, paragraph, remainder of line, page, blank line or block of text.

Selecting text

▪ To delete a block of text (words, sentences and paragraphs), text must first be highlighted or selected. Once text is selected, it may be deleted using the methods indicated in the Quick Feature Access.

▪ Text may be highlighted or selected using the mouse or the keyboard using the procedures indicated in the keystrokes on page 48.

Undeleting text

▪ Text may be restored after it has been deleted. Your insertion point should be in the location to which you wish the text to be restored when accessing this task. WordPerfect remembers your last three deletions and allows you to restore them.

Undeleting vs. Undo

▪ Undelete lets you restore the most recent deletion or up to three previous deletions at the insertion point. Undo lets you restore deleted information in its original location or reverse the last change or action made to the document.

▪ When using Undo to restore deleted text, you must use the command immediately after the deletion is made.

EXERCISE DIRECTIONS:

 In this exercise, you will open a file from the data disk as a read-only file and make the deletions indicated in the exercise.

1. Start with a clear screen.

2. [⌨] Create the exercise as shown in Part I

   OR

   [💾] Open **DIVE.11** from the data disk as a read-only file (Open As Copy).

3. Using the selection and deletion procedures indicated in Part II of the exercise, make the revisions.

4. After deleting the last paragraph (remainder of page), undelete it.

5. Using another deletion method, delete the last paragraph again.

6. Print one copy.

7. Close the file; *save as* **DIVE**.

PART I

DIVING VACATIONS
DIVING IN THE CAYMAN ISLANDS

Do you want to see sharks, barracudas and huge stingrays? Do you want to see gentle angels, too?

The Cayman Islands were discovered by Christopher Columbus in late 1503. The Cayman Islands are located just south of Cuba. The Caymans are the home to only about 125,000 year-around residents. However, they welcome approximately 200,000 visitors each year. Each year more and more visitors arrive. Most visitors come with colorful masks and flippers in their luggage ready to go scuba diving.

Because of the magnificence of the coral reef, scuba diving has become to the Cayman Islands what safaris are to Kenya. If you go into a bookstore, you can buy diving gear.

Now, you are ready to jump in!

Recommendations for Hotel/Diving Accommodations:

Sunset House, Post Office Box 4791, George Towne, Grand Cayman; (800) 854-4767.

Coconut Harbour, Post Office Box 2086, George Towne, Grand Cayman; (809) 949-7468.

Seeing a shark is frightening at first; they seem to come out of nowhere and then return to nowhere. But as soon as the creature disappears, you will swim after it. You will just want to keep this beautiful, graceful fish in view as long as you can.

PART II

Ctrl+Del.   (~~DIVING VACATIONS~~
DIVING IN THE CAYMAN ISLANDS

Double-click
Press Del.   (Do you want to see sharks, barracudas and ~~huge~~ stingrays?
\Do you want to see ~~gentle~~ angels, too?

Ctrl+Backspace
for word deletions {   The Cayman Islands were discovered by Christopher Columbus
in ~~late~~ 1503. The Cayman Islands are located ~~just~~ south of Cuba.
The Caymans are ~~the~~ home to only about 125,000 year-around
residents. However, they welcome approximately 200,000 visitors
each year. → ~~Each year more and more visitors arrive.~~ Most

⬭ *F8, →, Del*   visitors come with ~~colorful~~ masks and flippers in their luggage ^
Ctrl+Del.   (~~ready to go scuba diving.~~

Quadruple-click
Press Del.   { ~~Because of the magnificence of the coral reef, scuba diving~~
~~has become to the Cayman Islands what safaris are to Kenya. If~~
~~you go into a bookstore, you can buy diving gear.~~

         Now, you are ready to jump in!

Select w/mouse.
Click cut.   (~~Recommendations for~~ Hotel/Diving Accommodations:

Select w/mouse.   Sunset House, ~~Post Office~~ Box 4791, George Towne; Grand Cayman;
Press Del.   (800) 854-4767.

         Coconut Harbour, ~~Post Office~~ Box 2086, George Towne, Grand
Cayman; (809) 949-7468.

move mouse
pointer on left   ~~Seeing a shark is frightening at first; they seem to come~~
margin. Click right   ~~out of nowhere and then return to nowhere. But as soon as the~~
button. Choose   ~~creature disappears, you will swim after it. You will just want~~
Paragraph. Press   ~~to keep this beautiful, graceful fish in view as long as you can.~~
Delete

Lesson 3 ■ Exercise 11   47

NOTE: *While there are numerous methods to select and delete text, the methods below represent the most efficient way to accomplish the task. You may use whichever method you find most comfortable.*

SELECT TEXT

NOTE: *Use the left mouse button unless otherwise instructed.*

—USING MAIN MOUSE METHOD—

1. Position insertion point at beginning of text to select.
2. Hold mouse button down and drag over text.
3. Release mouse button.

—USING QUICKSELECT METHODS—

To select word:

1. Place insertion point anywhere on word.
2. Double-click.

To select sentence:

1. Place insertion point anywhere on sentence.
2. Triple-click.

OR

1. Place mouse pointer in left margin opposite desired sentence.
2. Click *right* mouse button.
3. Choose **Select Sentence**................... `S`

To select paragraph:

1. Place insertion point anywhere on paragraph.
2. Quadruple-click.

OR

1. Place mouse pointer in left margin opposite desired paragraph.
2. Click *right* mouse button.
3. Choose **Select Paragraph**................ `P`

To select page:

1. Place mouse pointer in left margin.
2. Click *right* mouse button.
3. Choose **Select Page**........................ `A`

To select entire document:

1. Place mouse pointer in left margin.
2. Click *right* mouse button.
3. Choose **Select All** .... `L`

To select block:

1. Click where selection is to begin.
2. Move mouse pointer to where selection will end.
3. Press **Shift** + click mouse.

—USING KEYBOARD—

F8, arrow keys

1. Position insertion point to the immediate left of text to be selected.
2. Hold down **Shift** key.
3. Press a desired option:

TO SELECT:	PRESS:
One character left	`◄`
One character right........................	`►`
One line up	`↑`
One line down	`↓`
To end of line	`End`
To start of line................................	`Home`
To end of word	`Ctrl` + `►`
To start of word..................	`Ctrl` + `◄`
Top of screen	`PgUp`
Bottom of screen............................	`PgDn`
To end of paragraph	`Ctrl` + `↓`
To start of paragraph...........	`Ctrl` + `↑`
To end of document.........	`Ctrl` + `End`
To beginning of document	`Ctrl` + `Home`

CANCEL SELECTION

Click anywhere outside the selection

OR

Press **F8**... `F8`

DELETE

To delete character:

1. Place insertion point immediately to the left of character or space to be deleted.
2. Press **Delete** key .... `Del`

OR

1. Place insertion point to the *right* of character to be deleted.
2. Press **Backspace** .... `Backspace`

To delete word:

1. Place insertion point anywhere in word to be deleted.
2. Press **Ctrl + Backspace**.
....  `Ctrl` + `Backspace`

To delete block of text:

1. Select (highlight) block of text to be deleted using selection procedures outlined above.
2. Click **Cut** button.................

   OR

   Press **Delete**................................. `Del`

   or **Backspace**...................... `Backspace`

   OR

   a. Click the *right* mouse button.

   b. Choose **Delete** .... `D`

UNDELETE
Ctrl + Shift + Z

1. Click **Edit**............................... `Alt` + `E`
2. Click **Undelete**................................... `N`
3. Select desired option:

   • **Restore**.. `R`
   to restore last deletion.

   • Click **Next** or **Previous** to..... `N` or `P`
   cycle through last 3 deletions.

4. Click **Restore**................................... `R`

NEXT EXERCISE...

EXERCISE 12

▪ OPEN A DOCUMENT ▪ REVEAL CODES ▪ SHOW SYMBOLS ▪ DELETE CODES

NOTES:

▪ As a document is created in WordPerfect, codes are inserted that determine the document's appearance. These codes are not displayed on the screen, but can be revealed when necessary either through the **Reveal Codes** or **Show Symbols** (¶) features.

Reveal Codes

▪ When the **Reveal Codes** feature is selected, the document window is divided into two parts. The top part is the normal editing area; the bottom part displays the same text with the codes displayed. The **divider line** splits the two parts of the window. An example of this screen and its symbols appears below:

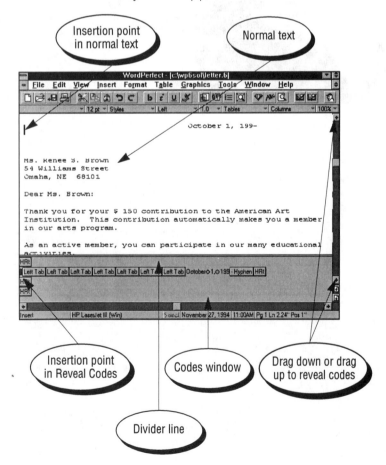

Show Symbols (¶)

▪ When the **Show Symbols** feature is selected, all the codes that were inserted when the document was created are displayed on screen as various symbols. A hard return code is represented by a paragraph symbol (¶); a tab code is represented by an arrow (→); a space is represented by a solid square (■). An example of a document with symbols displayed is shown below.

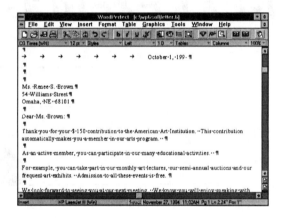

Delete Codes

- To delete a code in Reveal Codes mode, use the mouse pointer to click on the code (the insertion point, represented by a red indicator, appears before the code) and press the Delete key. Or, use the mouse pointer to drag the code out of the Reveal Codes window.

- To delete a code in Show Symbols mode, move the insertion point to the left of the code and press the Delete key.

- To combine two paragraphs into one, the hard returns that separate the paragraphs must be deleted. Therefore, deleting the paragraph symbols will delete the code. This may be done in either Reveal Codes or Show Symbols mode.

EXERCISE DIRECTIONS:

 In this exercise, you will edit an exercise you created earlier by deleting text.

1. Start with a clear screen.

2. Open **LETTER** (if you created it in Exercise 5).

   OR

   💾 Open **LETTER.12** from the data disk as a read-only file (Open As Copy).

3. Using any desired method, make the indicated deletions.

   HINT: To bring the date and closing to the left margin, making this letter full-block style, reveal codes or show symbols and delete the tab codes that precede the date until the date moves to the margin. Or, use the mouse to highlight the blank space to the left of the date and press the Delete key. Do the same for the closing.

4. Preview your work.

5. Print one copy.

6. Close the file; save the changes.

   OR

   💾 Close the file; *save as* **LETTER**.

REVEAL CODES

Alt + F3

Drag horizontal bar down to where Reveal Codes should begin.

OR

1. Click **View** .... Alt + V
2. Click **Reveal Codes** C
3. Place insertion point to the left of code to be deleted.

OR

Point to and click on code to be deleted.

4. Press **Delete** .... Del

To exit Reveal Codes:

Drag divider line up or down into document window

OR

Press **Alt + F3** .... Alt + F3

SHOW SYMBOLS (¶)

Ctrl + Shift + F3

1. Click **View** .... Alt + V
2. Click **Show ¶** .... S

   To exit Show Symbols:

   a. Click **View** .... Alt + V
   b. Click **Show ¶** .... S

October 1, 199-

Ms. Renee S. Brown
54 Williams Street
Omaha, NE 68101

Dear Ms. Brown:

Thank you for your $ 150 contribution to the American Art Institution. This contribution
~~automatically~~ makes you a member in our arts program.

As an active member, you can participate in our many ~~educational~~ activities.

For example, you can take part in ~~our~~ monthly art lectures, ~~our~~ semi-annual auctions and ~~our~~
frequent art exhibits. Admission to ~~all these~~ events is free.

We look forward to seeing you at our next meeting. ~~We know you will enjoy speaking with
our other members and participating in very stimulating conversation.~~

Sincerely,

Alan Barry
President

ab/yo

EXERCISE

▪ HARD SPACE ▪ CONVERT CASE

13

NOTES:

Hard Space

▪ To prevent two or more words from splitting during word wrap, a **hard space code** can be inserted between words. This feature is particularly useful when keyboarding first and last names, dates, equations and time.

```
Edit
 Undo              Ctrl+Z
 Redo              Ctrl+Shift+R
 Undo/Redo History...
 Undelete... Ctrl+Shift+Z
 Repeat...

 Cut               Ctrl+X
 Copy              Ctrl+C
 Paste             Ctrl+V
 Append
 Select                      ▶

 Paste Special...
 Links...
 Object...

 Find and Replace... F2
 Go To...          Ctrl+G

 Convert Case         | Lowercase
 Preferences...       | Uppercase
                      | Initial Capitals
```

Convert Case

▪ The **Convert Case** feature lets you change an existing block of text to all upper- or lowercase letters, or lowercase letters with initial caps. When you choose lowercase with initial caps, the first word in each sentence remains capitalized.

 The proofreaders' mark for inserting a hard space is:

The proofreaders' mark for capitalization is: ≡

EXERCISE DIRECTIONS:

 In this exercise, you will gain more practice inserting and deleting text. In addition, you will use the hard space and convert case features.

1. Start with a clear screen.

2. Open **BLOCK** (if you completed it in Exercise 6).

   OR

   💾 Open **BLOCK.13** from the data disk as a read-only file (Open As Copy).

3. Make the indicated revisions; insert a hard space where you see the ⌂ symbol.

4. After all revisions are made, undelete the last deleted sentence.

5. Convert ANNUAL AWARDS DINNER to lowercase with initial caps.

6. Undo this last change.

7. Spell check your document.

8. Print one copy.

9. Close the file; save the changes.

   OR

   💾 Close the file; save as **BLOCK**.

Today's Date

Mr. Thomas *T.* Walen
Updike Mechanics Company
23 Clogg Avenue
Atlanta, GA 30315

Dear Mr. Walen *, Mr. Walen*

CONGRATULATIONS! You have been nominated as the outstanding employee of the month. *We made your selection based on the recommendations of your supervisors.*

Selection The Committee that made your selection requires that you submit a photograph of yourself *to* to your supervisor so that we can display your picture in the company's executive offices. *immediate* *Mr. Quinn.* *will then* *throughout*
Updike Mechanics is proud of your accomplishments. We look forward to honoring you at our ANNUAL AWARDS DINNER on December 3.

Sincerely,

Paulette Manning
President

pm/yo

INSERT A HARD SPACE
Ctrl + Space

1. Type first word.
2. Click **Format** .... `Alt` + `R`
3. Click **Line** .... `L`
4. Click **Other Codes** .... `O`
5. Click **Hard Space** .... `P`

6. Click **Insert** .... `Enter`
7. Type next word.

CONVERT CASE

1. Select/highlight text to be converted.
2. Click **Edit** .... `Alt` + `E`

3. Click **Convert** .... `V`
4. Click a convert option:
   - **Lowercase** .... `L`
   - **Uppercase** .... `U`
   - **Initial Capitals** .... `I`

Lesson 3 ■ Exercise 13   55

LESSON 3
SUMMARY EXERCISE A

EXERCISE DIRECTIONS:

1. Start with a clear screen.
2. Open **REGRETS** if you completed it in Summary Exercise 2B.

   OR

   💾 Open **REGRETS.3A** from the data disk as a read-only file (Open As Copy).
3. Make the indicated revisions.
4. Convert PERSONNEL MANAGER to lowercase with initial caps.
5. Spell check your document.
6. Print one copy.
7. Close the file; save the changes.

   OR

   💾 Close the file; save as **REGRETS**.

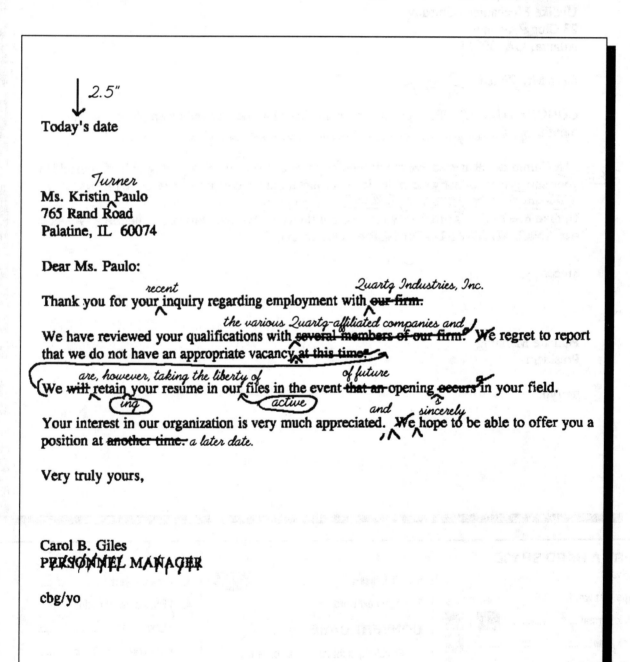

↓ *2.5"*

Today's date

Turner
Ms. Kristin Paulo
765 Rand Road
Palatine, IL 60074

Dear Ms. Paulo:

Thank you for your *recent* inquiry regarding employment with ~~our firm.~~ *Quartz Industries, Inc.*

We have reviewed your qualifications with ~~several members of our firm.~~ *the various Quartz-affiliated companies and* We regret to report that we do not have an appropriate vacancy ~~at this time.~~

We ~~will~~ *are, however, taking the liberty of* retain*ing* your resume in our *active* files in the event ~~that an~~ opening *of future* ~~occurs~~ in your field.

Your interest in our organization is very much appreciated. *and sincerely* We hope to be able to offer you a position at ~~another time.~~ *a later date.*

Very truly yours,

Carol B. Giles
~~PERSONNEL MANAGER~~

cbg/yo

LESSON 3
SUMMARY EXERCISE B

EXERCISE DIRECTIONS:

1. Start with a clear screen.
2. Open **OPEN** if you completed it in Summary Exercise 2A.

   OR

   💾 Open **OPEN.3B** from the data disk as a read-only file (Open As Copy).
3. Change the letter style to full block.
4. Make the indicated revisions.

5. Insert a hard space between times and a.m./p.m.
6. Spell check your document.
7. Undelete the last deleted paragraph.
8. Print one copy.
9. Close the file; save the changes.

   OR

   💾 Close the file; *save as* **OPEN**.

Today's date

Arco Industries, Inc,

Mr. Martin Quincy, *President*
641 Lexington Avenue
New York, NY 10022

Dear Mr. Quincy:

We are *very* pleased to announce the opening of a new subsidiary of our company, *COMPUSELLTRAIN.* We specialize in selling, training and service of portable personal computers.
service   *sales*

This may be hard to believe, but we carry *a full line of* portable personal computers that can do everything *your* a conventional desktop can. Our portables can run all of the same applications as your *computers* company's conventional PCs. With the purchase of a computer, we will train two employees *All of* in your firm on how to use an application of your choice. *The graphic capabilities are outstanding.*
the   *of*

For a free demonstration, call us at 212-456-9876 any business day from 9:00 a.m. to 5:00 p.m.

¶ *The rep for your area is Ms. Sally Hansen. She will phone you to discuss your possible needs.*

Very truly yours
~~Sincerely,~~

Theresa Mann
President

tm/yo

Undo the last deleted paragraph.

LESSON 4

Exercises 14–20

- Center and Flush Right Line

- Center Page Top to Bottom

- Justification

- Changing Font Face, Style and Size

- Font Appearance (Bold, Underline, Double Underline, Italics, Outline, Shadow, Small Caps, Redline and Strikeout)

- Ornamental Fonts

- Special Characters

- Remove Font Appearance

EXERCISE

14

▪ CENTER AND FLUSH RIGHT LINE ▪ CENTER PAGE TOP TO BOTTOM

NOTES:

Center Line

▪ WordPerfect lets you center a single line of text between left and right margins, on a tab, or in a column by selecting Line, Center from the Format main menu or by clicking the *right* mouse button anywhere in the document window and selecting Center.

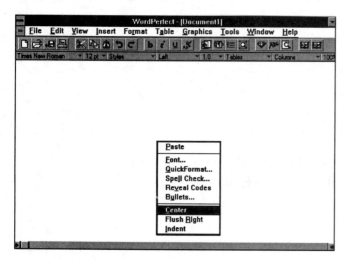

▪ Text may be centered before or after typing.

Flush Right Line

▪ The Flush Right feature aligns a single line or part of a line of text at the right margin. Flush right may be accessed by selecting Line, Flush Right from the Format main menu or by clicking the *right* mouse button anywhere in the document window and selecting Flush Right.

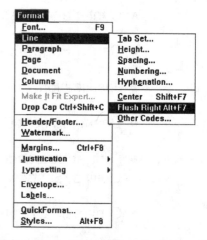

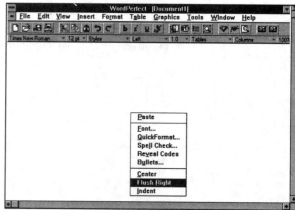

▪ Text may be right aligned before or after typing.

▪ To align a partial or full line of existing text at the right margin, make sure the line ends with a hard return.

Center Page Top to Bottom

■ Text may be centered vertically on a page (center page from top to bottom). If there are hard returns before or after the centered text, WordPerfect will include them in the vertical centering. Therefore, to vertically center text without additional blank lines, start the text at the top of the screen.

 The proofreaders' mark for centering is ⅂⅃ .

EXERCISE DIRECTIONS:

 In this exercise, you will create an announcement and center and right align text horizontally and vertically.

Part I

1. Begin the exercise at the top of a clear screen.

2. Use the default margins.

3. Center the page from top to bottom (vertically center).

4. Create the announcement on the right as indicated.

5. Preview your work.

6. Print one copy.

7. Save the exercise; name it **RSVP**.

8. Close the document window.

Part II

1. Begin the exercise at the top of a clear screen.

2. Use the default margins.

3. Type the exercise as shown.

4. Print one copy.

5. After completing the exercise, right align the address and phone number; center align hotel names.

6. Save the exercise; name it **EXPO**

7. Close the document window.

CENTER LINE
Shift + F7

New Text

1. Place insertion point at beginning of line to center.

2. Click **Format** .... `Alt` + `R`

3. Click **Line** .... `L`

4. Click **Center** .... `C`

5. Type text.

6. Press **Enter** .... `Enter`
   to return to left margin.

Existing Text (one line only)

1. Position insertion point before line to be centered.

2. • Click *right* mouse button anywhere in document window.

   • Click **Center** .... `C`

FLUSH RIGHT
Alt + F7

New Text

1. Place insertion point at beginning of text to flush right.

2. Click **Format** .... `Alt` + `R`

3. Click **Line** .... `L`

4. Click **Flush Right** .... `F`

5. Type text.

6. Press **Enter** .... `Enter`
   to return to left margin.

Existing Text (one line only)

1. Position insertion point before line to be flush right.

2. • Click *right* mouse button anywhere in document window.

   • Click **Flush Right** .... `R`

3. Press **Enter** .... `Enter`
   to return to left margin.

CENTER PAGE TOP TO BOTTOM (Vertically Center)

NOTE: Text will not appear vertically centered on the screen, but will appear centered on the page when previewed.

1. Place insertion point anywhere on page.

2. Click **Format** .... `Alt` + `R`

3. Click **Page** .... `P`

4. Click **Center** .... `C`

5. Click **Current Page** .... `P`

   OR

   Click **Current and Subsequent Pages** `S`

6. Click **OK** .... `Enter`

Celebrate
↓ *2*
On The Hudson

↓ *3*

NEW YEAR'S EVE DINNER DANCE

↓ *3*

HUDSON RIVER CLUB
↓ *2*

Call 555-9888
For Reservations

MEDIAMAX, INC.

12 River Road
Freemont, CA 94539
510-555-5555

FAX: 510-666-6666

Today's date

Ms. Lonny Brady, Manager
65 Oak Lane
Freemont, CA 94539

Dear Ms. Brady:

As per your request for information about hotels in the San Francisco area, the following hotels have agreed to offer discounted rates to all attendees of Computer Expo and are within 20 minutes of the Convention Center.

Fairmont Hotel
Grand Hyatt
Hyatt Regency
King George Hotel
Nikko
Westin St. Francis

Hotels listed below offer free overnight parking:

Fairmont Hotel
Nikko
Westin St. Francis

When you call to make your reservation, explain that you are attending the Computer Expo at the Convention Center. A limited number of rooms are available at preferred rates, so plan early.

Sincerely,

Marvin Brother
Computer Expo Coordinator

mb/

EXERCISE

JUSTIFICATION **15**

Justify

NOTES:

▪ **Justification** lets you align all text that follows the justification code until another justification code is entered. WordPerfect provides five alignment options:

• **Left** - all lines are even at the left margin but are ragged at the right margin (the default).

• **Center** - all lines are centered between the margins.

• **Right** - all lines are ragged at the left margin and are even at the right margin.

• **Full** - all lines are even at the left and right margins, except for the last line of the paragraph.

• **All** - all lines are even at the left and right argins,including the last line of the paragraph.

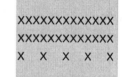

▪ Justification should be used to affect blocks of text, not individual lines.

▪ Justification may be changed before or after typing text.

▪ WordPerfect applies left justification to your text by default.

When you change justification of existing text, all text following the code changes. Do not be alarmed. Insert another justification code to return your text as desired.

EXERCISE DIRECTIONS:

In this exercise, you will create an announcement using center, left right, full and all justification.

1. Start with a clear screen.

2. Use the default margins.

3. Keyboard the letter on the right *exactly as shown*, including the circled, misspelled words.

4. Align text (center and flush right) where shown. Use full justification for paragraph text. Use all justification for the company name in the letterhead.

5. Spell check.

6. Preview your document.

7. Print one copy.

8. Save the file; name it **GLOBAL**.

9. Close the document window.

T H E   G L O B A L   T R A V E L   G R O U P

485 Madison Avenue
New York, NY 10034

PHONE: (212) 234-4566
FAX: (212) 345-9877

Today' Date

Mr. Astrit Ibrosi
45 Lake View Drive
Huntington, NY 11543

Dear Mr. Ibrosi:

Ms. Packer in our office has (refered) your letter to me. You had asked her to provide you with a list of hotels in the San Francisco area that have a business center which offers laptop rentals, fax services, and teleconferencing capabilities.

Since I am the representative for the San Francisco area, I have compiled a list of hotels that offer the services you requested. They appear below:

Regency Central
Surry Hotel
Fairmont Hotel
Renaissance Center
Marriott Mark
Grand Hyatt

When you are ready to make your reservations, please call our office. If you have any other travel needs, call GLOBAL. Our (expereinced) staff will give you prompt and (courtous) service and will answer all your travel questions.

Sincerely,

Marietta Dunn
Travel Representative

md/yo

JUSTIFY

Ctrl + L, Ctrl + R, Ctrl + E (center), Ctrl + J (full)

1. Place insertion point at beginning of text to receive justification change (new text).

   OR

   Select text to receive justification change (existing text).

2. Click **Format** .... `Alt` + `R`

3. Click **Justification** .... `J`

4. Click a justification option:

   • **Left** .... `L`

   • **Right** .... `R`

   • **Center** .... `E`

   • **Full** .... `F`

   • **All** .... `A`

   OR

• Click Justification......... `Left` button on Power bar.

• Click a justification option:

   • **Left**

   • **Right**

   • **Center**

   • **Full**

   • **All**

EXERCISE

CHANGING FONT FACE, STYLE AND SIZE

Font face   Font size

NOTES:

▪ A **font** is a complete set of characters in a specific face, style and size. Each set includes upper- and lowercase letters, numerals and punctuation. A font that might be available to you in WordPerfect is Arrus BLK BT.

▪ A **font face** (often called **typeface** or just **font**) is the design of a character. Each design has a name and is intended to convey a specific feeling.

▪ You should select typefaces that will make your document attractive and communicate its particular message. As a rule, use no more than two or three font faces in any one document.

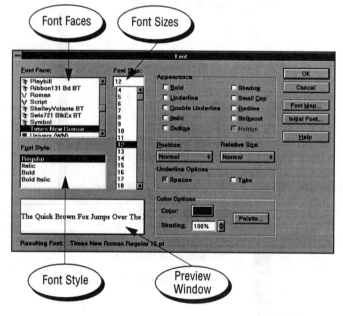

Font Faces   Font Sizes

Font Style   Preview Window

Font Faces

▪ There are basically three types of font faces: serif, sans serif, and script. A **serif** face has lines, curves or edges extending from the ends of the letter (**T**) while a **sans serif** face is straight-edged (**T**) and **script** looks like handwriting (𝒯).

Serif Font Face:

> Times New Roman

Sans Serif Font Face:

> Helvetica

Script Font Face:

> *Freestyle Script*

▪ A serif font face is typically used for document text because it is more readable. Sans serif is often used for headlines or technical material. Script typefaces are used for formal invitations and announcements.

▪ Font faces may be changed by selecting the desired font listed in the Font dialog box.

Or, it may be changed by clicking the Font Face button on the Power Bar (which drops down a list of font choices).

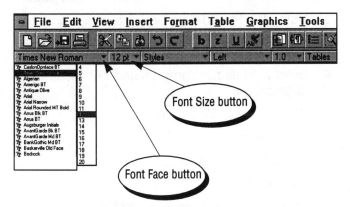

 The fonts that are available to you depend on your printer's capabilities.

■ The Font dialog box may be accessed by selecting Font from the Format main menu, double-clicking the Font Face or the Font Size button on the Power Bar, or clicking the *right* mouse button anywhere in the document window and selecting Font.

 In the Font dialog box, selected fonts are displayed in the Preview window at the lower left side and are described in the Resulting Font line.

Font Style

■ **Font style** refers to the slant and weight of letters, such as bold and italic.

> Times New Roman Regular
> *Times New Roman Italic*
> **Times New Roman Bold**
> ***Times New Roman Bold Italic***

■ Note the Font dialog box illustrated on the previous page. The Font Style box lists the styles or weights specially designed and available for the selected font. You may also apply attributes such as bold and italic, outline and small cap through the Appearance panel of the Font dialog box (this will be covered in the next exercises).

■ Fonts are also categorized as **monospaced** (fixed-pitch) or **proportional**.

> COURIER--MONOSPACED
> PALATINO--PROPORTIONAL

■ **Monospaced fonts**, such as Courier, allot the same horizontal space on the line for each character -- an **I** takes as much space as an **M**.

■ **Proportional fonts**, such as Times Roman, allot less space for letters such as **I** and more space for letters such as **M**.

Font Size

■ **Font size** generally refers to the height of the font, usually measured in points.

> Bookman 8 point
>
> Bookman 12 point
>
> Bookman 18 point
> Courier--10 pitch
> Courier--12 pitch

■ There are 72 points to an inch. However, monospaced font size may be expressed in characters per inch, such as Roman 10cpi. Use 10 to 12 point type size for document text and larger sizes for headings and headlines.

■ Font size may be changed in the Font dialog box or by clicking the Size button on the Power Bar (which drops down a list of font sizes).

■ The currently selected font, style and size is displayed in the Preview window and described in the Resulting Font line.

■ You can change fonts *before* or *after* typing text.

EXERCISE DIRECTIONS:

 In this exercise, you will change the font faces, styles and sizes of a previously created announcement.

1. Start with a clear screen.

2. Open **RSVP** if you completed it in Exercise 14.

   OR

   💾 Open **RSVP.16** from the data disk as a read-only file (Open As Copy).

To create the announcement shown on next page:

3. Using the Font dialog box, make the font face, font size, and font style changes indicated.

4. Enter the last paragraph using center justification.

5. Preview your document.

6. Print one copy.

7. Close the file; save the changes.

   OR

   💾 Close the file; *save as* **RSVP**.

CHANGE FONT FACE, FONT SIZE, AND FONT STYLE

F9

—*USING DIALOG BOX*—

1. Place insertion point where font change will begin (before typing).

   OR

   Select text to receive font change (after typing).

2. • Click **Format** .... `Alt` + `R`

   • Click **Font** .... `F`

   OR

   a. Click *right* mouse anywhere in the document window.

   b. Select **Font**

   OR

Double-click Font Face or Font Size button on Power Bar.

NOTE: *At Font dialog box, currently selected font is displayed in Preview window and described in resulting font line.*

3. In **Font Face** list, highlight desired font .... `F`

4. In **Font Style** box, highlight desired style .... `O`

5. In **Font Size** box, highlight desired size .... `S`

—*USING POWER BAR*—
(*FONT FACE AND FONT SIZE ONLY*)

1. Place insertion point where font change will begin (before typing).

OR

Select text to receive font change (after typing).

To change font face:

a. Click Font Face button ....  Times New Roman ▾

b. Select desired font from list.

To change font size:

a. Click Font Size button .... 12 pt ▾

b. Select desired size from list.

Celebrate) serif 60 pt bold

On The Hudson) sans serif 35 pt

NEW YEAR'S EVE DINNER DANCE) serif 28 pt bold

HUDSON RIVER CLUB) sans serif 28 pt

Call 555-9888
For Reservations) sans serif 10 pt

Our courteous staff will be glad to assist you at any time.
We are located at Four World Financial Center.) center sans serif 10 pt

EXERCISE

FONT APPEARANCE (BOLD, UNDERLINE, DOUBLE UNDERLINE, ITALIC)

NOTES:

- **Bold,** underline, double underline and *italic* are features used to emphasize or enhance text and are referred to as **appearance attributes**. These features work as on/off toggle switches. You must choose the command to turn on the feature; then choose the command to turn off the feature.

- The appearance of a font face is changed in the Font dialog box *(see illustration below)* or by using the style buttons shown above (there is no double underline button in the Toolbar).

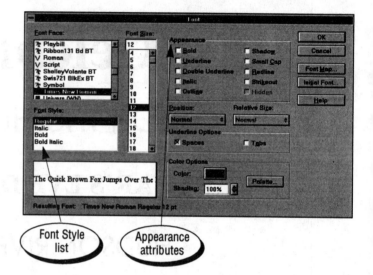

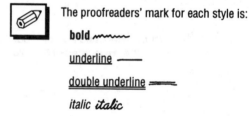

The proofreaders' mark for each style is:

bold 〰〰〰

underline ———

double underline ═══

italic *italic*

- As indicated in the previous exercise, Font Styles also adds bold and italics to a font face, but not all font faces have these styles added. If bold and italic are unavailable in the Font Style list box, they can be added as an appearance attribute.

- Text may be emphasized before or after typing text.

  NOTE: *Other appearance attributes (outline, shadow, small cap, redline, strikeout and hidden text) will be covered in the next lesson.*

 After bolding, underlining, double underlining or italicizing desired text, you must turn off the feature by repeating the procedure you used to turn on the feature.

EXERCISE DIRECTIONS:

 In this exercise, you will enhance a menu using varied font sizes and appearances.

1. Start with a clear screen.

2. ⌨ Keyboard the exercise as shown in the On Disk illustration

   OR

   💾 Open **FOOD.17** from the data disk as a read-only file (Open As Copy).

3. Center the page top to bottom.

4. Make the alignment, font face, appearance and size changes indicated in the exercise.

5. Preview your document.

6. Print one copy.

7. 💾 Close the file; *save as* **FOOD**.

APPEARANCE CHANGES

BOLD	*UNDERLINE*
Ctrl + B	Ctrl +U
ITALICS	*DOUBLE UNDERLINE*
Ctrl + I	*not applicable*

—USING FONT DIALOG BOX—

1. Place insertion point before text to receive appearance change (new text).

   OR

   Select/highlight text to receive appearance change (existing text).

2. • Click **Format** .... `Alt` + `R`

   • Click **Font** .... `F`

   OR

   Double-click Font Face .... `Times New Roman ▼` button on Power Bar.

3. • Click in box to select desired appearance change(s).

   • Click **OK** .... `Enter`

—USING TOOLBAR—

Click desired appearance button on Toolbar:

• Bold ....`b`

• Italics ....`i`

• Underline ....`u`

NOTE: Double underline must be selected on Font dialog box.

RETURN TO NORMAL OR TURN FEATURE OFF

1. Place insertion point where appearance change will end (new text).

   OR

   Select text to return to normal (existing text).

2. Click **Format**........................ `Alt` + `R`

   OR

   a. Click *right* mouse button.

   b. Click **Font** ....`F`

3. Click box to deselect appearance change.

4. Click **OK** .... `Enter`

   OR

   Click selected appearance button on Toolbar to turn feature off:

• Bold ....`b`

• Italics ....`i`

• Underline ....`u`

NOTE: Double underline must be deselected on Font dialog box.

ON DISK

The Sherwood Forest Inn) *center and set to sans serif 26 pt bold; press Enter key twice*
125 Pine Hill Road) *right align and set to sans serif*
Arlington, VA 22207) *12 pt bold italics*
703-987-4443

BREAKFAST MENU) *center*
sans serif 18 pt bold
double underline

BEVERAGES

Herbal Tea...$1.00
Coffee...$2.00
Cappuccino...$2.50

FRUITS

Berry Refresher...$3.00
Sparkling Citrus Blend...$3.00
Baked Apples...$3.50

center

GRAINS

Fruity Oatmeal...$3.50
Bran Muffins...$3.00
Whole Wheat Zucchini Bread...$3.00
Four-Grain Pancakes...$5.00

EGGS

Baked Eggs with Creamed Spinach...$6.50
Poached Eggs with Hollandaise Sauce...$6.00
Scrambled Eggs...$2.50
Sweet Pepper and Onion Frittata...$6.50

David Zeiss, Proprietor) *left align script 16 pt bold*

Set all headings to sans serif 12 pt bold, italics and underline Set all menu items to script 12 pt italics

DESIRED RESULT

The Sherwood Forest Inn

125 Pine Hill Road
Arlington, VA 22207
703-987-4443

BREAKFAST MENU

BEVERAGES

Herbal Tea...$1.00
Coffee...$2.00
Cappuccino...$2.50

FRUITS

Berry Refresher...$3.00
Sparkling Citrus Blend...$3.00
Baked Apples...$3.50

GRAINS

Fruity Oatmeal...$3.50
Bran Muffins...$3.00
Whole Wheat Zucchini Bread...$3.00
Four-Grain Pancakes...$5.00

EGGS

Baked Eggs with Creamed Spinach...$6.50
Poached Eggs with Hollandaise Sauce...$6.00
Scrambled Eggs...$2.50
Sweet Pepper and Onion Frittata...$6.50

David Zeiss, Proprietor

EXERCISE

18

FONT APPEARANCE (OUTLINE, SHADOW, SMALL CAPS, REDLINE AND STRIKEOUT)

NOTES:

- In addition to bold, underline and double underline, WordPerfect provides other emphasis styles. These include outline, shadow, small caps, redline and strikeout. **Redline** and **strikeout** emphasis styles are used to indicate text has been added, deleted or moved, and are useful when comparing the current document with a different version of a document. Redline displays on screen in red but usually appears shaded, underlined or with a series of vertical bars (depending on your printer) when printed. Note examples below:

  > outline
  > shadow
  > SMALL CAPS
  > redline
  > ~~strikeout~~

- Like the other appearance changes, these may be applied *before* or *after* typing text. They may be accessed using the same methods previously presented for the other appearance changes (*see previous exercise*).

- If your printer does not support italics, the printed copy will appear underlined. Some font appearances will not apply to certain font faces. For example, if you use outline or shadow on Courier, it simply appears bolded.

 The fonts and font appearances that are available to you depend on your printer's capabilities.

EXERCISE DIRECTIONS:

 In this exercise, you will enhance a flyer using bold, double underline, italics and shadow.

1. Start with a clear screen.

2. Open **GLOBAL** (if you completed it in Exercise 15).

   OR

   💾 Open **GLOBAL.18** from the data disk as a read-only file (Open As Copy).

3. Make the font face, size and appearance changes indicated in the exercise.

4. Preview your document.

5. Print one copy.

6. Close the file; save the changes.

   OR

   💾 Close the file; *save as* **GLOBAL**.

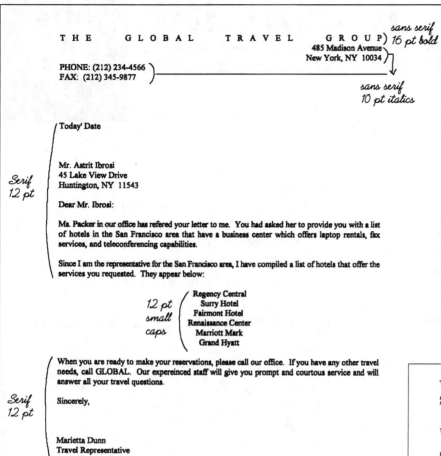

DESIRED RESULT

THE GLOBAL TRAVEL GROUP *sans serif 16 pt bold*
485 Madison Avenue
New York, NY 10034 *sans serif 10 pt italics*

PHONE: (212) 234-4566
FAX: (212) 345-9877

Serif 12 pt

Today' Date

Mr. Astrit Ibrosi
45 Lake View Drive
Huntington, NY 11543

Dear Mr. Ibrosi:

Ms. Packer in our office has refered your letter to me. You had asked her to provide you with a list of hotels in the San Francisco area that have a business center which offers laptop rentals, fax services, and teleconferencing capabilities.

Since I am the representative for the San Francisco area, I have compiled a list of hotels that offer the services you requested. They appear below:

12 pt small caps
Regency Central
Surry Hotel
Fairmont Hotel
Renaissance Center
Marriott Mark
Grand Hyatt

When you are ready to make your reservations, please call our office. If you have any other travel needs, call GLOBAL. Our expereinced staff will give you prompt and courtous service and will answer all your travel questions.

Serif 12 pt
Sincerely,

Marietta Dunn
Travel Representative

md/yo

OUTLINE/SHADOW/SMALL CAPS/REDLINE/STRIKEOUT

F9

1. Place insertion point before text to receive appearance change (before typing).

   OR

   Select/highlight text to receive appearance change (after typing).

2. Click **Format** .... `Alt` + `R`

   OR

   Click *right* mouse button anywhere in document window.

3. Click **Font** .... `F`

4. Click box to select desired appearance change.

5. Click **OK** .... `Enter`

NOTE: Outline, Shadow, Small Caps, Redline and Strikeout must be selected on Font menu.

RETURN TO NORMAL OR TURN FEATURE OFF

1. Place insertion point where appearance change will end (before typing).

   OR

   Select/highlight text to return to normal (after typing).

2. Click **Format** .... `Alt` + `R`

   OR

   Click *right* mouse button anywhere in document window.

3. Click **Font** .... `F`

4. Click box to deselect appearance change.

5. Click **OK** .... `Enter`

EXERCISE

▪ ORNAMENTAL FONTS ▪ SPECIAL CHARACTERS

19

NOTES:

Ornamental Fonts

▪ **Wingdings** and **Monotype Sorts** are ornamental or symbol font face collections that are used to enhance a document. Below and on the next page are Wingding and Monotype Sort font collections.

 A symbol font face must be available with your printer.

▪ The upper- and lowercase of the letter and character key provide different Wingdings and/or Monotype Sorts. To choose a Wingding or a Monotype Sort face, select the font face and then press the corresponding keyboard letter or character shown in the chart.

 Many of the symbols are the same in each font collection.

Wingding Sorts Font Collection

Monotype Sorts Font Collection

Special Characters

- Another source of ornamental fonts is the special character sets called **Iconic Symbols**.

- Special characters may be accessed by selecting <u>C</u>haracter from the <u>I</u>nsert main menu, or by pressing Ctrl + W. The following dialog box appears, with the most recently used character set selected:

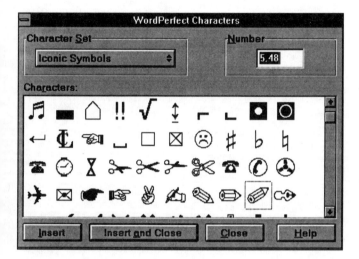

- Special character sets are also found as fonts. They can be accessed through the Font dialog box, and all begin with WP.

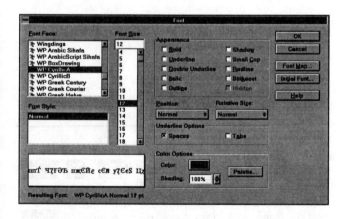

- You may change the size of a symbol font face as you would any other character, by changing the point size.

- Ornamental characters can be used to:

  - Separate items on a page:

  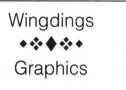

  - Emphasize items on a list:

  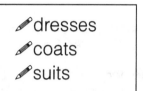

  - Enhance a page:

  - Add an in-line graphic:

  Save your document on 🖫

EXERCISE DIRECTIONS:

 In this exercise, you will add a symbol face to separate portions of a menu created earlier.

1. Start with a clear screen.

2. Open **FOOD** if you completed it in Exercise 17.

   OR

   💾 Open **FOOD.19** from the data disk as a read-only file (Open As Copy).

3. Enhance the document with symbols from the Wingding font collection and Special Characters where indicated in the exercise. Use any desired Wingding; use the special characters shown.

4. Make the other changes to font faces and alignments as directed in the exercise.

5. Preview your document.

6. Print one copy.

7. Close the file; save the changes.

   OR

   💾 Close the file; *save as* **FOOD**.

ADD A SYMBOL FONT

1. Position insertion point where symbol font will begin.

2. Press **F9** .... `F9`

   OR

   a. Click *right* mouse button anywhere in document window.

   b. Select Font.

   OR

   Click Font Face ....  button on Power Bar.

3. In Font Face list, choose Wingdings or Monotype Sorts.

4. Press the keyboard letter or character for the desired symbol *(see charts on previous pages)*.

5. To turn off symbol font, repeat step 3 and choose a different font.

INSERT SPECIAL CHARACTERS

1. Position insertion point to the left of where you wish to insert character.

2. Press **Ctrl + W** .... `Ctrl` + `W`

   OR

   a. Click **Insert** .... `Alt` + `I`

   b. Click **Character** .... `C`

3. Click **Character Set** `Alt` + `S`, `Space` list box to display character set list.

4. Click desired character set. .... `Enter`

5. Click desired symbol.

6. Click **Insert** .... `Alt` + `I`

   Click **Close** .... `Alt` + `C`

   OR

   Click **Insert and Close** .... `Alt` + `A`

Insert Special Character 5, 166;
space before and after each character.

The Sherwood Forest Inn

Insert special character 5, 167

**125 Pine Hill Road
Arlington, VA 22207
703-987-4443**

BREAKFAST MENU

BEVERAGES

Herbal Tea...$1.00
Coffee...$2.00
Cappuccino...$2.50

FRUITS

Berry Refresher...$3.00
Sparkling Citrus Blend...$3.00
Baked Apples...$3.50

Insert centered Wingdings (no Italics) here and insert one blank line

GRAINS

Fruity Oatmeal...$3.50
Bran Muffins...$3.00
Whole Wheat Zucchini Bread...$3.00
Four-Grain Pancakes...$5.00

EGGS

Baked Eggs with Creamed Spinach...$6.50
Poached Eggs with Hollandaise Sauce...$6.00
Scrambled Eggs...$2.50
Sweet Pepper and Onion Frittata...$6.50

Insert special character 5, 74

David Leis, Proprietor   *right align*

DESIRED RESULT

The ❦ Sherwood ❦ Forest ❦ Inn

**125 Pine Hill Road
Arlington, VA 22207
703-987-4443**

❧BREAKFAST MENU❧

BEVERAGES

Herbal Tea...$1.00
Coffee...$2.00
Cappuccino...$2.50

✦❖✦✖✦✖❖

FRUITS

Berry Refresher...$3.00
Sparkling Citrus Blend...$3.00
Baked Apples...$3.50

✦❖✦✖✦✖❖

GRAINS

Fruity Oatmeal...$3.50
Bran Muffins...$3.00
Whole Wheat Zucchini Bread...$3.00
Four-Grain Pancakes...$5.00

✦❖✦✖✦✖❖

EGGS

Baked Eggs with Creamed Spinach...$6.50
Poached Eggs with Hollandaise Sauce...$6.00
Scrambled Eggs...$2.50
Sweet Pepper and Onion Frittata...$6.50

David Leis❖Proprietor

EXERCISE

REMOVE FONT APPEARANCE

20

NOTES:

Remove Font Appearance

▪ If you decide you would like to remove the font appearance you applied to text, select/highlight the text where the style is to be removed and repeat the procedure used to apply the appearance change. You can also remove font appearances by deleting the codes that were inserted when the styles were applied. *(See Exercise 12, Deleting Codes.)*

Drag code off the screen

To delete a code in Reveal Codes mode:

• Use the mouse pointer to click on the code and press the Delete key, or

• Use the mouse pointer to drag the code out of the Reveal Codes window.

EXERCISE DIRECTIONS:

 In this exercise, you will delete appearance changes from a previously saved menu.

1. Start with a clear screen.

2. Open **FOOD** (if you completed it in Exercise 19).

   OR

   💾 Open **FOOD.20** from the data disk as a read-only file (Open As Copy).

3. Using any desired method, remove the font appearances indicated in the exercise.

4. Preview your document.

5. Print one copy.

6. Close the file; save the changes.

   OR

   💾 Close the file; *save as* **FOOD**.

The ✿ Sherwood ✿ Forest ✿ Inn

125 Pine Hill Road
Arlington, VA 22207
703-987-4443

➤❧BREAKFAST MENU❧➤ ⟩ *Remove double underline*

BEVERAGES

Herbal Tea...$1.00
Coffee...$2.00
Cappuccino...$2.50

●✧✖✧✖●

FRUITS

Berry Refresher...$3.00
Sparkling Citrus Blend...$3.00
Baked Apples...$3.50

●✧✖✧✖●

Remove
underline

GRAINS

Fruity Oatmeal...$3.50
Bran Muffins...$3.00
Whole Wheat Zucchini Bread...$3.00
Four-Grain Pancakes...$5.00

●✧✖✧✖●

EGGS

Baked Eggs with Creamed Spinach...$6.50
Poached Eggs with Hollandaise Sauce...$5.00
Scrambled Eggs...$2.50
Sweet Pepper and Onion Frittata...$6.50

David Leis✿Proprie...

DESIRED RESULT

The ✿ Sherwood ✿ Forest ✿ Inn

125 Pine Hill Road
Arlington, VA 22207
703-987-4443

➤❧BREAKFAST MENU❧➤

BEVERAGES

Herbal Tea...$1.00
Coffee...$2.00
Cappuccino...$2.50

●✧✖✧✖●

FRUITS

Berry Refresher...$3.00
Sparkling Citrus Blend...$3.00
Baked Apples...$3.50

●✧✖✧✖●

GRAINS

Fruity Oatmeal...$3.50
Bran Muffins...$3.00
Whole Wheat Zucchini Bread...$3.00
Four-Grain Pancakes...$5.00

●✧✖✧✖●

EGGS

Baked Eggs with Creamed Spinach...$6.50
Poached Eggs with Hollandaise Sauce...$5.00
Scrambled Eggs...$2.50
Sweet Pepper and Onion Frittata...$6.50

David Leis✿Proprietor

REMOVE FONT APPEARANCE

1. Select/highlight text to change appearance or return to normal.

2. Click *right* mouse button anywhere in document window.

    OR

    a. Click **Fo**rmat .... `Alt` + `R`

    b. Click **F**ont .... `F`

3. Click appearance change to remove.

    OR

    Click desired appearance button:

    • Bold .... `b`

    • Italic .... `i`

    • Underline .... `u`

OR

a. Reveal Codes .... `Alt` + `F3`

b. Drag code off screen.

LESSON 4
SUMMARY EXERCISE A

EXERCISE DIRECTIONS:

1. Start with a clear screen.

2. ⌨ Type the exercise as shown in the On Disk illustration.

   OR

   💾 Open **COLOR.4A** from the data disk as a read-only file (Open As Copy).

To create the flyer as shown in the Desired Result illustration:

3. Set top and bottom margins to .5".

4. Center the page from top to bottom.

5. Change the alignment, font face, size and style of the text as indicated in the exercise.

6. Insert any desired symbol font and special character where indicated.

7. Preview your document.

8. Print one copy.

9. 💾 Close the file; *save as* **COLOR**.

ON DISK

Increase Your Sales
Make an Impact with Color

ColorMasters
Full color documents have a greater
impact on clients

Our color printing service is
designed for short run orders, so it
has never been faster or more
affordable to capture your audience's
attention and increase sales.

Whether you need spot color or
photographs, simply send us your
disk or modem your computer files
and we will output them in full color.

Brochures
Reports
Flyers
Posters
Postcards
Overheads
Promo Kits
Presentations

4 to 72 Hour Service
Satisfaction Guaranteed

TechColor
87 Avenue of Americas New York NY 10033 212-555-6666

DESIRED RESULT

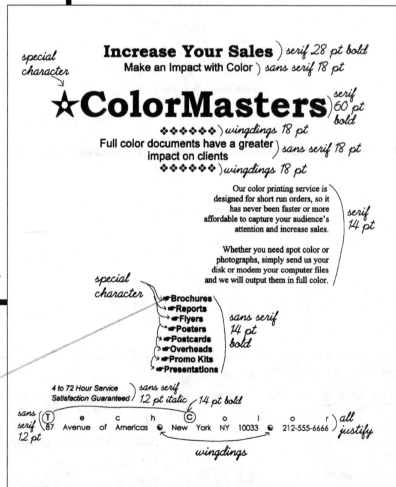

CTRL-W
Enter

82

LESSON 4
SUMMARY EXERCISE B

EXERCISE DIRECTIONS:

1. Start with a clear screen.

2. ⌨ Type the exercise as shown in the On Disk illustration.

   OR

   💾 Open **DESIGN 4B** from the data disk as a read-only file (Open As Copy).

   To create the flyer as shown in the Desired Result illustration on the next page:

3. Center the page from top to bottom.

4. Change the alignment, font face, size and style of the text as indicated in the exercise.

5. Insert any desired symbol font and special character where indicated.

6. Preview your document.

7. Print one copy.

8. Close the file; name it **DESIGN**.

   OR

   💾 Close the file, *save as* **DESIGN**.

ON DISK

Create a
Design with Color

4 Reasons Why

The world is a colorful place.
So, why not include color in all your
processing?

Color increases the visual impact of the
message and makes it more memorable.
Don't you want your ads to have impact and be noticed?

Color creates a feeling and helps explain
the subject. Greens and blues are cool, relaxing tones,
while reds and oranges scream with emphasis. Pastels
communicate a gentle tone.

Color creates a personality. You can make your
corporate forms and brochures have their own identity
and personality with color.

Color highlights information. An advertisement
or manual might have warnings in red, explanations in
black and instructions in blue.

Our color processing labs will take care of *all* your color processing needs. Just call **1-800-555-6666** for information. Our courteous staff is ready to assist you with any technical question.

**LABPRO
FOR
COLOR PROCESSING**

DESIRED RESULT

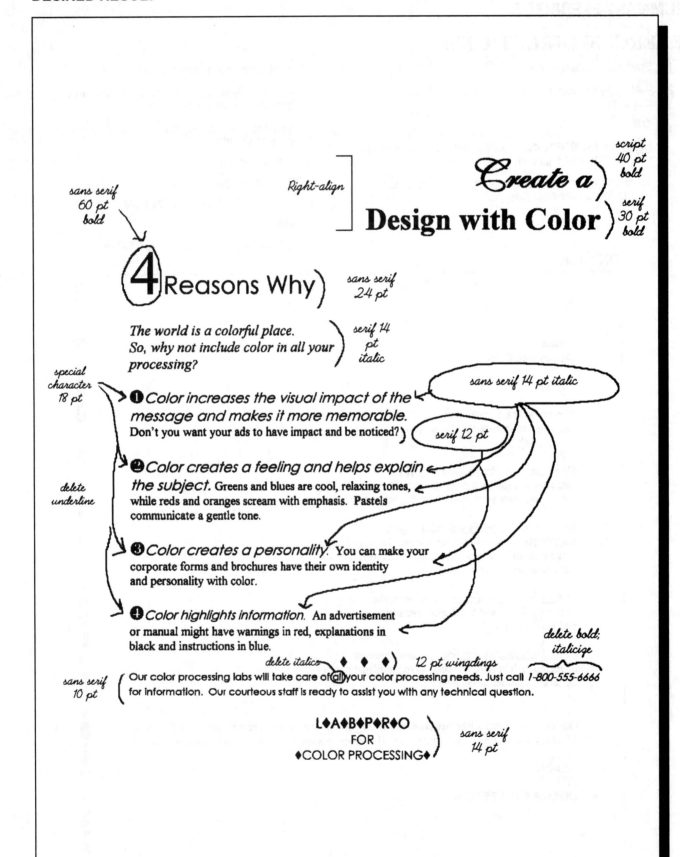

script 40 pt bold

serif 30 pt bold

Create a
Design with Color

Right-align

sans serif 60 pt bold

④ Reasons Why)

sans serif 24 pt

The world is a colorful place.
So, why not include color in all your
processing?

serif 14 pt italic

special character 18 pt

sans serif 14 pt italic

❶ *Color increases the visual impact of the*
message and makes it more memorable.
Don't you want your ads to have impact and be noticed?)

serif 12 pt

delete underline

❷ *Color creates a feeling and helps explain*
the subject. Greens and blues are cool, relaxing tones,
while reds and oranges scream with emphasis. Pastels
communicate a gentle tone.

❸ *Color creates a personality.* You can make your
corporate forms and brochures have their own identity
and personality with color.

❹ *Color highlights information.* An advertisement
or manual might have warnings in red, explanations in
black and instructions in blue.

delete bold; italicize

delete italics ♦ ♦ ♦) 12 pt wingdings

sans serif 10 pt

Our color processing labs will take care of all your color processing needs. Just call *1-800-555-6666*
for information. Our courteous staff is ready to assist you with any technical question.

L♦A♦B♦P♦R♦O
FOR
♦COLOR PROCESSING♦

sans serif 14 pt

84

LESSON 5

Exercises 21–27

- Line Spacing

- Indenting Text

- Format a One-Page Report

- Set Margins and Tabs

- Relative vs. Absolute Tabs

- Hanging Indent

- First-Line Indent

- Moving Text

- QuickFormat

- Linked Headings

- Copy and Paste

- Drag and Drop

- Make-It-Fit

EXERCISE

▪ LINE SPACING ▪ INDENTING TEXT

21

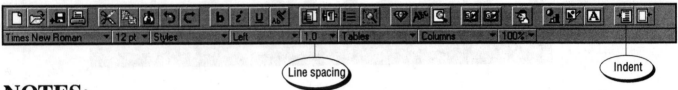

Line spacing

Indent

NOTES:

Line Spacing

▪ Use line spacing to specify the spacing between lines of text. A line spacing change affects text from the insertion point forward. Line spacing may also be applied to selected text. If your line spacing is set for double, two hard returns will result in four blank lines.

• The quickest way to change line spacing is to click the Line Spacing button on the Power bar and select a line spacing amount.

• If you want to preview the effect of the line spacing change on your document, set the line spacing amount in the Line Spacing dialog box (which appears after selecting Line, Spacing from the Format menu). The preview window illustrates the effect of your line spacing selection.

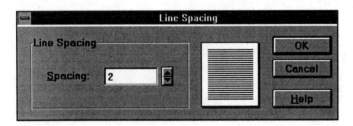

Indenting Text

▪ The **Indent** feature moves a complete paragraph one tab stop to the right and sets a temporary left margin for the paragraph.

▪ The **Double Indent** feature indents paragraph text one tab stop from both margins.

▪ Paragraphs may be indented before or after text is typed.

▪ Since text is indented to a tab setting, accessing the Indent feature once will indent text .5" to the right (or left and right); accessing it twice will indent text 1", etc.

▪ The Indent mode is ended by a hard return.

▪ Before accessing the Indent feature, be sure to position the insertion point to the left of the first word in the paragraph to be indented.

■ The Indent feature may be accessed by clicking the Indent button on the Toolbar or selecting Paragraph from the Format main menu, then selecting Indent or Double Indent from the resulting submenu.

Or, to indent from the left margin only, you may click the Indent button on the Toolbar 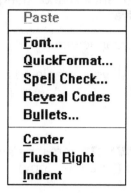 or click the *right* mouse button and select Indent.

 The proofreaders' symbol for indenting is: ⅀ or .⅀

EXERCISE DIRECTIONS:

 In this exercise, you will change line spacing, indent text and change fonts to create a flyer.

1. Start with a clear screen.

2. Open **DIVE** (if you completed it in Exercise 11).

   OR

   💾 Open **DIVE.21** from the data disk as a read-only file (Open As Copy).

3. Make the indicated revisions.

4. Full justify document text.

5. Spell check.

6. Preview your document.

7. Print one copy.

8. Save the file; name it **DIVE**.

   OR

   💾 Close the file; *save as* **DIVE**.

LINE SPACING

1. Place insertion point within paragraph where line spacing change will begin.

   OR

   Select text to receive line spacing change.

2. • Click Line Spacing .... `1.0`
      button on Power Bar.

   • Select line spacing amount.

   OR

   a. Click **Format** .... `Alt` + `R`

   b. Click **Line** .... `L`

   c. Click **Spacing** .... `S`

3. Type desired spacing amount............. `S`
   in **Spacing** text box

   EXAMPLES:

   1.5 = one and one-half space

   2 = double space

   3 = triple space

   OR

   Click increment arrows to select a line spacing amount.

4. Click **OK** .... `Enter`

INDENT/DOUBLE INDENT
F7/Ctrl + Shift + F7

—FOR LEFT INDENT ONLY—

   Click Indent button on .... `▤`
   Toolbar once for each .5" indention.

   OR

   a. Click *right* mouse button.

   b. Select Indent.

—FOR LEFT AND/OR RIGHT INDENT—

1. Place insertion point where indention should begin.

2. Click **Format** .... `Alt` + `R`

3. Click **Paragraph** .... `A`

4. Click **Indent** .... `I`

   OR

   Click **Double Indent** .... `D`

END INDENT MODE

   Press **Enter** .... `Enter`

Set body text to 14 pt

DIVING IN THE CAYMAN ISLANDS) *center and set to 18 pt sans serif bold*

Double space. Delete returns between paragraphs

Do you want to see sharks, barracudas, ~~and~~ stingrays? *and angelfish* ~~Do you want to see angels, too?~~

and The Cayman Islands were discovered by Christopher Columbus in 1503 ~~The Cayman Islands~~ are located south of Cuba. The Caymans are home to ~~only~~ about 25,000 year-around residents. However, they welcome ~~approximately~~ 200,000 visitors each year. Most visitors come with masks and flippers in their luggage.

~~Now, you are ready to jump in!~~

Hotel/Diving Accommodations:) *set to sans serif 14 pt bold*

Single space and double indent

(Sunset House,) *PO* Box 4791, George Town, Grand Cayman; (800) 854-4767.

(Coconut Harbour,) *PO* Box 2086, George Town, Grand Cayman; (809) 949-7468.

(Red Sail Sports,) PO Box 1588, George Town, Grand Cayman; (809) 854-4767.

Set circled hotels to italics

(Cayman Diving Lodge,) PO Box 11, East End, Grand Cayman; (809) 947-7555.

(Anchorage View,) PO Box 2123, Grand Cayman; (809) 947-4209.

DESIRED RESULT

DIVING IN THE CAYMAN ISLANDS

Do you want to see sharks, barracudas, stingrays and angelfish?

The Cayman Islands were discovered by Christopher Columbus in 1503 and are located south of Cuba. The Caymans are home to about 25,000 year-around residents. However, they welcome 200,000 visitors each year. Most visitors come with masks and flippers in their luggage.

Hotel/Diving Accommodations:

Sunset House, PO Box 4791, George Town, Grand Cayman; (800) 854-4767.

Coconut Harbour, PO Box 2086, George Town, Grand Cayman; (809) 949-7468.

Red Sail Sports, PO Box 1588, George Town, Grand Cayman; (809) 979-7965.

Cayman Diving Lodge, PO Box 11, East End, Grand Cayman; (809) 947-7555.

Anchorage View, PO Box 2123, Grand Cayman; (809) 947-4209.

Lesson 5 ▪ Exercise 21   89

EXERCISE

▪ FORMAT A ONE-PAGE REPORT ▪ SET MARGINS AND TABS

22

Page Margins

NOTES:

- A **report** or manuscript generally begins 2" from the top of the page and is prepared in double space. Each new paragraph begins .5" from the left margin (tab once). The title of a report is centered and keyed in all caps. A quadruple space follows the title.

- Margins vary depending on how the report is bound. For an unbound report, use margins of 1" on the left and right (the default).

Set Margins

- WordPerfect measures margins in inches.

- The default margins are 1" on all sides of the page.

- A left/right margin change affects text beginning with the paragraph in which the insertion point is placed. To change margins for the entire document, place the insertion point at the beginning (or within the first paragraph) of the text to receive the margin change.

- Margins may be changed by selecting Margins from the Format main menu or by clicking the Page Margins button [≡] on the Toolbar.

  NOTE: The Page Margins button is visible only if an 800 x 600 video display is chosen in Windows Setup.

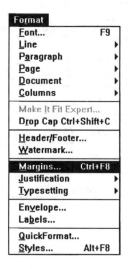

- Then, in the Margins dialog box which follows, enter precise settings for each margin.

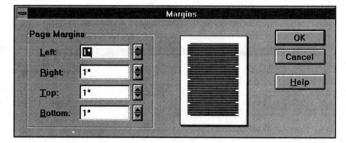

- Left and right margins may also be changed on the Ruler bar.

Margin markers

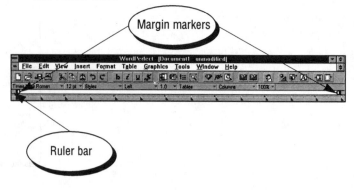

Ruler bar

- Using the Ruler bar to set margins lets you see the effects of margin changes as you make them.

- Drag (click and hold left mouse button) the left and/or right margin markers (the solid black part of the marker) to the desired position. Text adjusts to the new margins when the mouse button is released. As you drag the marker, note the margin position which displays in the lower right of the status bar.

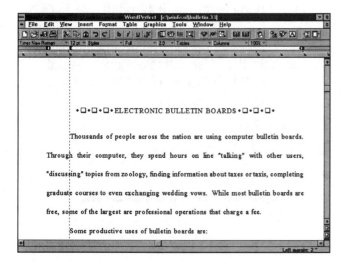

Set Tabs

- The Tab key indents a single line of text. Default tabs are set .5" apart. When the Tab key is pressed once, text will advance 1/2 inch; when the Tab key is pressed twice, text will advance 1 inch, etc.

- If you desire text to advance .8" each time the Tab key is pressed, you can do so by changing the tab settings.

- When you change tab settings in a document, changes take effect from that point forward.

- Tabs may be changed on the Ruler bar or by selecting Line/Tab Set from the Format main menu.

Setting Tabs on the Ruler Bar

- Tab settings are displayed on the Ruler Bar as left-pointing triangles which are set .5" apart. Left-pointing triangles represent left-aligned tab settings. (Other tab types will be covered in Lesson 9).

Ruler bar

Left aligned tab sets

- To set a new left-aligned tab, click anywhere on the Ruler bar where a new tab is desired; a new tab marker is inserted. To delete a tab setting, drag the tab marker (triangle) off the Ruler bar.

- Tabs may also be set using the Tab Set dialog box. This method lets you set and clear tab positions and tab types in one operation. You cannot, however, see the result of your changes on text until all settings have been made.

Relative vs. Absolute Tabs

- When you set tabs, you can measure them from the left edge of the page (absolute tabs) or from the left margin (relative tabs). Default tab settings are relative to the left margin. The left edge of the page begins at zero (0) on the tab set ruler.

- Relative and absolute tabs are set on the Tab Set dialog box.

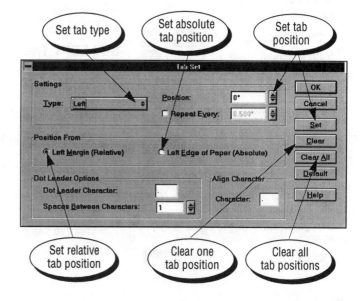

Set tab type

Set absolute tab position

Set tab position

Set relative tab position

Clear one tab position

Clear all tab positions

EXERCISE DIRECTIONS:

In this exercise, you will create a one-page report, setting new margins and tabs. You will also review line spacing and double indent procedures.

1. Start with a clear screen.

2. Set 1.5" left and right margins in the Margins dialog box.

3. Display the Ruler bar.

4. Drag the 2" tab marker off the Ruler bar (making the first tab stop 1" from the left margin or 2.5" from the left edge of the page).

    NOTE: To see the position of the tab marker, point to a marker and click and hold the left mouse button. Note tab position on bottom right of the Status bar.

5. Keyboard the report on the right.

    • Begin the title on Ln 2". Use any desired Wingding font before and after the heading as shown.

    • Set title to sans serif 14 point bold. Center the title.

    • Set subheadings to sans serif 12 point bold.

    • Set body text to serif 12 point.

6. Double space the first and last paragraphs; double indent and single space the middle paragraphs. Use the telephone special character before each middle paragraph.

7. Full justify paragraph text.

8. Spell check.

9. Preview your document.

10. Print one copy.

11. Save the file; name it **BULLETIN**.

SET MARGINS
(Left/Right, Top/Bottom)
Ctrl + F8

1. Place insertion point where margin change will begin.

2. Click Page Margins button............. on Toolbar.

    OR

    a. Click **Fo_r_mat** .... Alt + R

    b. Click **_M_argins** .... M

3. Click appropriate text box to change desired margin:

    • **_L_eft**............................. Alt + L

    • **_R_ight** .... Alt + R

    • **_T_op** .... Alt + T

    • **_B_ottom** .... Alt + B

4. Type margin amount.

    OR

    Click increment arrows to select margin amount.

5. Click **OK** .... Enter

—USING RULER BAR FOR LEFT/RIGHT MARGIN CHANGE—

1. Display Ruler bar.

    a. Click **_V_iew** .... Alt + V

    b. Click **_R_uler** .... R

2. Drag left and/or right margin markers to desired positions.

SET LEFT TABS
—USING RULER BAR—

To delete a tab:

a. Drag the tab marker (triangle) off the Ruler bar.

b. Click anywhere on Ruler bar to set a new tab.

—USING THE TAB SET DIALOG BOX—

1. • Click **Fo_r_mat** .... Alt + R

    • Click **_L_ine** L

    • Click **_T_ab Set**............................. T

    OR

Double-click a tab marker (triangle) on the Ruler bar.

2. Click how tabs are to be measured (Position From):

    Left _M_argin (Relative) .... Alt + M

    OR

    Left _E_dge of Paper................ Alt + E
    (Absolute)

    To clear desired tab setting:

    a. Click **_P_osition** text box .... Alt + P

    b. Type position of tab to be cleared.

    c. Click **_C_lear** C

    OR

    Click **Clear _A_ll** .... A
    to clear all tabs.

    To set desired tab:

    a. Click **_P_osition** text box ...... Alt + P

    b. Type position of tab to set.

    c. Click **_S_et** .... S

3. Click **OK** .... Enter
    when tabs are set as desired.

◆□◆□◆□◆ ELECTRONIC BULLETIN BOARDS ◆□◆□◆□◆

2.5" ←————→ *1"* ←————→ Thousands of people across the nation are using computer bulletin

boards. Through their computer, they spend hours on line "talking" with other users,

"discussing" topics from zoology, finding information about taxes or taxis, completing

graduate courses to even exchanging wedding vows.

PRODUCTIVE USES INCLUDE:

☎A system created by a car expert in Las Vegas lists
thousands of collectors' cars.

☎A system developed by a retired guidance counselor in Atlanta provides current information on
scholarships and loans.

☎A system set up by a hospital in West Virginia
offers detailed answers to medical questions for
people who do not want to travel long distances
necessary to see a doctor.

BASIC NEEDS:

Tab ————→ All you need to connect a bulletin board is a computer and a modem

connected to a telephone line.

BASIC COSTS:

Tab ————→ Besides the basic fee of subscribing to a bulletin board, the cost of

"talking" on your computer is the same as talking on your phone, since phone lines

are used for data transmission. While most bulletin boards are free, some of the

largest are professional operations that charge a fee.

EXERCISE

▪ HANGING INDENT ▪ FIRST-LINE INDENT

23

NOTES

Hanging Indent

- When all the lines in a paragraph are indented except the first line, a **hanging indent** is created.

- Note the effect of a hanging indented paragraph below. The second and succeeding lines of the paragraph indent to the first tab stop.

> This paragraph is an example of a "hanging indent." Note that all the lines in the paragraph are indented except the first line. This can be an effective way to emphasize paragraph text. This paragraph style is commonly used for bibliographies.

- A hanging indent may be set by selecting Paragraph, Hanging Indent from the Format main menu.

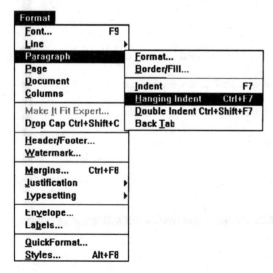

First-Line Indent

- A **first-line indent** lets you set the amount of space each paragraph indents. Each time you press Enter, the insertion point automatically begins at the indented setting. This feature eliminates the need to use the Tab key to indent each new paragraph.

- First-line indents may be set by clicking the Paragraph Format button on the Toolbar or by selecting Paragraph from the Format main menu, then selecting Format from the submenu.

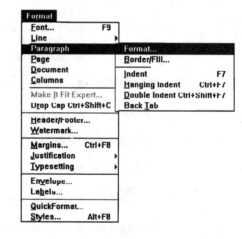

- In the Paragraph Format dialog box which follows, you may enter the amount you wish each paragraph to indent in the First Line Indent text box. You may also add extra spacing between paragraphs each time you press Enter in the Spacing Between Paragraphs text box.

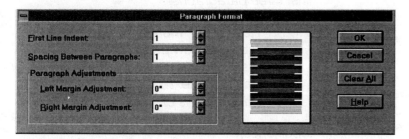

- First-line indents may also be set by dragging the first-line indent marker (the top left triangle) right on the Ruler bar to the desired first-line indent position. As the marker is being moved, the Status bar displays the exact position of the marker. This method allows you to see the effect of your change as the marker is moved.

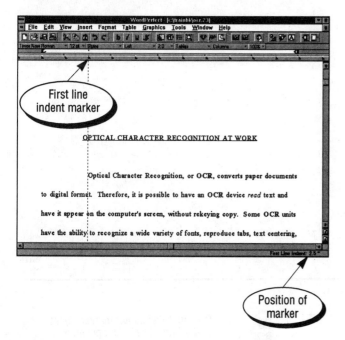

EXERCISE DIRECTIONS:

 In this exercise, you will create a one-page report, setting first-line indent for some paragraphs and hanging indents for others. You will also gain more practice using the line spacing, margins and font features.

1. Start with a clear screen.

2. Display the Ruler bar.

3. • Using the margin markers on the Ruler bar, set 1.5" left and right margins. (To set 1.5" right margin, drag the right margin marker to 7" on the Ruler bar.)

   • Using the Margins dialog box, set a .5" bottom margin.

4. Keyboard the report on the right:

   • Begin the title on Ln 2".

   • Use any desired special character before and after the title as shown.

   • Set title to sans serif 14 point bold.

   • Set body text to serif 12 point.

   • Set cities to a sans serif bold.

5. Set a 1" first line indent and double space the *first two paragraphs*.

6. Set hanging indents and single space the *last three paragraphs*.

   NOTE: Remember, there is no need to tab each new paragraph. The first-line indent automatically advances text 1" when a new paragraph is created.

7. Spell check.

8. Preview your document.

9. Print one copy.

10. Save the file; name it **OCR**.

HANGING INDENT
Ctrl + F7

1. Click **F**o**rmat** .... Alt + R
2. Click **P**a**ragraph** .... A
3. Click **H**anging Indent .... H

   To End Hanging Indent Mode:

   Press **Enter** .... Enter

FIRST-LINE INDENT

1. Place insertion point where indentation should begin.
2. Click **F**o**rmat** .... Alt + R

3. Click **P**a**ragraph** .... A
4. Click **F**ormat............................... F
5. Click **F**irst Line .... Alt + F
   Indent text box.
6. Enter first-line indent amount.

   OR

   Click increment arrows to select a first-line indent amount.
7. Click **OK** .... Enter

—USING RULER BAR—

1. Place insertion point where indentation should begin.

2. Drag first-line indent marker *right* to desired first-line indent position.

RETURN TO PREVIOUS SETTINGS

1. Place insertion point where reset adjustments should begin.
2. Click **F**o**rmat** .... Alt + R
3. Click **P**a**ragraph** .... A
4. Click **F**ormat............................... F
5. Click **Clear A**ll .... A
6. Click **OK** .... Enter

❀OPTICAL CHARACTER RECOGNITION AT WORK❀

Optical Character Recognition, or **OCR**, converts paper documents to digital format. Therefore, it is possible to have an **OCR** device *read* text and have it appear on the computer's screen, without rekeying copy. Some **OCR** units have the ability to recognize a wide variety of fonts, reproduce tabs, text centering, and other formatting. Most **OCR** units process pages three or four times faster than the average typist's 70 words per minute.

Here are some interesting ways in which companies use Optical Character Recognition to ease their work loads:

A **Boston** service bureau recently scanned and republished a client's large medical catalog, a project that would have otherwise been too time consuming to undertake.

A **New York**-based newspaper plans to create data files of their back issues, many of which were published in 1845.

A **Maryland** company needed to transfer files from an aging word processing system to a newer one. It discovered that printing the files from the old system and then scanning them into the new system was less expensive.

EXERCISE

24

▪ CUT AND PASTE ▪ DRAG AND DROP ▪ QUICKFORMAT

NOTES:

▪ **Cut and Paste** and **Drag and Drop** are features that let you move a block of text, a sentence, paragraph, page or column to another location in the same document or to another document.

Cut and Paste

▪ The **Cut** procedure allows you to cut or delete selected text from the screen and temporarily place it on the Clipboard (temporary storage buffer). The **Paste** procedure allows you to retrieve text from the Clipboard and place it in a desired location in the document.

▪ There are several procedures to cut and paste text. *(See keystrokes on page 100.)*

▪ Information remains on the Clipboard until you cut or copy another selection (or until you exit Windows). Therefore, you can paste the same selection into many different locations, if desired.

Drag and Drop

▪ The **Drag and Drop** method of moving text allows you to move selected text using your mouse. This method is convenient for moving a word(s) or a block of text from one location to another.

▪ Once text to be moved is selected, place the mouse pointer anywhere on the selected text and click and hold the *left* mouse button as you **drag** the highlighted text to the new location. The mouse pointer changes to a box with a dotted shadow to indicate that you are dragging text.

▪ When you reach the new location, release the mouse button to **drop** the text into place. Be sure to remove the selection highlight before pressing any key, so that you do not delete your newly moved text.

▪ If text was not reinserted at the correct point, you can undo it (Edit, Undo). It is sometimes necessary to insert or delete spaces, returns, or tabs after completing a move.

▪ If you wish to move an indented or tabbed paragraph, be sure the indent or tab code to the left of the text is moved along with the paragraph. To insure this, reveal codes and check that the cursor is to the left of the code to be moved before selecting text.

QuickFormat

- The QuickFormat feature allows you to copy formatting, such as font face, style and size, from one part of text to another.

- QuickFormat also allows you to link headings together so that when you make a format change to one heading, all the headings change and take on the same format.

- After accessing the QuickFormat feature, you must indicate in the dialog box which follows whether you wish to copy the format of a character, word or phrase, or copy the format of an entire heading.

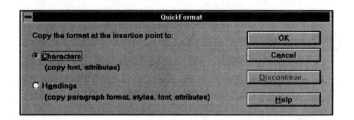

 The proofreaders' mark for moving is →or ⟳
or ← .

EXERCISE DIRECTIONS:

 In this exercise, you will move paragraphs, then format them using the QuickFormat feature.

1. Start with a clear screen.

2. ⌨ Type the exercise exactly as shown in On Disk illustration:

   • Use the default margins.

   • Start on Ln 1".

   • Use special characters for the numbers preceding each paragraph.

   OR

   💾 Open **TIPS.24** from the data disk as a read-only file (Open As Copy).

   To create Desired Result illustration:

3. Move the paragraphs in sequential numerical order.

   • Use the drag and drop procedure for the first move. Use the cut and paste procedure for the second move. Use any desired procedure for the remaining moves.

4. Set left margin to 2" and right margin to 1".

5. Center the heading and set text to sans serif 20 point bold.

6. Enter one return after each tip. Double indent text twice (1") below each tip.

7. Format number 1 to 20 point bold.

   • Using the QuickFormat feature, copy the Character formatting (point size change and bolding) to the remaining numbers.

8. Format the first tip (SLOW DOWN) to sans serif 14 point.

   • Using the QuickFormat feature, copy the Character formatting to the remaining tips.

9. Format the text below each tip to italics.

   • Using the QuickFormat feature, copy the Character formatting to the remaining text below each tip.

10. Center the page top to bottom.

11. Preview your document.

12. Print one copy.

13. Save the file; name it **TIPS**.

    OR

    💾 Close the file; *save as* **TIPS**.

MOVE

Block leave go cut, Click ins place then paste

Cut and Paste

1. Select text to be moved (cut).

2. • Click *right* mouse button

   • Click **Cut**..................................... C

   OR

   a. Click **Edit**............................ Alt + E

   b. Click **Cut**.................................... T

   OR

   Click **Cut** button on Toolbar.............. ✂

3. Position insertion point where text is to be reinserted.

4. • Click *right* mouse button.

   • Click **Paste**............................... P

   OR

   a. Click **Edit**........................... Alt + E

   b. Click **Paste**.............................. P

OR

Click **Paste** button on Toolbar.......... 📋

Drag and Drop

1. Select text to be moved.

2. Position mouse pointer on selected text.

3. Click and hold left mouse button. (A shadowed box appears.)

4. Drag text to new location.

5. Release mouse button.

QUICKFORMAT

1. Format a character, word or phrase with font face, style or size you want copied to other text.

2. Select the text that has formatting to be copied.

3. Click **QuickFormat** button on Toolbar 🖌

   OR

OR

a. Click **Format** .... Alt + R

b. Click **QuickFormat**....................... Q

OR

a. Click *right* mouse button.

b. Click **QuickFormat** .... Alt + Q

4. Click **Characters** .... Alt + C
   to format a character,
   word or phrase.

OR

Click **Headings** .... Alt + E
   to format an entire heading.

NOTE: The mouse pointer changes to a paintbrush.

5. Drag the paintbrush over the text you wish to format.

   To turn off QuickFormat:

   Repeat the procedure you used in step 3.

ON DISK

SIX TIPS FOR THE WORKAHOLIC

①SLOW DOWN. Make a conscious effort to eat, talk, walk and drive more slowly. Give yourself extra time to get to appointments so you are not always rushing.

③DRAW THE LINE. When you are already overloaded and need more personal time, do not take on any other projects. You will be just causing yourself more stress.

②LEARN TO DELEGATE. Let others share the load--you don't have to do everything yourself. You will have more energy and the end result will be better for everyone.

⑥TAKE BREAKS. Take frequent work breaks: short walks or meditating for a few minutes can help you unwind and clear your head.

⑤CARE FOR YOURSELF. Eat properly, get enough sleep and exercise regularly. Do what you can so that you are healthy, both mentally and physically.

④CUT YOUR HOURS. Be organized, but do not let your schedule run your life. Also, try to limit yourself to working eight hours a day--and not a minute more.

DESIRED RESULT

SIX TIPS FOR THE WORKAHOLIC

①SLOW DOWN.
Make a conscious effort to eat, talk, walk and drive more slowly. Give yourself extra time to get to appointments so you are not always rushing.

②LEARN TO DELEGATE.
Let others share the load--you don't have to do everything yourself. You will have more energy and the end result will be better for everyone.

③DRAW THE LINE.
When you are already overloaded and need more personal time, do not take on any other projects. You will be just causing yourself more stress.

④CUT YOUR HOURS.
Be organized, but do not let your schedule run your life. Also, try to limit yourself to working eight hours a day--and not a minute more.

⑤CARE FOR YOURSELF.
Eat properly, get enough sleep and exercise regularly. Do what you can so that you are healthy, both mentally and physically.

⑥TAKE BREAKS.
Take frequent work breaks: short walks or meditating for a few minutes can help you unwind and clear your head.

EXERCISE

▪ MOVING TEXT ▪ QUICKFORMAT ▪ LINKED HEADINGS

25

NOTES:

▪ As noted in the previous exercise, the QuickFormat feature may be used to link headings together so that when you make a format change to one heading, all the headings change and take on the same format.

▪ In order to link headings, you must first identify heading text by selecting (highlighting) the text that has the formatting you wish to copy. Then, click the QuickFormat button on the Toolbar. In the dialog box which follows, select Headings.

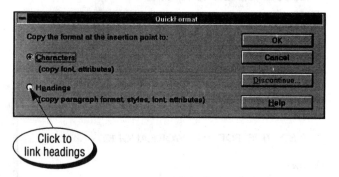

Click to link headings

▪ When the mouse pointer becomes a paintbrush, drag it over any text you wish to link. Each word or phrase you paint, receives a heading code. When you make a formatting change to text you identified as a heading, all "heading" text will take on the same format.

 If you move an indented or tabbed paragraph with formatting codes (double spacing, font changes, etc.), be sure the indent, tab and/or formatting code to the left of the text is moved along with the paragraph. To insure this, reveal codes and check that the insertion point is to the left of the code to move before selecting text.

EXERCISE DIRECTIONS:

 In this exercise, you will gain more practice moving text. You will also use the QuickFormat feature to link heading text and then make formatting changes to the linked text.

1. Start with a clear screen.

2. Open **BULLETIN** if you created it in Exercise 22.

 OR

 📇 Open **BULLETIN.25** from the data disk as a read-only file (Open As Copy).

3. Move the paragraphs as indicated. Use any procedure you desire to move the paragraphs.

4. Using QuickFormat, identify the side headings as heading text and change the side headings to a serif font.

5. Preview your document

6. Change one of the QuickFormat linked headings to serif 14 point italic (all side headings should change).

7. Print one copy.

8. Close the file; save the changes.

 OR

 📇 Close the file; *save as* **BULLETIN**.

◆□◆□◆□◆ ELECTRONIC BULLETIN BOARDS ◆□◆□◆□◆

Thousands of people across the nation are using computer bulletin boards. Through their computer, they spend hours on line "talking" with other users, "discussing" topics *ranging* from zoology, finding information about taxes or taxis, completing graduate courses to even exchanging wedding vows.

change side headings to serif 14 pt. italic

PRODUCTIVE USES INCLUDE:

move

☎A system created by a car expert in Las Vegas lists thousands of collectors' cars.

☎A system developed by a retired guidance counselor in Atlanta provides current information on scholarships and loans.

☎A system set up by a hospital in West Virginia offers detailed answers to medical questions for people who do not want to travel long distances necessary to see a doctor.

BASIC NEEDS:

All you need to connect a bulletin board is a computer and a modem connected to a telephone line.

BASIC COSTS:

Besides the basic fee of subscribing to a bulletin board, the cost of "talking" on your computer is the same as talking on your phone, since phone lines are used for data transmission. While most bulletin boards are free, some of the largest are professional operations that charge a fee.

move

DESIRED RESULT

◆□◆□◆□◆ ELECTRONIC BULLETIN BOARDS ◆□◆□◆□◆

Thousands of people across the nation are using computer bulletin boards. Through their computer, they spend hours on line "talking" with other users, "discussing" topics ranging from zoology, finding information about taxes or taxis, completing graduate courses to even exchanging wedding vows. While most bulletin boards are free, some of the largest are professional operations that charge a fee.

PRODUCTIVE USES INCLUDE:

☎A system set up by a hospital in West Virginia offers detailed answers to medical questions for people who do not want to travel long distances necessary to see a doctor.

☎A system developed by a retired guidance counselor in Atlanta provides current information on scholarships and loans.

☎A system created by a car expert in Las Vegas lists thousands of collectors' cars.

BASIC COSTS:

Besides the basic fee of subscribing to a bulletin board, the cost of "talking" on your computer is the same as talking on your phone, since phone lines are used for data transmission.

BASIC NEEDS:

All you need to connect a bulletin board is a computer and a modem connected to a telephone line.

EXERCISE

▪ **COPY AND PASTE** ▪ **DRAG AND DROP**

26

NOTES:

▪ **Copy and Paste** and **Drag and Drop** are features that let you copy text from one location to another.

▪ Copying leaves text in its original location while placing a duplicate in a different location in the same document or another document. (Copying text to another document will be covered in a later lesson.) In contrast, moving removes text from its original location and places it elsewhere.

Copy and Paste

▪ The procedure for copying text is similar to the procedure for moving text. *(See keystrokes on page 106.)*

▪ When text is copied, it remains on the screen while a copy of it is placed on the Clipboard.

▪ Text remains on the Clipboard until you copy another selection (or until you exit Windows). Therefore, you can paste the same selection into many different locations, if desired.

▪ Text is reinserted or retrieved from the Clipboard at the insertion point. Therefore, place the insertion point to the immediate left of where the text is to be reinserted before following the paste procedures outlined in the Quick Feature Access or the detailed keystrokes on page 106.

Drag and Drop

- Use the drag and drop method to copy selected text using your mouse.

- Once text to be copied is selected, place the mouse pointer anywhere on the selected text, press the Ctrl key while **dragging** text to the new location (a black shadowed box appears). Then **drop** a copy of the text into its new location by releasing the mouse button. Be sure to release the mouse button before releasing the Ctrl key.

- As with the Move feature, if text was not copied properly, you can undo it.

EXERCISE DIRECTIONS:

In this exercise, you will enhance a flyer created earlier using the copy procedure. In addition, you will gain practice using the QuickFormat and Link Headings feature.

1. Start with a clear screen.

2. Open **TIPS** if you completed it in Exercise 24.

   OR

   💾 Open **TIPS. 26** from the data disk as a read-only file (Open As Copy).

3. To link the side headings (the numbers and tips), use QuickFormat to identify the side headings and numbers as heading text. (In the previous exercise, this text was identified as character text.)

4. Using QuickFormat, change the first side heading and number to 18 point.

NOTE: *All tips and numbers should change to the new format.*

5. Using the letter "s" and the Wingding font, create a line of diamonds to the right of the first tip. Press the Tab key once before each line of diamonds.

6. Copy the line and paste it next to the remaining tips. Copy the tab code along with the line.

7. Type and center **To Summarize:** in serif 14 point bold as shown.

8. Copy each number and tip as shown:

   • Center align all tips.

   • Set font to serif 14 point.

9. Set the title to 25 point bold.

10. Preview your document.

11. Print one copy.

12. Close the file; save the changes.

    OR

    💾 Close the file; *save as* **TIPS**.

COPY AND PASTE

1. Select text to be copied.

2. Click *right* mouse button.

   Click **Copy** .... O

   OR

   a. Click **Edit** .... Alt + E

   b. Click **Copy** C

   OR

   Click Copy button on Toolbar .... 🔲

3. Position insertion point where text is to be reinserted.

4. • Click *right* mouse button.

   • Click **Paste** .... P

   OR

   a. Click **Edit** .... Alt + E

   b. Click **Paste** .... P

   OR

   Click Paste button on Toolbar .... 📋

DRAG AND DROP

1. Select text to be copied.

2. Position mouse pointer on selected text.

3. Press and hold **Ctrl** while clicking and holding left mouse button. (A black shadowed box appears.)

4. Drag text to new location.

5. Release mouse button.

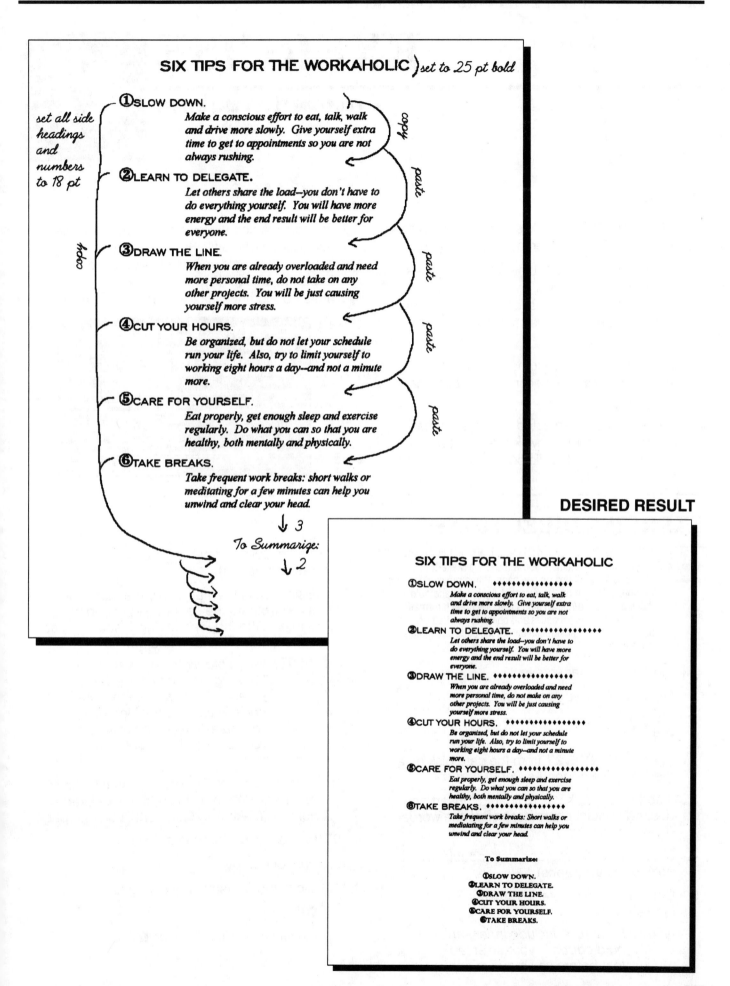

SIX TIPS FOR THE WORKAHOLIC)set to 25 pt bold

set all side
headings
and
numbers
to 18 pt

①SLOW DOWN.

Make a conscious effort to eat, talk, walk and drive more slowly. Give yourself extra time to get to appointments so you are not always rushing.

②LEARN TO DELEGATE.

Let others share the load--you don't have to do everything yourself. You will have more energy and the end result will be better for everyone.

③DRAW THE LINE.

When you are already overloaded and need more personal time, do not take on any other projects. You will be just causing yourself more stress.

④CUT YOUR HOURS.

Be organized, but do not let your schedule run your life. Also, try to limit yourself to working eight hours a day--and not a minute more.

⑤CARE FOR YOURSELF.

Eat properly, get enough sleep and exercise regularly. Do what you can so that you are healthy, both mentally and physically.

⑥TAKE BREAKS.

Take frequent work breaks: short walks or meditating for a few minutes can help you unwind and clear your head.

↓ 3

To Summarize:

↓ 2

copy   paste   paste   paste   paste   copy

DESIRED RESULT

SIX TIPS FOR THE WORKAHOLIC

①SLOW DOWN. ♦♦♦♦♦♦♦♦♦♦♦♦♦♦♦

Make a conscious effort to eat, talk, walk and drive more slowly. Give yourself extra time to get to appointments so you are not always rushing.

②LEARN TO DELEGATE. ♦♦♦♦♦♦♦♦♦♦♦♦♦♦♦

Let others share the load—you don't have to do everything yourself. You will have more energy and the end result will be better for everyone.

③DRAW THE LINE. ♦♦♦♦♦♦♦♦♦♦♦♦♦♦♦

When you are already overloaded and need more personal time, do not make on any other projects. You will be just causing yourself more stress.

④CUT YOUR HOURS. ♦♦♦♦♦♦♦♦♦♦♦♦♦♦♦

Be organized, but do not let your schedule run your life. Also, try to limit yourself to working eight hours a day—and not a minute more.

⑤CARE FOR YOURSELF. ♦♦♦♦♦♦♦♦♦♦♦♦♦♦♦

Eat properly, get enough sleep and exercise regularly. Do what you can so that you are healthy, both mentally and physically.

⑥TAKE BREAKS. ♦♦♦♦♦♦♦♦♦♦♦♦♦♦♦

Take frequent work breaks: Short walks or mediatating for a few minutes can help you unwind and clear your head.

To Summarize:

①SLOW DOWN.
②LEARN TO DELEGATE.
③DRAW THE LINE.
④CUT YOUR HOURS.
⑤CARE FOR YOURSELF.
⑥TAKE BREAKS.

EXERCISE

27

▪ COPYING TEXT ▪ MAKE IT FIT

NOTES:

- The **Make-It-Fit** feature lets you shrink or expand a document to fill a desired number of pages.

- If, for example, your document fills 1¼ pages, but you would like it to fit on one page, the Make-It-Fit Expert automatically adjusts margins, font size or line spacing so that the text will shrink to one page.

- You may return your document to the original number of pages by selecting Undo from the Edit menu.

- Make-It-Fit may be selected from the Format menu or by clicking the Make-It-Fit button on theToolbar. In the dialog box which follows,

you must indicate how many pages you wish your document to fill. In addition, you must indicate the items you would like Make-It-Fit Expert to adjust. If you do not want the margins affected, do not click the margin check boxes.

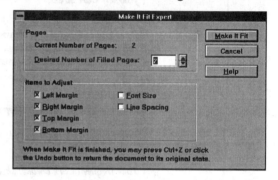

EXERCISE DIRECTIONS:

In this exercise, you will gain more practice moving and copying text. In addition, you will use the Make-It-Fit feature to keep all text on one page. When moving/copying the hotel information, be sure that the indent and bold codes are moved/copied along with the hotel information. To insure this, reveal codes and check to see that your insertion point is positioned before the code you intend to move/copy.

1. Start with a clear screen.

2. Open **DIVE** if you completed it in Exercise 21.

   OR

   💾 Open **DIVE.27** from the data disk as a read-only file (Open As Copy).

3. Insert paragraphs as indicated. Insert any desired special character before the words "Don't" as shown.

4. Single space paragraph text (double space between paragraphs).

5. Copy and move hotel information as indicated.

   NOTE: Be sure to include indent and bold codes in your selected text before you move or copy.

6. Using QuickFormat, bold each hotel name (as characters).

7. Using QuickFormat, apply the same font and size format to the second side heading (Hotels Offering Free Diving Instruction) as used in the first side heading.

   NOTE: When highlighting the first side heading format to copy, be sure you include the font face code in your highlighted text. To insure that you do, reveal your codes as you select the text.

8. Use the Make It Fit feature to shrink text to one page. You may include any desired items to make the document fit on one page.

9. Preview your document.

10. Print one copy.

11. Close the file; save the changes.

    OR

    💾 Close the file; *save as* **DIVE**.

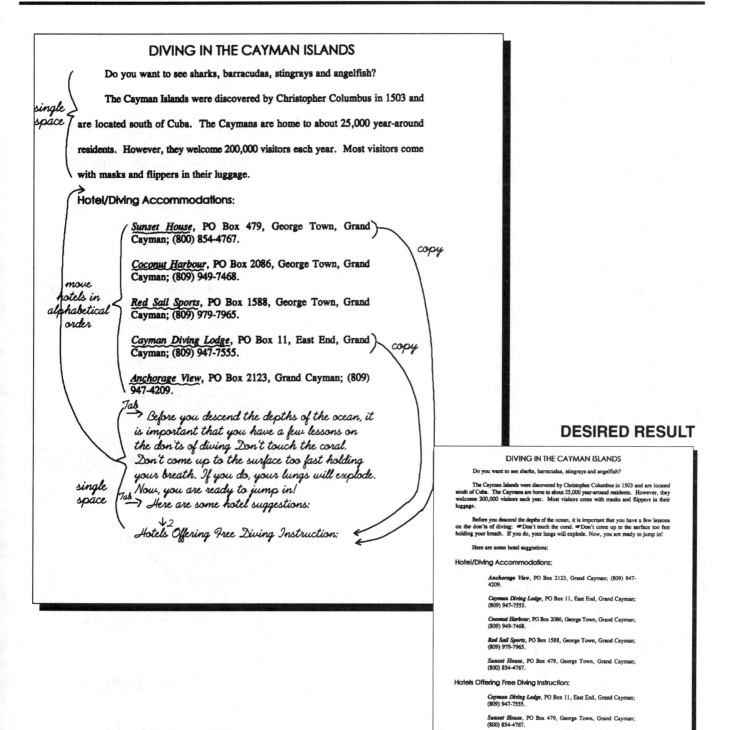

DESIRED RESULT

MAKE IT FIT

1. Click Make-it-Fit button on Toolbar ....
   OR
   a. Click **Format** .... `Alt` + `R`
   b. Click **Make It Fit Expert** .... `I`

2. Click **Desired Number of Filled Pages** text box.

3. Type number of pages .... `Alt` + `D` you wish document to be

4. Click desired items to automatically adjust:
   - **Left Margin** .... `Alt` + `L`
   - **Right Margin** .... `Alt` + `R`
   - **Top Margin** .... `Alt` + `T`
   - **Bottom Margin** .... `Alt` + `B`
   - **Font Size** .... `Alt` + `F`
   - **Line Spacing** .... `Alt` + `L`

5. Click **Make-It-Fit** .... `Enter`

To return document to its original state:

Click **Undo** button on Toolbar ....
OR
a. Click **Edit** .... `Alt` + `E`
b. Click **Undo** .... `U`
OR
Press **Ctrl + Z** .... `Ctrl` + `Z`

EXERCISE DIRECTIONS:

1. Start with a clear screen.

2. ⌨ Type a one-page report from the text shown in the On Disk illustration.

   OR

   💾 Open **BATS.5A** from the data disk as a read-only file (Open As <u>C</u>opy) and create a one page report.

To create the report as shown in the Desired Result illustration:

3. Use the default margins.

4. Display the Ruler bar. Drag the first tab marker to 1.8"; drag the second tab marker to 2.25".

5. Center and set the title to sans serif 14 point bold; set the body text to serif 12 point.

6. Double space body text.

7. Format bat species and their descriptions as follows:

   • Single space (double space between each).

   • Double indent.

   • Create a hanging indent for each.

   • Change the first bat species paragraph to italic. Use QuickFormat to copy the formatting to the other species paragraphs and link them as headings.

8. Move bat species (and their descriptions) into alphabetical order.

9. Spell check.

10. Preview your document.

11. Reformat the first bat species paragraph to a sans serif font. (All linked paragraphs should change to the new formatting.)

NOTE: When highlighting the first bat species paragraph before making the formatting change, be sure to include the QuickFormat code in your highlighted text. To ensure this, reveal your codes before selecting the text. Note the illustration below.

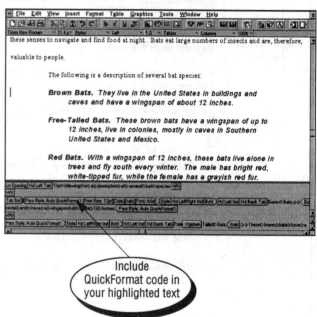

Include QuickFormat code in your highlighted text

12. Use Make It Fit to keep text on one page. Adjust font size, and top and bottom margins.

13. Print one copy.

14. Save the exercise; name it **BATS**.

    OR

    💾 Close the file; *save as* **BATS**.

BATS¶Do bats get in your hair? Do vampire bats exist? How blind
is a bat? These are questions you might ask yourself if you were
ever near a cave, an attic or another sheltered place.¶A bat is
the only mammal that can fly. They usually stay in dark places,
tend to live in colonies, come out only at night, and hang upside
down when they are resting. As night approaches, they head for
their feeding grounds. Bats have an excellent sense of smell and
hearing and depend on these senses to navigate and find food at
night.Bats eat large numbers of insects and are, therefore,
valuable to people. ¶The following is a description of several
bat species:¶Vampire Bats. These mammals feed on the blood of
other animals and live in Central and South America. Vampire
bats swallow about 1 tablespoon of blood a day. They leave their
victims with a small wound which heals quickly, but these bats
can carry rabies.¶Brown Bats. They live in the United States in
buildings and caves and have a wingspan of about 12 inches.
¶Free-Tailed Bats. These brown bats have a wingspan of up to 12
inches, live in colonies, mostly in caves in Southern United
States and Mexico. ¶Red Bats. With a wingspan of 12 inches,
these bats live alone in trees and fly south every winter. The
male has bright red, white-tipped fur, while the female has a
grayish red fur. ¶Now, to answer the questions asked earlier:
Bats do not get tangled in people's hair. Bats tend to be
frightened of people and will fly away. Bats are not blind. All
species of bats can see, but they see very poorly, especially at
night. But, vampire bats DO exist; they are one of several kinds
of bat species which have been described here.

DESIRED RESULT

BATS

Do bats get in your hair? Do vampire bats exist? How blind is a bat? These are questions you might ask yourself if you were ever near a cave, an attic or another sheltered place.

A bat is the only mammal that can fly. They usually stay in dark places, tend to live in colonies, come out only at night, and hang upside down when they are resting. As night approaches, they head for their feeding grounds. Bats have an excellent sense of smell and hearing and depend on these senses to navigate and find food at night. Bats eat large numbers of insects and are, therefore, valuable to people.

The following is a description of several bat species:

Brown Bats. *They live in the United States in buildings and caves and have a wingspan of about 12 inches.*

Free-Tailed Bats. *These brown bats have a wingspan of up to 12 inches, live in colonies, mostly in caves in Southern United States and Mexico.*

Red Bats. *With a wingspan of 12 inches, these bats live alone in trees and fly south every winter. The male has bright red, white-tipped fur, while the female has a grayish red fur.*

Vampire Bats. *These mammals feed on the blood of other animals and live in Central and South America. Vampire bats swallow about 1 tablespoon of blood a day. They leave their victims with a small wound which heals quickly, but these bats can carry rabies.*

Now, to answer the questions asked earlier: Bats do not get tangled in people's hair. Bats tend to be frightened of people and will fly away. Bats are not blind. All species of bats can see, but they see very poorly, especially at night. But, vampire bats DO exist; they are one of several kinds of bat species which have been described here.

EXERCISE DIRECTIONS:

1. Start with a clear screen.
2. ⌨ Keyboard the exercise shown in On Disk illustration below. Start at the top of the page (1").

   OR

   💾 Open **NEWS.5B** from the data disk as a read-only file (Open As Copy).
3. Use the default margins.
4. Clear all tab stops. Set a tab stop at 4.5" from the left edge of the paper.
5. Set all text to sans serif 12 point.
6. Insert today's date, the inside address and salutation as shown in illustration A on the right beginning on Ln 2".
7. Make the indicated revisions.
8. Type the paragraph at the bottom of Illustration A as shown, and move it as indicated.
9. Set 2" left and right margins for the paragraphs containing event descriptions.
10. Change the first event title to bold.
    - Use QuickFormat to copy the bold formatting to the other headings and link them as headings.
11. Change the first event description to italic.
    - Use QuickFormat to copy the italic formatting to the other descriptions and link them as headings.
12. Insert the closing as shown.
13. Spell check.
14. Reformat the first event heading to serif 14 point; reformat the event descriptions to serif. (All linked paragraphs should change to the new formatting.)
15. Change the inside address to read as follows:

    Ms. Cathy King, Director
    Corporate Training
    - Use drag and drop to move "Director" after "King".
16. Use Make it Fit to keep text on one page. Adjust font size as well as top and bottom margins.
17. Preview your document.
18. Print one copy.
19. Close the file; name it **NEWS**.

    OR

    💾 Close the file; *save as* **NEWS**.

ON DISK

I strongly urge you to attend this year's <u>Computer Expo</u>. In four days, you will pick up the latest computer news and discover new ways to put your computer to work -- in the office, in the lab, in the studio, in the classroom or in your home.

If you are interested in attending, call *Derek Brennan* at 1-800-555-5555. He will pre-register anyone who wishes to attend. This will save you long lines at the show. The preregistration fee is $150.00 Onsite registration will be an additional $25.00.

Here are some of the events you can look forward to:

Keynote Sessions.

These sessions will feature luminaries from the computer world who will offer you insights from industry.

Application Workshops.

Join a series of two-hour learning sessions which will provide guidelines, tips and "how-to's" on popular software packages.

Programmer/Developer Forums.

Veteran and novice computer users will brainstorm so you can learn about innovative advances and techniques.

ILLUSTRATION A

2"
↓
Today's date

Ms. Cathy King
Corporate Training Director
D.L. Morgan Company
55 Fourth Street
San Francisco, CA 94103

Dear Ms. King:

Remove underline; set to italics

I strongly urge you to attend this year's Computer Expo. In four
days, you will pick up the latest computer news and discover new
ways to put your computer to work -- in the office, in the lab,
in the studio, in the classroom or in your home.

If you are interested in attending, call *Derek Brennan* at 1-800-
555-5555. He will pre-register anyone who wishes to attend.
This will save you long lines at the show. The preregistration
fee is $150.00. Onsite registration will be an additional $25.00.

Here are some of the events you can look forward to:

move

Set 2" left and right margins
move

Keynote Sessions.
These sessions will feature luminaries from the computer world
who will offer you insights from industry. *DS*
Application Workshops.
Join a series of two-hour learning sessions which will provide
guidelines, tips and "how-to's" on popular software packages. *DS*
Programmer/Developer Forums.
Veteran and novice computer users will brainstorm so you can
learn about innovative advances and techniques.

Insert into alphabetical order

Interest Group Meetings.
These sessions will include Education Workshops for
teachers, resources and recommendations for the home
office worker, and ways to fully utilize your computer in
a law office.

Sincerely,

Kevin McKenzie
Expo Coordinator

km/yo

DESIRED RESULT

Today's date

Ms. Cathy King, Director
Corporate Training
D.L. Morgan Company
55 Fourth Street
San Francisco, CA 94103

Dear Ms. King:

I strongly urge you to attend this year's *Computer Expo*. In four days, you will pick up the latest computer news
and discover new ways to put your computer to work—in the office, in the lab, in the studio, in the classroom or in
your home.

Here are some of the events you can look forward to:

Application Workshops.
*Join a series of two-hour learning sessions which will provide
guidelines, tips and "how-to's" on popular software packages.*

Interest Group Meetings.
*These sessions will include Education Workshops for teachers,
resources and recommendations for the home office worker, and
ways to fully utilize your computer in a law office.*

Keynote Sessions.
*These sessions will feature luminaries from the computer world
who will offer you insights from industry.*

Programmer/Developer Forums.
*Veteran and novice computer users will brainstorm so you can
learn about innovative advances and techniques.*

If you are interested in attending, call Derek Brennan at 1-800-555-5555. He will pre-register anyone who
wishes to attend. This will save you long lines at the show. The preregistration fee is $150.00. Onsite registration
will be an additional $25.00.

Sincerely,

Kevin McKenzie
Expo Coordinator

km/yo

LESSON 6

Exercises 28–35

- Thesaurus

- Grammar Check (Grammatik)

- Creating a Memorandum

- Finding and Replacing Text

- Hyphenation

- Bullets and Numbers

- Document Information

EXERCISE

THESAURUS **28**

NOTES:

- The **Thesaurus** feature indicates the part of speech (e.g., noun or adjective), a list of synonyms within the part of speech, and the antonyms of selected words.

- The insertion point must be on the word you wish to look up before you access the feature.

- Thesaurus may be accessed by selecting Thesaurus from the Tools main menu or by pressing Alt + F1.

- Once Thesaurus is accessed, the following dialog box appears showing the **headword**, the part of speech, and a list of synonyms for the word appearing in the Word text box.

- Headwords are listed in the following order: nouns (n), verbs (v), adjectives (a) and antonyms (ant). Click the down scroll arrow to view other headwords, their parts of speech and synonyms.

- Words marked with bullets may be looked up by clicking the word and then clicking the Look Up button. This replaces the original word in the first column.

- Double-clicking a bulleted word displays a new list of synonyms in the column to its right.

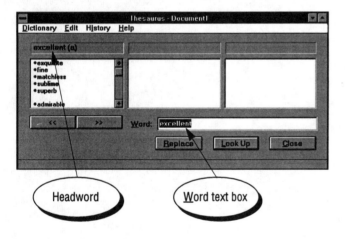

Headword   Word text box

- When you look up third column words, the first column words disappear, allowing the new word list to display in the third column. To redisplay earlier lists, click the arrow buttons at the bottom of the dialog box.

- The Thesaurus feature replaces verbs with the correct tense. For example, if you look up the word "inquiring," the replacement word would include "ing."

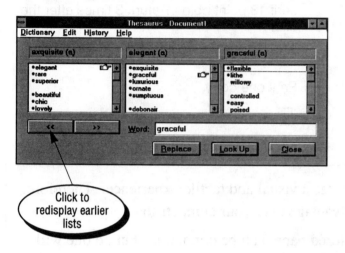

Click to redisplay earlier lists

EXERCISE DIRECTIONS:

 In this exercise, you will use the Thesaurus feature to substitute words marked in brackets.

1. Start with a clear screen.

2. ⌨ Keyboard exercise below.

   OR

   💾 Open **PAPER.28** from the data disk as a read-only file (Open As Copy).

3. Set 1.5" left and right margins.

4. Set a 1" first line indent.

5. Using the Thesaurus feature, substitute the words marked in brackets, as shown in On Disk illustration.

6. Center and bold the title COLOR PAPER in serif 18 point bold. Return 3 times after the title.

7. Center the exercise top to bottom.

8. Print one copy.

9. 💾 Close the file; *save as* **PAPER**.

Paper is an important part of publishing. Paper creates a visual and tactile experience. Therefore, using anything but white gives you a significant advantage over your competition.

Bright colors convey an urgent message. Neon colored paper can be obnoxious, but no one will ignore it and it is virtually impossible to lose in a stack of ordinary white paper.

Somber and dignified messages require a softer color paper. To convey the warmth of a sun-soaked vacation, you might try a paper that reflects the warm glow of a summer day.

THESAURUS
Alt + F1

1. Place insertion point on word to look up.

2. • Click **Tools**............................ Alt + T

   • Click **Thesaurus** .... T

3. Select a thesaurus option:

   To replace word:

   a. Highlight word to replace word in document.

   b. Click **Replace** .... R

To display headword synonyms:

a. Double-click bulleted word.

b. Select bulleted word.

c. Click **Look Up** L

To view list already examined:

a. Click **History** I

b. Click arrow .... buttons

4. Click **Close** C

ON DISK

set 1" first line indent

Paper is an (important) part of publishing. Paper (creates) a visual and tactile experience. Therefore, using anything but white gives you a (significant) advantage over your competition.

Bright colors (convey) an urgent message. Neon colored paper can be (obnoxious) but no one will ignore it, and it is (virtually) impossible to lose in a stack of ordinary white paper.

neon paper

(Somber) and dignified messages (require) a softer color paper. To (convey) the warmth of a sun-soaked vacation, you might try a paper that (reflects) the warm (glow) of a summer day.

DESIRED RESULT

COLOR PAPER

Paper is a significant part of publishing. Paper establishes a visual and tactile experience. Therefore, using anything but white gives you an important advantage over your competition.

Bright colors communicate an urgent message. Neon-colored paper can be offensive, but no one will ignore it. It is almost impossible to lose neon paper in a stack of ordinary white paper.

Serious and dignified messages demand a softer color paper. To impart the warmth of a sun-soaked vacation, you might try a paper that exhibits the warm radiance of a summer day.

EXERCISE

▪ **GRAMMAR CHECK (GRAMMATIK)**
▪ **CREATING A MEMORANDUM**

Grammatik

NOTES:

▪ **Grammatik** is WordPerfect's grammar check feature. It checks your document for spelling, errors in usage, punctuation and mechanics. Style errors (including clichés, jargon and wordiness) will not be detected, however.

▪ Grammatik checks for errors based on the default writing style, Quick Check. Other writing-style options are available:

- Spelling Plus
- Very Strict
- Formal Memo or Letter
- Informal Memo or Letter
- Technical or Scientific
- Documentation or Speech
- Student Composition
- Advertising
- Fiction

▪ When a writing style is selected, WordPerfect applies different grammar rules to detect different kinds of writing errors.

▪ Grammatik is accessed by selecting Grammatik from the Tools main menu or clicking the Grammatik button on the Toolbar. The following dialog box appears:

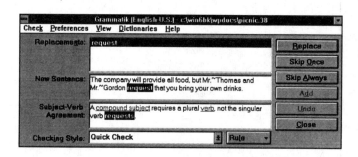

▪ When Grammatik detects an error, the windows display the following:

Replacements Displays how to correct the error.

New Sentence Displays the sentence correctly rewritten.

third window Displays the grammar rule that was violated by the error.

▪ Grammatik also flags spelling errors.

- To respond to grammar and spelling errors, click the appropriate button:

Replace Replaces the highlighted error with a new word.

Skip Once Ignores the highlighted error for this occurrence only and advances to the next detected error.

Skip Always Ignores the highlighted error for the entire document.

Add Adds a word to the Grammatik spelling dictionary.

Undo Reverses the last action.

Close Closes Grammatik.

Creating a Memorandum

- The **memo** is a written communication within a company. Some companies create memos on blank paper, while others use letterhead or preprinted forms. Memos may also be created using WordPerfect's Template feature *(see Lesson 13)*.

- A memo should begin 1" from the top of the page, which is the top of your screen. The word MEMORANDUM may be centered at the top of the page or it may be omitted.

- Memorandums are usually prepared with all parts beginning at the left margin.

- Re (in reference to) is often used in place of the word Subject in the memorandum heading.

- Memorandums are generally not centered vertically.

- Double space between each part of the memorandum heading. The body of the memo begins a double or triple space below the subject line.

- If copies are to be sent to others, a copy notation may be indicated as the last item on the page.

EXERCISE DIRECTIONS:

 In this exercise, you will create a memorandum and use Grammatik to check the grammar and spelling.

1. Start the exercise at the top of a clear screen.

2. Set the left and right margins to 1.25".

3. ⌨ Keyboard the memo on the right exactly as shown, including the circled, misspelled words and usage errors.

   OR

   💾 Open **PICNIC.29** from the data disk as a read-only file (Open As <u>C</u>opy).

4. Double indent WHAT YOU NEED TO KNOW paragraphs.

5. Using the Thesaurus feature, substitute the words marked in brackets.

6. Use Grammatik to grammar and spell check the document. Accept WordPerfect's suggestions for correcting grammar and spelling errors.

7. Insert a hard space between names, dates and times (where you see the ⌂ symbol).

8. Print one copy.

9. Save the exercise; name it **PICNIC**.

   OR

   💾 Close the file; *save as* **PICNIC**.

GRAMMAR CHECK

Alt + Shift + F1

1. Position insertion point at the beginning of document.

2. • Click **T**ools .... Alt + T

   • Click **G**rammatik .... G

   OR

   Click Grammatik button .... 🔲
   on Toolbar.

3. When an error is detected, click appropriate option:

   • **R**eplace .... R
   to replace highlighted error with new word.

   • Skip **O**nce .... O
   to ignore only this occurrence of highlighted error and advance.

   • Skip **A**lways .... A
   to skip all occurrences of highlighted error.

   • **A**dd .... D
   to add word to Grammatik spelling dictionary.

   • **U**ndo .... U
   to reverse last action.

   • **C**lose C
   to close Grammatik.

   To change writing style:

   a. Click **P**references .... P

   b. Click **C**hecking Styles C

   c. Click desired writing style.

   d. Click **S**elect .... Enter

set 1.25" left and right margins

TO: Staff

FROM: Janet Garcia

RE: **ANNUAL COMPANY PICNIC** — *bold*

DATE: Today's Date

This year, our picnic will be Saturday May△8△at Fairview Meadow Country Club. Fairview is a newly referbished facility that offers tennis courts, ball fields and excellent outdoor cooking and dining accomodations.

WHAT YOU NEED TO KNOW — *italics*

double indent

The swimming pool will be available to us exclusively between noon and 3:30△p.m. The Club has beach chairs, but you must bring your own towels.

The company will provide all food, but Mr.△Thomas and Mr.△Gordon requests that you bring your own drinks.

Employees are welcome to bring there children, so bring the family.

If you plan to attend, or if you have any other questions, call Joan Saunders at extention△104, by Thursday,△May 6.

yo

EXERCISE

FINDING AND REPLACING TEXT

NOTES:

▪ The **Find and Replace** feature scans your document and searches for occurrences of specified words, phrases or codes. Once the desired text or code is found, it can be edited or replaced.

▪ Find and Replace may be accessed from the Edit main menu. In the Find and Replace Text dialog box which appears, the word or phrase to search for must be typed in the Find text box; the replacement text or code is entered in the Replace With text box.

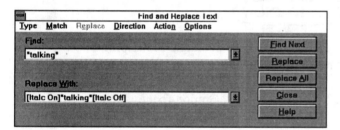

▪ WordPerfect scans the document and stops at the first occurrence of the specified word or code. Click the appropriate button to continue your search:

Find Next   Stops at the next occurrence.

Replace   Confirms each replacement.

Replace All   Replaces all occurrences without confirmation.

▪ To search for text exactly in the case it was typed (uppercase, lowercase or initial caps) or a specific font, choose Case or Font from the Match menu. If, for example, you wanted to find the word HELP and you did not select the Case option, both upper- and lowercase occurrences of the word would be found.

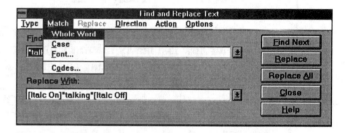

▪ Use the Whole Word option from the Match menu to select whole words only. For example, if you were searching for the word *the*, and you did not select the Whole Word option, WordPerfect would flag words in which *the* was a part of the word, like **the**se, **the**saurus, **the**sis, etc.

▪ Use the **Codes** option from the Match menu, to find codes such as Bold On, Bold Off, Left Tab, etc.

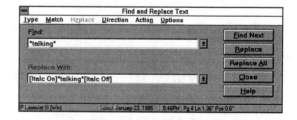

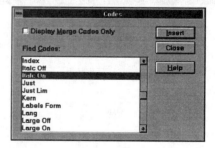

- The <u>W</u>ord Forms option in the <u>T</u>ype menu allows you to find and replace words based on the root form of the word. For example, if you select the <u>W</u>ord Forms option and you search for the word *call,* WordPerfect would find the words **call**s, **call**ed, **call**er, and **call**ing as well.

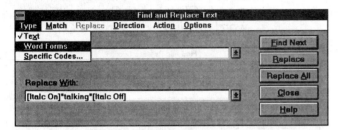

- Use the <u>S</u>pecific Codes option in the <u>T</u>ype menu to find a code that requires specific numbers or information, such as a margin code. For example, you could find a 1" left margin code and replace it with a 2" left margin code; or you could find a Times New Roman font code and replace with an Arial font code.

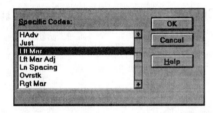

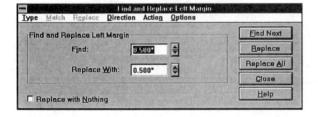

- WordPerfect searches in a forward direction. To search from the insertion point backward, select <u>B</u>ackward from the <u>D</u>irection menu.

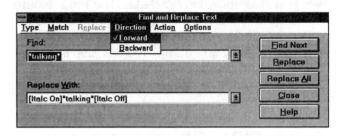

EXERCISE DIRECTIONS:

In this exercise, you will search for the words shown in brackets. The Find feature quickly places the insertion point on those words so you can use the Thesaurus feature to edit them. You will also search for and replace words within this document.

1. Start with a clear screen.

2. Open **BULLETIN** if you completed it in Exercise 25.

   OR

   💾 Open **BULLETIN.30** from the data disk as a read-only file (Open As Copy).

3. Use the Find feature to place your insertion point on each word marked in brackets. Then, use the Thesaurus feature to replace each word.

4. Search for each occurrence of the word "bulletin" and replace with BULLETIN.

5. Search for the word "talking" and replace with *talking*.

   HINT: In the Replace With text box, select Codes from the Replace menu. Click Italics On, type the word "talking"; click Italics Off.

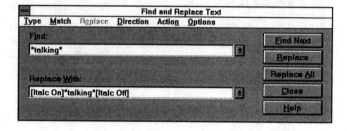

6. Print one copy.

7. Close the file; save the changes.

   OR

   💾 Close the file; *save as* **BULLETIN**.

FIND AND REPLACE TEXT/CODES

F2 then step 4

1. Place insertion point at top of document.

2. Click **Edit** .... Alt + E

3. Click **Find and Replace** .... F

4. Type text to be searched in **Find** text box.

5. Type replacement text in **Replace With** text box.

   To find specific text:

   a. Click **Match** .... M

   b. Click **Whole Word** .... W

      OR

      Click **Case** C

      OR

   a. Click **Font** .... F

   b. Type font information to be searched.

   c. Click **OK** .... Enter

   To find/replace codes:

   a. Click **Match** .... M

   b. Click **Codes** .... O

   c. Double-click code to be searched/replaced.

   d. Click **Close** C

   To find/replace specific codes:

   a. Click **Type** .... T

   b. Click **Specific Codes** .... S

   c. Double-click code to be searched.

   d. Type additional code information.

   e. Click **Close** C

6. Click **Find Next** .... Alt + F
   to search for each occurrence.

   OR

   a. Click **Replace** .... Alt + R

   b. Click **Replace All** .... Alt + A

7. Click **Close** C

◆□◆□◆□◆ ELECTRONIC BULLETIN BOARDS ◆□◆□◆□◆

Thousands of people across the nation are using computer bulletin boards. Through their computer, they spend hours on line "talking" with other users, "discussing" topics ranging from zoology, finding information about taxes or taxis, completing graduate courses to even exchanging wedding vows. While most bulletin boards are free, some of the largest are professional operations that (charge) a fee.

PRODUCTIVE USES INCLUDE:

☎A system set up by a hospital in West Virginia offers detailed answers to medical questions for people who do not want to travel long distances necessary to see a doctor.

☎A system (developed) by a retired guidance counselor in Atlanta provides current information on scholarships and loans.

☎A system (created) by a car expert in Las Vegas lists thousands of collectors' cars.

BASIC COSTS:

Besides the basic fee of subscribing to a bulletin board, the cost of "talking" on your computer is the same as talking on your phone, since phone lines are used for data transmission.

BASIC NEEDS:

All you need to (connect) a bulletin board is a computer and a modem connected to a telephone line.

EXERCISE

HYPHENATION

NOTES:

- **Hyphenation** produces a tighter right margin by dividing words that extend beyond the right margin rather than wrapping them to the next line. If text is full-justified and hyphenated, the sentences have smaller gaps between words.

- By default, WordPerfect's Hyphenation feature is set to off. In the off position, WordPerfect wraps any word extending beyond the right margin. When hyphenation is on, a word that starts before the left edge of the hyphenation zone and extends beyond the right edge of the zone will be hyphenated.

- Hyphenation may be accessed by selecting Line, Hyphenation from the Format main menu. In the Line Hyphenation dialog box which follows, you may change the width of the space a word must span before hyphenation divides it by changing the hyphenation zone. *Increase* the percentage of the zone to hyphenate *fewer* words; *decrease* to hyphenate *more* words.

Click to turn hyphenation on

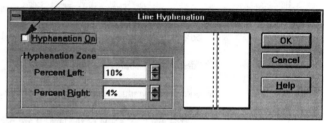

- To keep words such as sister-in-law or self-control together even if they span the hyphenation zone, type the word with a **hard hyphen** (Ctrl + -).

EXERCISE DIRECTIONS:

In this exercise, you will use the Find and Replace feature to search for a bolded OCR and replace it with an unbolded Optical Character Recognition. You will also hyphenate the document to produce a tighter right margin.

1. Start with a clear screen.

2. Open **OCR** if you completed it in Exercise 23.

   OR

   📁 Open **OCR.31** from the data disk as a read-only file (Open As Copy).

3. Delete blank lines at the top of your page so the document begins at 1".

4. Full justify the document.

5. Set the left hyphenation zone to 4%.

6. Hyphenate the document.

7. Set left and right margins to 1.75" for all paragraphs; set a 2" right margin for hanging indented paragraphs.

8. Insert the paragraph as shown using a hanging indent format.

9. Search for the word **OCR**. Replace all but the first occurrence with Optical Character Recognition.

   NOTE: When entering the search word, be sure to enter [Bold On] and [Bold Off] codes as part of that word.

10. Using Thesaurus, substitute the words marked in brackets.

11. Preview your document.

12. Print one copy.

13. Close the file; save the changes.

    OR

    📁 Close the file; *save as* **OCR**.

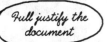
Full justify the document

❦OPTICAL CHARACTER RECOGNITION AT WORK❦

Optical Character Recognition, or **OCR**, converts paper documents to digital format. Therefore, it is ⟨possible⟩ to have an **OCR** device *read* text and have it appear on the computer's screen, without rekeying copy. Some **OCR** units have the ability to recognize a wide ⟨variety⟩ of fonts, reproduce tabs, text centering, and other formatting. Most **OCR** units process pages three or four times faster than the average typist's 70 words per minute.

Here are some interesting ways in which companies use Optical Character Recognition to ease their work loads:

A **Boston** service bureau recently scanned and republished a client's large medical catalog, a project that would have otherwise been too time consuming to ⟨undertake⟩.

A **New York**-based newspaper plans to create data files of their back issues, many of which were published in 1845.

A **Maryland** company needed to transfer files from an aging word processing system to a newer one. It discovered that printing the files from the old system and then scanning them into the new system was less ⟨expensive⟩.

At the supermarket checkout stand a laser beam "reads" the bar code on an item and gives the information -- item, price, etc., -- to the cash register.

DESIRED RESULT

❦OPTICAL CHARACTER RECOGNITION AT WORK❦

Optical Character Recognition, or **OCR**, converts paper documents to digital format. Therefore, it is feasible to have an **OCR** device *read* text and have it appear on the computer's screen, without rekeying copy. Some **OCR** units have the ability to recognize a wide collection of fonts, reproduce tabs, text centering, and other formatting. Most **OCR** units process pages three or four times faster than the average typist's 70 words per minute.

Here are some interesting ways in which companies use Optical Character Recognition to ease their work loads:

A **Boston** service bureau recently scanned and republished a client's large medical catalog, a project that would have otherwise been too time consuming to tackle.

A **New York**-based newspaper plans to create data files of their back issues, many of which were published in 1845.

At the supermarket checkout stand a laser beam "reads" the bar code on an item and gives the information--item, price, etc.,--to the cash register.

A **Maryland** company needed to transfer files from an aging word processing system to a newer one. It discovered that printing the files from the old system and then scanning them into the new system was less costly.

HYPHENATION

1. Position insertion point where hyphenation is to begin.
2. Click **For**mat .... `Alt` + `R`
3. Click **L**ine .... `L`
4. Click **Hyph**enation .... `E`

5. Click **Hyphenation On** check box .... `O`
6. Click **OK** .... `Enter`

   To change hyphenation zone:

   a. Click **Percentage Left** text box .... `L`

   b. Type a new left percentage.

c. Click **Percentage Right** text box..... `R`

d. Type a new right percentage.

e. Click **OK** .... `Enter`

EXERCISE

BULLETS AND NUMBERS

32

Bullet

NOTES:

- A **bullet** is a dot or symbol used to highlight points of information or to itemize a list that does not need to be in any particular order.

• red	• apple
• blue	• pear
• green	• orange

- Using the **Bullets and Numbers** feature, you can insert bullets automatically to create a bulleted list for each paragraph or item you type.

- The Bullets and Numbers feature also allows you to create numbered paragraphs for items that need to be in a particular order. The numbers you insert increment automatically.

> The Bullets and Numbers feature allows you to:
> 1.   Create numbered paragraphs.
> 2.   Create bulleted paragraphs.
> 3.   Use symbols instead of the traditional round dot or square bullet.

- The Bullets and Numbers feature is accessed by selecting Bullets & Numbers from the Insert main menu.

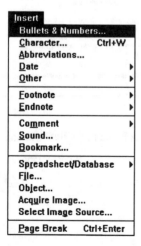

Insert	
Bullets & Numbers...	
Character...	Ctrl+W
Abbreviations...	
Date	▶
Other	▶
Footnote	▶
Endnote	▶
Comment	▶
Sound...	
Bookmark...	
Spreadsheet/Database	▶
File...	
Object...	
Acquire Image...	
Select Image Source...	
Page Break	Ctrl+Enter

- In the Bullets and Numbers dialog box which follows, you may select the bullet or number style you desire.

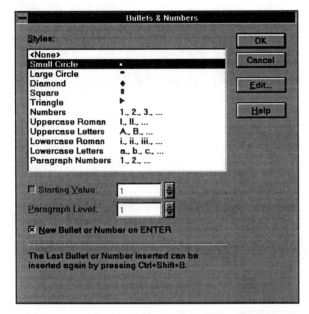

- Once the bullet or number style is chosen, you may type your text. By selecting New Bullet or Number on ENTER, the bullet or number is entered automatically each time the Enter key is pressed. The bullet or number begins at the left margin and the text automatically advances to the first tab stop.

- If you wish to insert bullets at a later point in the document, you can click the Bullet button on the Toolbar or press Ctrl + Shift + B; the bullet or number style you previously selected in the dialog box displays.

- You can add bullets and numbers to existing text by selecting/highlighting the text and then choosing Bullets & Numbers from the Insert main menu.

- Special characters may also be used as bullets. However, special characters will *not* automatically insert each time the Enter key is pressed (if that option was selected).

When using the Bullets and Numbers feature for numbered paragraphs, adding or deleting paragraphs will result in all paragraphs being automatically renumbered.

EXERCISE DIRECTIONS:

In this exercise, you will create a letter containing bulleted items and a numbered list.

1. Start with a clear screen.

2. Use the default margins.

3. Begin the exercise on Ln 2".

4. Format the full-block letter as shown.

5. Select a serif font face (Times New Roman).

6. Use the Bullets and Numbers feature to create the diamond bullets and numbered list.   Set 2" left and right margins for the bulleted and numbered items.

7. Spell check.

8. Set the left hyphenation zone to 4%.

9. Hyphenate the document.

10. Preview your work.

11. If necessary, use the Make-It-Fit feature to keep all text on one page. You may affect the fonts and bottom margin only.

12. Print one copy.

13. Save the exercise; name it **JOB**.

14. Close the document window.

CREATE A BULLETED OR NUMBERED LIST

1. Place insertion point where bulleted or numbered list is to begin.

2. Click **Insert** .... Alt + I

    Click **Bullets & Numbers** .... N

    OR

    Click **Ctrl + Shift + B** ..... Ctrl + Shift + B

OR

Click Insert Bullet button ....
on Toolbar.

CHANGE BULLET OR NUMBER STYLE

1. Click **Insert** .... Alt + I

2. Click **Bullets and Numbers** .... N

3. Click desired bullet or number style.

    To inset automatic bullet or number when Enter is pressed:

    Click New Bullet or Number on ENTER check box.

4. Click **OK** .... Enter

January 28, 199-

Ms. Harriet Denassos
78 Token Street
Marietta, GA 30068

Dear Harriet:

As per your request, I have outlined below the importance of using a resume to secure employment.

A resume is used to organize the important facts about you in a written document. It should contain brief but sufficient information to tell a prospective employer:

set 2" left and right margins

- What you can do.
- What is your level or education.
- What you have done.
- What you know.
- What kind of job you want.

Your resume should accomplish several objectives:

1. It will serve as your introduction.
2. It will save time for both the employer and applicant.
3. It will serve as a focus for, and improve, your personal interview. When you have outlined your outstanding qualities, you will find it easier to discuss them at an interview.
4. It will provide the employer with a visual reminder of what you said at the interview.

So, when you begin your preparation, proofread it carefully. Remember, your resume is a representation of yourself. It makes the first and last impression of who you are. Good luck in your job search.

Sincerely,

Susan Zantak
Counselor

sz

EXERCISE

▪ DOCUMENT INFORMATION

33

NOTES:

▪ The **Document Information** feature provides you with a statistical summary of your document. It lists the number of characters, words, lines, sentences, paragraphs and pages in your document. In addition, it indicates the average word length, average words per sentence, and maximum words per sentence. This is a particularly useful feature if you are required to submit a report with a specified word or page count.

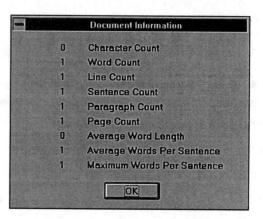

	Document Information
0	Character Count
1	Word Count
1	Line Count
1	Sentence Count
1	Paragraph Count
1	Page Count
0	Average Word Length
1	Average Words Per Sentence
1	Maximum Words Per Sentence

OK

EXERCISE DIRECTIONS:

 In this exercise, you will check your document for errors based on an Advertising writing style.

1. Start with a clear screen.

2. Use the default margins.

3. Begin the exercise on Ln 1.5".

4. ⌨ Keyboard the full-block letter on the right as shown including the circled, misspelled words.

   OR

   💾 Open **TOURS.33** from the data disk as a read-only file (Open As <u>C</u>opy).

5. Change text to a sans serif font.

6. Use the Date feature to insert today's date.

7. Change underlined text to italic in the first paragraph.

8. Change left and right margins to 2" for tour information.

9. Create bulleted paragraphs for tour information using any desired bullet style.

10. Full justify bulleted paragraphs.

11. Set left hyphenation zone to 4% and hyphenate the document.

12. Use QuickFormat to set tour titles to bold and italics.

13. Using the Thesaurus feature, substitute the words marked in brackets.

14. Starting with the second paragraph, search for "riding tours" and replace with "horseback riding tours."

15. Access document information. Note the number of words in this document.

16. Use Make It Fit, if necessary, to keep text on one page.

17. Spell check.

18. Print one copy.

19. Save the file; name it **TOURS**.

    OR

    💾 Close the file; *save as* **TOURS**.

Today's date

Ms. Christine Sabbio
876 North LaSalle Street
Chicago, IL 60601

Dear Ms. Sabbio:

You called last week inquiring about horseback riding tours in the United States, particulary the eastern half of the country with English-style riding.

Since I have been unable to reach you by phone, I am outlining in this letter some information about riding tours that I think will interest you.

set 2" left and right margins

EQUITABLE TOURS - This company offers riding tours of two to eight days and is located in Woodstock, Vermont. The cost ranges from $579 for four days to $1,229 for eight. They will arrange itinerries in Northern California and in Arizona.

EQUESTRIAN RIDES - This company offers riding tours from inn to inn through the Sugarbush, Vermont area between the Green Mountains and Lake Champlain. There are five-day rides at $795 and six-day rides for $960.

HOOFBEATS INTERNATIONAL - This company is located in New Jersey and offers instruction. They will arrange riding tours in upstate New York where participants may mix lessons with trail rides and stay at the farm or a nearby inn. The cost varies according to the program.

While there are many other riding tours availlable, I have outlined what I believe to be the best three. If you desire more information about riding tours, please call me.

Sincerely,

Paula Badar
Travel Agent

pb/yo

DOCUMENT INFORMATION

1. Click **File**.............................. `Alt` + `F`
2. Click **Document Info**.......................... `I`
3. Click **OK** .... `Enter`

EXERCISE

OUTLINING **34**

NOTES:

- An **outline** is used to organize information about a subject for the purpose of making a speech or writing a report. There are two types of outlines, a topic outline and a sentence outline.

- A **topic outline** summarizes the main topics and subtopics in short phrases, while a **sentence outline** uses complete sentences for each. Both of these outline types are organized using numbers. Outlines may, however, be organized using bullets or headings.

- The Outline feature is accessed by selecting **Outline** from the Tools main menu.

- An Outline Feature Bar displays, providing buttons for easy access to outline editing features. When you position your pointer over the buttons, a description of the button appears on the title bar.

- Outlines include several levels of information. A traditional outline, like the one illustrated on the right, uses Roman numerals to indicate the first outline level (I, II, III, etc.), capital letters to indicate the second outline levels (A, B, C, etc.), and Arabic numerals to indicate the third outline level (1, 2, 3, etc.). To use this format, you must change the default Paragraph outline type to Outline by selecting **Define Outline** from Options menu on the Feature Bar, or by clicking the drop-down arrow next to [Paragraph] and choosing Outline.

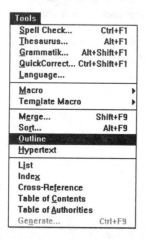

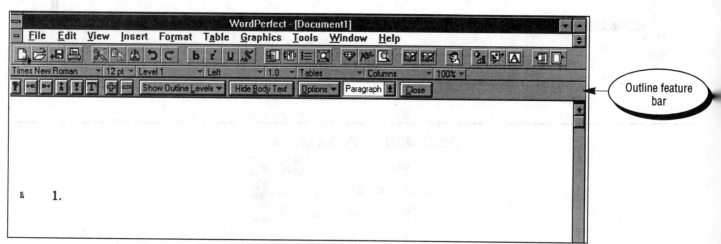

Outline feature bar

- When you begin your outline, symbols appear at the left of your screen, indicating non-outline text and the outline level of the text you type.

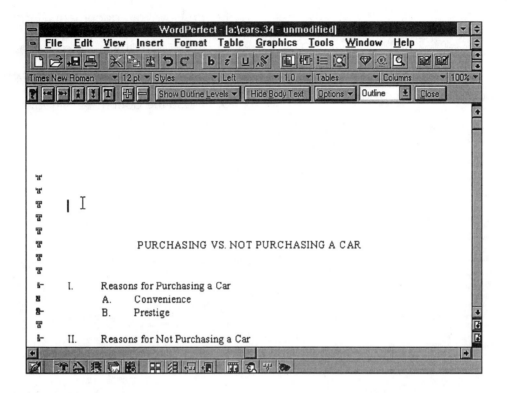

- While there are numerous outline styles available, we will concentrate on the **traditional outline style** is this exercise.

- An outline generally begins 2" from the top of the page and has a centered heading. A triple space follows the heading. The Outline feature is then accessed.

To advance from one level to the next:

- Use the Tab key, or

- Click the right-pointing arrow on the Feature Bar.

If you make an error by advancing too far to the next level:

- Press Shift + Tab, or

- Click the left-pointing arrow on the Feature Bar.

To type non-outline text below your outline:

- Select End Outline from the Options drop-down menu on the Feature Bar.

- Select Close.

EXERCISE DIRECTIONS:

 In this exercise, you will create a traditional outline.

1. Start with a clear screen.

2. Set 1.5" left and right margins.

3. Center the heading on approximately Ln 2".

4. Using the Outline feature and the outline style, create the topic outline on the right.

5. Spell check.

6. Preview your document (Page Zoom Full).

7. Print one copy.

8. Save the exercise; name it **CARS**.

9. Close the document window.

OUTLINE

1. Place insertion point where outline is to begin.

2. Click **Tools** .... Alt + T

3. Click **Outline** .... O

NOTE: The first outline level symbol and number of outline item you type appears.

To change outline style:

4. • Click **Options** .... Shift + Alt + O
   (on Feature Bar)

   • Click **Define** Outline .... D

   • Select desired outline style.

   • Click **OK** .... ⏎

NOTE: As you highlight a choice, a sample of the style appears in the Description areas.

Select Outline for this exercise.

To create outline:

5. Keyboard text for first level.

6. **Enter** .... ⏎

To advance to next level:

7. Press **Tab** .... Tab

   OR

   Click **right arrow** button .... ◄

   on Feature Bar.

8. Keyboard text for next level.

9. **Enter** .... ⏎

To type text for next level:

Repeat steps 5-7.

To return to previous level:

Press **Shift + Tab** .... Shift + Tab

OR

Click left arrow button .... ◄

on Feature Bar.

To end outline:

10. Click **Options** .... Shift + Alt + O
    (on Feature Bar)

11. Click **End** Outline .... E

12. Click **Close** (on Feature Bar) C

PURCHASING VS. NOT PURCHASING A CAR

I.   Reasons for Purchasing a Car
       A.   Convenience
       B.   Prestige

II.   Reasons for Not Purchasing a Car

       A.   Inconvenience
             1.   Expense of gasoline
             2.   Crowded roads
             3.   Parking problems
                   a.   Expensive parking garages
                   b.   Increasing tows
       B.   Hazards
             1.   Possibility of accidents
             2.   Unpredictable weather
       C.   Bad Financial Investment
             1.   High taxes
             2.   High interest rates
       D.   Continuing Costs
             1.   Fuel
             2.   Maintenance
                   a.   Brakes
                   b.   Oil
                   c.   Filter
                   d.   Tuneup
                         (1)   Points
                         (2)   Plugs
                         (3)   Timing

EXERCISE

▪ OUTLINING

35

NOTES:

- In this exercise, you will prepare a letter which includes a **paragraph outline**. Paragraph outline style is the default.

- A paragraph outline indicates the first levels as Arabic numbers, the second levels as lowercase letters, and the third levels as lowercase Roman numerals.

- In order to center the outline within the letter in this exercise, it is necessary to change your left and right margins to 2". After completing the outline, you must change your margins back to the default of 1" on the left and right. Double space before and after the outline.

- Be sure to end your outline before completing the letter.

EXERCISE DIRECTIONS:

 In this exercise, you will create a reporting using the Bullets and Numbers Feature.

1. Start with a clear screen.

2. Format the letter on the right in block style. Start on Ln 1.36".

3. Set the font for the document to serif 11 point.

4. Use the default margins for the letter.

5. Set left and right margins to 2" before beginning the outline.

6. After completing the outline:
   - End the outline feature
   - Reset the margins to 1".

7. Spell check.

8. Preview your document.

9. Print one copy.

10. Save the exercise; name it **CAREER**.

11. Close the document window.

Today's date

Mr. Ronald Mangano, Assistant Principal
New Dorp High School
465 New Dorp Lane
Staten Island, NY 10306

Dear Mr. Mangano:

I would once again like to make a presentation to your classes on *Choosing and Planning a Career.* A brief outline of my planned talk appears below:

1.   **CHOOSING AND PLANNING A CAREER**

     a.   Discovering the World of Work
     b.   Investigating Career Fields
             Medicine
             Business
        (1)   Marketing
        (2)   Brokerage
        (3)   Computer-related
             (a)   Technician
             (b)   Programmer
             (c)   Data Entry Operator
        (4)   Teaching
        (5)   Engineering

2.   **GETTING A JOB**

     a.   Being Interviewed
          i   How to dress
             (1)   What to say
     b.   Writing a Resume

While I may not have enough time to include all the material in my presentation, the outline will give you an overview of my topic. I look forward to addressing your classes on March 31.

Sincerely,

Janice Waller
Recruitment Representative

jw/yo

LESSON 6
SUMMARY EXERCISE A

EXERCISE DIRECTIONS:

1. Start with a clear screen.

2. Begin the exercise on Ln 1".

3. Set the title to 16 point bold. Use serif 12 point for the body text. Use italic and bold where shown.

4. Use the default margins.

5. Create the exercise shown below.

6. Use any bullet style for *Facts in Brief*.

7. Using the Thesaurus feature, substitute the words marked in brackets.

8. Print one copy.

9. Save the exercise; name it **BULLET**.

10. Close the document window.

BULLETS AND NUMBERS

Facts in Brief

- A bullet is a dot or symbol used to highlight points of information or ⟨itemize⟩ a list.
- The Bullets and Numbers feature ⟨allows⟩ you to insert bullets to ⟨create⟩ a bulleted list for each paragraph or item you type.
- The Bullets and Numbers feature also allows you to create numbered paragraphs.
- Each time the Enter key is pressed, the bullet or number is automatically inserted.
- You can add bullets and numbers to existing text.
- Special characters may also be used as bullets.

Inserting Bullets and Numbers Before Typing Text

1. Click **Insert**.
2. Click **Bullets and Numbers**.
3. Select a bullet or number style.
4. If you choose a number style, select a **Starting Value**.
5. If you ⟨want⟩ to insert a new bullet or number every time you press Enter, select **New Bullet or Number on ENTER**.
6. Click **OK**.

LESSON 6
SUMMARY EXERCISE B

EXERCISE DIRECTIONS:

1. Start with a clear screen.

2. Use the default margins.

3. Begin the exercise on Ln 1.5"

4. ⌨ Keyboard the text as shown in the On Disk illustration using a serif font.

   OR

5. 💾 Open **SERVICES.6B** from the data disk as a read-only file (Open As Copy).

   To create the flyer as shown in the Desired Result illustration, p. 145:

6. Set the title to script 24 point bold. Set the first word in the paragraph to sans serif 14 point bold; set the remaining paragraph to italic.

7. Set line spacing for the first paragraph (including the title) to 1.5".

8. Create a bulleted list for printing items as shown. Use any bullet style except a round dot.

9. Set bulleted items to a sans serif font.

10. Change the left margin for the bulleted items to 2".

11. Change margins to default for "Our Services include." Set text to italic.

12. Change the left margin to 2" and the right margin to 1.5" for the second set of bulleted paragraphs.

13. Create bulleted paragraphs for *Services* paragraphs.

14. Use QuickFormat to set *Services* titles to sans serif 14 point bold.

15. Center align company name and address and set text to sans serif. Set address and phone information to 10 point.

16. Search for WILLIAM H. BROWN and change to WILLIAM BROWN.

17. Access document information. Note the number of words in this document.

18. Use Make It Fit, if necessary, to keep text on one page.

19. Spell check.

20. Print one copy.

21. Save the exercise; name it **SERVICES**.

    OR

    💾 Close the file; *save as* **SERVICES**.

Printing With a Personal Touch...
Whether you are creating a one-time special event or developing a long-term corporate identity program, it is important to demonstrate quality and professionalism in your printed materials. At WILLIAM H. BROWN, you will find a Special Services Center, designed to handle your custom printing needs. We have been in business for over 30 years. Our commitment to quality and service stands tall in a very competitive marketplace. Let us help you with your personal printing needs for

Business cards
Stationery
Invitations and Announcements
Rubber Stamps
Business forms
Binders, Tabs, Folders
Signs, Banners, Name Plaques
Greeting Cards
Labels and Decals

Our Services include:

COMPLETE BUSINESS PACKAGE
Create a corporate identity package including business cards, letterhead and envelopes.

SALES AND MERCHANDISING SUPPORT
Printed announcements, banners, flyers and brochures.

PRESENTATIONS AND MEETING MATERIALS
Customized imprints on three-ring binders, divider tabs and covers.

SPECIAL OCCASIONS
Invitations, matchbooks and napkins for weddings, anniversaries, graduations and other special events.

BUSINESS FORMS
Internal business forms, carbonless invoices, work orders, receipts, memos, request forms and more.

WILLIAM H. BROWN, INC.
122 West 28 Street
New York, NY 10033
(212) 444-4444

Printing With a Personal Touch...

WHETHER *you are creating a one-time special event or developing a long-term corporate identity program, it is important to demonstrate quality and professionalism in your printed materials. At WILLIAM BROWN, you will find a Special Services Center, designed to handle your custom printing needs. We have been in business for over 30 years. Our commitment to quality and service stands tall in a very competitive marketplace. Let us help you with your personal printing needs for*

change left margin to 2"

- ◆ BUSINESS CARDS
- ◆ STATIONERY
- ◆ INVITATIONS AND ANNOUNCEMENTS
- ◆ RUBBER STAMPS
- ◆ BUSINESS FORMS
- ◆ BINDERS, TABS, FOLDERS
- ◆ SIGNS, BANNERS, NAME PLAQUES
- ◆ GREETING CARDS
- ◆ LABELS AND DECALS

change left margin to 1"

Our Services include:

change left margin to 2" and right margin to 1.5"

- • **COMPLETE BUSINESS PACKAGE**
  Create a corporate identity package including business cards, letterhead and envelopes.

- • **SALES AND MERCHANDISING SUPPORT**
  Printed announcements, banners, flyers and brochures.

- • **PRESENTATIONS AND MEETING MATERIALS**
  Customized imprints on three-ring binders, divider tabs and covers.

- • **SPECIAL OCCASIONS**
  Invitations, matchbooks and napkins for weddings, anniversaries, graduations and other special events.

- • **BUSINESS FORMS**
  Internal business forms, carbonless invoices, work orders, receipts, memos, request forms and more.

WILLIAM BROWN, INC.
122 WEST 28 STREET
NEW YORK, NY 10033
PHONE: 212-444-4444★FAX: 212-555-5555

LESSON 7

Exercises 36-44

- Two-Page Letter
- Hard vs. Soft Page Breaks
- Second-Page Heading
- Printing Multiple Pages
- Create a Table
- Move Within a Table
- Enter Text
- Two-Page Letter
- Bookmarks vs. QuickMarks
- Footnotes
- Endnotes
- Editing a Footnote or Endnote
- Creating Headers, Footers and Page Numbers
- Widow and Orphan Lines
- Page Numbering Placement
- Page Numbering Styles
- Moving Text from One Page to Another
- Using GoTo

EXERCISE

▪ A TWO PAGE LETTER ▪ HARD VS. SOFT PAGE BREAKS
▪ SECOND-PAGE HEADING ▪ PRINTING MULTIPLE PAGES

NOTES:

Hard vs. Soft Page Breaks

▪ WordPerfect assumes you are working on an 8½" x 11" page. Since WordPerfect uses default 1" top and bottom margins, there are exactly 9" of vertical space on a standard page for entering text.

▪ Therefore, when you enter text beyond Ln 9.83" (the last line of the 9 inches), WordPerfect automatically inserts a solid black and gray horizontal line across the screen to indicate the end of one page and the start of another; the status bar displays Pg 2.

NOTE: In Draft view, the hard page break is represented by a single line.

▪ When WordPerfect ends the page, this is referred to as a **soft page break**.

▪ To end the page before 9.83", you can enter a **hard page break** by selecting Page Break from the Insert main menu or pressing Ctrl + Enter. Text can still be added above the page break, but the hard page break will always begin a new page.

▪ A hard page break may be deleted by moving the insertion point to the end of the page before the hard page break, and pressing Delete or revealing your codes and deleting the [HPg] code.

Second-Page Headings

▪ A multiple-page letter requires a heading on the second and succeeding pages. The heading should begin at 1" and include the name of the addresses (to whom the letter is going), the page number, and the date.

Printing Multiple Pages

▪ As indicated in Exercise 8, WordPerfect allows you to specify how much of the document you wish to print: the full document, current page, multiple pages, selected text, document summary, or document on disk.

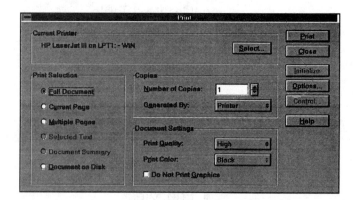

- When printing all pages in a multiple-page document, you must select Full Document, not the Current Page option. The insertion point may be on any page in the document when selecting this option.

- To print selected pages (pages 2 and 3, pages 3-5, etc.), select the Multiple Pages option, then enter the page range you wish to print in the Page(s) text box. Note the **Page(s)/Label(s)** text box and **print range** options shown below.

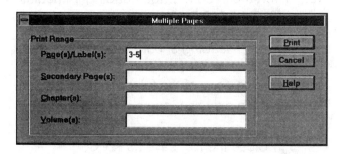

Type	To Print
3	Page 3
1,3,5	Pages 1, 3 and 5
4-	Page 4 to end of document
-2	The beginning of document through page 2
2-6	Pages 2 through 6
1-2 6	Pages 1, 2 and 6
2,5,9-11	Pages 2, 5, and 9 through 11.

- You may also print only odd pages, even pages, or both.

INSERT HARD PAGE BREAK

1. Place insertion point where new page is to begin.
2. Press **Ctrl + Enter** .... Ctrl + Enter

DELETE HARD PAGE BREAK

1. Place insertion point immediately after hard page break line.
2. Press **Backspace** .... Backspace

   OR

   a. Reveal Codes .... Alt + F3
   b. Place insertion point on hard page break code (HPg).
   c. Press **Delete** .... Del

PRINT SELECTED PAGES
F5

1. Click **File** .... Alt + F

   Click **Print** .... P

   OR

   Click Print button on Power Bar ....
2. Click **Multiple Pages** .... M
3. Click **Print** .... P

4. Click **Page(s)** text box .... A
5. Type selected page(s) using the following formats:

   3-9 ....= pages 3, 4, 5, 6, 7, 8 and 9
   3,6 ....= pages 3 and 6
   3-5,9 ....= pages 3, 4, 5 and 9
   -9.........= all pages before and including 9
   9-............= all pages after and including 9

PRINT ODD/EVEN PAGES

1. Follow steps 1-2, above.
2. Click **Options** .... O
3. Click **Print Odd/Even Pages** list box and select option:

   • **Both** .... B
   • **Odd** .... O
   • **Even** .... E
4. Click **OK** .... Enter
5. Click **Print** .... P or Enter

PRINT MULTIPLE PAGES

1. Click **File** .... Alt + F
2. Click **Print** .... P
3. Click in **Number of Copies** text box ... N

   OR

   Click increment arrows .. ↑ ↓ ← →
4. Type desired number of copies to print.
5. Click a print option:

   • **Full Document** .... F
   • **Current Page** .... P
   • **Multiple Pages** .... M
   • **Selected Text** L
   • **Document Summary** .... A
   • **Document on Disk** .... D
6. Click **Print** .... P

EXERCISE DIRECTIONS:

 In this exercise, you will create a two-page letter. Allow WordPerfect to insert the page break for you.

1. Start with a clear screen.
2. ⌨ Format the letter below and on the right in full-block style as a draft copy. (Draft copies are double spaced.)

   OR

   💾 Open **NYC.36** from the data disk as a read-only file (Open As Copy):
   - Set document line spacing to 2.
   - Create bulleted paragraphs as shown.
   - Add the remaining text below the bulleted paragraphs, as shown, to complete the letter.
   - Follow directions 6-12.
3. Use the default margins.
4. Begin the exercise on Ln 2.5"; set font to serif 12 point.

5. Use the Bullet feature to create the bullets on the first page.
6. Use the Paragraph Outline feature to create the numbered list on the last page. Be sure to choose the End Outline option after keyboarding item 3.
7. Spell check.
8. Print one copy of pages 2 and 3.
9. Reset line spacing to single for the document.
10. Insert the second-page heading immediately after the page break.
    NOTES: In future exercises, second page heading should be inserted as a header (see exercise 41).
11. Print one copy of the full document.
12. Save the exercise; name it **NYC**.

    OR

    💾 Close the file; *save as* **NYC**.
13. Close the document window.

Today's date

Mr. Brendon Basler
54 West Brook Lane
Fort Worth, TX 76102-1349

Dear Mr. Basler:

I am so glad to hear that you might be moving to Manhattan. You asked me to write and tell you what it is like living in Manhattan. Since I have been a New Yorker for most of my life and love every minute of it, I will describe to you what it might be like for you to live here.

- If you move to an apartment in Manhattan with a view, you might see the Empire State Building, the Metropolitan Life Tower, the Chrysler Building or even the Citicorp Center. Depending on where your apartment is located, you might even see the twin towers of the World Trade Center. The Brooklyn and Manhattan Bridges are off to the east and on a clear day you can see the Hudson River.

- Traffic in New York as well as waiting in long lines at the post office and the movie theaters can be very frustrating. However, after you have lived here for a short while, you will know the best times to avoid long lines.

- It is absolutely unnecessary and <u>very</u> expensive to own a car in Manhattan. The bus and subway system are excellent means to travel within the City.

- There is always something to do here. If you love the opera, ballet, theater, museums, art galleries, and eating foods from all over the world, then New York is the place for you.

Before you actually make the move, I suggest that you come here for an extended visit. Not everyone loves it here.

You mentioned that you would be visiting some time next month. I have listed on the next page some of the hotels (and their phone numbers) you might want to consider staying at while
Mr. Brendon Basler

Mr Brendon Basler
Page 2
Today's date

you are visiting. I have included those that would be in walking distance to your meeting locations. And, while you are attending your meetings, your family can take advantage of some of the sights and shopping near your hotel. I have called the hotels to be certain they can accommodate you and your family. They all seem to have availability at the time you are planning to visit.

1.   **Plaza Hotel** - located at 59th Street and Central Park South at the foot of Central Park. 1-800-228-3000.

2.   **The Pierre Hotel** - located at 61st Street and Fifth Avenue across the street from Central Park. 1-800-332-3442.

3.   **The Drake Swissotel** - located at 56th Street and Park Avenue. 212-421-0900.

Of course, you realize that there are many other hotel options available to you. If these are not satisfactory, let me know and I will call you with other recommendations.

Good luck with your decision. When you get to New York, I will show you some of the sights and sounds of the City. Hopefully, you will then be able to decide whether or not New York City is the place for you.

Sincerely,

Pamela Davis

pd/yo

EXERCISE

37

- **LETTERS WITH SPECIAL NOTATIONS**
- **BOOKMARKS**

NOTES:

Letters with Special Notations

- Letters may include special parts in addition to those learned thus far. The letter in this exercise contains a mailing notation, a subject line, and an enclosure and copy notations.

- When a letter is sent by a special mail service such as Express mail, Registered mail, Federal Express, Certified mail or by hand (via a messenger service), it is customary to include an appropriate notation on the letter. This notation is placed a double space below the date and typed in all caps.

- The **subject** identifies or summarizes the body of the letter. It is typed a double space below the salutation. A double space follows it. It may be typed at the left margin or centered in modified-block style. *Subject* may be typed in all caps or in upper- and lowercase. *Re* (in reference to) is often used instead of *Subject*.

- An **enclosure** (or attachment notation) is used to indicate that something else besides the letter is included in the envelope. The enclosure or attachment notation is typed a double space below the reference initials and may be typed in several ways (the number indicates how many items are enclosed in the envelope):

ENC.	Enclosure	Enclosures (2)
Enc.	Encls.	Attachment
Encl.	Encls (2)	Attachments (2)

- If copies of the document are sent to others, a **copy notation** is typed a double space below the enclosure/attachment notation (or the reference initials if there is no enclosure/attachment). A copy notation may be typed in several ways:

Copy to:	c:
Copy to	pc: (photocopy)

Bookmarks

- The **Bookmark** feature allows you to return quickly to a desired location in a document. This is a convenient feature if, for example, you are editing a large document and have to leave your work for a time. You could set a bookmark to keep your place. When you return to work, you can open your file, find the bookmark in your document and quickly return to the place you marked. Or, you might not have all the information needed to complete your document when you begin. Setting bookmarks will enable you to return to those sections of the document which need development or information inserted.

- You can have several bookmarks in a document; however, each bookmark must be named for easy identification. The bookmark name can be the first line of the paragraph or a one-word or character name.

- Your insertion point may be anywhere in the document when finding the bookmark.

- The Bookmark feature may be accessed by selecting Bookmark from the Insert main menu.

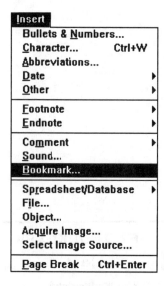

EXERCISE DIRECTIONS:

 In this exercise, you will set several bookmarks as you create your document, find them when you have completed your document, and insert additional information at each bookmark location.

1. Start with a clear screen.

2. Set absolute tab stops at 2" and 4.5".

3. Format the letter on the right in modified-block style.

4. Use the default margins.

5. Begin the exercise on Ln 2.5"; set font to serif 12 point.

6. Double indent the quotation paragraphs 1" from the left and right margins.

   NOTE: When you indent once, the text will advance 1" from the left margin, to the first tab stop you set (2" from the left edge of the page).

7. Set bookmarks where indicated; name the first one **1stINDENT**; the second, **3rdINDENT**; and the third, **copyto**.

8. Insert a hard-page break where indicated and include the second-page heading.

   NOTE: If necessary, adjust spacing at the top of the first page so that the second-page heading is properly positioned.

9. Spell check.

10. Save the exercise; name it **PREVIEW**.

11. Find the first bookmark, **1stINDENT**. Insert the following sentence at the bookmark location:

    Furthermore, they have captured the objects on film so true to life that anyone watching them is captivated.

12. Find the second bookmark, **3rdINDENT**. Insert the following sentence as the third indented paragraph:

    I will institute a program which will make schools throughout the country aware of their vocational potential.

13. Find the third bookmark, **copyto**. Insert a copy notation also to Tien Lee.

14. Spell check again.

15. Print three copies of page 1 and one copy of page 2.

16. Close your file; save the changes.

SET A BOOKMARK

1. Place insertion point where you want bookmark.

2. Click **Insert** .... Alt + I

3. Click **Bookmark** .... B

4. Click **Create** .... E

5. Click in **Bookmark Name** text box.

NOTE: The Bookmark Name text box displays text following the insertion point.

6. Click **OK** .... Enter
   to accept text as bookmark name.

   OR

   Type new bookmark name ....*name*

7. Click **OK** .... Enter

FIND BOOKMARK

1. Click **Insert** .... Alt + I

2. Click **Bookmark** .... B

3. Highlight name of bookmark to find.

4. Click **Go To** .... G

Today's date
↓2

REGISTERED MAIL
↓2
Ms. Elizabeth DeKan
Broward College
576 Southfield Road
Marietta, GA 30068
↓2
Dear Ms. DeKan:
↓2
Subject: Educational Films for High Schools and Colleges
↓2
Thank you for your interest in the films that we have available for high school and college
students. We are pleased to send you the enclosed flyer which describes the films in detail.
Also enclosed is a summary of those films that have recently been added to our collection since
the publication of the flyer.

There have been many positive reactions to our films. Just three weeks ago, a group of
educators, editors and vocational experts were invited to view the films at the annual
EDUCATORS' CONFERENCE. Here are some of their comments:

We will be sure to send the films in time for you to preview them. Please be sure to list the
date on which you wish to preview the film.

Mr. William R. Bondlow, Jr., president of the National Vocational Center in Washington,
D.C. and editor-in-chief of *Science Careers*, said,

(create bookmark)   I like the films very much. They are innovative and a
great benefit to all those interested in the earth
sciences as a professional career.

Ms. Andra Burke, a leading expert presently assigned to the United States Interior
Department, praised the films by saying that,

Ms. Elizabeth DeKan
Page 2
Today's date
↓3

(create book mark)   They are a major educational advance in career
placement, which will serve as a source of motivation
for all future geologists.

A member of the National Education Center, Dr. Lawrence Pilgrim, also liked the films and
said,

These are just some of the reactions we have had to our films. We know you will have a
similar reaction.

We would very much like to send you the films that you would like during the summer
session. You can use the summer to review them. It is important that your request be
received quickly since the demand for the films is great, particularly during the summer
sessions at colleges and universities throughout the country.

Cordially,

William DeVane
Executive Vice President
Marketing Department

wd/yo
Enclosures (2)
↓2
Copy to   Robert R. Redford
            Nancy Jackson

(create bookmark)

EXERCISE

▪ TWO-PAGE LETTER ▪ BOOKMARKS VS. QUICKMARKS

NOTES:

Bookmarks vs. QuickMarks

▪ **Bookmarks** are used when you want to return to more than one location in a single document. However, if you need to use only one bookmark in a document, you can set a **QuickMark**. A QuickMark is a generic bookmark.

▪ WordPerfect allows you to have only one QuickMark in a document. If you place a second QuickMark in a document, the first one will be deleted. Because only one QuickMark may be inserted in a document, it does not need to be named.

▪ WordPerfect automatically places a QuickMark at the insertion point location whenever you save a document.

▪ QuickMark can be accessed by selecting Bookmark from the Insert main menu, then selecting Set QuickMark in the Bookmark dialog box.

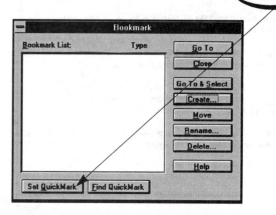

EXERCISE DIRECTIONS:

1. Start with a clear screen.

2. Open **DIVE** (if you saved it in Exercise 27).

   OR

   Open **DIVE.38** from the data disk as a read-only file (Open As Copy).

3. Create a two-page, full-block style letter from the document on the right.

4. Begin the exercise on Ln 2.5".

5. Insert the date and inside address as shown.

6. Set paragraph text to 12 point; set subject line text to 12 point bold.

7. Use the Case Convert feature to change the subject line from all caps to initial capitals.

8. Set a QuickMark at the beginning of the third paragraph.

9. Make the remaining revisions.

10. Enter an appropriate second-page heading.

11. Enter the following letter closing:

    Yours truly,

    John Rogers
    Travel Agent

    jr/yo

    enclosure

12. Spell check.

13. Find the QuickMark. Insert the following new paragraph at the QuickMark location:

    Some hotels do not have a beach. Instead, they have a cliff from which you can make entry into the ocean. When the sun sets, you can see the incredible sights down below.

14. Print one copy of the full document.

15. Save the document as a new file (Save As); name it **DIVING**.

16. Close the document window.

↓2.5"

Today's date

insert {
Mr. Kenyatta Belcher
80 Avenue P
Cambridge, MA 02138

Dear Ken,

SUBJECT:◄———— DIVING IN THE CAYMAN ISLANDS) *set to 12 pt*

◄————Do you want to see sharks, barracudas, stingrays and angelfish?

◄————The Cayman Islands were discovered by Christopher Columbus in 1503 and are located south of Cuba. The Caymans are home to about 25,000 year-around residents. However, they welcome 200,000 visitors each year. Most visitors come with masks and flippers in their luggage.

set a Quickmark ⟶ Before you descend the depths of the ocean, it is important that you have a few lessons on the don'ts of diving: ☞Don't touch the coral. ☞Don't come up to the surface too fast holding your breath. If you do, your lungs will explode. Now, you are ready to jump in!

◄———— Here are some hotel suggestions:

Hotel/Diving Accommodations:

Anchorage View, PO Box 2123, Grand Cayman; (809) 947-4209.

Cayman Diving Lodge, PO Box 11, East End, Grand Cayman; (809) 947-7555.

Coconut Harbour, PO Box 2086, George Town, Grand Cayman; (809) 949-7468.

Red Sail Sports, PO Box 1588, George Town, Grand Cayman; (809) 979-7965.

Sunset House, PO Box 479, George Town, Grand Cayman; (800) 854-4767.

Hotels Offering Free Diving Instruction:

Cayman Diving Lodge, PO Box 11, East End, Grand Cayman; (809) 947-7555.

Sunset House, PO Box 479, George Town, Grand Cayman; (800) 854-4767.

¶ *I am enclosing a brochure which will give you more details about the Cayman Islands. If you have any additional questions, please feel free to call me at any time.*

SET QUICKMARK

Ctrl + Shift + Q

1. Place insertion point where you want QuickMark placed.

2. Click **I**nsert .... Alt + I

3. Click **B**ookmark .... B

4. Click **Set Q**uickmark .... Q

FIND QUICKMARK

Ctrl + Q

1. Click **I**nsert .... Alt + I

2. Click **B**ookmark .... B

3. Click **F**ind QuickMark .... F

EXERCISE

FOOTNOTES

39

NOTES:

- A **footnote** is used in a document to give information about the source of quoted material. The information includes the author's name, the publication, the publication date and the page number from which the quote was taken.

- Footnotes are printed at the bottom of a page. A **separator line** separates footnote text from the text on the page.

- A **reference number** appears immediately after the quote in the text, and a corresponding footnote number or symbol appears at the bottom of the page.

- The Footnote feature automatically inserts the reference number after the quote, inserts the separator line, numbers the footnote and formats your page so that the footnote appears on the same page as the reference number.

- The actual note may be viewed in Page view if you scroll to the bottom of the page. To see how the page will format, select T**w**o Page from the **V**iew main menu or click the Zoom button on the Power Bar 🔍

- Footnotes may be inserted by selecting **F**ootnote, **C**reate from the **I**nsert main menu.

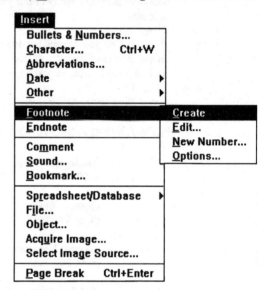

- The footnote screen displays the first footnote number ready for you to type the first footnote.

EXERCISE DIRECTIONS:

In this exercise, you will create a report with footnotes and include a QuickMark.

1. Start with a clear screen.

2. Create the report on the right in double space.

3. Use the default margins.

4. Begin the exercise on Ln 2".

5. Type until you reach each reference number; use the Footnote feature to insert the reference number and the footnote text.

6. Set a QuickMark at the end of the second paragraph.

7. Spell check.

8. Find the QuickMark. Insert the following sentences at the QuickMark location:

   It belongs to a class of animals called arachnids, the same family that spiders, mites and ticks also belong to. Scorpions live in warm countries in most parts of the world.

9. Print one copy.

10. Save the exercise; name it **SCORPION**.

11. Close the document window.

2"

THE SCORPION

What is the first thing you think of when you hear the word "scorpion"? Most people think of "sting," "unsightly insect" or "poisonous."

The scorpion is a small animal with a dangerous poisonous stinger in its tail. The scorpion is *not* an insect.

create QuickMark

Scorpions eat large insects and spiders, and are most active at night. "Scorpions capture and hold their prey with their pedipalps, which have teeth. They then stab the prey with their stingers."[1]

reference numbers

The scorpion's stinger is a curved organ in the end of its tail. Two glands at the base give out a poison that flows from two pores. "Of the more than forty species of scorpions found in the United States, only two are considered to be harmful to people."[2] While a scorpion's sting is painful, it does not usually cause death.

separator line

footnotes

[1]Gottfried, et al, *Biology* (New Jersey: Prentice-Hall, Inc., 1983), 461.

[2]Gottfried, 461.

FOOTNOTE

1. Keyboard to the first reference number.

   OR

   Place insertion point at the location of the first reference number.

2. Click **Insert** .... `Alt` + `I`

3. Click **Footnote** .... `F`

4. Click **Create** .... `C`

   NOTE: *A blank window appears displaying the separator line and the first assigned footnote number.*

5. Keyboard footnote text.

6. Click **Close** .... `C`
   to return to document.

   NOTE: *The reference number is automatically inserted in the document.*

EXERCISE

▪ ENDNOTES ▪ EDITING A FOOTNOTE OR ENDNOTE

NOTES:

▪ An **endnote** contains the same information as a footnote, but is printed at the end of a document or on a separate page and differs in format. Compare the endnote illustrations below with the footnotes in the previous exercise.

Endnotes at the End of a Document

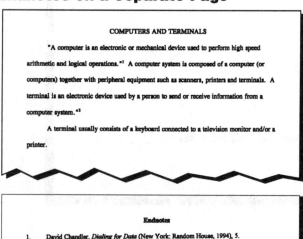

Endnotes on a Separate Page

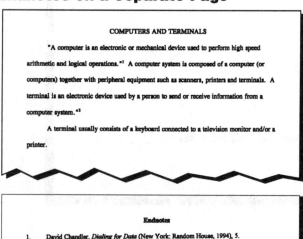

▪ When endnotes are created, they appear at the end of the document text. Each note number is indicated by an arabic numeral and a period. You may space twice after the period or use the Indent button before typing endnote text.

▪ To force endnotes onto a separate page, place the insertion point below the last line of document text and press Ctrl + Enter.

▪ It is possible to have both footnotes and endnotes in the same document.

▪ Like footnotes, endnotes may be viewed in Page view if you scroll to the bottom of the page. To see how the page will format, select Two Page from the View main menu or click Page Zoom Full button on the Power Bar ⊞

▪ The Endnote feature may be accessed by selecting Endnote from the Insert main menu.

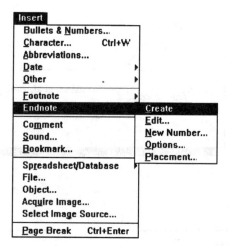

Editing a Footnote/Endnote

■ If you need to make a correction to the footnote/endnote, you may return to the footnote window and edit the note. When you edit, add, or delete footnotes or endnotes, WordPerfect renumbers and reformats them as necessary.

■ To edit a footnote or endnote, select Edit, Footnote (or Endnote), from the Insert main menu. Then, type the number of the footnote or endnote to edit in the Footnote (or Endnote) Number text box. This will place your insertion point at the footnote or endnote to be edited and display the footnote/endnote screen.

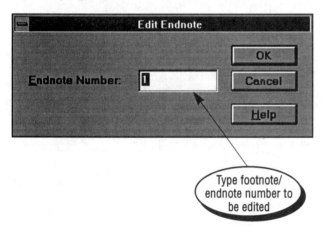

Type footnote/ endnote number to be edited

■ To move to the previous or next note, click the Previous or Next button on the footnote/endnote screen. Click the Close button to return to your document when you have completed your edits.

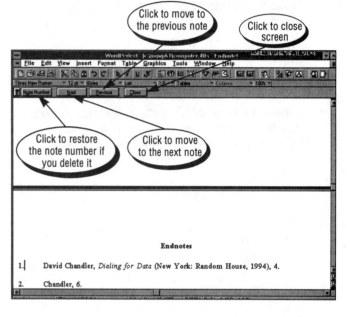

Click to move to the previous note

Click to close screen

Click to restore the note number if you delete it

Click to move to the next note

■ The Footnote Options dialog box allows you to edit the number style in the text or in the note. In addition, you may change the line style or the amount of space before and/or after the line separating the footnotes from the text.

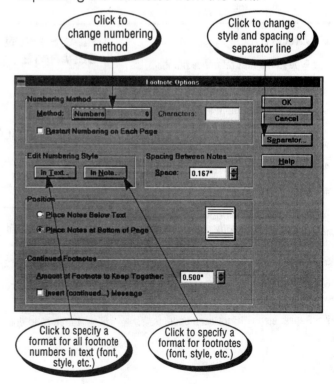

Click to change numbering method

Click to change style and spacing of separator line

Click to specify a format for all footnote numbers in text (font, style, etc.)

Click to specify a format for footnotes (font, style, etc.)

EXERCISE DIRECTIONS:

In this exercise, you will create a report with endnotes appearing on a separate page.

1. Start with a clear screen.

2. Create the report on the right in double space.

3. Use the default margins.

4. Begin the exercise on Ln 2".

5. Type until you reach each reference number; use the Endnote feature to insert the reference number and the endnote text.

6. Place the endnotes on a separate page.

7. Spell check.

8. Edit endnote number 1. Change the page number to 4.

9. Print one copy.

10. Save the exercise; name it **COMPUTER**.

11. Close the document window.

ENDNOTE

1. Type to the first reference number.

   OR

   Place insertion point at the location of the first reference number.

2. Click **I**nsert .... Alt + I

3. Click **E**ndnote .... E

4. Click **C**reate C

NOTE: A blank window appears with an automatically assigned reference number.

5. Type footnote text.

6. Click **C**lose C
   to return to document.

7. Repeat steps 1-6 for each endnote.

PLACE ENDNOTES ON SEPARATE PAGE

1. Place insertion point at last line of text.

2. Press **Ctrl + Enter** .... Ctrl + ⏎

EDIT FOOTNOTE/ENDNOTE

1. Click **I**nsert .... Alt + I

2. Click **E**ndnote .... E

3. Click **E**dit .... E

4. Keyboard footnote/endnote number to edit.

5. Click **OK** .... ⏎

6. Make desired correction.

7. Click **C**lose C
   to return to document.

FOOTNOTE/ENDNOTE OPTIONS

1. Click **I**nsert .... Alt + I

2. Click **E**ndnote .... E

3. Click **O**ptions .... O

4. Make desired option changes.

5. Click **OK** .... Enter

COMPUTERS AND TERMINALS

"A computer is an electronic or mechanical device used to perform high speed arithmetic and logical operations."[1] A computer system is composed of a computer (or computers) together with peripheral equipment such as scanners, printers and terminals. A terminal is an electronic device used by a person to send or receive information from a computer system."[2]

A terminal usually consists of a keyboard connected to a television monitor and/or a printer.

Endnotes

1. David Chandler, *Dialing for Data* (New York: Random House, 1994), 5.

2. Chandler, 6.

EXERCISE

CREATING HEADERS, FOOTERS AND PAGE NUMBERS

NOTES:

Headers and Footers

■ A **header** is text (such as a chapter title, a date, or a company name) which prints at the top of every page or every other page; a **footer** is text which prints at the bottom of every page or every other page.

■ After the desired header or footer text is typed once, the Header/Footer feature will automatically insert it on every page or on specific pages of your document.

■ You can create two different headers (specified as either A or B) and two different footers (specified as either A or B) at any place in the document. You can have only two headers and two footers active on any given page.

■ Headers/Footers may be accessed by selecting Header/Footer from the Format main menu, then, selecting Create in the Headers/Footers dialog box:

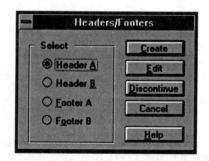

■ When you create a header or footer, the Header/Footer Feature Bar automatically displays. The Feature Bar provides options for creating and editing headers/footers. When you click outside the header/footer area, the Feature Bar becomes deactivated.

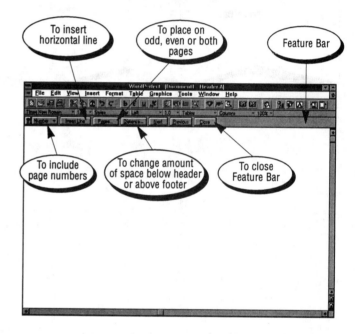

■ The header will print just below the top margin; the footer will print just above the bottom margin.

■ The distance between text and the header or footer may be changed. To do so, select Distance on the Feature Bar and make the desired adjustments.

■ You may insert a horizontal line below header or above footer text by selecting Insert Line on the Feature Bar.

■ Headers and footers display in *Page* or *Two Page view*.

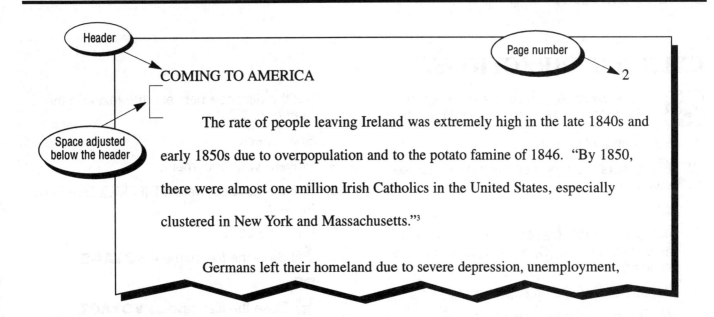

COMING TO AMERICA

The rate of people leaving Ireland was extremely high in the late 1840s and

early 1850s due to overpopulation and to the potato famine of 1846. "By 1850,

there were almost one million Irish Catholics in the United States, especially

clustered in New York and Massachusetts."[3]

Germans left their homeland due to severe depression, unemployment,

- If you plan to insert a header on the *left* side of your pages, insert page numbers on the top *right* side or bottom of your pages. Be sure that your header/footer text does not overlap or appear too close to the page number.

- Headers, footers and page numbers may be inserted after the document is typed.

 If you want header, footer and/or footnotes to align with the body text, you must set margins for the *document*, not for the page. If you want document font face, size and style to apply to header or footer text, you must change the initial font settings.

Editing Headers/Footers

- To edit a header or footer, you may click inside the header or footer or select Header/Footer, Edit from the Format main menu. Or, you may click the *right* mouse button while inside the header or footer and select Header/Footer, Edit.

Page Numbers

- Page numbers should be included on the second and succeeding pages of multiple-page documents. Page numbers may be included as part of header/footer text by selecting Number, then Page Number on the Feature bar, or they may be placed in a document independent of the header/footer. Position the insertion point where you desire the page number before selecting the Number button on the Feature Bar. *(Placing page numbers outside header/footer text will be covered in Exercise 42.)*

- Headers/footers and page numbers should not appear on the first page of a multiple-page document. Therefore, they must be suppressed on the first page by selecting Page, Suppress from the Format main menu.

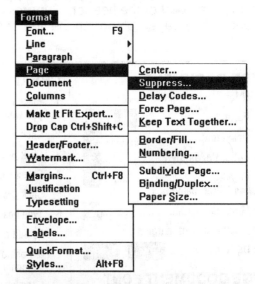

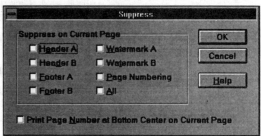

EXERCISE DIRECTIONS:

 In this exercise, you will create a report with footnotes, headers and page numbers.

1. Start with a clear screen.

2. Create the report on the right in double space.

OR

Open **VOYAGE.41** from the data disk as a read-only file (Open As Copy). Set line spacing to 2.

3. Begin the exercise on approximately Ln 2".

   NOTE: You must set margins, font face and font size for the document.

4. Use a serif 12 point font for the document.

5. Set 1.5" left and right document margins.

6. Create the header: DIFFICULTIES COMING TO AMERICA. Include a right-aligned page number as part of the header. Suppress the header and page number on the first page.

7. Set the distance between the text and the header to 0.35".

8. Spell check.

9. Preview your document.

10. Edit the header. Delete DIFFICULTIES from the title.

11. Print one copy.

12. Save the file; name it **VOYAGE**.

OR

Close the file; *save as* **VOYAGE**.

NOTE: While the exercise is shown in single space, you are to use double space. Your printed document will result in two or three pages, depending on the selected font, and footnotes will appear on the same pages as reference numbers.

13. Close the document window.

CHANGE DOCUMENT MARGINS

1. Click **Fo_r_mat** .... `Alt` + `R`
2. Click **Document** .... `D`
3. Click **Initial Codes Style** .... `S`
4. Click **Fo_r_mat** .... `R`
   in **Styles Editor** dialog box.
5. Click **Margins** .... `M`
6. Change left and right margins.
7. Click **OK** twice .... `Enter` , `Enter`

CHANGE DOCUMENT FONT STYLE OR SIZE

1. Click **Fo_r_mat** .... `Alt` + `R`
2. Click **Document** .... `D`
3. Click **Initial Font** .... `F`
4. Click desired option(s):
   - **Font Face** .... `Alt` + `F`
   - **Font Size** .... `Alt` + `S`
   - **Font Style** .... `Alt` + `O`
5. Click **OK** .... `Enter`

CREATE HEADERS/FOOTERS

1. Place insertion point on first page where you want new header/footer to appear.
2. Click **Format** .... `Alt` + `R`
3. Click **Header/Footer** .... `H`
4. Select **Header A** or **Header B** `A` or `B`
5. Click **Create** .... `C`
6. Type header/footer text.

   To add a page number:

   a. Position cursor where number will appear.
   b. Click **Number** .... `M`
      on Feature Bar.
   c. Click **Page Number** .... `P`

   To adjust distance between header/footer and document text:

   a. Click **Distance** .... `D`
      on Feature Bar.
   b. Type amount of space in text box.

   OR

   Click increment arrows.
7. Click **Close** .... `C`
   on Feature Bar.

SUPPRESS HEADER/ FOOTER/PAGE NUMBER ON FIRST PAGE

1. Place insertion point on page where text is to be suppressed.
2. Click **Format** .... `Alt` + `R`
3. Click **Page** .... `P`
4. Click **Suppress** .... `U`
5. Click appropriate check box to suppress desired item.
6. Click **OK** .... `Enter`

EDIT HEADER/FOOTER

1. Place insertion point on first page where you want change to occur.
2. Click **Format** .... `Alt` + `R`
3. Click **Header/Footer** .... `H`
4. Click **Edit** .... `E`

   OR

   a. Click anywhere inside header or footer.
   b. Click *right* mouse button.
   c. Click **Header/Footer**.
   d. Click **Edit**.
5. Edit header/footer text.
6. Click **Close** .... `M`
   on Feature Bar.

IMMIGRATION TO THE UNITED STATES
IN THE NINETEENTH CENTURY

The United States is sometimes called the "Nation of Immigrants" because it has received more immigrants than any other country in history. During the first one hundred years of US history, the nation had no immigration laws. Immigration began to climb during the 1830s. "Between 1830-1840, 44% of the immigrants came from Ireland, 30% came from Germany, 15% came from Great Britain, and the remainder came from other European countries."[1]

The movement to America of millions of immigrants in the century after the 1820s was not simply a flight of impoverished peasants abandoning underdeveloped, backward regions for the riches and unlimited opportunities offered by the American economy. People did not move randomly to America but emanated from very specific regions at specific times in the nineteenth and twentieth centuries. "It is impossible to understand even the nature of American immigrant communities without appreciating the nature of the world these newcomers left."[2]

The rate of people leaving Ireland was extremely high in the late 1840s and early 1850s due to overpopulation and to the potato famine of 1846. "By 1850, there were almost one million Irish Catholics in the United States, especially clustered in New York and Massachusetts."[3]

Germans left their homeland due to severe depression, unemployment, political unrest, and the failure of the liberal revolutionary movement. It was not only the poor people who left their countries, but those in the middle and lower-middle levels of their social structures also left. "Those too poor could seldom afford to go, and the very wealthy had too much of a stake in the homelands to depart."[4]

Many immigrants came to America as a result of the lure of new land, in part, the result of the attraction of the frontier. America was in a very real sense the last frontier--a land of diverse peoples that, even under the worst conditions, maintained a way of life that permitted more freedom of belief and action than was held abroad. "While this perception was not entirely based in reality, it was the conviction that was often held in Europe and that became part of the ever-present American Dream."[5]

---

[1]Lewis Paul Todd and Merle Curti, *Rise of the American Nation* (New York: Harcourt Brace Jovanovich, Inc., 1972), 297.

[2]John Bodner, *The Transplanted* (Bloomington: Indiana University Press, 1985), 54.

[3]E. Allen Richardson, *Strangers in This Land* (New York: The Pilgrim Press, 1988), 6.

[4] Richardson, 13.

[5]Richardson, 72.

EXERCISE

42

▪ **WIDOW AND ORPHAN LINES**
▪ **PAGE NUMBERING PLACEMENT** ▪ **PAGE NUMBERING STYLES**

NOTES:

Widow and Orphan Lines

▪ A **widow** line occurs when the last line of a paragraph is printed by itself at the top of a page. An **orphan** line occurs when the first line of a paragraph appears by itself on the last line of the page. Widow and orphan lines should be avoided.

▪ The Widow/Orphan Protect feature eliminates widows and orphans in a document and may be accessed by selecting Page, Keep Text Together from the Format main menu.

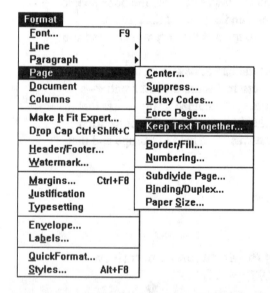

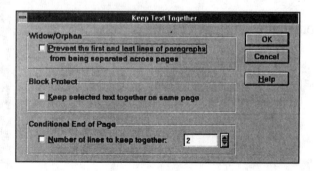

Page Numbering Placement

▪ As indicated in Exercise 41, page numbers may be included independent of the header/footer text by selecting Page, Numbering from the Format main menu.

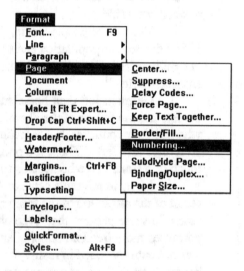

▪ WordPerfect provides numerous page numbering position options. Numbers may be inserted at the top or bottom left, center or right of a page. The Page Numbering dialog box (which appears after Format, Page, Numbering is selected) displays the page numbering position you select on the sample facing pages.

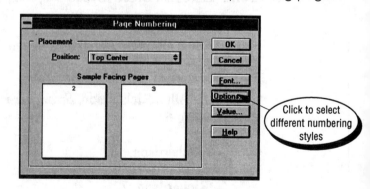

Click to select different numbering styles

Page Numbering Styles

■ WordPerfect provides five different numbering styles. Numbering styles may be selected by clicking Options on the Page Numbering dialog box shown on the previous page.

Numbers	1, 2, 3, 4, 5, etc.
Lowercase Letter	a, b, c, d, e, f, etc.
Uppercase Letter	A, B, C, D, E, F, etc.
Lowercase Roman	i, ii, iii, iv, v, etc.
Uppercase Roman	I, II, III, IV, V, etc.

■ Once selected, the numbering style displays in the Page Numbering Options dialog box in the sample facing pages preview.

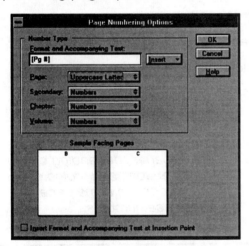

EXERCISE DIRECTIONS:

 In this exercise, you will create a report with footnotes, a header, and bottom centered page numbers. Remember to suppress headers and page numbers on the first page.

NOTE: When a quotation is longer than two sentences, it is single spaced and indented. In this exercise, you will indent the quoted material, as directed.

1. Start with a clear screen.

2. ⌨ Create the report on the right. Set line spacing to 2.3".

   NOTE: You must set margins, font face and font size for the document.

   OR

   💾 Open **USA.42** from the data disk as a read-only file (Open As Copy).

3. Begin the exercise on approximately Ln 2".

4. Use a serif 13 point font for the document.

5. Set 1.5" left and right document margins.

6. Set the title to 14 point bold.

7. Use widow and orphan protection.

8. Indent and single space the quoted text, as indicated.

9. Create the following header:

   BUILDING THE UNITED STATES OF AMERICA

10. Include an Uppercase Roman page number on the bottom center of the second and succeeding pages.

11. Spell check.

12. Edit the header to read:

    BUILDING THE U. S. A.

13. Preview your document.

14. Print one copy.

15. Save the file; name it **USA**.

16. Close the document window.

    NOTE: While the exercise is shown in single space, you are to use double space. Your printed document will result in two or three pages, depending on the selected font, and footnotes will appear on the same page as reference numbers.

INSERTING PAGE NUMBERS

1. Place insertion point at beginning of document or page.
2. Click **Format** .... `Alt` + `R`
3. Click **Page** .... `P`
4. Click **Numbering** .... `N`
5. Click **Position** list box .... `P`
6. Click a page number position option:
   - **No Page Numbering** .... `N`
   - **Top Left** .... `L`
   - **Top Center** .... `C`
   - **Top Right** .... `R`
   - **Alternating Top** .... `A`
   - **Bottom Left** .... `B`
   - **Bottom Center** .... `O`
   - **Bottom Right** .... `T`
   - **Alternating Bottom** .... `E`

To change numbering style:

a. Click **Options** .... `O`
b. Click **Page** list box .... `Alt` + `P`
c. Select a numbering method option:
   - **Numbers** .... `N`
   - **Lowercase Letter** .... `L`
   - **Uppercase Letter** .... `U`
   - **Lowercase Roman** .... `O`
   - **Uppercase Roman** .... `P`

7. Click **OK** .... `◄`
   until you return to document.

SET WIDOW/ORPHAN PROTECTION

1. Place insertion point on page where you want protection to begin.
2. Click **Format** .... `Alt` + `R`
3. Click **Page** .... `P`
4. Click **Keep Text Together** .... `K`
5. Click **Prevent the First and Last Lines of Paragraphs from Being Separated Across Pages** check box .... `P`
6. Click **OK** .... `◄`

IMMIGRATION'S IMPACT IN THE UNITED STATES

The opportunity to directly transfer a skill into the American economy was great for newcomers prior to the 1880s. "Coal-mining and steel-producing companies in the East, railroads, gold- and silver-mining interests in the West, and textile mills in New England all sought a variety of ethnic groups as potential sources of inexpensive labor."[1] Because immigrants were eager to work, they contributed to the wealth of the growing nation. During the 1830s, American textile mills welcomed hand-loom weavers from England and North Ireland whose jobs had been displaced by power looms. It was this migration that established the fine-cotton-goods trade of Philadelphia. "Nearly the entire English silk industry migrated to America after the Civil War, when high American tariffs allowed the industry to prosper on this side of the Atlantic."[2]

Whether immigrants were recruited directly for their abilities or followed existing networks into unskilled jobs, they inevitably moved within groups of friends and relatives and worked and lived in clusters.

As the Industrial Revolution progressed, immigrants were enticed to come to the United States through the mills and factories who sent representatives overseas to secure cheap labor. An example was the Amoskeag Manufacturing Company, located along the banks of the Merrimack River in Manchester, New Hampshire. In the 1870s, the Amoskeag Company recruited women from Scotland who were expert gingham weavers. Agreements were set specifying a fixed period of time during which employees would guarantee to work for the company.[3]

In the 1820s, Irish immigrants did most of the hard work in building the canals in the United States. In fact, Irish immigrants played a large role in building the Erie Canal. American contractors encouraged Irish immigrants to come to the United States to work on the roads, canals, and railroads, and manufacturers lured them into the new mills and factories.

"Most German immigrants settled in the middle western states of Ohio, Indiana, Illinois, Wisconsin and Missouri."[4] With encouragement to move west from the Homestead Act of 1862, which offered public land free to immigrants who intended to become citizens, German immigrants comprised a large portion of the pioneers moving west. "They were masterful farmers and they built prosperous farms."[5]

---

[1]E. Allen Richardson, *Strangers in This Land* (New York: The Pilgrim Press, 1988), 67.

[2]John Bodnar, *The Transplanted* (Bloomington: Indiana University Press, 1985), 54.

[3]Bodnar, 72.

[4]David A. Gerber, *The Making of An American Pluralism* (Chicago: University of Illinois, 1989), 124.

[5]Bodnar, 86.

EXACERCISE

EXERCISE

43

▪ MOVING TEXT FROM ONE PAGE TO ANOTHER ▪ USING GO TO

NOTES:

▪ The procedure for moving blocks of text from one page to another is the same as moving blocks of text on the same page. However, when moving text from one page to another, the **Go To** feature may be used to advance quickly to the page where the text is to be reinserted. Or, it may be used at any time to move the insertion point quickly to a specific location in your document.

▪ Go To may be accessed from the <u>E</u>dit main menu or by pressing Ctrl + G.

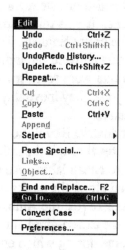

Edit	
<u>U</u>ndo	Ctrl+Z
<u>R</u>edo	Ctrl+Shift+R
U<u>n</u>do/Redo History...	
U<u>n</u>delete... Ctrl+Shift+Z	
Rep<u>e</u>at...	
Cu<u>t</u>	Ctrl+X
<u>C</u>opy	Ctrl+C
Paste	Ctrl+V
Appen<u>d</u>	
Se<u>l</u>ect	▶
Paste <u>S</u>pecial...	
Lin<u>k</u>s...	
<u>O</u>bject...	
<u>F</u>ind and Replace... F2	
Go To...	Ctrl+G
Con<u>v</u>ert Case	▶
Pr<u>e</u>ferences...	

EXERCISE DIRECTIONS:

In this exercise, you will move paragraphs from one page to another. After moving the paragraph in this exercise, it may be necessary to move the second page heading appropriately.

1. Start with a clear screen.

2. Open **PREVIEW** if you completed it in Exercise 37.

   OR

   💾 Open **PREVIEW.43** from the data disk as a read-only file (Open As <u>C</u>opy).

3. Make the indicated revisions.

4. Using the Thesaurus, replace the words marked in brackets. Be sure replacement words maintain the same tense/endings as original words.

5. Print one copy.

6. Close the file; save the changes.

   OR

   💾 Close the file; *save as* **PREVIEW**

MOVE TEXT USING GO TO

1. Select text to be moved.

2. Click **<u>E</u>dit** .... `Alt` + `E`

3. Click **Cu<u>t</u>** .... `T`

   OR

   a. Click *right* mouse button.

   b. Click **Cut** .... `C`

4. Press **Ctrl + G** .... `Ctrl` + `G`

5. Click in **Page <u>N</u>umber** .... `Alt` + `N` text box.

6. Type page number to go to.

   OR

   Click increment button to desired page number.

7. Click **OK** .... `↵`

8. Place insertion point where text is to be reinserted.

9. Click **<u>E</u>dit** .... `Alt` + `E`

10. Click **<u>P</u>aste** .... `P`

    OR

    a. Click *right* mouse button.

    b. Click **Paste** .... `P`

— Today's date

REGISTERED MAIL

Ms. Elizabeth DeKan
Broward College
576 Southfield Road
Marietta, GA 30068

Dear Ms. DeKan:

Subject: Educational Films for High Schools and Colleges

Thank you for your interest in the films that we have available for high school and college students. We are pleased to send you the enclosed flyer which describes the films in detail. Also enclosed is a summary of those films that have recently been added to our collection since the publication of the flyer.

move to next page

There have been many positive reactions to our films. Just three weeks ago, a group of educators, editors and vocational experts were invited to view the films at the annual EDUCATORS' CONFERENCE. Here are some of their comments:

Ⓐ We will be sure to send the films in time for you to preview them. Please be sure to list the date on which you wish to preview the film.

Mr. William R. Bondlow, Jr., president of the National Vocational Center in Washington, D.C. and editor-in-chief of *Science Careers*, said,

insert Ⓑ

I like the films very much. They are innovative and a great benefit to all those interested in the earth sciences as a professional career. Furthermore, they have captured the objects on film so true to life that anyone watching them is captivated.

Ⓒ Ms. Andra Burke, a leading expert presently assigned to the United States Interior Department, praised the films by saying that,

move to next page

Ms. Elizabeth DeKan
Page 2
Today's date

insert Ⓒ   They are a major educational advance in career placement, which will serve as a source of motivation for all future geologists.

A member of the National Education Center, Dr. Lawrence Pilgrim, also liked the films and said,

move to previous page Ⓑ   I will institute a program which will make schools throughout the country aware of their vocational potential.

These are just some of the reactions we have had to our films. We know you will have a similar reaction.

insert Ⓐ

We would very much like to send you the films that you would like during the summer session. ~~You can use the summer to review them.~~ It is important that your request be received quickly since the demand for the films is great, particularly during the summer sessions ~~at colleges and universities throughout the country.~~

Cordially,

William DeVane
Executive Vice President
Marketing Department

wd/yo
Enclosures (2)

Copy to   Robert R. Redford
             Nancy Jackson
             Tien Lee

EXERCISE

▪ MOVING TEXT FROM ONE PAGE TO ANOTHER ▪ USING GO TO

44

NOTES:

- Moving paragraphs in this exercise will not affect footnote placement since WordPerfect makes the necessary adjustments.

- To change page number style from Uppercase Roman to Numbers, you can delete the page number position code [Pg Num Pos] and reinsert a new one.

EXERCISE DIRECTIONS:

 In this exercise, you will move text from one document to another.

1. Start with a clear screen.

2. Open **USA** if you completed it in Exercise 42.

 OR

 💾 Open **USA.44** from the data disk as a read-only file (Open As Copy).

3. Make the indicated revisions.

4. Full justify the document.

5. Using the Thesaurus, replace the words marked in brackets. Be sure replacement words maintain the same tense/endings as original words.

6. Change page number method from Uppercase Roman to Numbers.

7. Print one copy.

8. Close the file; save the changes.

 OR

 💾 Close the file; *save as* **USA**.

full justify and hyphenate entire document

IMMIGRATION'S IMPACT IN THE UNITED STATES

The opportunity to directly transfer a skill into the American economy was great for newcomers prior to the 1880s. "Coal-mining and steel-producing companies in the East, railroads, gold- and silver-mining interests in the West, and textile mills in New England all sought a variety of ethnic groups as potential sources of inexpensive labor."[1] Because immigrants were eager to work, they contributed to the wealth of the growing nation. During the 1830s, American textile mills welcomed hand-loom weavers from England and North Ireland whose jobs had been displaced by power looms. It was this migration that established the fine-cotton-goods trade of Philadelphia. "Nearly the entire English silk industry migrated to America after the Civil War, when high American tariffs allowed the industry to prosper on this side of the Atlantic."[2]

single space & indent quote from the left and right

[1] E. Allen Richardson, *Strangers in This Land* (New York: The Pilgrim Press, 1988), 67.

[2] John Bodnar, *The Transplanted* (Bloomington: Indiana University Press, 1985), 54.

insert Ⓐ ——→ BUILDING THE U. S. A.

Whether immigrants were recruited directly for their abilities or

followed existing networks into unskilled jobs, they inevitably moved

within ~~groups~~ of friends and relatives and worked and lived in clusters.

As the Industrial Revolution progressed, immigrants
were enticed to come to the United States through the mills
and factories who sent representatives overseas to secure
cheap labor. An example was the Amoskeag Manufacturing
Company, located along the banks of the Merrimack River in
Manchester, New Hampshire. In the 1870s, the Amoskeag
Company recruited women from Scotland who were expert
gingham weavers. Agreements were set specifying a fixed
period of time during which employees would guarantee to
work for the company.[3]

move where indicated

In the 1820s, Irish immigrants did most of the hard work in building

Ⓐ

the canals in the United States. In fact, Irish immigrants played a large role

in building the Erie Canal. American contractors encouraged Irish

immigrants to come to the United States to work on the roads, canals, and

railroads, and manufacturers ~~lured~~ them into the new mills and factories.

"Most German immigrants settled in the middle western states of

Ohio, Indiana, Illinois, Wisconsin and Missouri."[4] With encouragement to

---

[3]Bodnar, 72.

[4]David A. Gerber, *The Making of An American Pluralism* (Chicago:
University of Illinois, 1989), 124.

ⒾⒾ *change to Arabic numbers*

BUILDING THE U. S. A.

move west from the Homestead Act of 1862, which offered public land free

to immigrants who intended to become citizens, German immigrants

⟨comprised⟩ a large portion of the pioneers moving west. "They were

masterful farmers and they built prosperous farms."[5]

---

[5]Bodnar, 86.

 change to Arabic numbers

EXERCISE DIRECTIONS:

1. Start with a clear screen.
2. ⌨ Create a two-page letter *in any style* from the text below. Include a proper heading for the second page.

   OR

   💾 Open **CHOICES.7A** from the data disk as a read-only file (Open As Copy).
3. Use the default margins.
4. Send the letter Special Delivery, and include an appropriate subject line.

To format the numbered items:

a. Set left margin to 1.5".
b. Using the Bullets and Numbers feature, create the numbered paragraphs.
c. When you complete typing the numbered items, reset the left margin to 1".

5. Spell check.
6. Print one copy.
7. Save the file; name it **CHOICES**.

OR

💾 Save the file; *save as* **CHOICES**.

Today's date Ms. Tricia P. Blane 40 East 78 Street New York, NY 10035 Dear Ms. Blane:¶I have received your letter requesting advice on how to make a wise decision in your purchase of a personal computer. There are many factors you must consider when you are ready to purchase a PC, but those outlined below are the most significant: ¶1. **The Microprocessor** - The heart of the machine is the microprocessor which is the most critical component to consider. The microprocessor controls the speed with which the computer responds. Certain software requires a specific speed to run. Therefore, you must decide what software you want to run and then ask the salesperson for a computer whose microprocessor will run your desired software. ¶2.**Random Access Memory** - Certain software programs require a certain amount of working memory, or RAM to operate; four megabytes is practically a minimum these days, and the smallest hard disk available is usually about 125 megabytes. ¶3.**The Screen & Graphics Card** - The color screens of a few years ago were difficult to view when doing word processing. But the color screens today are excellent and are a must if you intend to do desktop publishing or other graphics applications. An important factor in selecting a graphics card is their resolution, that is, how many dots make up the display on the screen vertically and horizontally. A VGA card, or "video graphics adaptor" generally displays 800 dots horizontally and 600 dots vertically. But you can purchase graphics cards with higher resolution, giving you 1,024 horizontal and 768 vertical dots. ¶You do realize, of course, that the cost of a computer depends upon the quality of the parts you assemble. Be sure to go to a reliable vendor. You might get a better price from a mail-order retailer, but if you *need service* -- you might have a problem. ¶I am enclosing an article from a recent PC magazine which compares several models. Stop by my office any time and I will show you my computer. I might also suggest that you try out different varieties. The more research you do, the better qualified you will be to make a purchasing decision. ¶Sincerely, Rose Jaffe Consultant rj:yo enclosure copy to: Jabar Hammond Paul Salow

LESSON 7
SUMMARY EXERCISE B
EXERCISE DIRECTIONS:

1. Start with a clear screen.

2. ⌨ Create the report below.

   OR

   💾 Open **NUWORLD.7B** from the data disk as a read-only file (Open As Copy).

3. Set a 1.5" left document margin.

4. Include a bold, right-aligned header: LABOR IN COLONIAL AMERICA; and a page number (in any style) on the second and succeeding pages. You may place the page number wherever desired.

5. Set the title to 14 point bold.

6. Turn on widow/orphan protection.

7. Full justify the document.

8. Spell check.

9. Print one copy.

10. Save the file; name it **NUWORLD**.

    OR

    💾 Save the file; *save as* **NUWORLD**.

11. Close the document window.

LABOR IN COLONIAL AMERICA¶Labor was a key issue in colonial America. The American labor force consisted of indentured servants, redemptioners from Europe, slaves from Africa and the colonists themselves. ¶Indentured servants were the first source of foreign labor to arrive in the new world. Scores came from England between 1698 and 1700. "Out of 3,257 people who left for America, 918 of them were on their way to Maryland, a major port of indentured servants and redemptioners."[1]¶The new world offered much to the Europeans. Most European laborers desired the political and economic freedoms of America. The British capitalists offered those who wanted to come to America, but could not afford it, the opportunity to do so by having them agree to surrender a portion of their life to work as a laborer in return for having those expenses paid. This was the beginning of indentured servants. ¶Why were people so willing to enter into a life of servitude in a new country? Conditions in Europe during this period were poor. Political and economic problems existed. People were lured to the new world by its promise for religious freedom and an opportunity for a better life. ¶The colonists realized that in the development of a new country, labor is the most important element of production. They recognized the importance of a good labor supply. Because the supply of good white servants infrequently met the demand, more than half of all persons who came to America, south of England, were servants. ¶The contract of servitude was simple. Europeans who were unable to pay their own passage across the Atlantic become bond servants for a period of years to some colonial master who paid for them. "It was a legal contract by which the servant bound himself to serve the master in such employments as the master might assign for a given length of time usually in a specified plantation."[2] The contract included other clauses. A more skilled worker might collect wages and also be excluded from field labor. Education was included in a child's indenture. "Four years for each adult was the average time of servitude. Children usually worked until they were 21."[3] ¶Servitude was cruel; it subjected large numbers of people to a hard, laborious, and dangerous way of life. Many who came found the work too difficult; they were not ready for this type of life. "In the first few years, it killed fifty or seventy-five out of every hundred."[4]

---

[1]Emerson Smith, *Colonists in Bondage*, (New York: Holt Rinehart and Winston, Inc., 1975), 308.

[2]Smith, 45.

[3]Smith, 47.

[4]Percy Brackson and John Falcon, *History of Agriculture in Northern United States*, (New York: Alfred A. Knopf, Inc., 1974), 117.

LESSON 8

Exercises 45-54

- Opening Multiple Documents

- Sizing WIndows

- Copying Text From One Document to Another

- Moving Text From One Document to Another

- Inserting a File

- Inserting a Macro

- Recording/Playing a Macro with a Pause

EXERCISE

▪ OPENING MULTIPLE DOCUMENTS ▪ SIZING WINDOWS

NOTES:

- WordPerfect lets you open and work with up to nine documents at one time. This is a convenient feature for moving and/or copying text from one document to another.

- The area where you type your document is called the **document window**.

- You may open multiple files individually or all at once in the same operation. To open multiple files from the Open File dialog box, select each of the desired files, then click OK.

- **Windowing** lets you view those documents as you work with them.

Arranging Multiple Windows (Documents)

Cascaded Windows

- When you open more than one document window, you can decide how you want them arranged. One option is to **cascade** them. Cascaded windows overlap so that the title bar of each window is displayed.

- The **active window** is indicated by the shaded title bar. When you type or apply features, the document in the active window will be affected. To change the active window, click the title bar of the desired window. The active window will display the active document.

- Note the illustration below of four open documents which are cascaded:

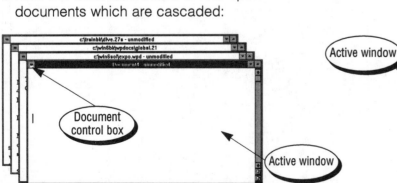

Tiled Windows

- Another arrangement option is to **tile** document windows. This allows you to view several documents at one time. Tiled windows are arranged on the screen with no overlapping. You may choose to tile your document horizontally or vertically. Vertically tiled documents are arranged side by side while horizontally tiled documents are tiled one below the other. The active window is indicated by the shaded title bar. Note the illustrations below of three vertically and horizontally tiled documents.

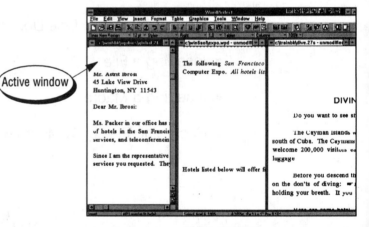

Vertically tiled

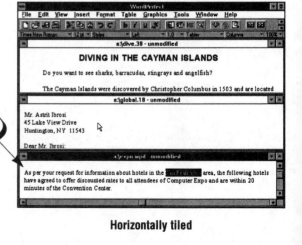

Horizontally tiled

- You can switch between document windows whether they are currently displayed or not by selecting <u>W</u>indow from the main menu and choosing the document you want.

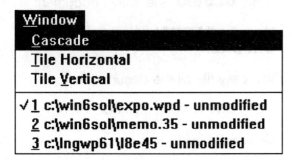

Closing a Document Window

- As you close each document window, you can save its contents. To close a window, double-click the document control box (the bar to the left of the title bar) or select <u>C</u>lose from the <u>F</u>ile menu.

Sizing Windows

Maximizing a Window

- When you begin a new document, WordPerfect provides a full-screen or **maximized** window ready for you to begin typing. The controls in the WordPerfect title bar let you size and arrange WordPerfect in the Windows screen. The controls to the left and right of the menu bar allow you to size and arrange the current document window.

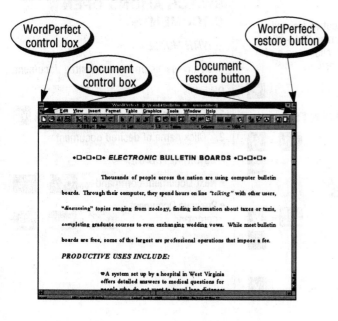

Minimizing a Window

- When you **minimize** a window, your document is reduced to a small rectangle. This allows you to view several documents at one time. To minimize a window, click on the document restore button ▓ (up/down arrow) to the right of of main menu bar.

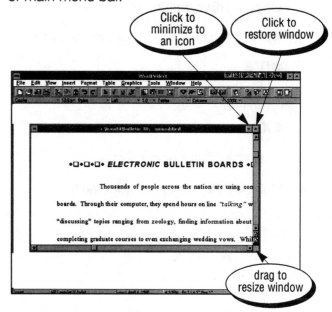

- You can size the window to the exact size you want by dragging the frame of the document window. To change the size of the window in two directions at once, drag the corner of the window.

- To minimize the minimized window to an icon, click the document minimize button ▼. This lets you keep several documents open at the same time.

EXERCISE DIRECTIONS:

In this exercise, you will open several documents and arrange the multiple windows.

1. Open a NEW document.

2. Open the following files in one operation:

   DIVE

   GLOBAL

   EXPO

3. Cascade all the documents.

4. Make **DIVE** the active document.

5. Make **GLOBAL** the active document.

6. Minimize **GLOBAL**; then maximize **GLOBAL**.

7. Vertically tile all the documents.

8. Make **EXPO** the active document.

9. Close each window.

   NOTE: *Four windows should be displayed. Three windows contain open documents; one window contains a blank, untitled document.*

OPEN MULTIPLE DOCUMENTS

Ctrl + O

1. Click Open button .... 🖳
   on Toolbar.

   OR

   a. Click **F**ile .... `Alt` + `F`

   b. Click **O**pen .... `O`

2. Select name of each file to be opened.

   • To select consecutive files, drag from first filename in desired group to last filename.

   • Click name of first file in group, use scroll bar/box as needed to bring last file of desired group into view, then press Shift + click (press Shift while you click) name of last file.

   • To select non-consecutive files, click first filename, then press Ctrl + click (press Ctrl while you click) name of each additional file desired.

3. Click **OK** .... ◄

CASCADE DOCUMENTS

1. Click **W**indow .... `Alt` + `W`

2. Click **C**ascade .... `C`

TILE DOCUMENTS

1. Click **W**indow .... `Alt` + `W`

2. Click **T**ile Horizontal .... `T`

   OR

   Click Tile **V**ertical .... `V`

SWITCH AMONG OPEN DOCUMENTS

—WITH MOUSE—

Click any visible portion of desired document.

OR

1. Click **W**indow .... `Alt` + `W`

2. Click name of desired document.

—FROM KEYBOARD—

• Next Document command ..... `Ctrl` + `F6`

• Previous Document command .... `Ctrl` + `Shift` + `F6`

NEXT EXERCISE

EXERCISE

46

COPYING TEXT FROM ONE DOCUMENT TO ANOTHER

NOTES:

- The procedure to copy text from one document to another is the same as copying text from one location to another in the same document.

- Windowing makes it easy to copy text in one document and place it in another, since you can actually see where the text is coming from and where it is going.

REMINDER: Copying text leaves text in its original location and pastes a copy of it in its new location.

- When you have successfully copied all the text you want from a file, close that file. Then, tile your windows again to provide larger windows for the remaining documents.

EXERCISE DIRECTIONS:

 In this exercise, you will open several documents, tile them and copy some text from each to a create a new document. This procedure may also be used for moving text from one document to another.

1. Open a NEW document.
2. ⌨ Keyboard the letter exactly as shown on the right.

   OR

   💾 Open **HOTELS.46** from the data disk as a read-only file (Open As Copy).
3. Use the default margins; begin the exercise on Ln 2.5".
4. Open **GLOBAL, EXPO** and **DIVE** if you completed them in a previous exercise.

   OR

   💾 Open **GLOBAL.46, EXPO.46** and **DIVE.46** from the data disk as a read-only file (Open As Copy).
5. Tile all the documents.
6. Copy the letterhead from **GLOBAL** to the top of the NEW document. Copy the remaining indicated text in each document into the NEW document. Leave a double space before and after each insert.

NOTE: The document to be copied from must be the active document. When you are ready to place the text, the new document must become the active document. Follow keystrokes carefully.

7. Close all documents except the NEW document.
8. Maximize the NEW document window.
9. Change text in small caps to normal.
10. Make any necessary adjustments to the text. Avoid awkward paragraph breaks.
11. Insert an appropriate page 2 heading in the NEW document.
12. Set a .5" bottom margin on the second page.
13. Spell check the NEW document.
14. Close and save the NEW document; name it **HOTELS**.
15. Print one copy of **HOTELS**.
16. Close the document window.

MOVE/COPY TEXT FROM ONE OPEN DOCUMENT TO ANOTHER

1. Open each file from which text is to be copied or moved.
2. Open a new file to receive the moved/copied text.

NOTE: To make the Copy/Move procedure easier, tile the open documents.

3. Click in the window where text is to be moved/copied *from.*
4. Highlight text to copy/move.

   To copy text:
   a. Click **Edit** .... Alt + E C
   b. Click **Copy** C

   OR
   Click Copy button........................ 🖺 on Toolbar.

   OR
   Press **Ctrl + C** .... Ctrl + C

   To cut (move text):
   a. Click **Edit** .... Alt + E T
   b. Click **Cut** .... T

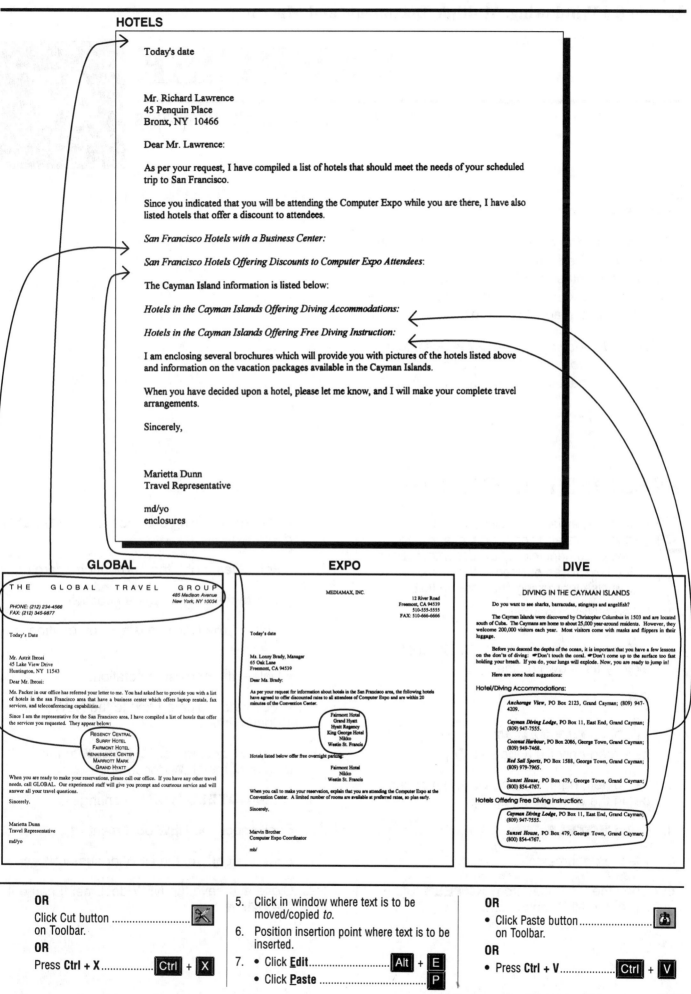

HOTELS

Today's date

Mr. Richard Lawrence
45 Penquin Place
Bronx, NY 10466

Dear Mr. Lawrence:

As per your request, I have compiled a list of hotels that should meet the needs of your scheduled trip to San Francisco.

Since you indicated that you will be attending the Computer Expo while you are there, I have also listed hotels that offer a discount to attendees.

San Francisco Hotels with a Business Center:

San Francisco Hotels Offering Discounts to Computer Expo Attendees:

The Cayman Island information is listed below:

Hotels in the Cayman Islands Offering Diving Accommodations:

Hotels in the Cayman Islands Offering Free Diving Instruction:

I am enclosing several brochures which will provide you with pictures of the hotels listed above and information on the vacation packages available in the Cayman Islands.

When you have decided upon a hotel, please let me know, and I will make your complete travel arrangements.

Sincerely,

Marietta Dunn
Travel Representative

md/yo
enclosures

GLOBAL

THE GLOBAL TRAVEL GROUP
485 Madison Avenue
New York, NY 10034
PHONE: (212) 234-4566
FAX: (212) 345-9877

Today's Date

Mr. Astrit Ibrosi
45 Lake View Drive
Huntington, NY 11543

Dear Mr. Ibrosi:

Ms. Packer in our office has referred your letter to me. You had asked her to provide you with a list of hotels in the san Francisco area that have a business center which offers laptop rentals, fax services, and teleconferencing capabilities.

Since I am the representative for the San Francisco area, I have compiled a list of hotels that offer the services you requested. They appear below:

REGENCY CENTRAL
SURRY HOTEL
FAIRMONT HOTEL
RENAISSANCE CENTER
MARRIOTT MARK
GRAND HYATT

When you are ready to make your reservations, please call our office. If you have any other travel needs, call GLOBAL. Our experienced staff will give you prompt and courteous service and will answer all your travel questions.

Sincerely,

Marietta Dunn
Travel Representative

md/yo

EXPO

MEDIAMAX, INC.
12 River Road
Freemont, CA 94539
510-555-5555
FAX: 510-666-6666

Today's date

Ms. Lonny Brady, Manager
65 Oak Lane
Freemont, CA 94539

Dear Ms. Brady:

As per your request for information about hotels in the San Francisco area, the following hotels have agreed to offer discounted rates to all attendees of Computer Expo and are within 20 minutes of the Convention Center.

Fairmont Hotel
Grand Hyatt
Hyatt Regency
King George Hotel
Nikko
Westin St. Francis

Hotels listed below offer free overnight parking:

Fairmont Hotel
Nikko
Westin St. Francis

When you call to make your reservation, explain that you are attending the Computer Expo at the Convention Center. A limited number of rooms are available at preferred rates, so plan early.

Sincerely,

Marvin Brother
Computer Expo Coordinator

mb/

DIVE

DIVING IN THE CAYMAN ISLANDS

Do you want to see sharks, barracudas, stingrays and angelfish?

The Cayman Islands were discovered by Christopher Columbus in 1503 and are located south of Cuba. The Caymans are home to about 25,000 year-around residents. However, they welcome 200,000 visitors each year. Most visitors come with masks and flippers in their luggage.

Before you descend the depths of the ocean, it is important that you have a few lessons on the don'ts of diving: ☞Don't touch the coral. ☞Don't come up to the surface too fast holding your breath. If you do, your lungs will explode. Now, you are ready to jump in!

Here are some hotel suggestions:

Hotel/Diving Accommodations:

Anchorage View, PO Box 2123, Grand Cayman; (809) 947-4209.

Cayman Diving Lodge, PO Box 11, East End, Grand Cayman; (809) 947-7555.

Coconut Harbour, PO Box 2086, George Town, Grand Cayman; (809) 949-7468.

Red Sail Sports, PO Box 1588, George Town, Grand Cayman; (809) 979-7965.

Sunset House, PO Box 479, George Town, Grand Cayman; (800) 854-4767.

Hotels Offering Free Diving Instruction:

Cayman Diving Lodge, PO Box 11, East End, Grand Cayman; (809) 947-7555.

Sunset House, PO Box 479, George Town, Grand Cayman; (800) 854-4767.

OR

Click Cut button .... on Toolbar.

OR

Press **Ctrl + X** .... `Ctrl` + `X`

5. Click in window where text is to be moved/copied *to.*

6. Position insertion point where text is to be inserted.

7. • Click **Edit** .... `Alt` + `E`
   • Click **Paste** .... `P`

OR

• Click Paste button .... on Toolbar.

OR

• Press **Ctrl + V** .... `Ctrl` + `V`

EXERCISE

MOVING TEXT FROM ONE DOCUMENT TO ANOTHER

47

NOTES:

▪ The procedure to move text from one document to another is the same as moving text from one location to another in the same document. Windowing makes it easy to move text from one document and place it in another.

REMINDER: Moving text cuts (removes) text from its original location and pastes it in the new location.

EXERCISE DIRECTIONS:

 In this exercise, you will open two documents and copy and move text from one document into a new document. Follow the keystrokes outlined in the previous exercise for moving and copying text.

1. Open a NEW document.

2. ⌨ Keyboard the letter (NEW DOCUMENT) exactly as shown on the right.

   OR

   💾 Open **CAYMAN.47** from the data disk as a read-only file (Open As Copy).

3. Set .5" left, right, top and bottom margins; begin the exercise on Ln 2.5".

4. Open **HOTELS**.

5. Tile the documents.

6. Copy the letterhead from **HOTELS** to the top of the NEW document.

7. Make the following changes to the **HOTELS** document:

   • Set .5" left, right, top and bottom margins.

   • Delete the second page heading.

   • Delete "The Cayman Island information is listed below:"

   • Delete the enclosure notation.

   • Move the indicated text to the NEW document.

8. Copy the closing from **HOTELS** to the bottom of the NEW document.

9. Close **HOTELS**; save the changes.

10. Spell check the NEW document.

11. Print one copy of the NEW document.

12. Close and save the NEW document; name it **CAYMAN**.

NEW DOCUMENT (CAYMAN)

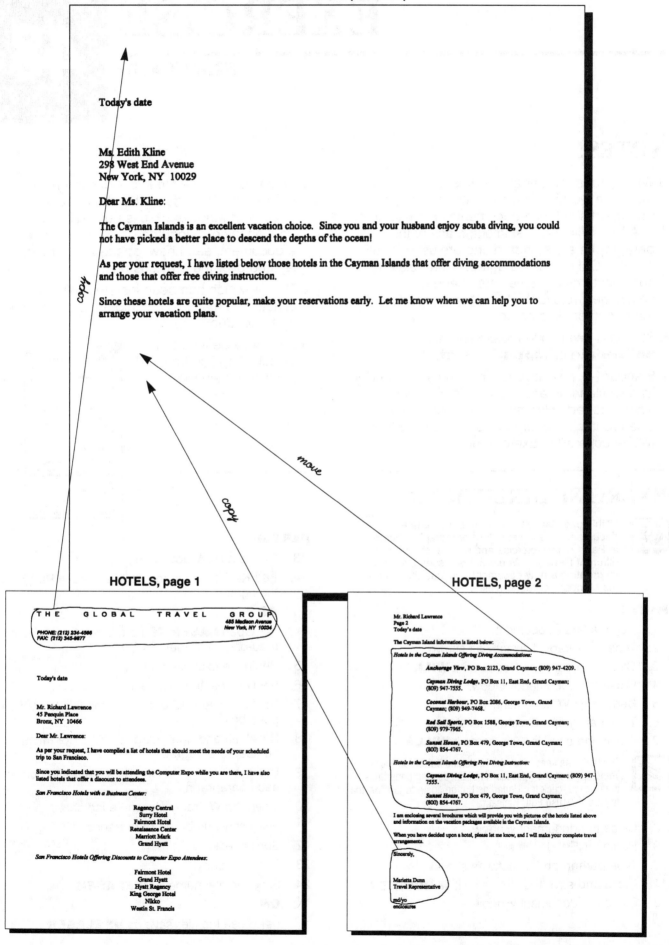

Today's date

Ms. Edith Kline
298 West End Avenue
New York, NY 10029

Dear Ms. Kline:

The Cayman Islands is an excellent vacation choice. Since you and your husband enjoy scuba diving, you could not have picked a better place to descend the depths of the ocean!

As per your request, I have listed below those hotels in the Cayman Islands that offer diving accommodations and those that offer free diving instruction.

Since these hotels are quite popular, make your reservations early. Let me know when we can help you to arrange your vacation plans.

copy

move

copy

HOTELS, page 1

THE GLOBAL TRAVEL GROUP
485 Madison Avenue
New York, NY 10034
PHONE: (212) 234-4566
FAX: (212) 345-8877

Today's date

Mr. Richard Lawrence
45 Penquin Place
Bronx, NY 10466

Dear Mr. Lawrence:

As per your request, I have compiled a list of hotels that should meet the needs of your scheduled trip to San Francisco.

Since you indicated that you will be attending the Computer Expo while you are there, I have also listed hotels that offer a discount to attendees.

San Francisco Hotels with a Business Center:

Regency Central
Surry Hotel
Fairmont Hotel
Renaissance Center
Marriott Mark
Grand Hyatt

San Francisco Hotels Offering Discounts to Computer Expo Attendees:

Fairmont Hotel
Grand Hyatt
Hyatt Regency
King George Hotel
Nikko
Westin St. Francis

HOTELS, page 2

Mr. Richard Lawrence
Page 2
Today's date

The Cayman Island information is listed below:

Hotels in the Cayman Islands Offering Diving Accommodations:

Anchorage View, PO Box 2123, Grand Cayman; (809) 947-4209.

Cayman Diving Lodge, PO Box 11, East End, Grand Cayman; (809) 947-7555.

Coconut Harbour, PO Box 2086, George Town, Grand Cayman; (809) 949-7468.

Red Sail Sports, PO Box 1588, George Town, Grand Cayman; (809) 979-7965.

Sunset House, PO Box 479, George Town, Grand Cayman; (800) 854-4767.

Hotels in the Cayman Islands Offering Free Diving Instruction:

Cayman Diving Lodge, PO Box 11, East End, Grand Cayman; (809) 947-7555.

Sunset House, PO Box 479, George Town, Grand Cayman; (800) 854-4767.

I am enclosing several brochures which will provide you with pictures of the hotels listed above and information on the vacation packages available in the Cayman Islands.

When you have decided upon a hotel, please let me know, and I will make your complete travel arrangements.

Sincerely,

Marietta Dunn
Travel Representative

md/yo
enclosures

EXERCISE

INSERTING A FILE

48

NOTES:

■ When preparing certain types of documents, the same wording is often used for many of the paragraphs in those documents. For example, in A Last Will and Testament, many of the paragraphs are standard and are used for all clients. Only those paragraphs that relate to specific items or names are changed; sometimes, relevant information is inserted after the document is created.

■ Standard text is often referred to as **boilerplate** or **repetitive text**.

■ Standard or repetitive text may be saved under its own filename and inserted into a document when needed. Repetitive text may also be inserted into a document as a macro. (Macros will be covered in Exercise 50.)

■ When you insert a file into a document, the inserted file is made part of the current document window. This is quite different from opening a document. When you open a document, each new, opened document is layered over the previous one.

■ The file which has been inserted will remain intact. You may insert it into another document when needed.

■ A file may be inserted by selecting File from the Insert main menu.

Insert	
Bullets & Numbers...	
Character...	Ctrl+W
Abbreviations...	
Date	▶
Other	▶
Footnote	▶
Endnote	▶
Comment	▶
Sound...	
Bookmark...	
Spreadsheet/Database	▶
File...	
Object...	
Acquire Image...	
Select Image Source...	
Page Break	Ctrl+Enter

EXERCISE DIRECTIONS:

In this exercise, you will create a separate document for each standard paragraph indicated in Part I of the exercise and save each under a different filename. You will then assemble a report by creating a new document and inserting one of the standard paragraph files.

PART I

1. Begin a NEW document.
2. Type paragraph 1 exactly as shown.
3. Close and save the file; name it **WILL1**.
4. Close the document window.
5. Begin a NEW document.
6. Type paragraph 2 exactly as shown.
7. Close and save the file; name it **WILL2**.

To create the lines, click the Underline button on the Toolbar, press the Spacebar until the desired underlines are created; click the Underline button again to turn off the feature. Or, use Edit, Repeat.

8. Close the document window.
9. Begin a NEW document.
10. Type paragraph 3 exactly as shown.
11. Close and save the file; name it **WARRANTY**.
12. Close the document window.

PART II

13. Create a NEW document.
14. ⌨ Keyboard the report illustrated in Part II on the right.

    OR

    💾 Open **LASER.48** from the data disk as a read-only file (Open As Copy).

15. Begin the exercise on Ln 2".
16. Set line spacing to single.
17. Set font to serif 12 point. Set the title to serif 14 point bold.
18. Reset left and right margins to 1.5" for the numbered paragraphs.
19. Use the Bullets and Numbers feature to number each paragraph.
20. Insert the Warranty file where indicated.
21. Full justify numbered paragraphs.
22. Spell check.
23. Print one copy.
24. Save the file; name it **USELASER**.

    OR

    💾 Close the file; *save as* **USELASER**.

WILL1

I, *, of *, do make, publish and declare this to be my Last Will and Testament, hereby revoking all wills and codicils heretofore made by me.

WILL2

IN TESTIMONY WHEREOF, I have to this my Last Will and Testament, subscribed my name and affixed my seal, this * day of *, 199*.

_____
        *

Signed, sealed, published and declared by the above-named testator, as and for his Last Will and Testament, in our presence, and we at his request, in his presence and in the presence of each other, do hereunto, sign our names and set down our addresses as attesting witnesses, all on this * day of * 199*.

_____ residing at _____

_____ residing at _____

_____ residing at _____

WARRANTY

Trinitron warrants this unit will be free of defects in workmanship and materials for a period of one year from the date of purchase. This warranty does not cover damages resulting from accident, misuse or neglect. If your laser pointer fails to operate properly under normal use during the warranty period because of a defect in workmanship or material, Trinitron will repair or replace (at our option) the laser pointer with no cost to you except for shipping.

FACTS ABOUT LASER POINTER HIGHLIGHTER

The Trinitron Laser Pointer Highlighter is a unique device which allows you to point to relevant drawings, illustrations, or other references when you are conducting a lecture. All you need to do is aim the red laser beam at whatever it is you are referring to. Your audience will be immediately focused. Using the Trinitron Laser Pointer is a professional way to conduct a presentation, especially when there is a need to make reference to charts, etc. Here are some facts and safety tips:

1. **POWER.** Use two 9-volt alkaline batteries which are supplied. An AC Adaptor/Charger and a three-hour rechargeable Ni-cad power pack are optional.

2. **SAFETY.** The Trinitron Highlighter laser pointer complies with all electrical and safety regulations covering class II laser products. Staring into the beam should be avoided. **Do not direct the beam toward a person's eye.**

3. **BATTERIES.** The Trinitron Highlighter laser pointer uses two 9-volt alkaline batteries which are installed.

4. **OPERATION.** Slide the on/off safety switch up to turn on the laser pointer. Turn it off after use to prevent accidental use and drainage of batteries. To use the pointer, aim it at the object or area to be highlighted. Turn on the laser by pressing the on/off red bar-switch. Releasing the switch turns off the laser.

5. **WARRANTY.** *Insert Warranty file here*

INSERT A FILE

1. Place insertion point where you want file inserted.
2. Click **Insert** .... `Alt` + `I`
3. Click **File** .... `I`
4. Type or select name of document to insert.
5. Click **Insert** .... `Enter`

EXERCISE

INSERTING A FILE

49

NOTES:

▪ When you created the standard paragraphs for the will in Exercise 48, you inserted an asterisk (*) in locations where variable information would be inserted.

To insert the appropriate text at the asterisk locations:

• Use the Find feature to locate the asterisk quickly.

• Backspace to delete the asterisk.

• Insert the appropriate information.

NOTE: A keystroke review of setting first-line paragragh indents and finding text/codes has been provided for this lesson.

EXERCISE DIRECTIONS:

 In this exercise, you will create a last will and testament by inserting previously saved files containing standard paragraphs.

1. Start with a clear screen.

2. ⌨ Keyboard the last will and testament as indicated on the right.

   OR

   💾 Open **LASTWILL.49** from the data disk as a read-only file (Open As <u>C</u>opy).

3. Use the default margins.

4. Begin the exercise on Ln 2".

5. Set font to serif 14 point bold for title; set body text to serif 12 point.

6. Set a paragraph indent of 2" for the first, second and third paragraphs (Alt + R, A, F).

7. Insert the noted files.

8. Using the Find feature, locate each asterisk and insert the appropriate information, as indicated.

9. Spell check.

10. Print one copy.

11. Save the assembled document; name it **LASTWILL**.

12. Close the document window.

LAST WILL AND TESTAMENT
OF
JOHN RICHARD ADAMS

¶ Insert
WILL 1   **John Richard Adams*   4↓ ** 105 Oakwood Lane*
                                              Goshen, NY

FIRST: I direct that all my just debts, the expenses of my last illness and funeral and the expenses of administering my estate be paid as soon as convenient.

SECOND: I give all my articles of personal, household or domestic use or adornment, including automobile and boats, to my wife, Mary Adams, or, if she does not survive me, to my children, Thomas Adams and Betsy Adams, as shall survive me, in shares substantially equal as to value.

THIRD: I give and devise all my residential real property, and all my interest in any policies of insurance thereon, to my wife, Mary Adams, if she survives me or if she does not survive me, to my surviving children, to be held by them jointly.

¶ Insert   **third*   ** January * 1995*
WILL 2   **John Richard Adams*

SET FIRST LINE PARAGRAPH INDENT

1. *Click **Format**........................ Alt + R
2. Click **Paragraph** .... A
3. Click **Format**............................ F
4. Click **First Line Indent**.......... Alt + F
5. Type increment amount, or click increment arrows to move to desired measurement (from left margin).
6. Click **OK** .... ↵

FIND TEXT/CODES
F2

1. Place insertion point at top of document.
2. Click **Edit** .... Alt + E
3. Click **Find and Replace**................. F
4. Type text to be found in **Find** box.
5. Click **Find Next**..................... Alt + F
   to find next occurrence.

   OR

   Click **Close** .... Alt + C
6. Repeat step 5 for each find.

EXERCISE

RECORDING A MACRO

NOTES:

▪ A **macro** is a saved series of commands and keystrokes which may be played with a single keystroke or mouse click.

▪ Macros may be used to record repetitive phrases like the complimentary closing of a letter. When the phrase is needed, it is played with a single keystroke.

▪ A macro may also be used to automate a particular task, like changing margins and/or line spacing. Rather than press many keys to access a task, it is possible to record the process and play it with one keystroke.

▪ The macro exercises in this text will not cover programming commands. *(See your WordPerfect documentation for macro programming command information.)*

▪ To record a macro, select Macro, Record from the Tools main menu.

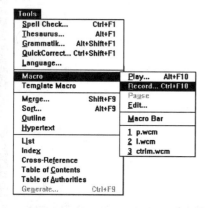

▪ In the Record Macro dialog box which follows, keyboard the name of your macro in the Filename text box. Then, select Record.

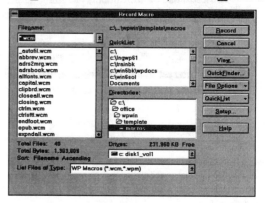

▪ Unless you specify another location to record to, WordPerfect automatically saves macros in the C:\OFFICE\WPWIN\TEMPLATES\MACROS subdirectory and assigns a .wcm extension.

▪ Record a macro carefully. When recording begins, the mouse pointer changes to a warning circle and Macro Record displays on the Status bar. Any key or mouse action will be recorded into the macro.

▪ To stop recording, click the Stop Macro Play or Record button on the Macro bar.

The Macro bar provides a quick way to access macro-related tasks.

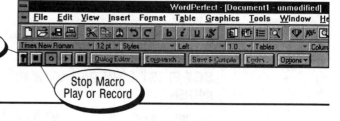

EXERCISE DIRECTIONS:

In this exercise, you will create several macros. You will play them back in subsequent exercises.

1. Start with a clear screen.

2. Create macro #1 in a serif 12 point font. Use italics and bold as shown; name it **P**. Insert a hard space (Ctrl + Spacebar) between the words.

3. Close the document window.

4. Create macro #2 in a script 14 point font; name it **C**. Insert a hard space between the words.

5. Close the document window.

6. Create macro # 3 in a serif 12 point and a sans serif 14 point font as shown; name it **DT**.

7. Close the document window.

8. Create macro # 4 in serif 12 point; name it **CL**.

Macro #1: P

PsA Micro**Computer** Systems, Inc.

Macro #2: C

CompuTechnology Group, Inc.

Macro #3: DT

Document**Tech** *Publishing* Assistant

Macro #4: CL

Very truly yours,

David Altmann, Esq.

da/yo

RECORD A MACRO

Ctrl + F10, name macro, record it, Ctrl + F10

1. Click **T**ools............................ `Alt` + `T`
2. Click **M**acro.. `M`
3. Click **R**ecord....................................... `R`

4. Type macro name.
5. Click **R**ecord .... `Alt` + `R`
6. Type keystrokes to be recorded.

   To stop recording macro:

   a. Click **T**ools....................... `Alt` + `T`

b. Click **M**acro.................................. `M`
c. Click **R**ecord................................. `R`

OR

Click Stop Record button on.............. ▣
Macro bar.

EXERCISE

RECORDING A MACRO **51**

NOTES:

■ In Exercise 50, you created macros for repetitive phrases. In this exercise, you will create command macros that will automate tasks like changing line spacing, changing margins, and printing, saving and closing a document.

■ While recording a macro, you may use a command that accesses a dialog box. To record selections from the dialog box, change the settings and proceed as usual. However, you may want to record the dialog box itself so that you can change settings when you play the macro. In that case, at the right end of the title bar, click the check box that appears only while recording a macro, then click OK and proceed as usual. If the OK button is dimmed, you probably need to enter a placeholder name or two characters in a text box. Enter text—it will not appear when you play the macro.

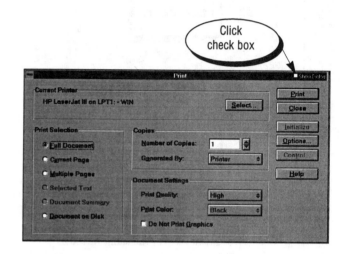

Click check box

EXERCISE DIRECTIONS:

 In this exercise, you will create 3 macros to automate tasks. Steps for creating each macro should be followed after Tools, Macro, Record has been accessed.

1. Start with a clear screen.

2. Keyboard your name.

   NOTE: Text must be on the screen before creating the macro to print.

3. Create macro #1 (print, save and close a document); name it **SA**.

4. Create macro #2 (change line spacing); name it **L**.

5. Close the document window.

6. Create macro #3 (change margins to 1.5"); name it **M**.

7. Close the document window.

| Macro #1: **SA** |

1. Click Print button on the Toolbar. 🖨
2. Click Print.
3. Click Save button on Toolbar. 💾
4. Click *Show dialog* check box on Save As dialog box.
5. Enter a new character or filename space in Filename text box.
6. Click OK.
7. Click File on main menu.
8. Click Close.

NOTE: The Macro feature bar disappears. To end the macro, click Tools, Macro, Record.

| Macro #2: **L** |

1. Click Line Spacing button on Power bar. `1.0 ▾`
2. Click Other.
3. Click up increment arrow and select 1.3".
4. Click OK.

| Macro #1: **M** |

1. Press Ctrl + F8.
2. Click Left margin up increment arrow and select 1.5".
3. Click Right margin up increment arrow and select 1.5".
4. Click OK.

RECORDING A MACRO INCLUDING A DIALOG BOX

1. Click **Tools**............ `Alt` + `T`
2. Click **Macro** .... `M`
3. Click **Record** .... `R`
4. Keyboard macro name.

5. Click **Record** .... `R`

—*WHEN DIALOG BOX IS ACCESSED*—

   a. Click check box at right end of title bar.

   b. If OK button is dimmed, type a space in text box.

   c. Click **OK** .... `↵`

EXERCISE
PLAYING A MACRO
52

NOTES:

▪ Once a macro has been recorded and saved, it can be *played* into your document whenever desired.

▪ **Macro play** may be accessed by selecting Macro, Play from the Tools main menu.

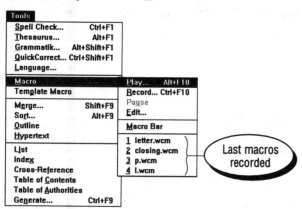

▪ In the Play Macro dialog box which follows, keyboard the macro name to play in the Filename text box. Or, select a macro from the filenames listed in the window. You will notice there are macros listed that you did not create.

WordPerfect has provided you with numerous macros to automate a variety of tasks. To determine what each macro does, click the macro and note the displayed explanation at the bottom of the dialog box.

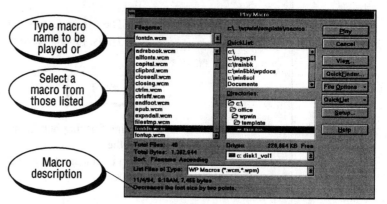

▪ The last macro you recorded or played is displayed on the Macro menu. You can select a macro to play back from the macros listed. *(See Illustration of drop-down menu.)*

EXERCISE DIRECTIONS:

In this exercise, you will create a legal letter, and where indicated, play two macros you created earlier. You will note that this document contains a re line, which is commonly used in legal correspondence. "Re" means "in reference to" or "subject." Press the Enter key twice before and after typing the "re" line.

1. Start with a clear screen.

2. Create the letter shown on the right.

3. Use the default margins.

4. Begin the exercise on Ln 2.5".

5. Set the font to serif 12 point.

6. Full justify paragraphs.

7. Play back the **P** and **C** macros wherever they appear in the text.

8. Spell check.

9. Preview your document.

10. Print one copy.

11. Save the file; name it **SETTLE**.

Today's date

Thomas Wolfe, Esq.
Wolfe, Escada & Yates
803 Park Avenue
New York, NY 10023

Dear Mr. Wolfe:

Re: [Macro P] vs.
        ABC Manufacturing Company

I am enclosing a copy of the Bill of Sale that transfers all Gordon's assets to [Macro P].

In addition, you asked us to represent [Macro C] in their $200,000 payment to [Macro P]. Because of this payment, [Macro C] became subrogated to the claim made by [Macro P], and [Macro P] cannot settle this matter without the approval of [Macro C].

[Macro C] would also be entitled to recover some portion of any judgment recovered by [Macro P] in the above action. In order to get a settlement in this matter, we will need to obtain a release of ABC Manufacturing Company by [Macro C].

Let's discuss this so that we can quickly settle this matter.

enclosure

PLAY A MACRO
Alt + F10

1. Position insertion point where macro is to play.

2. Click **Tools** .... `Alt` + `T`

3. Click **Macro** .... `M`

4. Click **Play** .... `P`

5. Double-click desired macro to play.

OR

a. Type the name of macro to play.

b. Click **Play** .... `Enter`

EXERCISE

PLAYING A MACRO

53

NOTES:

▪ As indicated in Exercise 52, WordPerfect provides you with numerous macros to automate tasks. In this exercise, you will play one of WordPerfect's macros.

EXERCISE DIRECTIONS:

 In this exercise, you will create a News Release, a document that is prepared and sent to various newspapers and magazines announcing a new product of a company. Each time the product name appears, you will play one of the macros you created earlier. In addition, you will use WordPerfect's fontup.wcm macro (which automatically increases the font size two points) to increase the font size of the title.

1. Start with a clear screen.

2. Create the News Release shown on the right.

3. Set the font for the document to serif 12 point.

4. Play the **M** macro to set your margins.

5. Begin the exercise on Ln 2". Use the Date Text feature to insert the current date.

6. Play the **DT** macro whenever Document**Tech** *Publ*ishing Assistant appears in the text.

7. Select the title text. Play the fontup.wcm macro to increase the font size of the title.

8. Spell check.

9. Play the **SA** macro; when prompted, name your document **DOCUMENT**.

   NOTE: The SA macro will print, save and close your file.

PRESS RELEASE
For Immediate Release

↓ *2*

For more information contact: Corine Cardoza

↓ *3*

INTRODUCING the Document**Tech** *Pub*lishing Assistant

↓ *2*

Cambridge, Massachusetts, March 7, 199-

↓ *2*

The Document**Tech** *Pub*lishing Assistant is the first in a series of publishing products that put together three distinct technologies—digital scanning, laser imaging and xerography—into one simplified publishing solution. The Document**Tech** *Pub*lishing Assistant provides high quality, low cost and quick turnaround. Document**Tech** *Pub*lishing Assistant eliminates complicated pre-press operations. It has a built-in scanner and quickly captures text, line art and photos, and converts them to digital masters.

Even booklet marking becomes easier. Document**Tech** *Pub*lishing Assistant has a signature booklet feature which will automatically turn out 11 x 17 or digest size (8.5 x 11) collated sets ready to be stitched, folded and trimmed. Document**Tech** *Pub*lishing Assistant prints an amazing 135 pages per minute and has a concurrent input/output capability. This means that while you are publishing one job, you'll be scanning, revising and readying others. Furthermore, Document**Tech** *Pub*lishing Assistant comes in a networked version.

###

EXERCISE

RECORDING/PLAYING A MACRO WITH A PAUSE

NOTES:

- A macro may be created with a pause so that you can give input while it is playing. When you record a macro with a pause, a PAUSE code is entered at the point where information will be inserted. When the macro is played, it will pause for you to type the variable text.

- Macro tasks can be easily accessed from the Macro bar. Therefore, before recording your macro, display the Macro bar (Tools, Macro, Macro Bar).

- To insert a pause while recording a macro, click the Pause button on the Macro bar. Whatever keystrokes or commands you execute while the Macro Pause is in effect will be ignored by the Macro Recorder. To resume recording, click the Pause button again (to turn Pause off), then continue with the keystrokes or commands you want in your recorded macro.

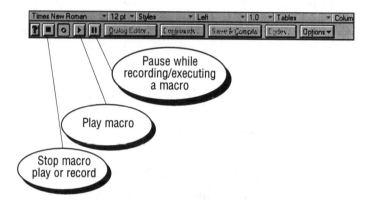

- To play a macro with a pause, select Macro, Play from the Tools main menu. When the playback stops, type the variable information in the pause location. Then, click the Pause button on the Macro bar to resume playback.

EXERCISE DIRECTIONS:

 In this exercise, you will record two macros that contain pauses and play them.

Part I

1. Start with a clear screen.

2. Access the Macro Bar.

3. Create macro #1 as shown in the Part I illustration, inserting a pause code where indicated; name it **S**.

4. Close the document window.

5. Create macro #2 as shown, inserting a pause code where indicated; name it **R**.

6. Close the document window.

Part II

7. Start with a clear screen.

8. Play the **M** macro to change the left and right margins.

9. Create the letter shown in Part II illustration.

10. Begin the exercise on Ln 2.5".

11. Use the Date Text feature to insert the current date.

12. Play each macro where indicated.

13. Full justify paragraphs.

14. Spell check.

15. Print one copy.

16. Save the exercise; name it **PAUSE**.

PART I

Macro #1: S

We shall expect your remittance in the amount of (PAUSE) within the next ten days.

Macro #2: R

Our last reminder to you that your account was past due was mailed to you on (PAUSE).

Today's date

Mr. Andrew S. Stone
321 Saxony Place
Indianapolis, IN 46204

Dear Mr. Stone:

Your account is now more than thirty days past due. **[Macro R - January 8]**.

[Macro S - $288.94]

We do value your patronage. The best way to maintain a good working relationship is to have a good credit record. If you have any questions, please feel free to phone me.

Sincerely,

Taylor Jones
Credit Manager

tj/yo

DISPLAY MACRO BAR

1. Click **Tools**..................**Alt** + **T**
2. Click **Macro**.................................**M**
3. Click **Macro Bar**.............................**M**

RECORD MACRO WITH PAUSE

1. Click **Tools**..................**Alt** + **T**
2. Click **Macro**.................................**M**
3. Click **Record**................................**R**
4. Type macro name.
5. Click **Record**.............................**Enter**

6. Type keystrokes to be recorded until you reach place where you wish to pause.
7. Click Pause button..............................**⏸**
   on Macro bar.
8. Click Pause button again....................**⏸**
   on Macro bar.
9. Continue typing keystrokes to be recorded.

To stop recording macro:

Click Stop Macro Play........................**◼**
or Record button on Macro bar.

PLAY MACRO WITH PAUSE
Alt + F10

1. Place insertion point where macro is to be played back.
2. Click **Tools**..................**Alt** + **T**
3. Click **Macro**.................................**M**
4. Click **Play**...................................**P**
5. Type name of macro to be played.
6. Click **Play**...................................**P**
7. Type desired text when macro pauses.
8. Click **Pause** button..........................**P**
   on Macro bar (to deselect) to play remainder of macro.

EXERCISE DIRECTIONS:

1. Create the following macro in italics; name it **TRIN**:

   TriniTron Laser Highlighter

2. Clear your screen.

3. Create the letter below in any style.

4. Play the macros indicated.

5. Insert the document, **WARRANTY**, where indicated. Double indent this paragraph .5" from the margins.

6. Spell check.

7. Print one copy.

8. Save the exercise; name it **CLIENT**.

9. Close the document window.

[Macro M] Today's date   Ms. Rosetta Stone   751 Hamlin Place   Old Bridge, NJ   08754   Dear Ms. Stone: ¶I am delighted to learn that you have purchased a **[Macro TRIN]** and that you are enjoying the use of it. I am sorry that you did not receive the warranty card which should have been enclosed with your **[Macro TRIN]**. ¶I do not have any loose warranty cards that I can send you. However, I will state the warranty policy in the paragraph below. ¶**[Insert WARRANTY.]** ¶Show this letter with the indicated warranty policy, along with your bill of sale, to your local dealer. He will then repair your **[Macro TRIN]**. ¶If you should have any problems, let me know. I know you will get many years of enjoyment from your **[Macro TRIN]**. Sincerely,   Shirley Chen   Customer Service   sc/yo **[Macro SA]**

EXERCISE DIRECTIONS:

1. Create the following macro in italics; name it **AD**:

   RideTheTrack ExerciSer

2. Close the document window.

3. Create the advertisement below.

4. Begin on Ln 2".

5. Play the macros indicated.

6. Spell check.

7. Play macro **SA** where indicated.

[Macro M]

DISCOVER AN EXCITING NEW WAY TO
ACHIEVE WELLNESS OF BODY AND MIND

[Macro L]

According to medical fitness experts, regular aerobic exercise is essential for achieving all-around wellness. Aerobic exercise helps you prevent illness, feel better physically and mentally, boost your energy level, and increase the years on your life. That's why you need **[Macro AD]**. **[Macro AD]** will provide you with the following benefits:

[Return to Single Space]

- you can burn more fat than on other exercisers and burn up to 1,100 calories per hour!
- you can improve your cardiovascular fitness and lower your overall cholesterol level.
- you'll feel more mentally alert, relaxed, positive and self-confident.

[Macro L]

With regular workouts on a **[Macro AD]**, you'll feel wonderful because you're doing something positive for yourself.

Seven out of ten **[Macro AD]** owners use their machines an average of three times per week.

Call your **[Macro AD]** representative today at 1-800-555-4444 to receive a FREE video and brochure.

[Macro AD]
[Macro SA; name the file WORKOUT]

LESSON 9

Exercises 55-68

- Newspaper Columns

- Parallel Columns

- Tables

EXERCISE

NEWSPAPER COLUMNS

55

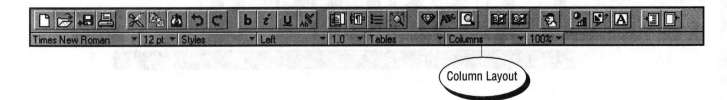

Column Layout

NOTES:

- The **newspaper column** feature allows text to flow from one column to another.

- WordPerfect provides two types of newspaper columns: *regular newspaper columns*, in which text flows down one column to the bottom of a page then starts again at the top of the next column, and *balanced newspaper columns*, in which each column is adjusted on the page so that they are equal in length.

REGULAR NEWSPAPER COLUMNS

Newspaper columns allow text to flow from one column to another. This is an example of a regular newspaper column. When text reaches the bottom of one column, it automatically wraps to the top of the next column. The gutter space is set by WordPerfect, but may be changed, as desired.

BALANCED NEWSPAPER COLUMNS

This is an example of a balanced newspaper column. Each column is adjusted on the page so that they are equal in length. No matter how much text is typed, the columns will always balance so that they are equal in length.

- Newspaper columns are particularly useful when creating newsletters, pamphlets, brochures, lists or articles.

- The Column feature is accessed by selecting Columns from the Format main menu, then selecting Define.

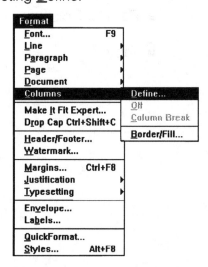

- To create newspaper columns quickly without accessing the dialog box, click the Columns button on the Power bar and specify the desired number of columns.

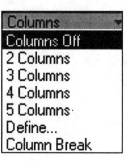

- In the Columns dialog box which appears, define the Number of Columns and the column Type you desire. You may also adjust the Spacing Between Columns (sometimes called the **gutter space**) and the width of each column. If you choose not to make any adjustments, the default settings will apply.

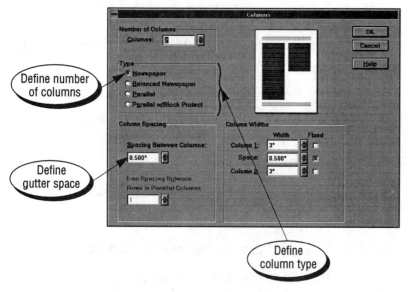

Define number of columns

Define gutter space

Define column type

- After defining the columns and clicking OK, you have turned on the Column feature. You must turn off the Column feature when you have completed your columnar document if you plan to continue the document without columns.

- To include a vertical line between columns, select Border/Fill from the drop-down menu, then click the Border Style list box in the Column Border dialog box. Click the vertical line between columns illustration from the samples which display.

- Columns may be created before or after typing text.

- You can retrieve text from a file into newspaper columns. When retrieving text from a file into columns, be sure your insertion point is within the Column mode.

- Click the mouse in the desired column to move the insertion point quickly from column to column.

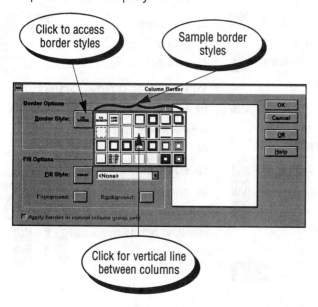

Click to access border styles

Sample border styles

Click for vertical line between columns

EXERCISE DIRECTIONS:

 In this exercise, you will create a two-column report using newspaper columns.

1. Start with a clear screen.

2. Use the default margins.

3. ⌨ Begin the exercise at the top of the screen.

   OR

   💾 Open **COCOA.55** from the data disk as a read-only file (Open As Copy).

4. Type the title in sans serif 18 point bold as shown; press Enter twice.

5. Create the article on the right using a two-column, *regular* newspaper-style format. Use the default gutter space between columns.

6. Set column text to serif 14 point.

7. Set line spacing to 2.

8. Insert a vertical line (border) between columns.

9. Full justify document text.

10. Spell check.

11. If necessary, use Make It Fit to keep all text on one page.

12. Preview your document.

13. Change the column type to balanced newspaper.

14. Print one copy.

15. Save the exercise; name it **COCOA**.

    OR

    💾 Close the file; *save as* **COCOA**.

16. Close the document window.

CREATE TEXT COLUMNS (Newspaper)

1. Place insertion point where column is to begin.

   OR

   Select existing text to include in columns.

2. • Click **Columns** .... [Columns ▼] button on Power Bar.

   • Click **Define**.

   OR

   • Click **Format** .... [Alt] + [R]

   • Click **Columns** .... [C]

   • Click **Define**.

3. Click a column type:

   • **Newspaper** .... [N]

   • **Balanced Newspaper** .... [B]

   • **Parallel** .... [P]

   • **Parallel with Block Protect** .... [A]

4. Change none, either, or both of the following options as desired:

   • Click **Columns** .... [C]

     Type desired number of columns.

   • Click **Spacing Between Columns** .... [S]

     Type desired distance.

5. Click **OK** .... [Enter]

INCLUDE VERTICAL LINE BETWEEN COLUMNS

1. Click **Format** .... [Alt] + [R]

2. Click **Columns** .... [C]

3. Click **Border/Fill** .... [B]

4. Click **Border Style** list box.

5. Click a desired border style.

6. Click **OK** .... [Enter]

TURN OFF COLUMNS

1. Place insertion point where column is to be turned off.

2. Click **Format** .... [Alt] + [R]

3. Click **Columns** .... [C]

4. Click **OFF** .... [O]

MOVE INSERTION POINT FROM COLUMN TO COLUMN

Click in desired column.

OR

TO MOVE TO:	PRESS:
Top of column	[Alt] + [Home]
Last line of column	[Alt] + [End]
Previous column	[Alt] + [←]
Previous column	[Alt] + [→]

CHOCOLATE

CHOCOLATE is probably the world's favorite food. You can drink it hot or cold, or eat it as a snack or as part of a meal. It is made into pies, cakes, cookies, candy, ice cream and even breakfast cereal. It is nourishing, energy-giving and satisfying.

Chocolate came to us from Mexico, by way of Europe. When the Spanish explorer Cortez arrived at the court of Montezuma, the Aztec Emperor, he found him drinking a cold, bitter drink called Chocolatl. It was made from seeds of the cacao tree, ground in water and mixed with spices. Montezuma gave Cortez the recipe and some cacao and vanilla beans. Cortez took them back to Spain, where the Spanish king and queen quickly improved the drink by adding sugar and having it served hot. For about a hundred years, chocolate was exclusively a royal Spanish treat. But once the secret leaked out, the upper classes in most of the European capitals were soon sipping hot chocolate. The Dutch settlers brought chocolate to the American colonies, and in 1765 a man named Baker started a chocolate mill near Boston.

A hundred years later a man in Switzerland found a way to make solid sweet milk chocolate, and a great candy business was born. Chocolate companies like Nestle and Hershey need a lot of cacao beans. About one-third of the supply, over 350 thousand tons, is imported each year from the African country of Ghana. Ghana is the world's largest supplier of cacao beans. For many years, chocolate was made by hand. Now, machines do most of the work.

THE CHOCOLATE FACTORY has been specializing in the finest chocolate products for over 50 years. Stop in and sample some of our outstanding chocolate delights.

EXERCISE

NEWSPAPER COLUMNS WITH CUSTOM WIDTHS

56

NOTES:

▪ WordPerfect allows you to create columns with custom widths. As indicated in the Columns dialog box, the default width of a two-column table using default margins is 3"; the gutter space is .5". To change the column width, click the Column 1 and/or Column 2 text box and type the desired width.

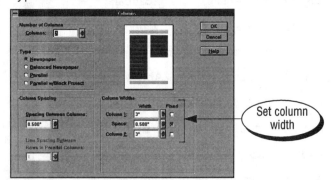

Set column width

▪ Column widths may also be changed by dragging the left and right column width markers on the Ruler bar. (Select Ruler Bar from the View main menu.)

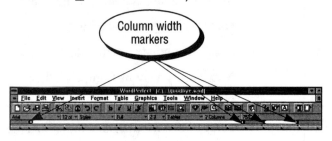

Column width markers

 Type the centered heading before you turn the Columns feature on.

EXERCISE DIRECTIONS:

 In this exercise, you will create an article using a two-column, newspaper-style format in which the second column is narrower than the first. The text does not fill up the first column and requires that you force the insertion point to the top of the second column. This is done by pressing Ctrl + Enter when you are ready to move to the top of the second column. You will also change your line spacing back to single space when you begin the second column.

1. Start with a clear screen.

2. ⌨ Type the exercise on the following page as shown.

   OR

   💾 Open **GOODBYE.56** from the data disk as a read-only file (Open As Copy).

3. Begin the exercise on Ln 2".

   To create the heading:

4. Type the heading in sans serif 24 point bold italic; set the "V" to 56 points.

   To make the ampersand (&):

5. Type a "k".

   • Set the size to 72 points.

   • Change the font to Wingdings. (The k changes to an ampersand.)

6. Press Enter once. Right align GUIDEBOOKS; set the size to 24 point bold.

   To create the remaining exercise:

7. Begin the column text on Ln. 4.4"

8. Create a two-column, regular newspaper-style format.

9. Change the width of column one to 5.5"; change the width of column two to 1.5". Use the default gutter space between columns.

10. Set column one text to sans serif 12 point; set column two text to sans serif 10 point bold.

11. Full justify column one text.

12. Set line spacing to 2 for the first column; set line spacing to 1 for the second column.

13. Spell check.

14. Preview your document.

15. Print one copy.

16. Save the exercise; name it **GOODBYE**.

    OR

    💾 Close the file; *save as* **GOODBYE**.

17. Close the document window.

VACATION PLANNING & GUIDEBOOKS

It can be very exciting to plan a vacation. There are a number of ways to go about it. Of course, you could have a travel agent make all the arrangements. But it is more exciting to investigate all the possibilities of travel.

First, you can check the hundreds of guidebooks which can be purchased at bookstores. Then, you can send away to the government tourist offices in the country you are planning to visit. They will send you lots of free literature about the country --places to visit and a list of accommodations. The travel advertisements in your newspaper will tell you where the bargains are. After you have planned your trip by looking through the guidebooks listed to the right, ask your travel agent to do the actual booking.

Enjoy!

OFFICIAL AIRLINE GUIDE

RUSSELL'S NATIONAL MOTOR COACH GUIDE

STEAMSHIP GUIDE

HOTEL AND RESORT GUIDE

RESTAURANTS, INNS AND MUSEUMS GUIDE

SIGHTSEEING GUIDE

FARM VACATIONS AND ADVENTURE TRAVEL GUIDE

CREATE COLUMNS WITH CUSTOM WIDTHS

1. Place insertion point where column is to begin.
2. Click **Format** .... `Alt` + `R`
3. Click **Columns** .... `C`
4. Click **Define** .... `D`
5. Click **Column 1** text box .... `Alt` + `1`
6. Type desired width. ....*number*, `Enter`
7. Click **Column 2** text box .... `Alt` + `2`
8. Type desired width. ....*number*, `Enter`

NOTE: Repeat procedure for each additional column.

9. Click **OK** .... `Tab` , `Enter`

EXERCISE

PARALLEL COLUMNS

57

NOTES:

- WordPerfect's **parallel column** feature allows text to move across the columns.

Monday	Meeting with John Smith at 9:00 a.m.
Tuesday	Lunch appointment with Randy Grafeo to discuss merger.

- Parallel columns are particularly useful when creating a list, script, itinerary, minutes of a meeting, or any other document in which text is read horizontally.

- The procedure for creating parallel columns is the same as creating newspaper style columns, except the column Type must be changed to Parallel in the Columns dialog box.

- After text is entered in the first column, enter a **hard page break** (Ctrl + Enter) to force the insertion point to move to the next column. After text is entered in the second column, a hard page break must be entered to force the insertion point to the third column. A hard page break is also needed to move the insertion point back to the first column.

 Be sure to type heading before you turn on the Column feature.

Click for parallel columns

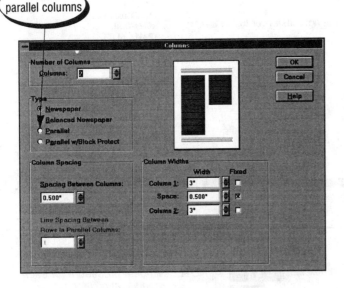

EXERCISE DIRECTIONS:

In this exercise, you will create minutes of a meeting using unequal parallel columns (the first column will be narrower than the second).

1. Start with a clear screen.

2. Use the default margins.

3. Begin the exercise on Ln 2".

4. Center the main heading in sans serif 18 point bold italics. Use any desired special character before and after the heading as shown. Center the minor headings in sans serif 12 point italics. Enter twice after the date.

5. Center four special characters to separate the date from the body text. Enter three times after the special characters.

6. Create a two column, parallel-style format.

7. Change the width of column one to 1.5"; change the width of column two to 4.5". Use the default distance between columns.

8. Set the side headings to sans serif 12 point italics; set the body text to serif 12 point.

9. Spell check.

10. Preview your document.

11. Print one copy.

12. Save the exercise; name it **AGELESS**.

13. Close the document window.

⪦⪧ *PERFECTION PLUS, INCORPORATED* ⪦⪧
MINUTES OF MEETING

March 29, 199-

⪦ ⪧ ⪦ ⪧

Present	Robin Jones, Quincy Garin, Zachary Malavo, Wendy Carley, Bill McKinley, Andrew Yang, Shirley DeChan.
Research	Mr. Malvo announced the development of a new product line. Several new chemical formulas were developed for a cream which will reduce skin wrinkling. The cream will be called **Ageless**.
Publicity	To launch this new product, Ms. Carley announced that promotions would be made at all the high-end New York department stores. Samples of the product will be given away at demonstration counters. Press releases will be sent to members of the press.
Advertising	The advertising budget was estimated at $5,223,000. Several advertising agencies were asked to submit presentations, and a decision will be made by the Advertising Committee as to which agency will represent this new line.
Sales	Mr. Garin, National Sales Manager, projected that sales could reach $10,000,000 the first year.
Adjournment	The meeting was adjourned at 4:00 p.m. Another meeting has been scheduled for Tuesday of next week to discuss future research and marketing of this new product.

EXERCISE

TABULAR COLUMNS

58

NOTES:

- Tabs may be used to align columns of information. However, since WordPerfect does have a Table feature which will organize information into columns and rows without using tabs or tab settings, using tab settings to align columns is not the most efficient way to tackle this task.

- Nonetheless, it is important for you to understand how tabs are used for tabular columns and the tab types available in WordPerfect (other than left aligned).

  NOTE: Tables will be introduced in Exercise 60.

- When you change tab settings in a document, changes take effect from that point forward.

- There are four different tab types. Each tab type is represented on the Ruler bar by a triangle pointing in a different direction.

▗ Left
▲ Center
◢ Right
⬠ Decimal
▚ Dot Left
⏢ Dot Center
◢ Dot Right
⏢ Dot Decimal

- Note the effect each tab type has on text:

Left-Aligned Tab

Text moves to the right of the tab as you type. (Represented by a left-pointing triangle on the Ruler bar ◣ .)

```
XXXXXXXXX
XXXXX
XXXXXX
```

Centered Tab

Text centers at the tab stop. (Represented by an up-pointing triangle on the Ruler bar ▲ .)

```
XXXXXXXXX
  XXXX
 XXXXX
```

Right-Aligned Tab

Text moves to the left or backwards from the tab as you type. (Represented by a right-pointing triangle on the Ruler bar ◢ .)

```
XXXXXXXXX
     XXXX
   XXXXXX
```

Decimal-Aligned Tab

Text before the decimal point (or other designated alignment character) moves to the left of the tab. Text you type after the decimal point moves to the right of the tab. The decimals (or other align character) stay aligned. (Represented by an up-pointing triangle with a middle dot on the Ruler bar ⬠ .)

```
123.65
 56.77
  4.66
```

*NOTE: Columns of text are generally horizontally centered between existing margins. To determine where to set tabs so they appear horizontally centered, it is necessary to create a **set-up line**. The set-up line is a blueprint for setting tab stops.*

To create a set-up line:

- *Center the longest line of each column and the space between the columns.*

- *Move the insertion point to the first character in each column of the set-up line and note the POS indicator. (You will set a tab stop at these positions.)*

- *Delete the set-up line.*

- *Clear all tabs.*

- *Set new tabs at noted positions.*

■ Tabs may be set on the Ruler bar or by selecting Line, Tab Set from the Format main menu.

Setting Tabs on the Ruler Bar

■ As noted in Exercise 22, tab settings are displayed on the Ruler bar as left-pointing triangles which are set .5" apart. Left-pointing triangles represent left-aligned tab settings (which is the default setting).

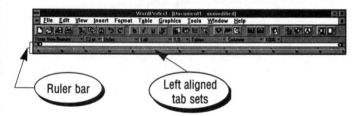

■ **To set a new left-aligned tab**, click anywhere on the Ruler bar where a new tab is desired; a new tab marker is inserted. To delete a tab setting, drag the tab marker (triangle) off the Ruler bar.

■ **To set right-aligned centered or decimal tabs**, you must first change the tab type. After the tab type is selected, each click on the Ruler bar will insert the tab type you have chosen. *(See keystrokes on next page.)*

■ Tabs may also be set using the Tab Set dialog box. This method lets you set and clear tab positions and tab types in one operation. You cannot, however, see the result of your changes on text until all settings have been made.

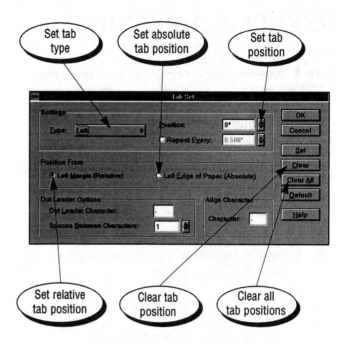

Relative vs. Absolute Tabs

■ When you set tabs, you can measure them from the left edge of the page (absolute tabs) or from the left margin (relative tabs). Default tab settings are relative to the left margin. The left edge of the page begins at zero (0) on the tab set ruler.

■ Relative and absolute tabs are set in the Tab Set dialog box.

EXERCISE DIRECTIONS:

 In this exercise, you will create a four-column, tabular document in which the first and second columns are left aligned, the third is right aligned and the fourth is decimal-aligned.

1. Start with a clear screen.

2. Use the default margins.

3. Set the document text to serif 12 point. Center the title lines; press Enter three times.

4. To determine where tab stops should be set, create the set-up line:

    a. Center the longest line in each column, including the intercolumn space (leave 10 spaces between columns).

    b. Using the directional keys or clicking the mouse, move the insertion point to the left of the first character in the first and second columns, to the right of the last character in the third column, and to the decimal in the fourth column, and note its horizontal position on Pos indicator.

    c. Delete the set-up line.

5. Set absolute tabs.

6. Clear all default tabs.

7. Set the appropriate tab for each column at the noted horizontal position.

    NOTE: After creating the set-up line, your tab positions should be: 2.3", 3.84", 5.39" and 5.99".

8. Type the remaining exercise.

9. Vertically center the exercise (Alt + R, P, C, P, ENTER).

10. Preview your document.

11. Print one copy.

12. Save the exercise; name it **PHONE**.

13. Close the document window.

SET TABS

—USING THE TAB SET DIALOG BOX—

1. Click **Format** .... `Alt` + `R`
2. Click **Line** .... `L`
3. Click **Tab Set** .... `T`

   To set tab type:
   - Click **Type** pop-up list .... `Alt` + `T`
   - Select desired tab type.

   To set desired tab:
   - Click **Position** text box ...... `Alt` + `P`
   - Type position of tab to set.
   - Click **Set** .... `S`

To indicate how tabs are to be measured:
(Position From)

Left **Margin** (Relative) .... `Alt` + `M`

OR

Left **Edge** of Paper .... `Alt` + `E`
(Absolute)

To clear desired tab setting:
   - Click **Position** text box .... `Alt` + `P`
   - Type position of tab to clear.
   - Click **Clear** .... `C`

   OR

   - Click **Clear All** .... `A`
     to clear all tabs.

—USING THE RULER BAR—

1. Click **View** .... `Alt` + `V`
2. Click **Ruler Bar** .... `R`

3. Point to bottom of Ruler Bar and click right mouse button.

4. Select **Clear All Tabs** .... `A`

5. Point to bottom of ruler bar, click right mouse button and select a tab type:

   Left .... `L`
   Center .... `C`
   Right .... `R`
   Decimal .... `D`
   ...**Left** .... `E`
   ...**Right** .... `I`
   ...**Decimal** .... `M`

6. Click anywhere on ruler bar where new tab is desired.

   To delete a tab:
   - Drag the tab marker (triangle) off the Ruler Bar.

LONG DISTANCE CALLS from BETHLEHEM, PA
Destination, Number Called, Minutes and Charges
June 1995

left tab   *left tab*   *right tab* *decimal tab*

Washington, DC	202-444-5555	28	$3.83
New Haven, CT	203-436-5555	1	.19
New York, NY	212-628-5555	52	4.94
New Haven, CT	203-436-5555	10	1.04

EXERCISE

TABULAR COLUMNS WITH DOT LEADERS

59

NOTES:

▪ A **dot leader** is a series of dots that connect one column to another to keep the reader's eye focused.

```
✓▸ Left
 ▴ Center
 ◂ Right
 ▴ Decimal
 ⋮ Dot Left
 ⋮ Dot Center
 ◂ Dot Right
 ⋮ Dot Decimal
```

▪ To create dot leaders, select a dot leader tab type when you set your tabs. The dot leader tabs are indicated with dots below each tab type.

▪ After all tab settings are made, use the Tab key to advance to each column. The dot leaders will automatically appear preceding those columns which contain a dot leader tab setting.

EXERCISE DIRECTIONS:

In this exercise, you will format a three-column tabular document in which the first column has a left-aligned tab setting, the second column has a decimal tab with a preceding dot leader, and the third column has a right-aligned tab setting with a preceding dot leader.

1. Start with a clear screen.

2. Use the default margins.

3. Center the title lines. Set font to serif 14 point bold for the main heading; set remaining document text to serif 12 point. Set second subheading to italics. Press Enter three times.

4. Set absolute tabs.

5. Clear all default tabs.

6. Create a set-up line:

   a. Center the longest line in each column, including the intercolumn space (leave 8 spaces between columns).

   b. Move the insertion point to the left of the first character in first column, and note the horizontal position.

   c. Move the insertion point to the decimal point in the second column, and note the horizontal position.

   d. Move the insertion point one character to the right of the last character in the sec ond column, and note the horizontal position.

7. Using the Tab Set dialog box, set a left-aligned tab for the first column, a decimal tab with a dot leader for the second column, and a right-aligned tab with a dot leader for the third column at the noted horizontal positions.

8. Type the remainder of the exercise.

9. Vertically center the exercise.

10. Preview your document.

11. Print one copy.

12. Save the exercise; name it **WAGES**.

13. Close the document window.

RAPID MESSENGER SERVICE
Employee Hourly Wages and Total Earnings
for 1995

left tab	*decimal tab*	*right tab*
Charles Palenlogis ..	$10.50 ...	$24,500
Gina Lombardi	7.80	26,876
Robin M. Alter	9.25	9,876
Jose Hernandez	8.50	18,450
Seung Kim	7.50	22,988

EXERCISE

▪ **CREATE THE TABLE STRUCTURE** ▪ **MOVE WITHIN A TABLE**
▪ **ENTERING TEXT IN A TABLE**

NOTES:

- The **Table** feature allows you to organize information into columns and rows without using tabs or tab settings.

- A table consists of **rows**, which run horizontally and are identified by number (1, 2, 3, etc.), and **columns**, which run vertically and are identified by letter (A, B, C, etc.). The rows and columns intersect to form empty boxes, called **cells**. Note the example below of a table with three rows and four columns:

	Column A	Column B	Column C	Column D
Row 1				
Row 2				
Row 3				

- Text, graphics, numbers or formulas are entered into cells after you have defined the structure of your table—that is, how many columns and rows you require for your table. (Formulas will not be covered in this text.)

Create the Table Structure

- Select <u>C</u>reate from the <u>T</u>able main menu. In the Create Table dialog box which follows, indicate the desired number of <u>C</u>olumns and <u>R</u>ows.

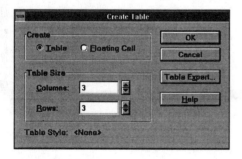

- You can also create tables quickly by clicking the Table QuickCreate button on the Power Bar and dragging the mouse pointer to select the desired number of rows and columns.

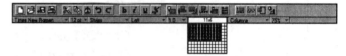

- The columns adjust automatically to fit between the left and right margins.

- You can create a table with up to 64 columns and 32,767 rows.

- After the table is created, the Tables Toolbar automatically appears.

Tables toolbar

Move Within a Table

- The insertion point moves in a table the same way it moves in a document. You may use the mouse to click in the desired cell, or you may use keystrokes to move around the cells *(see keystrokes on page 224)*.

- If there is no text in a cell, the directional arrow keys move the insertion point from cell to cell; otherwise, they move the insertion point through text in the cell.

- When the insertion point is in a table cell, the status bar indicates the cell location by displaying the cell's column letter and row number.

Status bar
indicates cell location
of insertion point

Entering Text in a Table

- As you enter text in a table cell, the cell expands downward to accommodate the text.

- Use the Tab key to advance the insertion point from one cell to the next, even at the end of the row.

 Pressing Enter in a cell extends the cell vertically. It will not advance you to the next cell.

 Double-clicking on the Table QuickCreate button on the Power bar [Tables ▼] will bring you to the Create Table dialog box.

EXERCISE DIRECTIONS:

 In this exercise, you will create a table with 4 columns and 5 rows.

1. Start with a clear screen.

2. Use the default margins.

3. Center the page from top to bottom.

4. Center the title as shown. Set the main title to sans serif 14 point bold; set the second and third lines of the title to 12 point; set the third line to italics. Press the Enter key 3 times.

5. Create the table shown on the right using 4 columns and 5 rows.

6. Enter the table text as shown. Bold the column headings.

7. Preview your document.

8. Print one copy.

9. Save the exercise; name it **CRUISE**.

10. Close the document window.

CREATE A TABLE STRUCTURE

1. Position insertion point at left margin where you want table to appear.

2. • Click Table QuickCreate button on Power bar.

   • Drag to select desired number of columns and rows.

   • Release mouse.

   OR

   • Click **T**able .... Alt + A

   • Click **C**reate C

   • Click **C**olumns text box ...... Alt + C
     and type desired number.

   OR

   • Click increment buttons to select number of columns.

   • Click **R**ows text box .... Alt + R
     and type desired number.

   OR

   • Click increment buttons to select number of rows.

   • Click **OK** .... Enter

ENTER TEXT IN TABLES

1. Click cell to receive text.

2. Type text.

3. Press **Tab** .... Tab
   to advance to next cell

   OR

Use the following insertion point movements:

TO MOVE:	PRESS:
One cell right	Tab
One cell left	Shift + Tab
One cell down	Alt + ↓
One cell up	Alt + ↑
First cell in row	Home , Home
Last cell in row	End , End
Top line of multi-line cell	Alt + Home
Bottom line of multi-line cell	Alt + End

FESTIVAL TRAVEL ASSOCIATES

WORLD CRUISE SEGMENTS
SPRING 1995

DESTINATION	DEPARTS	NO. OF DAYS	COST
Panama Canal	March 6	13	$2,529
Trans Pacific	March 19	11	$4,399
Israel to New York	March 19	18	$5,299
Naples to New York	March 19	11	$3,499

EXERCISE

JUSTIFICATION WITHIN TABLE CELLS

NOTES:

- WordPerfect allows you to change the justification of text for a cell, column or the entire table.

- You may left, center, right, full, all, or decimal align text either during the table creation process or afterward.

Left	**Decimal Align**: .1 10.0 1000.00
Center	**Full justify** needs more than one line to show its effect.
Right	**All justify** also needs more than one line to show its effect.

- To align text in a table, place the insertion point in any cell or select (highlight) several cells or columns in which you wish to align text and select Format from the Table main menu. In the Format dialog box which follows, click the Justification list box and select the desired justification option.

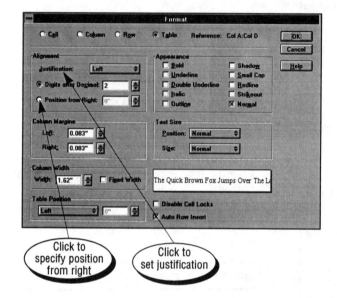

Click to specify position from right

Click to set justification

- After text is decimal aligned, it aligns at the right edge of the cell. To better position a column or table of decimal-aligned text, you can specify its position from the right of the cell in the table Format dialog box.

- You may also set appearance attributes (bold, italic, etc.) for cell, column or table text within the Format dialog box.

- To identify column letters and row numbers easily, you can display them on screen by clicking the Column/Row Indicators button on the Table Toolbar.

 It is easier to align text after it has been entered in the table.

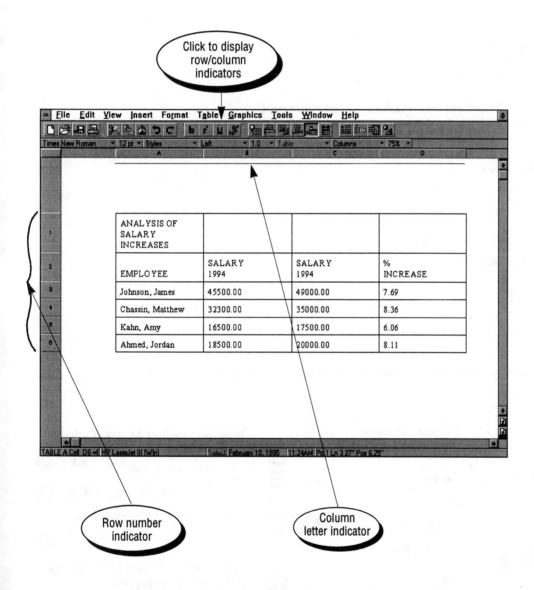

EXERCISE DIRECTIONS:

 In this exercise, you will create a table and center title and column headings, as well as decimal align and position columns B, C and D text.

1. Start with a clear screen.

2. Use the default margins.

3. Create the table as shown in illustration A on the right using four columns and six rows. Use a serif 12 point font.

4. Display column letters and row numbers.

To create Desired Result illustration:

5. Center align and bold the title and column headings.

6. Decimal align columns B, C and D text. Position column B and C text 0.06" from the right of the cell; position column D text 0.08" from the right of the cell.

7. Center the page top to bottom.

8. Preview your document.

9. Print one copy.

10. Save the exercise; name it **SALARY**.

11. Close the document window.

ALIGN TEXT WITHIN CELLS, COLUMNS OR TABLE

1. Place insertion point in table.

   OR

   Select a cell, several cells or columns to receive alignment change.

2. Click *right* mouse button.

   OR

   Click **Table** .... `Alt` + `A`

   OR

   Click **Table Format** button .... 🖮
   on Tables Toolbar and skip to step 4.

3. Click **Format** .... `O`

4. Select desired option:

   Cell .... `E`

   Column .... `L`

   Table .... `T`

5. Click **Justification** list box ..... `Alt` + `J`

6. Click desired justification (alignment) option:

   Left .... `L`

   Right .... `R`

   Center .... `C`

   Full .... `F`

   All .... `A`

   Decimal align .... `D`

To position text from the right of cell:

a. Click **Column** or .... `Alt` + `L` or `A`
   Table radio button.

b. Click **Position from Right** .. `Alt` + `R`

c. Type amount of **Position from.**

7. Click **OK** .... `Enter`

DISPLAY COLUMN LETTERS AND ROW NUMBERS

Click Column/Row Indicator button .... 🖮
on Table Toolbar.

ILLUSTRATON A

ANALYSIS OF SALARY INCREASES			
EMPLOYEE	SALARY 1994	SALARY 1995	% INCREASE
Johnson, James	45500.00	49000.00	7.69
Chassin, Matthew	32300.00	35000.00	8.36
Kahn, Amy	16500.00	17500.00	6.06
Ahmed, Jordan	18500.00	20000.00	8.11

DESIRED RESULT

ANALYSIS OF SALARY INCREASES			
EMPLOYEE	SALARY 1994	SALARY 1995	% INCREASE
Johnson, James	45500.00	49000.00	7.69
Chassin, Matthew	32300.00	35000.00	8.36
Kahn, Amy	16500.00	17500.00	6.06
Ahmed, Jordan	18500.00	20000.00	8.11

EXERCISE

JUSTIFICATION WITHIN TABLE CELLS

62

NOTES:

■ Since columns C, D and E in this exercise contain text that is considerably shorter than the column headings, it would be more visually attractive to center the text in those columns. Since column D is decimal aligned, the only way to "center" the text in this column is to position it from the right edge of the column. *(See keystrokes, Exercise 61.)*

EXERCISE DIRECTIONS:

 In this exercise, you will create the table structure, then edit it to align text in columns.

1. Start with a clear screen.

2. Use the default margins.

3. Center the title using serif 14 point bold; press Enter twice. Center the two subtitles using serif 12 point italic; press Enter three times.

4. Create the table shown on the right in serif 12 point. Determine the columns and rows needed. Set column headings to sans serif 12 point bold.

5. Vertically center the exercise.

6. Align column text as follows:

   • Center all column headings.

   • Right-align column A text.

   • Center-align columns C and D text.

   • Decimal-align column E text.

   • Position column E data 0.6" from the right of the column.

7. Preview your document.

8. Print one copy.

9. Save the exercise; name it **PURCHASE**.

10. Close the document window.

MIDDLETOWN HIGH SCHOOL

Spring Supply Order
1995

Catalog Number	Description	Quantity	Unit	Unit Price
239A	Staplers	10	box	4.24
22222D	Paper Clips	12	box	1.25
4D2	Blotters	12	each	5.05
90-4P	Memo Pads	10	ream	10.01
1P2	Disks	12	box	7.88
T999-1	Markers	19	box	8.65
9B	Chalk	50	box	.98

EXERCISE

63

▪ INSERTING AND DELETING COLUMNS AND ROWS ▪ DELETING A TABLE

NOTES:

■ One or more rows and/or columns may be inserted or deleted in a table before or after the insertion point position.

■ To insert a column or row, select Insert from the Table main menu. In the Insert Columns/Rows dialog box which follows, you must indicate if you wish to insert a column or a row, and if you wish to insert the column or row before or after the insertion point position.

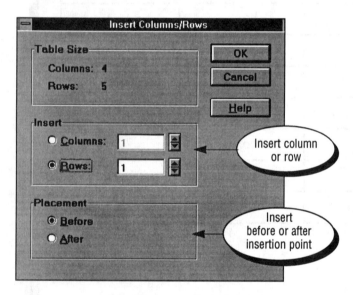

■ The text in the inserted column or row takes on the same formatting as the row or column of the insertion point.

■ To delete a column or row, select Delete from Table main menu. In the Delete dialog box which follows, you must indicate whether you wish to delete a column or row and the number of columns or rows to delete (if you did not select/highlight them first).

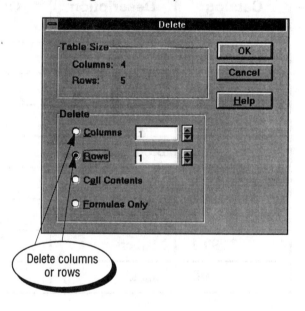

■ The entire table may also be deleted by selecting the entire table, then selecting <u>D</u>elete from the T<u>a</u>ble main menu.

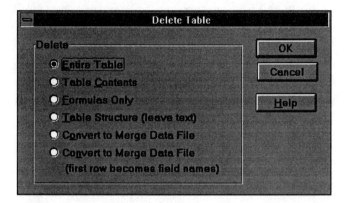

 To insert a new row at the end of a table, press the Tab key in the last cell.

 When a column or row is deleted, the contents of that column or row are also deleted.

EXERCISE DIRECTIONS:

 In this exercise, you will insert one column and one row in a preiously created table.

1. Start with a clear screen.

2. Open **CRUISE** if you completed it in Exercise 60.

   OR

   ⊟ Open **CRUISE.63** from the data disk as a read-only file (Open As <u>C</u>opy).

3. Set top and bottom margins to .25".

4. Insert one column after DESTINATION and enter the text as shown.

   NOTE: Once the new column is inserted, Column A becomes shorter and truncates the text in that column. In the next exercise, you will learn to adjust column widths so that columns A and B have more space and columns C, D and E have less space.

5. Insert one row at the end of the table and enter the text as shown.

6. Preview your file.

7. Print one copy.

8. ⊟ Close your file; save the changes.

   OR

   Close the file; *save as* **CRUISE**.

INSERT ROWS/COLUMNS

1. Place insertion point inside table, before or after where desired insertion is to occur.

2. Click **T<u>a</u>ble**..........................`Alt` + `A`

3. Click **<u>I</u>nsert**................................`I`

   OR

   Click *right* mouse button and select **Insert**.

4. Click button of item to insert:

   • **<u>C</u>olumns**............................`Alt` + `C`

   • **<u>R</u>ows**..................................`Alt` + `R`

5. Type number of columns or rows to be inserted.

   OR

   Click increment arrows to desired number.

6. Click Placement radio button:

   • **<u>B</u>efore**..............................`Alt` + `B`

   • **<u>A</u>fter**..................................`Alt` + `A`

7. Click **OK**...............................`Enter`

DELETE ROWS/COLUMNS

1. Place insertion point in column or row to delete.

   OR

   Select columns or rows to delete.

2. Click **T<u>a</u>ble**..........................`Alt` + `A`

3. Click **<u>D</u>elete**.............................`D`

   OR

   Click *right* mouse and select **Delete**.

4. Click button of item to be deleted:

   • **<u>C</u>olumns**............................`Alt` + `C`

   • **<u>R</u>ows**..................................`Alt` + `R`

5. Type number of columns or rows to delete.

6. Click **OK**.............................`Enter`

DELETE TABLE OR CELL CONTENTS

1. Select entire table.

2. Click **T<u>a</u>ble**..........................`Alt` + `A`

3. Click **<u>D</u>elete**.............................`D`

4. Click a delete option:

   • **<u>E</u>ntire Table**......................`Alt` + `E`

   • **Table <u>C</u>ontents**..................`Alt` + `C`

   • **<u>T</u>able Structure** (leave text) `Alt` + `T`

5. Click **OK**...............................`Enter`

FESTIVAL TRAVEL ASSOCIATES

WORLD CRUISE SEGMENTS
SPRING 1995

Insert column

Insert row

DESTINATION	PORTS	DEPARTS	NO. OF DAYS	COST
Panama Canal	New York, Cartegena, Panama Canal, Acapulco	March 6	13	$2,529
Trans Pacific	Los Angeles, Ensenada, Kona, Honolulu Fiji, Auckland	March 19	11	$4,399
Israel to New York	Haifa Kusadasi, Istanbul, Athens, Naples, Cannes, New York	March 19	18	$5,299
Naples to New York	Naples, Cannes, Lisbon, Southhampton, New York	March 19	11	$3,499
Trans-Atlantic	Fort Lauderdale, Madiera, Lisbon, Gibralter, Genoa	April 16	15	$2,599

EXERCISE

INSERT AND DELETE COLUMNS AND ROWS

64

NOTES:

▪ Remember, click the Undo button on the
Toolbar if you accidentally delete a column
or row, or if you insert a row in the wrong place.

EXERCISE DIRECTIONS:

In this exercise, you will create a
two-column table. You will then edit it to
include additional columns and rows.

Part I

1. Start with a clear screen.

2. Use the default margins.

3. Center the main title using sans serif 14
   point bold; center the subtitle using sans
   serif 12 point italic. Press Enter three times.

4. Create the table as shown in Part I on the
   right. Determine the columns and rows
   needed.

5. Vertically center the exercise.

6. Print one copy.

7. Save the exercise; name it **ROSEWOOD**.

Part II

8. Insert one column and three rows and the
   new text, as shown in Part II illustration.

9. Align column text as follows:

   • Center all column headings.

   • Decimal-align columns B and C data.

   • Position columns B and C data 0.6 from
     the right of the column.

10. Preview your document.

11. Print one copy.

12. Close the file; save the changes.

13. Close the document window.

ROSEWOOD FURNITURE COMPANY
Quarterly Sales and Salary Report

Name	Sales
Addison, Judy	113456.27
Chung, Mark	150888.99
Mannoff, Harrison	176911.89
Rivers, Sally	210333.00
Sanchez, Roberta	98400.35

ROSEWOOD FURNITURE COMPANY
Quarterly Sales and Salary Report

Name	Sales	Commission
Addison, Judy	113456.27	3000.28
Chung, Mark	150888.99	4234.00
Mannoff, Harrison	176911.89	3200.12
Rivers, Sally	210333.00	5876.23
Sanchez, Roberta	98400.35	987.99
Tomassi, Charles	223333.99	6210.00
Zarev, Rina	86100.00	800.99
Zyon, Paul	120000.00	3856.00

EXERCISE

CHANGE COLUMN WIDTHS

65

NOTES:

▪ **Column widths** may be changed using a specific measurement or by dragging the vertical lines between columns to the desired width.

▪ To adjust column widths and see the immediate effect of the change on the table as it is being made, place the mouse pointer on a vertical line between a column to be sized. (To adjust table size, place mouse pointer on the far left or right vertical line.) The pointer's shape changes to a table sizing arrow ↔. Press and hold the mouse as you drag the dotted line left or right to the desired width or table size.

(Table sizing arrow)

ANALYSIS OF SALARY INCREASES				
EMPLO YEE	YEARS OF SERVIC E	SALARY 1994	SALARY 1994	% INCREASE

▪ You can also adjust column widths and margins and see the immediate effect by dragging the column margin markers on the Ruler bar (Alt + V, R).

(Drag table sizing marker to change table size)   (Drag column width markers to change column width)

WordPerfect - [a:\salary.40]

ANALYSIS OF SALARY INCREASES			

(Size Column to Fit)

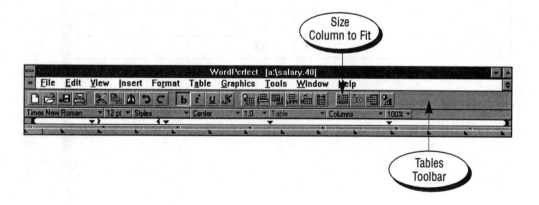

(Tables Toolbar)

- The **Size-Column-to-Fit** feature allows you to adjust the width of a cell or column automatically to fit the width of the text.

After highlighting the cell or column containing the widest text, click the Size-Column-to-Fit button 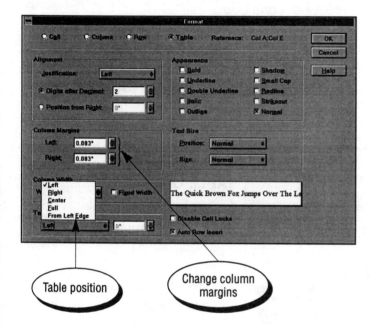 on the Tables Toolbar or click the *right* mouse button and select Size Column to Fit.

- You may also adjust column widths and margins using a specific measurement in the Format dialog box.

Horizontal Positioning of a Table

- WordPerfect sets column widths in a table to spread out evenly between the margins whether your table contains two or ten columns. When you change column width, WordPerfect keeps the same left margin. This means the table is no longer centered across the page.

- To center the table horizontally, click the Table Position list arrow in the Format dialog box *(see above)* and select Center.

- You may also position the table to the left or right of the page, or a specific amount from the left edge of the page.

Table position

Change column margins

EXERCISE DIRECTIONS:

 In this exercise, you will insert 2 columns and 2 rows. You will then adjust the column widths to make the table more visually attractive.

1. Start with a clear screen.

2. Open **SALARY** if you completed it in Exercise 61.

   OR

   Open **SALARY.65** from the data disk as a read-only file (Open As Copy).

3. Insert 2 rows and 1 column and enter text as shown.

4. Delete Amy Kahn's row.

5. Center-align YEARS OF SERVICE column.

6. Use the Size-Column-to-Fit feature to adjust column widths in all columns as shown.

   NOTE: To prevent the first column from adjusting to the size of the title, ANALYSIS OF SALARY INCREASES, insert a hard return after title text as shown.

7. Horizontally center the table on the page.

8. Preview the exercise.

9. Print one copy.

10. Close the file; save the changes.

    OR

    Close the file; *save as* **SALARY**.

CHANGE COLUMN WIDTH/MARGINS

To See Immediate Changes:

1. Place mouse pointer on a vertical line separating the column until it changes to a table sizing arrow ┼┼.

2. Drag sizing arrow left or right to desired width.

OR

1. Place insertion point in the table.

2. Display Ruler bar .. `Alt` + `Shift` + `F3`

3. Drag markers and guides to change the table:

OR

1. Place insertion point in cell containing longest text.

2. Click *right* mouse button.

3. Click **Size-Column-to-Fit** button on Tables Toolbar.

OR

Press **Ctrl + period** (.) .... `Ctrl` + `.` to expand current column.

OR

Press **Ctrl + comma** (,) .... `Ctrl` + `,` to shrink current column.

To Set Specific Settings:

1. Place insertion point in column to format.

   OR

   Select several columns to format.

2. Click **Table** .... `Alt` + `A`

3. Click **Format** .... `O`

4. Select desired button of item to be formatted:

   • **Column** .... `Alt` + `L`

   • **Table** .... `Alt` + `A`

   To set column margins:

   a. Click in **Column Margins** ... `Alt` + `L` **Left** text box.

   b. Type a left column .... *number* margin amount.

   c. Click in **Column Margins** ... `Alt` + `R` **Right** text box.

   d. Type a right column .... *number* margin amount.

   To set column widths:

   a. Click in **Width** text box ...... `Alt` + `T`

   b. Type a column width amount ... *number*

   To keep width of current column same regardless of changes to other columns:

   Click **Fixed Width** .... `Alt` + `X`

5. Click **OK** .... `Enter`

HORIZONTALLY POSITION TABLE ON PAGE

1. Place insertion point in table.

2. Click **Table Format** button .... `⌨` on Tables Toolbar.

   OR

   • Click *right* mouse button.

   • Select **Format**.

   OR

   • Click **Table** .... `Alt` + `A`

   • Click **Format** .... `F`

3. Click **Table** radio button .... `Alt` + `A`

4. Click **Table Position** list box and select desired position:

   • **Left** .... `L`

   • **Right** .... `R`

   • **Center** .... `C`

   • **Full** .... `F`

   • **From Left Edge** .... `E`

   Type amount from left edge.

5. Click **OK** .... `Enter`

insert one column

ANALYSIS OF SALARY INCREASES				
EMPLOYEE	*YEARS OF SERVICE*	SALARY 1994	SALARY 1995	% INCREASE
Johnson, James	*5*	45500.00	49000.00	7.69
Chassin, Matthew	*3*	32300.00	35000.00	8.36
Kahn, Amy	*2*	16500.00	17500.00	6.06 *delete row*
Ahmed, Jordan	*1*	18500.00	20000.00	8.11
Zano, Anthony	*8*	*38000.00*	*41500.00*	*9.21*
Lee, Kim	*4*	*25400.00*	*27000.00*	*6.30*

insert two rows

EXERCISE

JOIN AND SPLIT TABLE CELLS

66

NOTES:

▪ **Joining cells** lets you remove the dividing lines between cells to create a single, larger cell which may be used for a heading.

ORIGINAL TABLE

TABLE WITH JOINED CELLS

4 cells are joined here.		
2 cells are joined here.		4 cells are joined here.

▪ **Splitting cells** lets you divide cells.

ORIGINAL TABLE

TABLE WITH SPLIT CELLS

The cell below is split into 4 columns.	The 2 cells below are split into 3 columns.	The cell on the right is split into 2 rows.	

▪ Remember, column widths automatically spread out evenly between the margins whether your table contains two or ten columns. After making changes to column widths, therefore, reposition your table to center on the page.

EXERCISE DIRECTIONS:

 In this exercise, you will adjust the column widths of a previously created table, insert a new row and join cells, move the title to the new row, and reposition the table horizontally.

1. Start with a clear screen.

2. Open **CRUISE** if you completed it in Exercise 63.

   OR

   💾 Open **CRUISE.66** from the data disk as a read-only file (Open As Copy).

3. Display row and column indicators.

4. Set column A width to 1.38"; set column B width to 1.31".

   NOTE: See Exercise 65 keystrokes for procedures to set column widths using a specific setting.

5. Use the Size-Column-to-Fit feature to size columns C, D and E.

6. Center align column headings and text in column D.

7. Insert one row before the column heading row and join the cells.

8. Move the centered titles into the newly created row.

9. Reposition the table to center on the page.

10. Preview your document.

11. Print one copy.

12. Close the file; save the changes.

    OR

    💾 Close the file; *save as* **CRUISE**.

FESTIVAL TRAVEL ASSOCIATES

WORLD CRUISE SEGMENTS
SPRING 1995

DESTIN ATION	PORTS	DEPARTS	NO. OF DAYS	COST
Panama Canal	New York, Cartegena, Panama Canal, Acapulco	March 6	13	$2,529
Trans Pacific	Los Angeles, Ensenada, Kona, Honolulu Fiji, Auckland	March 19	11	$4,399
Israel to New York	Haifa, Kusadasi, Istanbul, Athens, Naples, Cannes, New York	March 19	18	$5,299
Naples to New York	Naples, Cannes, Lisbon, Southhampton, New York	March 19	11	$3,499
Trans-Atlantic	Fort Lauderdale, Madiera, Lisbon, Gibralter, Genoa	April 16	15	$2,599

DESIRED RESULT

FESTIVAL TRAVEL ASSOCIATES

WORLD CRUISE SEGMENTS
SPRING 1995

DESTINATION	PORTS	DEPARTS	NO. OF DAYS	COST
Panama Canal	New York, Cartegena, Panama Canal, Acapulco	March 6	13	$2,529
Trans Pacific	Los Angeles, Ensenada, Kona, Honolulu Fiji, Auckland	March 19	11	$4,399
Israel to New York	Haifa, Kusadasi, Istanbul, Athens, Naples, Cannes, New York	March 19	18	$5,299
Naples to New York	Naples, Cannes, Lisbon, Southhampton, New York	March 19	11	$3,499
Trans-Atlantic	Fort Lauderdale, Madiera, Lisbon, Gibralter, Genoa	April 16	15	$2,599

JOIN CELLS

1. Select cells to be joined.
2. Click **Table** .... Alt + A
3. Click **Join** .... J
4. Click **Cell** C

    OR

   • Click *right* mouse button.
   • Select **Join Cells**.

SPLIT CELLS

1. Select cells to be split.
2. Click **Table** .... Alt + A
3. Click **Split** .... S
4. Click **Cell** C
5. Select desired option:

   • **Columns** C
   • **Rows** .... R

6. Type desired number .... *number*
7. Click **OK** .... Enter

EXERCISE

▪ ADDING BORDERS AND FILLS TO A TABLE ▪ USING TABLE EXPERT

67

NOTES:

Table Lines and Borders

- A **table border** is a line (or lines) that surrounds a table. A **table line** divides the columns and rows to form the cells. By default, tables print with a single line around the outer edge (table border) and with single lines that divide columns and rows (table lines). Note the example below:

- WordPerfect lets you change the table border and table line style, and provides you with numerous line types.

THICK BORDER AND DASHED TABLE LINES

- To change table lines and borders, place the insertion point in the table, and select Lines/Fill from the Table menu. Then, in the Table Lines/Fill dialog box, click the Table button.

- To select a table line style, click the Table and Line Style buttons in the Table Lines/Fill dialog box and choose a style from the drop-down palette or list.

- To select a border line style, click the Table and Border buttons in the Table Lines/Fill dialog box and choose a style from the drop-down palette or list.

- For each line and border type you select, you will see a sample in the preview window.

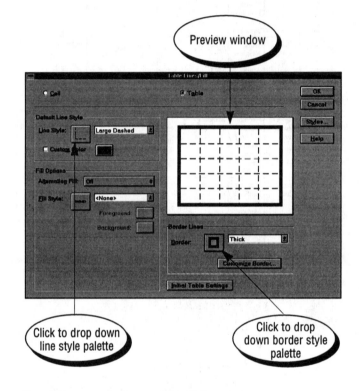

Preview window

Click to drop down line style palette

Click to drop down border style palette

Inside and Outside Lines

- You may also change the line type of inside and outside lines. Lines that surround the selection are **outside lines**; lines within the selection are **inside lines**.

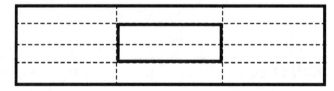

- Inside and outside line styles may be changed by selecting the cells to affect, then selecting Lines/Fill from the Table Toolbar. In the Table Lines/Fill dialog box which follows, select the Outside and/or Inside button and choose a line style from the drop-down palette or list.

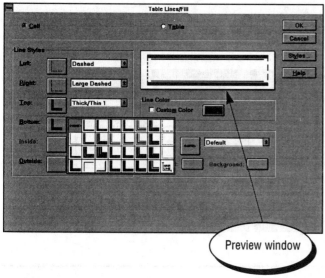

Preview window

Individual Lines

■ Changing the line type of individual lines is an effective way of emphasizing data within a cell. Note the table below in which the bottom and right lines of cell A1 are Heavy and the top, left and right lines of cell B2 are Double, while the bottom line of that cell is Thin/Thick1. All lines around cell C3 are Thick.

bottom and right lines: heavy		
	top, left and right lines: double; bottom line:	
		all lines around this cell are thick

■ There are many variations you can experiment with to emphasize data or make your table visually appealing.

■ Or, you may choose to eliminate all the lines, making the table look like tabular columns:

NAME OF STOCK	PURCHASE PRICE	NO. SHARES
R & L	$ 60.00	100
TECH LABS	45.35	80
ASTEC IND.	14.85	250
X-MATION	2.50	800
IDM	50.00	8
NORDAK INDUSTRIES	101.44	1,000

■ When you remove all lines, the table appears to be double spaced; it is not. While table lines are not visible, they are still part of the table structure.

■ Individual line styles may be changed by placing the insertion point in the individual cell, or selecting a group of cells to affect. Then, in the Table Lines/Fill dialog box, click the specific line button and choose a line style from the drop-down palette or list. (See Table Lines/Fill dialog box illustrated below).

■ While color shading options are available for lines and borders, you need a color printer to output color.

Fills (Shading/Patterns)

■ The Fill feature lets you emphasize a cell, row, column, or group of cells by adding a pattern or shade. The shading options are indicated as percents of black. Note the samples below:

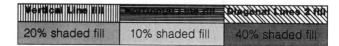

| 20% shaded fill | 10% shaded fill | 40% shaded fill |

■ Fills may be changed in the Table Lines/Fill dialog box by clicking the Fill Style button and choosing a fill option from the drop-down palette or list.

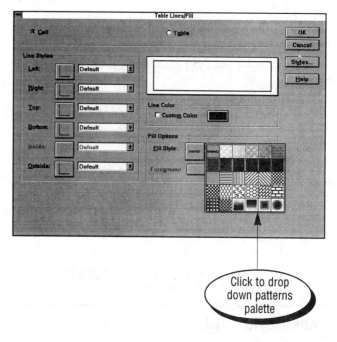

Click to drop down patterns palette

Using Table Expert

■ WordPerfect provides a quick way to enhance the appearance of tables through its Table Expert feature. Table Expert provides 40 predefined formatting styles from which you can select to apply to your table. Table Expert may be accessed by clicking the Table Expert button on the Tables Toolbar . In the Table Expert dialog box which follows, available styles are listed on the left, and a preview window displays the selected style.

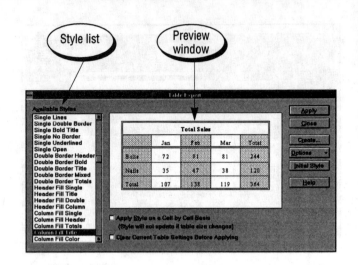

EXERCISE DIRECTIONS:

In this exercise, you will change lines and borders and add fill to a previously created table.

Part I

1. Start with a clear screen.

2. Open **CRUISE** if you completed it in Exercise 66.

   OR

   Open **CRUISE.67** from the data disk as a read-only file (Open As Copy).

3. Use the Lines/Fill feature to edit the table as shown:

   • Use a Thick/Thin1 table border.

   • Use a Dashed line style for table lines.

   • Use a 5% Fill to shade the column headings.

4. Preview the exercise.

5. Print one copy.

6. Close the file; save the changes.

   OR

   Close the file; *save as* **CRUISE**.

Part II

7. Start with a clear screen.

8. Open **SALARY**.

   OR

   Open **SALARY.67** from the data disk as a read-only file (Open As Copy).

9. Using the Table Expert feature, apply the Column Fill Title Style to your table as shown.

10. Change the title to sans serif 16 point bold.

11. Preview the exercise.

12. Print one copy.

13. Close the file; save the changes.

    OR

    Close the file; *save as* **SALARY**.

    NOTE: You might want to experiment with other table styles. Select another and apply it to this table.

TABLE LINES AND BORDERS

1. Place insertion point in table.

2. Click T**a**ble .... `Alt` + `A`

3. Click **L**ines/Fill .... `L`

4. Click T**a**ble button .... `Alt` + `A`

5. Click **L**ine style button .... `Alt` + `L`

6. Click desired line style from drop-down palette or list.

7. Click **B**order style button .... `Alt` + `B`

8. Click desired border style from drop-down palette or list.

9. Click **OK** .... `Enter`

INSIDE/OUTSIDE AND INDIVIDUAL LINES

1. Select cells to affect.

   OR

   Place insertion point in cell to affect.

2. Click T**a**ble .... `Alt` + `A`

3. Click **L**ines/Fill .... `L`

PART I

FESTIVAL TRAVEL ASSOCIATES

WORLD CRUISE SEGMENTS
SPRING 1995

DESTINATION	PORTS	DEPARTS	NO. OF DAYS	COST
Panama Canal	New York, Cartegena, Panama Canal, Acapulco,	March 6	13	$2,529
Trans Pacific	Los Angeles, Ensenada, Kona Honolulu Fiji, Auckland	March 19	11	$4,399
Israel to New York	Haifa, Kusadasi, Istanbul, Athens, Naples, Cannes, New York	March19	18	$5,299
Naples to New York	Naples, Cannes, Lisbon, South hampton, New York	March 19	11	$3,499
Trans-Atlantic	Fort Lauderdale, Madiera, Lisbon, Gibraltar, Genoa	April 16	15	$2,599

PART II

ANALYSIS OF SALARY INCREASES

EMPLOYEE	YEARS OF SERVICE	SALARY 1994	SALARY 1994	% INCREASE
Johnson, James	5	45500.00	49000.00	7.69
Chassin, Matthew	3	32300.00	35000.00	8.36
Ahmed, Jordan	1	18500.00	20000.00	9.21
Zano, Anthony	8	38000.00	41500.00	9.21
Lee, Kim	4	25400.00	27000.00	6.30

4. Click **Current Cell** .... `Alt` + `C`
   or **Selection.**

5. Click line to affect:

   • **Left** .... `L`

   • **Right** .... `R`

   • **Top** .... `T`

   • **Bottom** .... `B`

   • **Inside** .... `I`

   • **Outside** .... `O`

   NOTE: When changing all sides of a single cell, the Inside option will have no effect.

6. Click desired line style from drop-down palette or list.

7. Click **OK** .... `Enter`

FILLS AND PATTERNS

1. Follow steps 1-4, above.

2. Click **Fill Style** .... `F`

3. Click desired fill style from drop-down palette.

4. Click **OK** .... `Enter`

EXERCISE

JOIN AND SPLIT TABLE CELLS

68

NOTES:

▪ Remember, joining cells lets you remove the dividing lines between cells, while splitting cells lets you divide them.

EXERCISE DIRECTIONS:

 In this exercise, you will edit a previously created table by joining and splitting cells, and changing lines and border fills.

1. Open **ROSEWOOD** if you completed it in Exercise 64.

   OR

   🖫 Open **ROSEWOOD.68** from the data disk as a read-only file (Open As Copy).

2. Display the column and row indicators.

3. Use the Size-Column-to-Fit feature to size column A.

4. Set the width of columns B and C widths to 1.55" in the Format dialog box.

5. Insert two rows before the column heading row and join the cells in each row.

6. Move the centered titles into the newly created row and right align them. Italicize the column headings.

7. Join the cells in the row below the column headings.

8. Reposition the table to center on the page.

9. Using the Table Expert feature, apply the Header Fill Title Style to your table.

10. Use the Waves fill style for the joined rows.

11. Split the name column (not the name column heading) into two columns.

12. Using the Drag and Drop feature, move each first name into the second column; delete the comma after the last name.

13. Insert dashed inside lines within the name column.

14. Use a button fill to shade Charles Tomassi's name.

15. To highlight the Sales and Commission cells for Charles Tomassi, use a Thick/Thin 1 border for the left, top and right cells and a double line border for the bottom cells as shown.

16. Use a button table border for the entire table.

17. Preview the exercise.

18. Print one copy.

19. Close the file; save the changes.

    OR

    🖫 Close the file; *save as* **ROSEWOOD**.

ROSEWOOD FURNITURE COMPANY
Quarterly Sales and Salary Report

Name	Sales	Commission
Addison, Judy	113456.27	3000.28
Chung, Mark	150888.99	4234.00
Mannoff, Harrison	176911.89	3200.12
Rivers, Sally	210333.00	5876.23
Sanchez, Roberta	98400.35	987.99
Tomassi, Charles	223333.99	6210.00
Zarev, Rina	86100.00	800.99
Zyon, Paul	120000.00	3856.00

DESIRED RESULT

ROSEWOOD FURNITURE COMPANY
Quarterly Sales and Salary Report

Name		Sales	Commission
Addison	Judy	113456.27	3000.28
Chung	Mark	150888.99	4234.00
Mannoff	Harrison	176911.89	3200.12
Rivers	Sally	210333.00	5876.23
Sanchez	Roberta	98400.35	987.99
Tomassi	Charles	223333.99	6210.00
Zarev	Rina	86100.00	800.99
Zyon	Paul	120000.00	3856.00

EXERCISE DIRECTIONS:

1. Start with a clear screen.

2. Set .5" left and right margins.

3. Create the table shown below using 3 columns and 22 rows.

4. Display row and column indicators.

5. Join cells in the first row and center all title lines. Set first two title lines to sans serif 14 point bold; set third line to italics 12 point.

6. Change column B and C widths to 1.5" and column A width to 4.5".

7. Keyboard column text in serif 12 point; bold where indicated. Use a hard tab (Ctrl + Tab) to insert a tab where necessary.

8. Right-align text in columns B and C.

9. Edit the table as follows:

   • Reposition the table so it is centered horizontally.

   • Create a dotted border around the table; remove the table lines.

   • Use a 10% fill to shade the rows as shown.

   • Use a heavy double line around the Net Income amount as shown.

10. Center the exercise top to bottom (vertically center).

11. Preview the exercise.

12. Print one copy.

13. Save the exercise; name it **IS**.

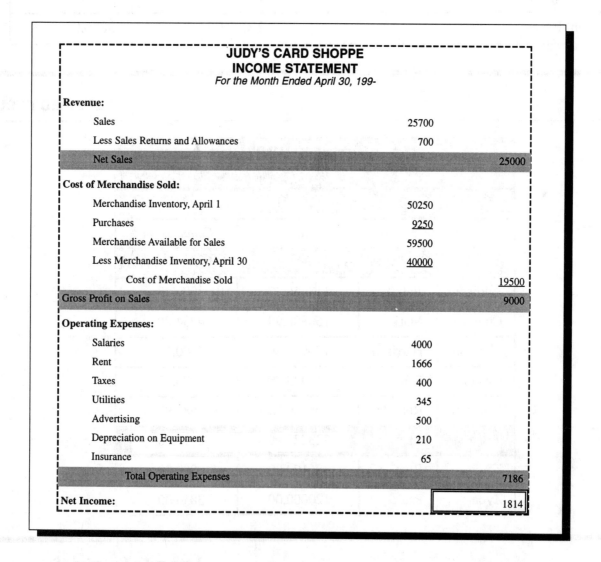

JUDY'S CARD SHOPPE
INCOME STATEMENT
For the Month Ended April 30, 199-

Revenue:		
Sales	25700	
Less Sales Returns and Allowances	700	
Net Sales		25000
Cost of Merchandise Sold:		
Merchandise Inventory, April 1	50250	
Purchases	9250	
Merchandise Available for Sales	59500	
Less Merchandise Inventory, April 30	40000	
Cost of Merchandise Sold		19500
Gross Profit on Sales		9000
Operating Expenses:		
Salaries	4000	
Rent	1666	
Taxes	400	
Utilities	345	
Advertising	500	
Depreciation on Equipment	210	
Insurance	65	
Total Operating Expenses		7186
Net Income:		1814

LESSON 9
SUMMARY EXERCISE B

EXERCISE DIRECTIONS:

PART I

1. Start with a clear screen.

2. Set left and right margins to .5".

3. Begin the exercise on Ln 2.5".

4. Create the memo below, inserting the table as shown.

5. Use eight rows and four columns for the table; set table text to a sans serif font.

6. Adjust the table size so the table is indented from the left and right margins.

7. Remove table and border lines; use a dotted border around row 1 and 2 as shown.

8. Join cells in row 1.

9. Use a button fill to shade row 2.

10. Preview the exercise.

11. Print one copy.

12. Save the exercise; name it **COURSES**.

PART II

13. Using Table Expert, apply the Row Fill Single style to the table.

14. Print one copy.

15. Save the exercise; name it **COURSES1**.

16. Close the document window.

NOTE: To make the table appear indented on both sides, you may need to adjust the table size.

PART I

TO: GUIDANCE PERSONNEL

FROM: Cynthia Greenskill, Chairperson

RE: Fall Computer Offerings

DATE: Today's

Listed below is a tentative schedule of computer classes that our department will be offering in the fall. Please be sure to use the correct code when registering students for the courses listed.

Fall Course Offerings			
COURSE TITLE	COURSE CODE	TIME OF CLASS	INSTRUCTOR
Database	DB3	10:00 A.M.	Winston
Spreadsheets	SS101	9.20 A.M.	Rosen
Basic	BC1	11:00 A.M.	Grande
Desktop	DTP1	12:40 P.M.	Giordano
Word Processing	WP3	1:50 P.M.	Pilgrim

If you have any questions regarding the above, please call me. Preliminary scheduling will begin on Monday of next week.

cg/

PART II

TO: GUIDANCE PERSONNEL

FROM: Cynthia Greenskill, Chairperson

RE: Fall Computer Offerings

DATE: Today's

Listed below is a tentative schedule of computer classes that our department will be offering in the fall. Please be sure to use the correct code when registering students for the courses listed.

Fall Course Offerings			
COURSE TITLE	COURSE CODE	TIME OF CLASS	INSTRUCTOR
Database	DB3	10:00 A.M.	Winston
Spreadsheets	SS101	9:20 A.M.	Rosen
Basic	BC1	11:00 A.M.	Grande
Desktop	DTP1	12:40 P.M.	Giordano
Word Processing	WP3	1:50 P.M.	Pilgrim

If you have any questions regarding the above, please call me. Preliminary scheduling will begin on Monday of next week.

cg/

LESSON 10

Exercises 69–76

- Calculating in Tables
- Using Formulas
- Using the Quick Sum Feature
- Formatting
- Copying Formulas
- Data Fill
- Using Functions
- Sorting by Line

EXERCISE

69

▪ CALCULATING IN TABLES ▪ USING FORMULAS ▪ FORMATTING

NOTES:

▪ WordPerfect lets you perform calculations for addition, subtraction, multiplication and division within a table cell. In addition, WordPerfect provides you with powerful spreadsheet capabilities found in a spreadsheet program.

▪ To calculate within a table, you may enter a **formula** directly in the table cell where the answer should appear.

▪ The formula tells WordPerfect which cells are to be calculated and what type of calculation is to be performed. **Cells** are identified by using their locations (A1, B3, C4). The type of calculation is identified by one of the following symbols:

    +   addition
    -   subtraction
    *   multiplication
    /   division

▪ Since cell locations, not the values themselves, are used to develop formulas, the formula B2+B3+B4 will result in the addition of the values in those cell locations.

▪ To enter a formula, access the **Formula Bar** from the Table main menu (Alt+A, R). Then, click in the formula Edit box and type the formula. Click the check mark to insert the formula into the cell.

▪ The Feature bar lets you create and insert formulas into tables and contains many frequently used spreadsheet options.

▪ When the insertion point is in a cell that contains a formula, the formula will appear in the Status bar.

▪ The exercises in this Lesson will cover simple calculations for addition, subtraction, multiplication and division. Subsequent exercises will cover simple spreadsheet features. Refer to software documentation for specialized calculations and detailed spreadsheet features.

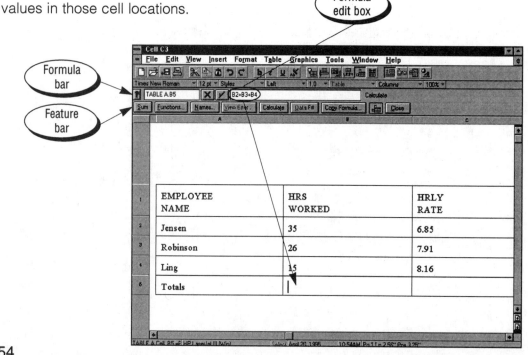

254

Using the Quick Sum Feature

■ To calculate the sum of values in table cells quickly (a more practical way to add values than the formula indicated on the previous page), place the insertion point in the cell where the answer is to appear and select Sum from the Feature bar. The cells above or to the left of the insertion point will be added.

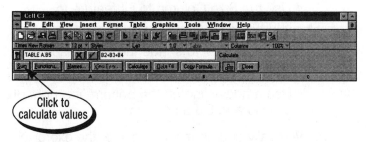

Click to calculate values

■ **Formatting** lets you change the appearance of numbers in a table. Since the numbers in columns C and D below are currency, you can format them to display two decimal places and a dollar sign to look like this:

EMPLOYEE NAME	HRS. WORKED	HRLY RATE	TOTAL EARNINGS
Jensen	35	$6.85	$239.75
Robinson	26	$7.91	$205.40
Ling	15	$8.16	$122.40
Totals	76	$22.91	$567.55

■ To format numbers, select **Number Type** from the Table main menu. In the Number Type dialog box which follows, click the radio button of what is to be affected: Cell, Column or Table. Then, click the desired format. A preview window displays the format style.

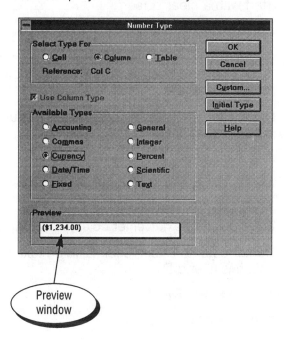

Preview window

EXERCISE DIRECTIONS:

In this exercise, you will create a table and perform multiplication and addition calculations.

1. Start with a clear screen.

2. Use the default margins.

3. Create the table shown in illustration A using 4 columns and 6 rows. Use a serif 12 point font for the text.

4. Display the Formula bar and row and column indicators.

5. Change column A width to 2".

   NOTE: You will adjust remaining columns later.

6. Enter column text. Center column headings.

7. Center column B text; decimal-align text in columns C and D.

To create desired result:

8. Edit the table as follows:

   • Enter the formula B2*C2 in cell D2 to calculate the amount for Cans Tomato Paste.

   • Enter formulas to calculate AMOUNT for the remaining items.

   • Use the Quick Sum feature to find totals for QTY, UNIT PRICE and AMOUNT.

   • Format columns C and D for currency.

   • Use the Size Column to Fit feature to shorten columns B, C and D.

   • Use a 10% fill to shade the row as shown in the Desired Result illustration.

   • Use a heavy line on the bottom and right of cell C6 and D6 as shown.

9. Vertically and horizontally center the exercise.

10. Preview the document.

11. Print one copy.

12. Save the file; name it **RECEIPT**.

13. Close the document window.

CALCULATE IN TABLES

—USING FORMULAS—

1. Create the table.

2. Click **Table** .... Alt + A

3. Click **Formula Bar** .... R

   OR

   Place insertion point in table.

   Click right mouse button and select **Formula Bar**.

4. Click in **Formula Edit** box.

5. Click in cell where answer should appear. (Cell location appears in formula.)

6. Click on first cell to be calculated.

   OR

   • Type first cell location to be calculated. (e.g., A1) in **Formula Edit** box.

7. Type calculation symbol:

   + (addition) .... +

   - (subtraction) .... -

   * (multiplication) .... *

   / (division) .... /

8. Click in next cell to be calculated.

   OR

   Type next cell location to be calculated in **Edit** box.

9. Click check mark on Formula bar to insert formula into cell.

—USING QUICK SUM FEATURE—

1. Place insertion point in cell where answer should appear.

2. Click **Sum** on Feature Bar .... Ctrl + =

FORMAT NUMBERS

Alt + F12

1. Place insertion point in column or row where numbers are to be formatted.

2. Click **Table** .... A

3. Click **Number Type** .... U

4. Click what is to be formatted:

   • **Cell** C

   • **Column** .... O

   • **Table** .... T

5. Click a desired format:

   • **Accounting** .... A

   • **Commas** .... M

   • **Currency** .... R

   • **Date/Time** .... D

   • **Fixed** .... F

   • **General** (the default) .... G

   • **Integer** I

   • **Percent** .... P

   • **Scientific** .... S

   • **Text** X

   • **Percent** .... P

ILLUSTRATION A

DESCRIPTION	QTY	UNIT PRICE	AMOUNT
Cans Tomato Paste	25	0.25	
Cases Potato Chips	11	8.45	
Cases Pop Corn	14	3.15	
Turkeys	12	7.12	
TOTALS			

DESIRED RESULT

DESCRIPTION	QTY	UNIT PRICE	AMOUNT
Cans Tomato Paste	25	$0.25	$6.25
Cases Potato Chips	11	$8.45	$92.95
Cases Pop Corn	14	$3.15	$44.10
Turkeys	12	$7.12	$85.44
TOTALS	62	$18.97	$228.74

EXERCISE

70

■ CALCULATING IN TABLES ■ COPYING FORMULAS

NOTES:

■ In Exercise 69, you entered the same formula several times to calculate the AMOUNT column. WordPerfect's Copy Formula feature lets you copy a formula you enter in one cell to another cell or to a group of cells.

■ Formulas may be copied by placing the insertion point in the cell that contains the formula to be copied, then selecting **Copy Formula** from the Table main menu or clicking Copy Formula on the Formula bar. In the Copy Formula dialog box which appears, you must indicate the **source cell** (the cell to be copied) and the **destination cell(s)** (the cells to receive the copied formula).

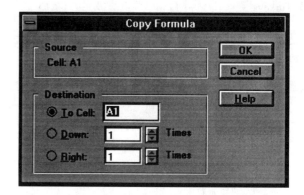

EXERCISE DIRECTIONS:

In this exercise, you will create a table and enter formulas to perform subtraction and addition calculations. You will then copy the formula you enter in the Difference and First Half Total columns to calculate the remaining items in those columns.

1. Start with a clear screen.
2. Use the default margins.
3. ⌨ Create the table shown in Illustration A on the right using 5 columns and seven rows. Use a serif 12 point font for the text. Join the cells in the first row.

   OR

   💾 Open **COMPARE.70** from the data disk as a read-only file (Open As Copy).
4. Center all title lines in the first row. Set font size to 14 point for the first 3 lines.
5. Enter the table text as shown.
6. Center and bold column headings in row 2.
7. Edit the table as follows:
   - Enter the formula C3-B3 in cell D3 to calculate the difference between first and second quarter sales for disk drives.

   - Copy the formula down to calculate the difference for the other items.
   - Enter the formulas B3+C3 in cell E3 to calculate the FIRST HALF TOTAL for disk drives.
   - Copy the formula down to calculate the FIRST HALF TOTAL for the other items.
   - Find TOTALS for columns B, C, D and E in row 7.
   - Decimal align and format all money columns for currency.
   - Use a 5% fill to shade column E.
8. Vertically center the exercise.
9. Preview the exercise.
10. Print one copy.
11. Save the file; name it **COMPARE**.

    OR

    💾 Close the file; *save as* **COMPARE**.
12. Close the document window.

258

ILLUSTRATION A

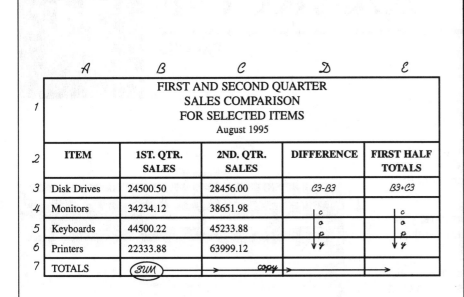

	$\mathcal{A}$	$\mathcal{B}$	$\mathcal{C}$	$\mathcal{D}$	$\mathcal{E}$
1	FIRST AND SECOND QUARTER SALES COMPARISON FOR SELECTED ITEMS August 1995				
2	ITEM	1ST. QTR. SALES	2ND. QTR. SALES	DIFFERENCE	FIRST HALF TOTALS
3	Disk Drives	24500.50	28456.00	C3-B3	B3+C3
4	Monitors	34234.12	38651.98	copy	copy
5	Keyboards	44500.22	45233.88		
6	Printers	22333.88	63999.12		
7	TOTALS	SUM →	copy →	→	

DESIRED RESULT

FIRST AND SECOND QUARTER SALES COMPARISON FOR SELECTED ITEMS August 1995				
ITEM	1ST. QTR. SALES	2ND. QTR. SALES	DIFFERENCE	FIRST HALF TOTALS
Disk Drives	$24,500.50	$28,456.00	$3,955.50	$52,956.50
Monitors	$34,234.12	$38,651.98	$4,417.86	$72,886.10
Keyboards	$44,500.22	$45,233.88	$733.66	$89,734.10
Printers	$22,333.88	$63,999.12	$41,665.24	$86,333.00
TOTALS	$125,569.72	$176,342.98	$50,772.26	$301,912.70

COPY A FORMULA

1. Place insertion point in cell that contains formula to be copied.
2. Click **Table** .... Alt + A
3. Click **Copy Formula** .... Y

   OR

   Click **Copy Formula** on Formula bar.
4. Click **To Cell** radio button ...... Alt + T
5. Type first cell where formula is to be copied *TO*.
6. Click radio button to indicate destination direction of copied formula:

   • **Down** .... Alt + D

   • **Right** .... Alt + R
7. Type number of times formula is to be copied in direction indicated.
8. Click **OK** .... ↵

EXERCISE 71

DATA FILL

NOTES:

■ **Data fill** is a fast method of entering sequential numbers in a column or row. With this feature, you can enter sequential numbers in any increment (e.g., 2, 4, 6, 8 or 5, 10, 15, 20).

■ In addition to entering and repeating numbers, you can also repeat values such as Roman numerals, days of the week, months, and quarters.

■ To enter sequential numbers for a column or row, at least two cells containing the values must be entered first to establish a pattern. Then, highlight the cells that contain the pattern of values as well as the empty cells to receive the remaining values. Select Data Fill from the Table menu or click the Data Fill button on the Feature bar.

Click for options

ABC PHARMACY						
PART-TIME PAYROL						
WEEK ENDING October 1995						
Employee Number	Employee Name	Hourly Rate	Hours Worked	Gross Pay	Taxes	Net Pay
110	Harrison	8.45	16			
112	Williams	7.35	18			
	Bhatt	6.85	22			
	Robinson	8.65	30			
	Townsend	5.55	28			
	Arries	7.35	14			
	Valor	9.10	16			
	Caston	7.85	20			

EXERCISE DIRECTIONS:

In this exercise, you will create a table and perform multiplication and subtraction calculations for a payroll. You will copy the formulas you enter in each column for the first employee to the other employees. Taxes are computed by multiplying the GROSS PAY by 20% (D3*.20). In addition, you will enter employee numbers using the Data Fill feature.

1. Start with a clear screen.

2. Use the default margins.

3. ⌨ Create the table shown in illustration A on the right using 7 columns and 10 rows. Join the cells in the first row.

   OR

   💾 Open **ABC.71** from the data disk as a read-only file (Open As Copy).

4. Center titles in row 1 using a serif 14 point bold font for the first line and serif 12 point italic font for the second and third lines.

5. Enter column text as shown using a serif 12 point font.

6. Display the Formula bar.

7. Edit the table as follows:

   • Center, bold and italicize column headings.

   • Use the Data Fill feature to enter the remaining employee numbers.

• Enter the formulas as shown in the exercise to calculate each column.

• Copy each formula down to the remaining employees in the column.

• Decimal-align money columns.

• Format all money columns for currency.

• Center-align EMPLOYEE NUMBER and HOURS WORKED column text.

• Position hourly rate column text 0.400" from the edge of the cell.

• Use the Size Column to Fit feature for columns D, E, F and G.

• Using Table Expert, apply the Single Underlined table style.

• Reposition the table so it is centered horizontally.

8. Vertically center the exercise.

9. Preview the exercise.

10. Print one copy.

11. Save the file; name it **ABC**.

12. Close the document file.

    OR

    💾 Close the file; *save as* **ABC**.

ILLUSTRATION A

	A	B	C	D	E	F	G
1			**ABC PHARMACY** *PART-TIME PAYROLL* *WEEK ENDING October 1995*				
2	Employee Number	Employee Name	Hourly Rate	Hours Worked	Gross Pay	Taxes	Net Pay
3	110	Harrison	8.45	16	C3*D3	E3*.20	E3-F3
4	112	Williams	7.35	18			
5		Bhatt	6.85	22			
6		Robinson	8.65	30			
7		Townsend	5.55	28			
8		Arries	7.35	14			
9		Valor	9.10	16			
10		Caston	7.85	20			

DESIRED RESULT

ABC PHARMACY
PART-TIME PAYROLL
WEEK ENDING October 1995

Employee Number	Employee Name	Hourly Rate	Hours Worked	Gross Pay	Taxes	Net Pay
110	Harrison	$8.45	16	$135.20	$27.04	$108.16
112	Williams	$7.35	18	$132.30	$26.46	$105.84
114	Bhatt	$6.85	22	$150.70	$30.14	$120.56
116	Robinson	$8.65	30	$259.50	$51.90	$207.60
118	Townsend	$5.55	28	$155.40	$31.08	$124.32
120	Arries	$7.35	14	$102.90	$20.58	$82.32
122	Valor	$9.10	16	$145.60	$29.12	$116.48
124	Caston	$7.85	20	$157.00	$31.40	$125.60

DATA FILL

1. Display the....................[Alt] + [A], [R]
   Formula Bar.

2. Enter the first two numbers in the column
   or row to establish a pattern.

3. Highlight the first two numbers and the
   remaining column or row.

4. Click **Data Fill** ....[Alt] + [Shift] + [D]
   on the Formula Bar.

EXERCISE

USING FUNCTIONS

72

NOTES:

■ To find an **average**, you might add the numbers to be averaged and then divide by the number of items. For example, to find the average list price in this exercise, the formula would look like:

$$(B4+B5+B6)/3$$

■ Rather than use the formula described above to find an average, you can use a **function**, a built-in formula that performs a special calculation automatically.

■ To average the values in B4 through B6 in this exercise, the Average function would be written in cell B9 as:

$$AVE(B4:B6)$$

To access the functions available in WordPerfect:

• Place your insertion point in the cell where you wish to insert a function.

• Select Functions on the Formula bar.

Click to calculate values

> NOTE: If Formula bar is not displayed, press Alt + A, R.

The functions are listed in the Table Functions dialog box window.

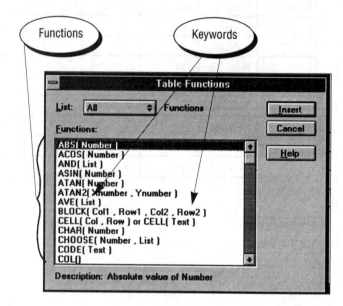

Functions   Keywords

■ You will note that each function begins with a name. You must replace **keywords** indicated in parentheses with data, names, cell or range addresses. Those functions which display *List* as the keyword after the function name require that you indicate the range of cells to be affected.

■ In previous exercises, you used the Sum button on the Formula bar to add values above the insertion point. The Sum button actually enters a SUM function formula into your cell, which looks like this:

$$SUM(C4:C6)$$

> NOTE: You will find the SUM function listed in the *Functions* list window.

■ You will be introduced to several of the most commonly used functions in this exercise. When you become comfortable with this concept, you can experiment with the numerous functions available in WordPerfect.

■ The other functions that will be used in this exercise include:

• COUNT   counts all cells in a range or block.

• MAX   indicates the highest value in a range or block.

• MIN   indicates the lowest value in a range or block.

EXERCISE DIRECTIONS:

In this exercise, you will create a table and perform subtraction, multiplication and addition calculations. Then, you will use functions to find the average, count, maximum and minimum values in the ranges specified.

1. Start with a clear screen.

2. Use the default margins.

3. Create the table shown below using six columns and 12 rows. Join the cells in the first row.

4. Right-align title lines in row 1 using a serif 14 point bold font for the first line and a serif 12 point italics font for the second line.

5. Display the Formula bar.

6. Enter column headings and column text using a serif 12 point font. Center and bold column headings.

7. Using Table Expert, apply the Fancy Buttons table style.

8. Use Horizontal Lines style to fill row 3.

9. Edit the table as follows:

   • Enter the formulas, as shown, in the indicated cells.

   • Copy the formulas down for each product.

• Use the SUM function to total the LIST PRICE column, and copy the formula to the remaining columns.

• Use the AVE function to average the LIST PRICE column, and copy the formula to the remaining columns.

• Repeat this procedure using the MAX, MIN and COUNT functions, and copy the formulas to the remaining columns.

   NOTE: While you could simply count the items yourself, this exercise is for practice purposes. You would normally use this function if you needed to count numerous items in a list.

• Decimal-align money columns.

• Format all money columns for currency.

10. Vertically center the exercise.

11. Preview the exercise.

12. Print one copy.

13. Save the file; name it **PRICE**.

14. Close the document window.

	A	B	C	D	E	F
1				**MATTHEW'S DRESS SHOP** *Price Worksheet for December 1994*		
2	PRODUCT	LIST PRICE	DISCOUNT	SALE PRICE	SALES TAX	TOTAL PRICE
3						
4	RED GOWN	745	185	B4-C4	D4*.08	D4+E4
5	BLUE JACKET	985	265			
6	BRN SLACKS	395	98			
7						
8	TOTALS	SUM(B4:B6)				
9	AVERAGE	AVE(B4:B6)				
10	MAXIMUM	MAX(B4:B6)				
11	MINIMUM	MIN(B4:B6)				
11	COUNT	COUNT(B4:B6)				

USE FUNCTIONS

1. Place insertion point in cell where function is to be inserted.

2. Click **T**able .... **A**

3. Click Fo**r**mula Bar .... **R**

4. Click **F**unctions .... **F**
   on Feature bar.

5. Double-click desired function.

If (List) is indicated in function:

6. Type range of cells to be affected (C5:C8).

   OR

   If another prompt is indicated in function:

   Replace keywords with data, names, cell or ranges addresses.

7. Click check mark .... [✓]

   OR

   Press **Enter** .... [↵]
   to insert formula.

EXERCISE 73

USING FUNCTIONS

NOTES:

■ If two question marks (??) appear in a cell after you perform a calculation or use a function, it means that the formula you used is invalid.

■ If you would like to delete a formula, click in the cell or highlight the cells that contain the formula(s) you wish to delete. Then, select, Delete, Cell Contents from the Table main menu.

EXERCISE DIRECTIONS:

 In this exercise, you will create a letter with an inserted table. You will also gain more practice using formulas and functions to perform calculations.

1.   Start with a clear screen.

2.   Use the default margins for the document; set 1.5" margins for the table.

3.   Use a serif 11 point font for the document.

4.   Begin the exercise approximately 1.36" from the top of the page.

5.   Create the exercise on the right as shown using the appropriate number of columns and rows for the table.

6.   Center column headings in row 1.

7.   Edit the table as follows:

   • Use the Size Column to Fit feature for CITY/STATE column.

   • Decimal-align money columns.

   • Center-align dates in column 1.

   • Format all money columns for currency with two decimal places.

   • Enter the SUM function in cell C7 to find the TOTAL of LODGING expenses (cells C2:C6).

   • Enter the AVE (average) function in cell C8 to find the average LODGING costs.

   • Enter the COUNT function in cell C9 to find how many items are listed.

   • Enter the MAX function in cell C10 to find the maximum value in the list.

   • Enter the MIN function in cell C11 to find the minimum value in the list.

   • Copy the formulas for SUM, AVE, COUNT, MAX and MIN to the remaining items in the row.

   • Using Table Expert, apply the Header Fill Column style.

   • Use a 10% fill to shade rows 7-11 as shown.

   • Use dotted lines for rows 7-11.

   • Reposition the table so it is centered horizontally.

8.   Preview the exercise.

9.   Print one copy.

10. Save the file; name it **EXPENSES**.

11. Close the document file.

1.36"

Today's date

Freed, Frank & Mulligan, Inc.
Attention Mr. Weston Freed
543 Main Street
Detroit, MI 48236

Ladies and Gentlemen:

We have reviewed Alison Jackson's expenses for September. We find that all is in order. The following is a summary:

DATE	CITY/ STATE	LODGING	AUTO	FOOD
Aug. 1	Miami, FL	$1,000.00	$195.00	$189.00
Aug. 7	New York, NY	$450.00	$45.00	$215.00
Aug. 14	Newton, MA	$189.00	$87.50	$105.65
Aug. 21	Redding, PA	$175.00	$80.00	$125.50
Aug. 28	Wayne, NJ	$250.00	$105.00	$85.00
TOTAL				
AVG				
COUNT				
MAX				
MIN				

We will file all the necessary end-of-quarter papers as we have in the past. I think we should get an earlier start next year in preparation of an audit. We should discuss how to proceed at our next meeting.

Sincerely,

Matthew Tyler
Comptroller

mt/

EXERCISE

SORTING BY LINE

74

NOTES:

- WordPerfect's **Sort** feature lets you arrange text alphabetically or numerically in ascending order (from A to Z or 1 to 25) or descending order (Z to A or 25 to 1).

- A **line sort** is used to arrange lists or columns of text and/or numbers.

- Each line is considered a **record**. A record is information about one person or one thing.

- Before you perform a sort, be sure your data is set up properly. A line record must end with a hard or soft return and records should have one tab per column. You can, however, type a list at the left edge of the screen and sort it.

- In addition to sorting lines, WordPerfect lets you sort paragraphs, merge records (to be covered in Lesson 11), merge parallel columns and merge rows of a table.

  NOTE: By default, WordPerfect sorts by line in ascending order.

- To begin the sort, place your insertion point in the first column to be sorted and follow the keystroke procedures outlined at the end of this exercise.

- Sort may be accessed by selecting Sort from the Tools main menu. In the Sort dialog box which follows, you are required to indicate certain information:

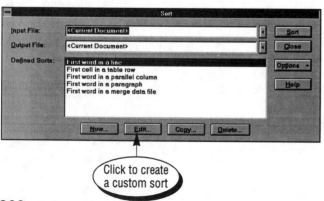

Click to create a custom sort

The *Input File (Source)* text box requires you to indicate the name of the file you wish to sort. Since your file is already onscreen, *<Current Document>* (the default) is automatically entered in the text box.

The *Output File (Destination)* text box requires you to indicate the name of the file where you wish to save the sorted text. If you want the sorted text to be saved to another file, enter the filename in the text box. If you want the sorted text to appear onscreen, *<Current Document>* (the default) is already entered for you.

The *Defined Sorts* options text box requires you to indicate the type of sort you are performing: first word in a line, first cell in a table row, first word in a parallel column, first word in a paragraph, or first word in a merge data file.

 It is important to save your document before you begin a sort. If your sort produces unexpected results, you can close your file without saving it, open the file again, and repeat the sort process.

- To activate the sort, click Sort or press Enter.

- After activating the sort, WordPerfect will arrange the record lines in ascending order starting with "the first word in a line," as the Defined Sort text box selection indicates. If you want to sort your records in descending order or based on the second word in the line, you would need to perform a custom sort.

266

- To perform a custom sort, click the <u>E</u>dit button at the bottom of the Sort dialog box. In the Edit Sort dialog box which follows, you must provide additional information.

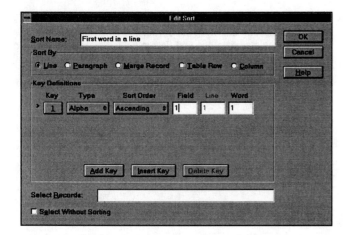

<u>S</u>ort Name requires you to confirm the type of sort you are performing: first word in a line, first cell in a table row, first word in a parallel column, first word in a paragraph, or first word in a merge data file.

Sort By requires you to reconfirm the type of sort you are performing. The Sort By option is selected based on the option you chose in the Sort dialog box.

Key Definitions options require you to indicate how you want the material sorted: the _Key_ field to sort, the _Type_ of sort, the _Sort Order_, the _Field_ and the _Word_ to use in the sort.

Key	Refers to the item (field and word in the field). Key 1 (the default) is the primary sort item. Key 2 is the secondary sort item.
Type	Refers to the kind of data to be sorted: <u>A</u>lpha(betic) or <u>N</u>umeric.
Sort Order	Refers to whether you want the sort in <u>A</u>scending (↑) or <u>D</u>escending (↓) order.
Field	Refers to column of text. In tabulated data, the first field is the left margin, the second field is the first tab stop, the third field is the second tab stop, etc.
Word	Refers to which word in the field (column) you wish to sort on—first (1), second (2), third (3), last (-1), second from last (-2), etc.

EXERCISE DIRECTIONS:

 In this exercise, you will sort the names in ascending order (alphabetically A-Z). Be sure to set tabs for each column.

1. Start with a clear screen.

2. Set the left margin to 3"; use the default right margin.

3. Create the exercise shown on the right. Set an absolute tab at 4.6".

4. Center the exercise vertically.

5. Save the exercise; name it **SORT**. *DO NOT EXIT THE DOCUMENT.*

6. Using the first word in a line sort, arrange the name column alphabetically (ascending order).

7. Save the sorted text to a new file; name it **SORT1**.

8. Sort the second column alphabetically (field is "2").

 To sort the second column, you must customize it by selecting Edit from the Sort dialog box. Remember, in tabulated data, the first field is the left margin, the second field is the first tab stop, etc. Therefore, for this sort, be sure to enter the field as 2.

9. Save the sorted text to a new file; name it **SORT2**.

10. Print one copy of **SORT2**.

11. Close the document window.

TO SORT (BY LINE)
Ctrl + F9

1. Open document you wish to sort.

2. Click **Tools**.......................... Alt + T

3. Click **Sort** .... R

4. Click **Input File**.................... Alt + I

   • Type filename to be sorted.

   OR

   • Use the default (<Current Document>) if document to be sorted is onscreen.

5. Click **Output File** text box...... Alt + O

   • Type file to be sorted *To.*

   OR

   • Use the default (<Current Document>) if document to be sorted is onscreen.

6. Click **Defined Sorts** option .... Alt + F

7. Choose a sort option.

To custom sort:

   a. Click **Edit** .... Alt + E

   b. Click **Sort Name**.............. Alt + S

   c. Specify the type of sort to be performed.

   d. Click a Sort By option:

   • **Line** .... Alt + L

   • **Paragraph** .... Alt + P

   • **Merge Record**........ Alt + M

   • **Table Row**.............. Alt + T

   • **Column**.................. Alt + C

   e. Click and select Type of sort:

   • **Alpha(betic)**

   • **Numeric**

   f. Click and select Sort Order:

   • **Ascending** (↑)............. A

   • **Descending** (↓) .... D

—*IN FIELD TEXT BOX*—

8. Type field number to be sorted.

—*IN WORD TEXT BOX*—

9. Type word number to be sorted.

10. Click **OK**.................... Enter

11. Click **Sort** .... Alt + S or Enter

Watson, Patricia	Publicity
Tracey, Frank	Ethics
Brittany, Margaret	Policy/Action
Harrison, George	Convention
Cooper, Latoya	Newsletter
Zarin, William	Convention
Chassin, Matthew	Membership

EXERCISE

SORTING BY LINE

75

NOTES:

▪ This exercise contains a centered heading. If you were to sort this exercise, WordPerfect would include the heading in the sort.

▪ To sort columns containing other text, select the text to be sorted first; then, perform the sort. For this exercise, you can place the insertion point anywhere in the second column; then, perform the sort.

 When you specify the field to sort in the Sort dialog box, remember that you are sorting Field 3. WordPerfect considers the left margin field one, the first tab, field two, and the third tab, field three.

EXERCISE DIRECTIONS:

 In this exercise, you will create tabular columns and sort the second column numerically in ascending order and then in descending order.

1. Start with a clear screen.

2. Set the left margin to 1.75". Use the default right margin.

3. Create the exercise shown on the right. Set a decimal tab at 6.0".

4. Center the exercise vertically.

5. Save the exercise; name it **DEBT**. *DO NOT EXIT THE DOCUMENT.*

6. Sort the second column numerically in ascending order.

7. Save the sorted text to a new file; name it **DEBT1**.

8. Sort the second column numerically in descending order.

9. Save the sorted text to a new file; name it **DEBT2**.

10. Print **DEBT1**.

11. Close the document window.

270

OUTSTANDING ACCOUNTS
OCTOBER

ABC Carpets	4,4456.87
R & R Jewelers	786.77
Alison's Sweet Shoppe	234.56
Harrison Taylor, Ltd.	2,192.33
P & A Brands, Inc.	456.99
Jolson Brothers	1,443.98

SORT SELECTED TEXT

1. Place insertion point on first line to be sorted.

   OR

   Select text to be sorted.

2. Click **Tools** .... `Alt` + `T`

3. Click **Sort** .... `R`

4. Follow steps 4-11 in previous exercise.

EXERCISE

SORTING WITHIN A TABLE

76

NOTES:

■ In the previous exercises, you sorted one column of records alphabetically or numerically in ascending or descending order. In other words, you sorted on one key field.

■ It is possible to sort one column of records (Key 1 field) and then subsort another column (Key 2 field) within the first column. Note the illustration below of records sorted on one column and subsorted on another.

COMPUTER INSTRUCTORS' ASSOCIATION
MEMBERSHIP LIST
1994

TITLE	FIRST	LAST	ADDRESS	CITY	ST	ZIP
Ms.	Barbara	Center	43 Beverly Road	Beverly Hills	CA	90210
Ms.	Donna	Brown	76 York Avenue	Santa Monica	CA	90087
Ms.	Rose	Casen	500 Carlin Way	Venice	CA	90122
Mr.	Paul	Rivlin	14 Hidden Hills	Stone Mountain	GA	30088
Ms.	Sharon	Walker	34 Prince Street	Bronx	NY	10456
Mr.	Nick	Batos	43 Wilmer Street	Brooklyn	NY	11230
Mr.	Roy	Porter	235 Belmill Road	Brooklyn	NY	11244
Ms.	Jaime	Leigh	111 John Street	New York	NY	10033
Ms.	Pamela	Jones	66 West 66 Street	New York	NY	10056
Mr.	Richard	Zarin	12 Circle Drive	Dallas	TX	78666
Mr.	Miles	Brown	1640 Ocean Avenue	Lubbock	TX	79410
Ms.	Natasha	Alesi	77 Midi Drive	San Marcos	TX	78666
Mr.	Jay	Stanis	9 Times Road	Orem	UT	84057

TABLE sorted by STATE (key 1) ↑   ↑
and subsorted by CITY(key 2)

■ In this exercise, for example, you are directed to create a membership list using a table format and sort the records by STATE then subsort the records by LAST name. Since you are performing both a sort and a subsort and not using the default sort (alphabetically by line) you must create a custom sort (click Edit in the Sort dialog box). Note the Edit Sort dialog box which follows.

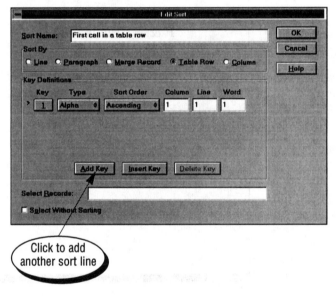

Click to add another sort line

■ If your insertion point was inside the table when you accessed the Sort feature, WordPerfect automatically entered Table Row as the Sort By option. The default in Key 1 is set for an Alpha, Ascending sort order on Column 1. (Column 1 is column A.) Unless you change the settings, the first word in the first line of each cell in column A will be used as the basis for the sort.

- Since we wish to sort the records by STATE, which is in column 6, the Key 1 entry for column must be changed to 6. Since there is only one word in the field, the Word entry remains 1.

- To include another sort line (to subsort the records by LAST name) and make entries for Key 2, you must click the Add Key button.

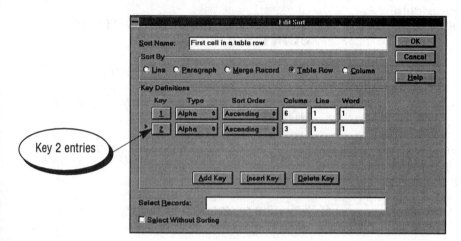

Key 2 entries

- Note the Key 2 entries: since LAST is the third column, the column number to be sorted is 3, and since there is only one word in the field, the Word to be sorted is 1. Since the sort and subsort will be alphabetical ascending, the Type is entered as Alpha and the Sort order is Ascending in both cases.

EXERCISE DIRECTIONS:

 In this exercise, you will perform several sorts and subsorts. Remember, since there is other text in the exercise besides the columns (the title lines and column headings), be sure to select the text to be sorted before starting the sort procedure. DO NOT INCLUDE TITLES AND COLUMN HEADINGS WHEN SELECTING THE COLUMNS.

1. Start with a clear screen.

2. Use the default margins.

3. Create the table shown on the right. Center the main title in serif 14 point; center the subtitles in serif 12 point. Use 7 columns and 14 rows to create the table.

   OR

   Open **JOIN.76** from the data disk as a read-only file (Open As Copy) and skip to step 8.

4. Center and bold the column headings.

5. Use the Size Column to Fit feature to size each column.

6. Center the exercise horizontally and vertically.

7. Save the exercise; name it **JOIN**. *DO NOT EXIT THE DOCUMENT.*

8. Sort the records in alphabetical order by LAST name.

9. Save the sorted text to a new file; name it **JOIN1**.

10. Sort the records in numerical order by ZIP.

11. Save the sorted text to a new file; name it **JOIN2**.

12. Sort the records in alphabetical order by STATE and subsort in alphabetical order by LAST name.

13. Save the sorted text to a new file; name it **JOIN3**.

14. Sort the records in numerical order by ZIP and subsort in alphabetical order by LAST name.

15. Save the sorted text to a new file; name it **JOIN4**.

16. Select File Options, Print from the Open File dialog box. Print one copy of **JOIN1**, **JOIN2**, **JOIN3**, and **JOIN4**.

17. Close the document window.

COMPUTER INSTRUCTORS' ASSOCIATION
MEMBERSHIP LIST
1995

TITLE	FIRST	LAST	ADDRESS	CITY	ST	ZIP
Mr.	Nick	Batos	43 Wilmer Street	Brooklyn	NY	11230
Ms.	Pamela	Jones	66 West 66 Street	New York	NY	10056
Mr.	Roy	Porter	235 Belmill Road	Broooklyn	NY	11244
Ms.	Sharon	Walker	34 Prince Street	Bronx	NY	10456
Ms.	Rose	Casen	500 Carlin Way	Venice	CA	90122
Mr.	Paul	Rivlin	14 Hidden Hills	Stone Mountain	GA	30088
Ms.	Barbara	Center	43 Beverly Road	Beverly Hills	CA	90210
Ms.	Natasha	Alesi	77 Midi Drive	San Marcos	TX	78666
Mr.	Jay	Stanis	9 Times Road	Orem	UT	84057
Mr.	Miles	Brown	1640 Ocean Avenue	Lubbock	TX	79410
Ms.	Jaime	Leigh	111 John Street	New York	NY	10033
Ms.	Donna	Brown	76 York Avenue	Santa Monica	CA	90087
Mr.	Richard	Zarin	12 Circle Drive	Dallas	TX	78666

LESSON 10
SUMMARY EXERCISE A

EXERCISE DIRECTIONS:

1. Start with a clear screen.
2. Use the default margins.
3. ⌨ Create the table as shown below.
   - Use the appropriate number of columns and rows.
   - Enter and align the text in serif 12 point as shown.
   - Use the Size Column to Fit feature to size the columns.
   - Format money column for currency with two decimal places.
   - Horizontally and vertically center the exercise.

   OR

   💾 Open **BRANCH.10A** from the data disk as a read-only file (Open As Copy) and skip to step 5.

4. Join cells in rows 1, 2 and 13.
5. Total the STAFF and SALES columns using the SUM function.
6. Use any desired fill or pattern or highlight the cells shown.
7. Preview the exercise.
8. Print one copy.
9. Sort the records in descending order by SALES.
10. Print one copy.
11. Sort the records alphabetically by STATE and subsort alphabetically by BRANCH.
12. Print one copy.
13. Save the file; name it **BRANCH**.
14. Close the document window.

		BALIWANE SPORTSWEAR **New Branches/Locations/Gross Sales As of January 31, 199-**		
BRANCH	**CITY**	**STATE**	**STAFF**	**SALES**
Paramount	New York	NY	18	$350,000.00
Sunview	Hollywood	CA	12	$125,000.00
Seaview	Portland	ME	8	$100,000.00
Cornielle	Providence	RI	20	$450,000.00
Astro Center	Houston	TX	19	$99,000.00
Mountainaire	Troy	NY	6	$95,000.00
Sunnyvale	New York	NY	16	$150,000.00
Downtown Center	Dallas	TX	16	$183,000.00
Beverly Road	Beverly Hills	CA	8	$259,865.00
TOTALS				

LESSON 10
SUMMARY EXERCISE B

EXERCISE DIRECTIONS:

1. Start with a clear screen.
2. Use the default margins.
3. Create the table as shown below.
   - Use the appropriate number of columns and rows.
   - Enter and align the text in serif 12 point as shown.
   - Use Size Column to Fit to size the columns.
   - Format money columns for currency with two decimal places.
   - Horizontally and vertically center the exercise

   OR

   💾 Open **QTRSALES.10B** from the data disk as a read-only file (Open As Copy) and skip to step 5.
4. Join cells in row 1.
5. Find the COMMISSION for each salesperson. Each employee receives a 5% commission on sales.

   ✎ Multiply SALES by .05 for Julie Aronson, then copy the formula down to the other employees.

6. Find QUARTERLY SALARY by adding the BASE SALARY to the COMMISSION earned for Julie Aronson, then copy the formula down to the other employees.
7. Use the functions to find TOTALS, AVERAGES, HIGHEST, and LOWEST in the BASE SALARY column, then copy the formulas to the other columns.
8. Align column headings and column text as shown.
9. Sort the records alphabetically by NAME.
10. Use any desired table border.
11. Use a 10% fill to shade the rows where shown.
12. Use any desired cell border for Matt Chasin and his sales amount.
13. Use any desired line style to separate the rows below the names.
14. Print one copy.
15. Save the file; name it **QTRSALES**.
16. Close the document window.

TRANSPORT CAR DEALERS				
QUARTERLY SALES AND SALARY REPORT April-June				
NAME	**BASE SALARY**	**SALES**	**COMMISSION**	**QTR. SALARY**
Aronson, Julie	$1,500.00	$113,456.55		
Blair, Pamela	$1,400.00	$123,098.90		
*Chasin, Matt	$1,200.00	*$334,987.00		
Rivera, Jose	$1,500.00	$88,465.90		
Song, Lauren	$1,400.00	$175,987.00		
Rao, Neomi	$1,500.00	$187,007.66		
Fabian, John	$1,300.00	$275,876.99		
Yerman, Jill	$1,500.00	$289,886.00		
TOTALS				
AVERAGES				
HIGHEST				
LOWEST				

*Highest Sales for Quarter

LESSON 11

Exercises 77–84

- Creating the Form File

- Creating the Data File

- Merging the Form and Data Files

- Merging Selected Records

- Merging with Conditions

- Preparing Envelopes while Merging

- Merging a Form File with a Data Table

EXERCISE

CREATING A FORM FILE

77

NOTES

- The **Merge** feature allows you to mass produce letters, envelopes, mailing labels and other documents so they appear to be personalized.

- A form file (the form letter) is combined with a data file (the names and addresses of those who will receive the letters) to produce a **merged document**. The same data file may then be used to produce the envelopes and/or labels, thus making it unnecessary to type the name and address list a second time.

- The **form file** contains information that does not change. All formatting, margins, spacing, etc., as well as graphics and paper size information, should be included in the form file.

- Codes are inserted where variable information will be placed. Variable information changes from letter to letter, such as the inside address and salutation.

- Each piece of variable information is called a **field**.

- In the exercise illustrated on page 283, the inside address and salutation are divided into fields, with each field given a name (if a name is not given, WordPerfect will number each field).

  Each field is named for what will eventually be inserted into that location. The first field is named *title*, the second is named *first*, the third is named *last*, the fourth is named *address*, the fifth is named *city*, the sixth is named *state*, and the seventh field is named *zip*. The illustration shows how fields display on the screen after the codes are entered.

- As you enter each field name, include spacing between the fields as you want it to appear when text is inserted in the letter.

- The same field name can be inserted in the letter as many times as desired. Note that Field(TITLE) and Field(LAST) are used twice since the letter contains two occurrences of someone's title and last name.

- When you complete the form file, print one copy to use as reference as you prepare the data file.

 The data file must contain the same fields as the form file. Otherwise, the final document will not merge properly.

- After the form file is created, it must be saved. Do not use an extension in your filename. The extension .FRM will be appended by WordPerfect.

- To create a form file for a letter, select Merge from the Tools main menu.

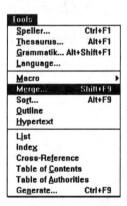

- In the Merge dialog box which follows, select Form to indicate that you are creating a form file.

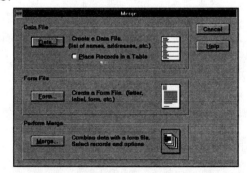

FORM FILE

Today's date

FIELD(TITLE) FIELD(FIRST) FIELD(LAST)
FIELD(ADDRESS)
FIELD(CITY), FIELD(STATE) FIELD(ZIP)

Dear FIELD(TITLE) FIELD(LAST):

You are cordially invited to attend our annual spring fashion show. The show will take place at the Plaza Hotel in New York City Friday evening, June 22 at 7:30 p.m. Refreshments will be served.

We appreciate your contributions and continued support of the Fashion Institute. We know you will see several outstanding collections at the showing. Please let me know if you plan to attend by calling my office any day between 9:00 a.m. and 5:00 p.m.

We look forward to you attending this special event.

Sincerely,

Thomas Mann
President
Fashion Institute

tm/yo

DATA FILE

FIELDNAMES(TITLE;FIRST;LAST;ADDRESS;CITY;STATE;ZIP)ENDRECORD

Mr. ENDFIELD
PeterENDFIELD
RinglerENDFIELD
23 Preston AvenueENDFIELD
BellemoreENDFIELD
NYENDFIELD
ENDRECORD

Mr. ENDFIELD
FredENDFIELD
LeBostENDFIELD
98-67 Kew Gardens RoadENDFIELD
Forest HillsENDFIELD
NYENDFIELD
11432ENDFIELD
ENDRECORD

Ms. ENDFIELD
MaryENDFIELD
McCleanENDFIELD
765 Bellmill RoadENDFIELD
RoslynENDFIELD
NYENDFIELD
11577ENDFIELD
ENDRECORD

Ms. ENDFIELD
LorraineENDFIELD
OelserENDFIELD
1275 BroadwayENDFIELD
New YorkENDFIELD
NYENDFIELD
10028ENDFIELD
ENDRECORD

MERGED DOCUMENTS

Today's date

Mr. Fred LeBost
98-67 Kew Gard
Forest Hills, NY

Dear Mr. LeBost

You are cordially
the Plaza Hotel i
served.

We appreciate yo
will see several o
attend
by calling my off

We look forward

Sincerely,

Thomas Mann
President
Fashion Institute

tm/yo

Today's date

Ms. Mary McClean
765 Bellmill Road
Roslyn, NY 11577

Dear Ms. McClean

You are cordially i
the Plaza Hotel in
served.

We appreciate you
will see several ou
attend
by calling my offic

We look forward t

Sincerely,

Thomas Mann
President
Fashion Institute

tm/yo

Today's date

Mr. Peter Ringler
23 Preston Avenu
Bellemore, NY

Dear Mr. Ringler

You are cordially
the Plaza Hotel i
served.

We appreciate yo
will see several o
attend
by calling my off

We look forward

Sincerely,

Thomas Mann
President
Fashion Institute

tm/yo

Today's date

Ms. Lorraine Oelser
1275 Broadway
New York, NY 10028

Dear Ms. Oelser:

You are cordially invited to attend our annual spring fashion show. The show will take place at the Plaza Hotel in New York City Friday evening, June 22 at 7:30 p.m. Refreshments will be served.

We appreciate your contributions and continued support of the Fashion Institute. We know you will see several outstanding collections at the showing. Please let me know if you plan to attend by calling my office any day between 9:00 a.m. and 5:00 p.m.

We look forward to you attending this special event.

Sincerely,

Thomas Mann
President
Fashion Institute

tm/yo

- In the Create Merge File dialog box which follows, you must indicate whether you wish to start your document in a new window or use the file in the active window. Since, it is likely that you have a blank screen, use the default.

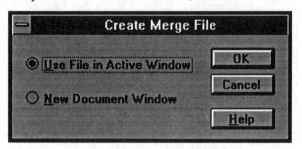

- In the Create Form File dialog box which follows, you must specify if you want to associate a data file with this form file. However, since you have not created the data file yet, select None.

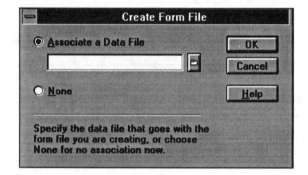

- Keyboard to the first field location (first variable).

- Click Insert Field button on Feature bar and click OK. The Merge Feature bar provides a quick way to access merge-related tasks.

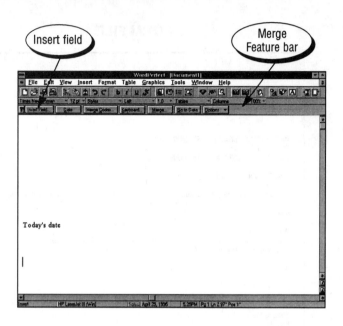

- In the Insert Field Name or Number dialog box which follows, click the Field text box and keyboard the first field name.

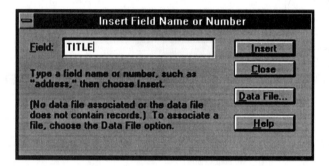

- Repeat the previous procedure for each variable to be inserted in the letter.

EXERCISE DIRECTIONS:

 In this exercise, you will create a form letter file. Follow the procedures outlined above or the keystrokes outlined on the next page.

1. Start with a clear screen.

2. Create the form letter file as shown on the right using a serif 12 point font.

3. Use the default margins.

4. Begin the exercise on Ln 2.5".

5. Spell check.

6. Print one copy. (Keep your printout for reference as you complete the next exercise.)

7. Save the file; name it **INVITE**.

    NOTE   The extension .FRM will be appended by WordPerfect.

8. Close the document window.

2.5"

Today's date

FIELD(TITLE) FIELD(FIRST) FIELD(LAST)
FIELD(ADDRESS)
FIELD(CITY), FIELD(STATE) FIELD(ZIP)

Dear FIELD(TITLE) FIELD(LAST):

You are cordially invited to attend our annual spring fashion show. The show will take place at the Plaza Hotel in New York City Friday evening, June 22 at 7:30 p.m. Refreshments will be served.

We appreciate your contributions and continued support of the Fashion Institute. We know you will see several outstanding collections at the showing. Please let me know if you plan to attend by calling my office any day between 9:00 a.m. and 5:00 p.m.

We look forward to you attending this special event.

Sincerely,

Thomas Mann
President
Fashion Institute

tm/yo

CREATE A FORM FILE
Shift + F9

1. Open a new document.
2. Click **Tools** .... `Alt` + `T`
3. Click **Merge** .... `E`
4. Click **Form** .... `F`
5. • Click Associate a Data File text box.

    • Keyboard data filename.

    OR

    • Click None.

6. Click **OK** .... `Enter`
7. Keyboard to first field location.
8. Click **Insert Field** ..... `Alt` + `Shift` + `I`
    on Feature Bar.
9. Click **OK** .... `Enter`
10. Keyboard name of first field ..... *field name* (TITLE, for example) in text box.
11. Click **Insert** .... `Alt` + `I`
12. Repeat steps 7-10 for each field.

13. Keyboard remainder of document.
14. Click **Close** .... `C`
    on Feature Bar.

    NOTE: Save this file as usual.

EXERCISE

CREATING THE DATA FILE

78

NOTES:

■ The **data file** contains the inside addresses and salutations of the people receiving the letter you created in the form file.

■ A data file may contain many **records**. A record is a collection of related information about one person. The information in each record is divided into **fields**. *The fields used in the form file MUST match the information used in the data file.*

■ To create a data file, select Merge from the Tools main menu, then select Data from the Merge dialog box.

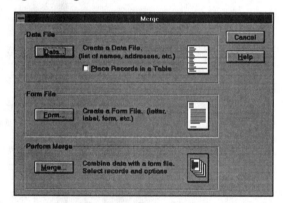

■ If you have information in the current document, you are prompted to indicate whether you want to use the current document or open a new one.

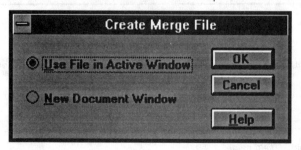

The Create Data File dialog box then appears:

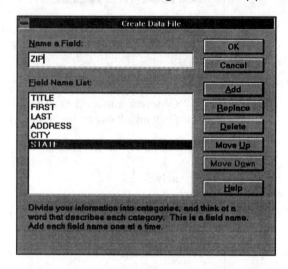

■ The field names are entered by typing the name of the field in the Name a Field text box, then selecting Add. *Be sure the data file fields match the fields used in the form file.*

■ It is not necessary, however, to enter variable information more than once where fields are used more than once. For example, WordPerfect will insert the information that relates to TITLE, LAST in the salutation during the merge process.

- After all field names are entered and you click OK, you can add the actual data (names and addresses) in the Quick Data Entry dialog box which follows. After entering the names and addresses of all the fields for the first record, select New Record and repeat the procedure for each person to receive a letter.

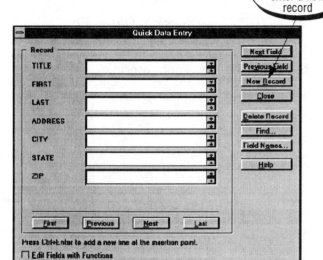

Click to enter a new record

- Note the illustration below left. It shows one record in a data file as it appears on the screen after the data is entered in the Quick Data Entry dialog box. Fields end with the **ENDFIELD** command and a hard return. An **ENDRECORD** command ends a record, and a **hard page break** separates the records.

- Note, too, that the information for each field matches the fields used in the form file (shown on bottom right). Since the comma used after the city was inserted in the form file, it should not be entered again in the data file. Otherwise, two commas will result when the documents are merged.

- After the data file is created, it must be saved.

DATA FILE   **FORM FILE**

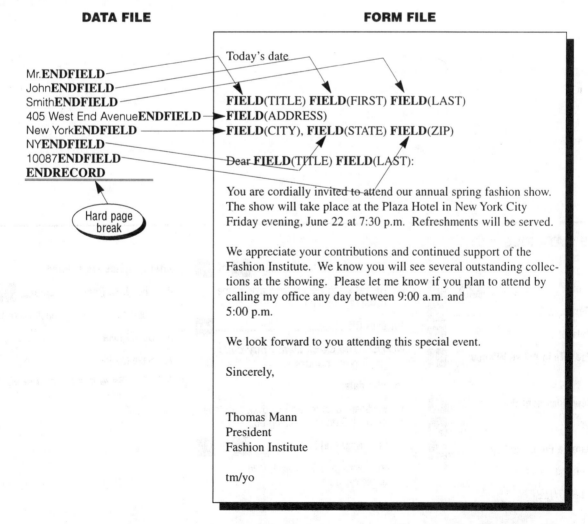

Mr.**ENDFIELD**
John**ENDFIELD**
Smith**ENDFIELD**
405 West End Avenue**ENDFIELD**
New York**ENDFIELD**
NY**ENDFIELD**
10087**ENDFIELD**
ENDRECORD

Hard page break

Today's date

FIELD(TITLE) **FIELD**(FIRST) **FIELD**(LAST)
FIELD(ADDRESS)
FIELD(CITY), **FIELD**(STATE) **FIELD**(ZIP)

Dear **FIELD**(TITLE) **FIELD**(LAST):

You are cordially invited to attend our annual spring fashion show. The show will take place at the Plaza Hotel in New York City Friday evening, June 22 at 7:30 p.m. Refreshments will be served.

We appreciate your contributions and continued support of the Fashion Institute. We know you will see several outstanding collections at the showing. Please let me know if you plan to attend by calling my office any day between 9:00 a.m. and 5:00 p.m.

We look forward to you attending this special event.

Sincerely,

Thomas Mann
President
Fashion Institute

tm/yo

EXERCISE DIRECTIONS:

 In this exercise, you will create a data file. In the next exercise, you will merge the data and form files.

1. Start with a clear screen.

2. Create a data file from the records on the right. Be sure the fields in the data file match the fields used in the form file.

3. Use the default margins.

4. Begin the exercise on Ln 1" (top of screen).

5. Save the exercise; name it **INVITE**.

   NOTE: The extension .DAT will be appended by WordPerfect.

6. Close the document window.

CREATE DATA FILE

Shift + F9

1. Click **Tools**............................ Alt + T

2. Click **Merge**................................. E

3. Click **Data** .... D

4. Click **Use File in Active Window** .... U

   OR

   Click **New Document Window** .... N

5. Click **OK** .... ↵

6. Click **Name a Field** text box .... N

7. Keyboard first field name.

   EXAMPLE: TITLE

8. Click **Add** or **Enter**.................. A or ↵

9. Repeat steps 7-9 for each field name (used in form file).

10. Click **OK** .... ↵

NOTE: The Quick Data Entry dialog box appears.

To enter data:

1. Keyboard data for first field.........*data text* in Quick Data Entry dialog box.

2. Click **Next Field** or **Enter** .... X or ↵

3. Repeat steps 1-2 for each field to receive data.

After all fields are entered:

4. Click **New Record** or **Enter** .... R or ↵

5. Repeat steps 1-4 for each record.

6. Click **Close** C

7. Save the file.

NOTE: Save this file as usual.

FIELDNAMES(TITLE;FIRST;LAST;ADDRESS;CITY;STATE;ZIP)**ENDRECORD**

Mr. **ENDFIELD**
Peter**ENDFIELD**
Ringler**ENDFIELD**
23 Preston Avenue**ENDFIELD**
Bellemore**ENDFIELD**
NY**ENDFIELD**
11010**ENDFIELD**
ENDRECORD

Mr. **ENDFIELD**
Fred**ENDFIELD**
LeBost**ENDFIELD**
98-67 Kew Gardens Road**ENDFIELD**
Forest Hills**ENDFIELD**
NY**ENDFIELD**
11432**ENDFIELD**
ENDRECORD

Ms. **ENDFIELD**
Mary**ENDFIELD**
McClean**ENDFIELD**
765 Belmill Road**ENDFIELD**
Roslyn**ENDFIELD**
NY**ENDFIELD**
11577**ENDFIELD**
ENDRECORD

Ms. **ENDFIELD**
Lorraine**ENDFIELD**
Oelser**ENDFIELD**
1275 Broadway**ENDFIELD**
New York**ENDFIELD**
NY**ENDFIELD**
10028**ENDFIELD**
ENDRECORD

EXERCISE

79

▪ MERGING THE FORM AND DATA FILES ▪ MERGING SELECTED RECORDS

NOTES:

■ Once the form and data files have been created, they may be merged to create a third document which contains personalized copies of the form file.

■ The **final, merged third document** will appear as separate pages, each page representing a record. This document may be saved under its own filename. Saving the merged third document under its own filename is particularly helpful if you wish to edit individual pages of the document. For example, a postscript (or P.S.) or special mailing notation might be added to selected letters.

■ To merge the form and data files, select <u>M</u>erge from the <u>T</u>ools main menu. In the Merge dialog box which follows, select Merge.

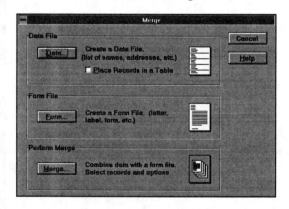

■ In the Perform Merge dialog box which follows, enter the filenames of the form and data files you wish to merge. The Output File text box option requires you to indicate how you wish the merged document to output. Descriptions of your output options are listed below.

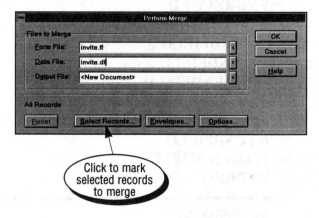

Click to mark selected records to merge

<Current Document>	merges to the current document window, showing you the merge on the screen and allowing you to save as a third document.
<New Document>	merges to a new document window, showing you the merge on the screen and allowing you to save as a third document (the default).
<Printer>	merges directly to the printer without showing the merge on the screen or allowing you to save as a third document on a disk.
Select File...	merges to a file you specify without showing the merge on the screen.

If the form and data files do not merge properly, check each file to see that the fields used in the form file have information that matches the fields used in the data file.

Merging Selected Records

- It is possible to merge selected records rather than all the records contained in the data file by marking them at the beginning of the merge process.

- To mark specific records to merge, click Select Records in the Perform Merge dialog box. In the Select Records dialog box which follows, click Mark Records. This produces a list of records in the Record List text box window with a check box next to each record. Click the check box to indicate the records you wish to merge.

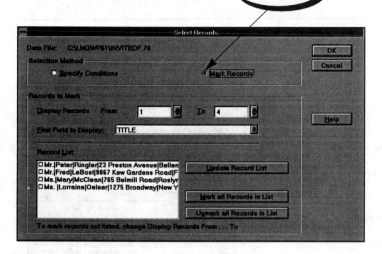

Click to mark records

 If you want most but not all records marked, click Mark all Records in List. Then, click those few records you do not want marked to deselect them.

 To help you select records by CITY, for example, click First Field to Display. Select city from drop-down list, then click Update Record List.

EXERCISE DIRECTIONS:

In this exercise, you will merge the form file created in Exercise 77 with the data file created in Exercise 78 and mark selected records for the merge.

1. Start with a clear screen.

2. Merge the form file **INVITE.FRM** with the data file **INVITE.DAT** to a NEW document.

3. Merge and print letters to Ms. Oelser and Ms. McClean only.

4. Save the merged letters under a new document name: **INVITE.FI**.

5. Close the document window.

MERGE FORM AND DATA FILES

Shift + F9

1. Click **Tools** .... `Alt` + `T`

2. Click **Merge** .... `E`

3. Click **Merge** .... `M`

4. Click **Form File** text box .... `Alt` + `F`

5. Keyboard name of form file .....*form name* or click pop-up arrow, select file.

6. Click **Data File** text box .... `Alt` + `D`

7. Keyboard name of data file ....*data name*

   OR

   a. Click **Data File** text box ..... `Alt` + `D`

   b. Click **Select File** .... `S`

   c. Click desired data file.

   d. Click **OK** .... `↵`

8. Change output, as desired.

9. Select records as desired, click **OK**.

10. Click **OK** .... `↵`

To change output:

1. Click **Output File** text box ...... `Alt` + `U`

2. Click **Output File** list button .. `Alt` + `O`

3. Click an Output Option:

   <Current Document>

   <New Document>

   <Printer>

   Select File .... `S`

To merge selected records:

1. Click **Select Records** .... `Alt` + `S`

2. Click **Mark Records** .... `A`

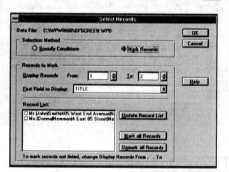

3. For each record you wish to merge, click check box of records.

   (See Select Records dialog box, above.)

4. Click **OK** .... `↵`

To change order of field display:

1. Click **First Field to Display** .... `F`

2. Click list button and select field.

3. Click **Update Record List** ...... `Alt` + `U`

FORM FILE

Today's date

FIELD(TITLE) FIELD(FIRST) FIELD(LAST)
FIELD(ADDRESS)
FIELD(CITY), FIELD(STATE) FIELD(ZIP)

Dear FIELD(TITLE) FIELD(LAST):

You are cordially invited to attend our annual spring fashion show. The show will take place at the Plaza Hotel in New York City Friday evening, June 22 at 7:30 p.m. Refreshments will be served.

We appreciate your contributions and continued support of the Fashion Institute. We know you will see several outstanding collections at the showing. Please let me know if you plan to attend by calling my office any day between 9:00 a.m. and 5:00 p.m.

We look forward to you attending this special event.

Sincerely,

Thomas Mann
President
Fashion Institute

tm/yo

INVITE.FRM

DATA FILE

FIELDNAMES(TITLE;FIRST;LAST;ADDRESS;CITY;STATE;ZIP)ENDRECORD

Mr. ENDFIELD
PeterENDFIELD
RinglerENDFIELD
23 Preston AvenueENDFIELD
BellemoreENDFIELD
NYENDFIELD
11010ENDFIELD
ENDRECORD

Mr. ENDFIELD
FredENDFIELD
LeBostENDFIELD
98-67 Kew Gardens RoadENDFIELD
Forest HillsENDFIELD
NYENDFIELD
11432ENDFIELD
ENDRECORD

Ms. ENDFIELD
MaryENDFIELD
McCleanENDFIELD
765 Bellmill RoadENDFIELD
RoslynENDFIELD
NYENDFIELD
11577ENDFIELD
ENDRECORD

Ms. ENDFIELD
LorraineENDFIELD
OelserENDFIELD
1275 BroadwayENDFIELD
New YorkENDFIELD
NYENDFIELD
10028ENDFIELD
ENDRECORD

INVITE.DAT

+

MERGED DOCUMENTS

=

Today's date

Mr. Fred LeBost
98-67 Kew Garde
Forest Hills, NY

Dear Mr. LeBost:

You are cordially
the Plaza Hotel in
served.

We appreciate you
will see several o
by calling my offi

We look forward

Sincerely,

Thomas Mann
President
Fashion Institute

tm/yo

Today's date

Mr. Peter Ringler
23 Preston Avenue
Bellemore, NY 110

Dear Mr. Ringler:

You are cordially i
the Plaza Hotel in
served.

We appreciate your
will see several out
by calling my office

We look forward to

Sincerely,

Thomas Mann
President
Fashion Institute

tm/yo

Today's date

Ms. Mary McClea
765 Bellmill Road
Roslyn, NY 1157

Dear Ms. McClea

You are cordially
the Plaza Hotel in
served.

We appreciate you
will see several ou
by calling my offi

We look forward t

Sincerely,

Thomas Mann
President
Fashion Institute

tm/yo

Today's date

Ms. Lorraine Oelser
1275 Broadway
New York, NY 10028

Dear Ms. Oelser:

You are cordially invited to attend our annual spring fashion show. The show will take place at the Plaza Hotel in New York City Friday evening, June 22 at 7:30 p.m. Refreshments will be served.

We appreciate your contributions and continued support of the Fashion Institute. We know you will see several outstanding collections at the showing. Please let me know if you plan to attend by calling my office any day between 9:00 a.m. and 5:00 p.m.

We look forward to you attending this special event.

Sincerely,

Thomas Mann
President
Fashion Institute

tm/yo

EXERCISE

CREATING THE FORM FILE AND DATA FILES

NOTES:

- In this exercise, you will create a form file which contains more variables than the previous exercise. Note that the same field name is assigned to variables that contain the same information (TITLE, LAST).

- When creating a data file where fields are used more than once, it is not necessary to repeat the variable information. In this exercise, for example, WordPerfect will insert the information that relates to TITLE, LAST and AMOUNT in the appropriate places during the merge process.

EXERCISE DIRECTIONS:

1. Start with a clear screen.
2. Create the form letter file as shown in Illustration A using a serif 12 point font.
3. Use the default margins.
4. Begin the exercise on Ln 2.5"
5. Spell check.
6. Print one copy. (Keep your printout for reference when creating the data file.)
7. Save the exercise; name it **DUE**.

NOTE: WordPerfect will append .FRM as the file extension

8. Close the document window.
9. Create the data file from the records shown in Illustration B.
10. Use the default margins.
11. Begin the exercise on Ln 1".
12. Save the file; name it **DUE**.

NOTE: WordPerfect will append .DAT as the file extension.

13. Close the document window.

ILLUSTRATION A

Today's date

FIELD(TITLE) FIELD(FIRST) FIELD(LAST)
FIELD(ADDRESS)
FIELD(CITY), FIELD(STATE) FIELD(ZIP)

Dear FIELD(TITLE) FIELD(LAST):

Just a brief reminder. FIELD(TITLE) FIELD(LAST), that your account is now past due. As you can see from the enclosed statement, you still have an outstanding balance of $FIELD(AMOUNT). This balance was due on FIELD(DATE).

We need your cooperation so that we can continue to give you the service we have provided you for many years.

Please mail your remittance for $FIELD(AMOUNT) today, so we are not forced to send your account to our collection agency.

Cordially,

Brenda Nadia
Collection Manager

bn/yo
Enclosure

ILLUSTRATION B

FIELDNAMES(TITLE;FIRST;LAST;ADDRESS;CITY;STATE;ZIP)**ENDRECORD**

Ms. **ENDFIELD**
Vanessa**ENDFIELD**
Jackson**ENDFIELD**
48 Endor Avenue**ENDFIELD**
Brooklyn**ENDFIELD**
NY**ENDFIELD**
11221**ENDFIELD**
256.98**ENDFIELD**
March 1**ENDFIELD**
ENDRECORD

Mr. **ENDFIELD**
Kenneth**ENDFIELD**
Hall**ENDFIELD**
5 Windsor Drive**ENDFIELD**
West Long Branch**ENDFIELD**
NJ**ENDFIELD**
07764**ENDFIELD**
450.50**ENDFIELD**
March 15**ENDFIELD**
ENDRECORD

Mr. **ENDFIELD**
Glenn**ENDFIELD**
Babbin**ENDFIELD**
187 Beach 147 Street**ENDFIELD**
Queens**ENDFIELD**
NY**ENDFIELD**
11694**ENDFIELD**
128.86**ENDFIELD**
February 28**ENDFIELD**
ENDRECORD

Ms. **ENDFIELD**
Stefanie**ENDFIELD**
Eaton**ENDFIELD**
137 Brighton Avenue**ENDFIELD**
Perth Amboy**ENDFIELD**
NJ**ENDFIELD**
08861**ENDFIELD**
612.75**ENDFIELD**
February 15**ENDFIELD**
ENDRECORD

Ms. **ENDFIELD**
Shirley**ENDFIELD**
Kee**ENDFIELD**
876 Ocean Parkway**ENDFIELD**
Brooklyn**ENDFIELD**
NY**ENDFIELD**
11244**ENDFIELD**
449.08**ENDFIELD**
April 15**ENDFIELD**
ENDRECORD

EXERCISE

MERGING THE FORM AND DATA FILES WITH CONDITIONS

81

NOTES:

▪ In addition to marking specific data records to merge, you can define **conditions** that data records must meet to be included in the merge. In this exercise, for example, if you wanted to merge letters for only those individuals who owe more than $200, you could direct WordPerfect to select the record only if it meets the condition(s) you define. If you wanted to merge letters for only those individuals who live in New Jersey and owe more than $200, you would set two conditions for your merge.

▪ To define conditions for the merge, select M<u>e</u>rge from the <u>T</u>ools main menu, then select M<u>e</u>rge. After specifying the files to merge in the Perform Merge dialog box, click <u>S</u>elect Records.

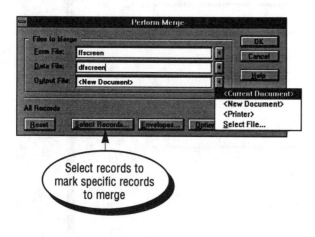

Select records to mark specific records to merge

▪ In the Select Records dialog box which appears, a table displays with four rows which represent conditions, and three columns which represent fields. To select a field in which to enter a condition, click the list button below each field column.

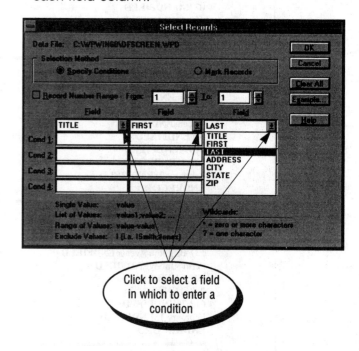

Click to select a field in which to enter a condition

■ A record is selected for merge if it meets any one of the conditions you define the selection criteria, which can include any of the following:

CRITERIA	RECORDS THAT WILL BE SELECTED	EXAMPLES
Single value	All records in which the selected field matches the value.	NJ
List of values	All records in which the selected field matches one of the values.	NJ;NY
Range of values	All data records in which the selected field is within the range of values.	NJ-NY
Excluded values	All records in which the selected field does not match the value.	!NY
Zero or more characters wildcard	All records in which the selected field is a possible match of the wildcard value.	New*
One-character wildcard	All records in which the selected field is a possible match of the wildcard value.	1008?

EXERCISE DIRECTIONS:

In this exercise, you will merge the form and data files you created in previous exercises based on specific criteria.

1. Start with a clear screen.

2. Merge the form file **DUE.FRM** with the data file **DUE.DAT** to a NEW document.

3. Define the following criteria for the merge: Merge and print letters for only those individuals who live in *New Jersey* and owe *more than* $200.

In the STATE field, enter single value NJ; in the AMOUNT field, enter single value >200.

4. Print the full document (one copy of each merged letter).

5. Save the merged letters under a new document name, **DUE.FI**.

6. Close the document window.

MERGE WITH CONDITIONS

1. Click **Tools**............................ Alt + T
2. Click **Merge**.................................. E
3. Click **Merge**.................................. M
4. Click **Form File** text box........ Alt + F
5. Keyboard name of form file.....*form name* or click pop-up arrow, select file.
6. Click **Data File** text box......... Alt + D

7. Keyboard name of data file.......*data name*

OR

   a. Click **Data File** text box..... Alt + D
   b. Click **Select File** .... S
   c. Click desired data file.
   d. Click **OK**................................ Enter

To merge with conditions:

   a. Click **Select Records** .... S
   b. Click **Specify Conditions** .... S
   c. **Press Alt + 1** .... Alt + 1
      to select first field on which to set a condition. (A list from data file will display).
   d. Click Field list arrow and select a field on which you will set a condition. (For this exercise, select STATE).

   e. Keyboard selection criteria. (For this exercise, type NJ).
   f. Press **Tab**................................. Tab
      to select another field on which to set a condition.

      OR

      Press **Alt + 2** .... Alt + 2
      to add another condition to the first field.
   g. Click Field list arrow and select a field on which you will set a condition. (For this exercise, select AMOUNT.)
   h. Keyboard selection criteria. (For this exercise, type >200.)
   i. Repeat steps f-g to select another field to set conditions or to add conditions to a field which has been selected.

8. Click **OK** .... Enter

FORM FILE

Today's date

FIELD(TITLE) FIELD(FIRST) FIELD(LAST)
FIELD(ADDRESS)
FIELD(CITY), FIELD(STATE) FIELD(ZIP)

Dear FIELD(TITLE) FIELD(LAST):

Just a brief reminder, FIELD(TITLE) FIELD(LAST), that your account is now past due. As you can see from the enclosed statement, you still have an outstanding balance of $FIELD(AMOUNT). This Balance was due on FIELD(DATE).

We need your cooperation so that we can continue to give you the service we have provided you for many years.

Please mail your remittance for $FIELD(AMOUNT) today, so we are not forced to send your account to our collection agency.

Cordially,

Brenda Nadia
Collection Manager

bn/yo
Enclosure

DATA FILE

FIELDNAMES(TITLE:FIRST:LAST:ADDRESS:CITY:STATE:ZIP)ENDRECORD
Ms. ENDFIELD
VanessaENDFIELD
JacksonENDFIELD
48 Endor AvenueENDFIELD
BrooklynENDFIELD
NYENDFIELD
11221ENDFIELD
256.98ENDFIELD
March 1ENDFIELD
ENDRECORD

Mr. ENDFIELD
KennethENDFIELD
HallENDFIELD
5 Windsor DriveENDFIELD
West Long BranchENDFIELD
NJENDFIELD
07764ENDFIELD
450.50ENDFIELD
March 15ENDFIELD
ENDRECORD

Mr. ENDFIELD
GlennENDFIELD
BabbinENDFIELD
187 Beach 147 StreetENDFIELD
QueensENDFIELD
NYENDFIELD
11694ENDFIELD
128.86ENDFIELD
February 28ENDFIELD
ENDRECORD

Ms. ENDFIELD
StefanieENDFIELD
EatonENDFIELD
137 Brighton AvenueENDFIELD
Perth AmboyENDFIELD
NJENDFIELD
08861ENDFIELD
612.75ENDFIELD
February 15ENDFIELD
ENDRECORD

Ms. ENDFIELD
ShirleyENDFIELD
KeeENDFIELD
876 Ocean ParkwayENDFIELD
BrooklynENDFIELD
NYENDFIELD
11244ENDFIELD
449.08ENDFIELD
April 15ENDFIELD
ENDRECORD

+

MERGED DOCUMENTS

=

Mr. Kenneth Hall
5 Windsor Drive
West Long Branch,

Dear Mr. Hall:

Just a brief reminde
enclosed statement,
March 15.

We need your coop
for many years.

Please mail your re
collection agency.

bn/yo
Enclosure

Today's date

Ms. Stefanie Eaton
137 Brighton Avenue
Perth Amboy, NJ 08861

Dear Ms. Eaton:

Just a brief reminder, Ms. Eaton, that your account is now past due. As you can see from the enclosed statement, you still have an outstanding balance of $612.75. This balance was due on February 15.

We need your cooperation so that we can continue to give you the service we have provided you for many years.

Please mail your remittance for $612.75 today, so we are not forced to send your account to our collection agency.

Cordially,

Brenda Nadia
Collection Manager

bn/yo
Enclosure

EXERCISE

CREATING AND MERGING FORM AND DATA FILES

82

NOTES:

▪ In the previous exercises, you divided each individual's name into three fields: TITLE, FIRST and LAST. You could have, however, used one field name (NAME) to represent an entire individual's name. It is only necessary to break down a field if you intend to selectively merge the documents on that field. In the previous exercises, for example, if you break down the name field into three fields, you can then selectively merge letters addressed by gender or title (doctors).

 Keep the number of fields used in the form file consistent with the number of fields used in the data file.

▪ In the exercise on the right, there are nine different field names in the form file. While the address field contains one line in some records and two lines in others (some contain a company name), there are, nonetheless, nine

ENDFIELD notations for each record in the data file. (Fields can be one or several lines.) To add a second line to a field in the Quick Data Entry dialog box, press Ctrl + Enter.

 It is important that you click Clear All in the Select Records dialog box so that previous settings will not interfere with the new merge.

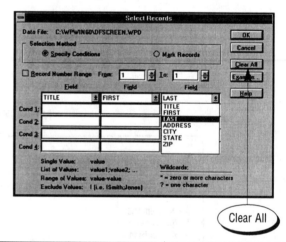

Clear All

EXERCISE DIRECTIONS:

 In this exercise, you will create and merge the form and data files based on specific conditions.

1. Start with a clear screen.

2. Create the form file as shown in illustration A on the right, using a 12 point font.

3. Use the default margins.

4. Begin the exercise on Ln 2.5".

5. Spell check.

6. Save the file; name it **BUY.FRM**.

7. Begin a NEW document.

8. Create the data file from the records shown in illustration B on the right.

9. Use the default margins.

10. Begin the exercise on Ln 1".

11. Save the file; name it **BUY.DAT**.

12. Begin a NEW document.

13. Merge the form file with the data file to a NEW document.

14. Define the following criteria for your merge:

   • Merge and print letters for companies located in *Texas* and *California* (TX;CA).

15. Print the full document (one copy of each merged letter).

16. Save the merged letters under a new document name: **BUY.FI**.

17. Close the document window.

ILLUSTRATION A

↓ .25"

Today's date

FIELD(NAME)
FIELD(ADDRESS)
FIELD(CITY), FIELD(STATE) FIELD(ZIP)

Dear FIELD(TINAME):

We received your order for FIELD(QUAN) FIELD(SOFTPKG) software packages. We will process it immediately. To expedite the order, we are arranging to have the software shipped directly from our warehouse in FIELD(CITY).

The cost of the software packages totals $FIELD(AMOUNT). We would appreciate payment as soon as you receive your order.

Thank you, FIELD(TINAME), for your confidence in our company. I know you will be satisfied.

Sincerely,

Yolanda Reeves
Sales Manager

yr/yo

ILLUSTRATION B

FIELDNAMES(NAME;ADDRESS;CITY;STATE;ZIP;TINAME;QUAN;SOFTPKG;AMOUNT)
ENDRECORD

Mr. Jason Lochner**ENDFIELD**
Computerland Associates
65 Linden Boulevard**ENDFIELD**
Houston**ENDFIELD**
TX**ENDFIELD**
77069**ENDFIELD**
Mr. Lochner**ENDFIELD**
two**ENDFIELD**
Microsoft Office**ENDFIELD**
810.76**ENDFIELD**
ENDRECORD

Ms. Rose Zaffarano**ENDFIELD**
Richmond Tile Company
645 Hammond Drive**ENDFIELD**
Los Angeles**ENDFIELD**
CA**ENDFIELD**
90210**ENDFIELD**
Ms. Zaffarano**ENDFIELD**
three**ENDFIELD**
Excel**ENDFIELD**
1,221.98**ENDFIELD**
ENDRECORD

Ms. Valerie Vetri**ENDFIELD**
70 Klondike Avenue**ENDFIELD**
Cleveland**ENDFIELD**
OH**ENDFIELD**
44199**ENDFIELD**
Ms. Vetri**ENDFIELD**
four**ENDFIELD**
Pagemaker**ENDFIELD**
235.85**ENDFIELD**
ENDRECORD

Mr. Deepa Lakani**ENDFIELD**
Knoll Stationery Supplies
87 Rockhill Road**ENDFIELD**
San Diego**ENDFIELD**
CA**ENDFIELD**
88912**ENDFIELD**
Mr. Lakhani**ENDFIELD**
two**ENDFIELD**
WordPerfect 6.1 for Windows**ENDFIELD**
512.34**ENDFIELD**
ENDRECORD

Ms. Diane Nordquist**ENDFIELD**
43-98 Sela Drive**ENDFIELD**
Dallas**ENDFIELD**
TX**ENDFIELD**
76767**ENDFIELD**
Ms. Nordquist**ENDFIELD**
two**ENDFIELD**
Microsoft Word**ENDFIELD**
555.87**ENDFIELD**
ENDRECORD

EXERCISE

- CREATING AND MERGING FORM AND DATA FILES
- PREPARING ENVELOPES WHILE MERGING

NOTES:

- WordPerfect makes it possible for you to create envelopes while merging a letter or other form file. *(Creating envelopes and labels independent of a merge, and with Templates, will be covered in Lesson 12.)*

- After specifying the form file and data filenames to merge in the Perform Merge dialog box, click Envelopes.

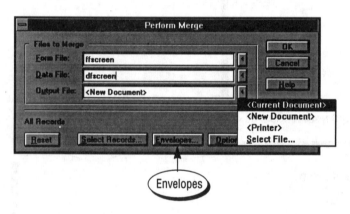

- In the Envelope dialog box which appears, specify the envelope size you require in the Envelope Definitions text box, or select one from the drop-down list. If the envelope size you want is not listed, you can create one. However, the range of envelope definitions you can create depends on the capabilities of your printer.

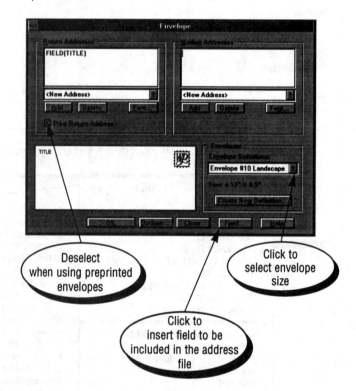

- You must then enter the fields in the Mailing Addresses window that will be needed for the envelopes. That is, include only the fields used in the inside address. Click Field and highlight field to be inserted, then select Insert.

- You may also include a return address (your address) by keyboarding it in the Return Addresses window. However, since most companies use a preprinted return address, this feature would be used mostly for personal correspondence.

- To prepare envelopes for the records in this exercise, use NAME, ADDRESS, CITY, ST and ZIP as your inside address fields.

- The merged envelopes follow the last merged letter. After your letters have printed, be sure your printer is loaded with the necessary envelopes.

EXERCISE DIRECTIONS:

1. Start with a clear screen.

2. Create the form letter file as shown in illustration A on the right, using a serif 12 point font.

3. Use the default margins.

4. Begin the exercise on Ln 2.5".

5. Spell check.

6. Save the file; name it **SHOW.FRM**.

7. Begin a NEW file.

8. Create the data file from the records shown in illustration B on the right.

9. Use the default margins.

10. Begin the exercise on Ln 1".

11. Save the file; name it **SHOW.DAT**.

12. Merge the form file with the data file to a NEW document.

13. Prepare an envelope for each letter in the merge. (Deselect Print Return Address.)

14. Print the full document (one copy of each merged letter).

15. Save the merged letters (and envelope text) under a new document name, **SHOW.FI**.

16. Close the document window.

CREATE ENVELOPES WHILE MERGING

1. Click **Tools** .... Alt + T

2. Click **Merge** .... E

3. Click **Merge** .... M

4. Enter name of **Form File**.

5. Enter name of **Data File**.

6. Set output file as <New Document>.

7. Click **Envelopes** .... Alt + E

   The Envelope dialog box appears.

8. Select an envelope size from Envelope Definitions (use your printer's default).

9. Click **Mailing Address** .... Alt + M
   text box.

10. Click **Field** .... Alt + I
    Data file's Field Name
    list appears.

11. Select first field name needed for address.

12. Click **Insert** .... Alt + I

13. Repeat steps 9-11 for each field of mailing address.

14. Set desired Return Address criteria:

    • For no Return Address,
      deselect **Print Return Address**.

• To include Return Address,
  select **Print Return Address**,

AND

• Keyboard desired address in **Return Addresses** text box.

15. Click **OK** .... Enter
    to return to **Perform Merge** box.

16. Click **OK** .... Enter
    to perform merge.

ILLUSTRATION A

↓ 2.5"

Today's date

FIELD(NAME)
FIELD(ADDRESS)
FIELD(CITY), FIELD(STATE) FIELD(ZIP)

Dear FIELD(TILAST):

As a preferred client of Taks Department Store, we are extending this invitation to you for our spring fashion show. The evening of FIELD(DATE) at FIELD(TIME) has been reserved for this private showing of our spring fashions.

We are confident that you will find our spring collection refreshing and exciting.

Please join us for refreshments after the show where you can meet many of the designers. We look forward to seeing you on FIELD(DATE).

Sincerely,

Amanda Desmond
Collections Department

ad/yo

ILLUSTRATION B

FIELDNAMES(NAME;ADDRESS;CITY;STATE;ZIP;TILAST;DATE;TIME)ENDRECORD

Ms. Claude Montane**ENDFIELD**
456 Winding Woods Way
Manalapan**ENDFIELD**
NJ**ENDFIELD**
07609**ENDFIELD**
Ms. Montane**ENDFIELD**
January 16**ENDFIELD**
6:30 p.m.**ENDFIELD**
ENDRECORD

Ms. Maria Vasquez**ENDFIELD**
1111 Chiffon Avenue
Woodbridge**ENDFIELD**
NJ**ENDFIELD**
00723**ENDFIELD**
Ms. Vasquez**ENDFIELD**
January 20**ENDFIELD**
8:30 p.m.**ENDFIELD**
ENDRECORD

Ms. Gladys Graff**ENDFIELD**
23 East 60 Street
New York**ENDFIELD**
NY**ENDFIELD**
10021**ENDFIELD**
Ms. Graff**ENDFIELD**
January 21**ENDFIELD**
8:30 p.m.**ENDFIELD**
ENDRECORD

Ms. Harriet Feiwell**ENDFIELD**
Ragtime Sportswear, Inc.
1248 Seventh Avenue**ENDFIELD**
New York**ENDFIELD**
NY**ENDFIELD**
10045**ENDFIELD**
Ms. Feiwell**ENDFIELD**
January 22**ENDFIELD**
8:30 p.m.**ENDFIELD**
ENDRECORD

EXERCISE

MERGING A FORM FILE WITH A DATA TABLE

84

NOTES:

- In this exercise, you will create a form file from the letter illustrated on page 305. However, the data file will be created using a table format (learned in Lesson 9) rather than a text format (used in previous exercises).

- A table organizes information into columns and rows. In a **data table** used with a merge, the columns represent **fields** and the rows represent **records**.

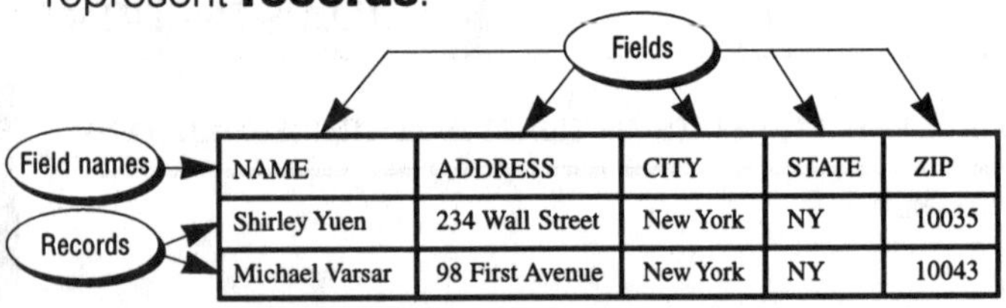

(Diagram showing a table with "Fields" pointing to the columns, "Field names" pointing to the header row, and "Records" pointing to the data rows)

NAME	ADDRESS	CITY	STATE	ZIP
Shirley Yuen	234 Wall Street	New York	NY	10035
Michael Varsar	98 First Avenue	New York	NY	10043

- To create a Data Table File, select Merge from the Tools main menu, then click Place Records in a Table check box, and click Data.

- After entering the actual data in the Quick Data Entry dialog box, WordPerfect places your data in a table.

- Note the illustration B, on the right, of data entered in a data table. Remember, each *column* is a **field** and each *row* is a **record**.

- WordPerfect divides the cell space across a page based on the number of fields to be used. When data is entered into the cells, it may break in awkward places *(see illustration)* since space is limited across the 8.5" x 11" page. However, the lines will print correctly in the merged document.

- When you enter a two-line address in the Quick Data Entry dialog box, press Ctrl + Enter to indicate the start of a new line.

- Remember, as you move to each column, the status line indicates the cell position: A1, B1, etc.

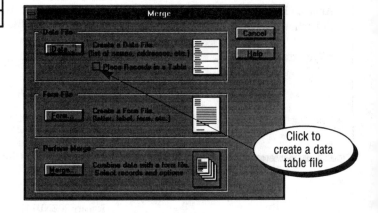

Click to create a data table file

EXERCISE DIRECTIONS:

1. Start with a clear screen.
2. Create the form file from the letter shown in Illustration A on the right.
3. Use the default margins.
4. Begin the exercise on Ln 2.5".
5. Spell check.
6. Save the file; name it **MISTAKE.FRM**.
7. Begin a NEW document.
8. Create a data table file using the following information:

```
Mr. Harold Dembo
Holistic, Inc.
654 Sanborn Street
Denver, CO 80202
8768
654.85
682.75
```

```
Ms. Jennifer Downing
7659 Utica Avenue
San Antonio, TX 78202
6543
76.99
109.10
```

```
Mr. Daniel Davis
Acme Plumbing Supply
90 Plaza Z
Milwaukee, WI 53212
7888
333.33
386.86
```

NOTE: After entering your data, your table should look like illustration B on the right.

9. Save the file; name it **MISTAKE.DAT**.
10. Merge the form file with the data table file to a NEW document.
11. Print the full document (one copy of each merged letter).
12. Saved the merged letters under a new document name, **MISTAKE.FI**.
13. Close the document window.

ILLUSTRATION A

 2.5"

Today's date

FIELD(TITLE) FIELD(FIRST) FIELD(LAST)
FIELD(ADDRESS)
FIELD(CITY), FIELD(ST) FIELD(ZIP)

Dear FIELD(TITLE) FIELD(LAST):

Thank you for your check No. FIELD(CKNO), in the amount of $FIELD(AMT). We notice that you erroneously deducted a discount, even though the discount period has expired.

We know this is an oversight. We are returning your check No. FIELD(CKNO), and we would appreciate your sending us another check for $FIELD(NWAMT) to cover the correct amount.

Thank you for your attention to this matter.

Sincerely,

Arnold Zahn
Credit Manager

az/yo

TITLE	FIRST	LAST	ADDRESS	CITY	ST	ZIP	CKNO	AMT	NWAMT
Mr.	Harold	Dembo	Holistic, Inc. 654 Sanborn Street	Denver	CO	80202	8768	654.85	682.75
Ms.	Jennifer	Downing	7659 Utica Avenue	San Antonio	TX	78202	6543	76.99	109.10
Mr.	Daniel	Davis	Acme Plumbing Supply 90 Plaza Z	Milwaukee	WI	53212	7888	333.33	386.86

CREATE DATA TABLE FILE

1. Click **T**ools.................... `Alt` + `T`
2. Click **M**erge.. `E`
3. Click **P**lace Records in a Table .... `P`
4. Click **D**ata... `D`
5. Keyboard first field name, press **Enter**.
6. Repeat step 4 for each field name.
7. Click **OK**. .... `↵`

NOTE: Table appears at top of screen with field names in top row.

8. At Quick Data Entry form, keyboard data. When finished, click **Close**.

OR

Click **C**lose .... `Alt` + `C`

9. Follow steps below to enter data directly into table.

To enter data directly into table:

1. Keyboard data for first field beginning with cell A1.

NOTE: Text may break awkwardly. Use Enter key only when you intend to begin a new line.

2. Press **Tab**...................................... `Tab` to move to next cell.

3. Keyboard data for each remaining field to complete the first row (record).

4. At end of last row, press **Tab** .... `Tab` to insert a new row.

5. Repeat steps 1-4 for each new record.

6. Save file as usual.

EXERCISE DIRECTIONS:

1. Create a form file and a data file from the information below.

2. Format the form file using any letter style. Use a serif 12 point font.

3. Create the data file using either a text or table file format.

   NOTE: The data file shown below was formatted as a data table file.

4. Name the form file, **TRAVEL.FRM**; name the data file, **TRAVEL.DAT**.

5. Merge the form and data files to a NEW document.

6. Save the merged letters under a new document name, **TRAVEL.FI**.

7. Prepare envelopes.

8. Print one copy of the merged file and the envelopes.

9. Close the document window.

FORM FILE

Today's date¶FIELD(NAME)
FIELD(ADDRESS)
FIELD(CITY)
FIELD(ST)
FIELD(ZIP)¶Dear Traveler:¶Thank you for your inquiry about a cruise to FIELD(PORT). We
are enclosing a brochure on FIELD(TITLE) which might be of interest to you if you should
decide to sail to FIELD(PORT). There are two sailings scheduled during the FIELD(SEASON):
FIELD(MONTH1) and FIELD(MONTH2). ¶If you would like more information about a vacation
of a lifetime, call FIELD(REP), who is one of the representatives in our office who will be
delighted to help you. ¶Sincerely,
Susan Crawford
Travel Administrator
sc/yo
Enclosure

DATA FILE

NAME	ADDRESS	CITY	ST	ZIP	PORT	TITLE	SEASON	MONTH1	MONTH2	REP
Ms. Beverly Oberlin	65 Court Street	Bangor	ME	04141	Spain	*Hidden Treasures*	spring	March 27	April 15	Sarah
Mr. Wayne Viscosa	ABC, Incorporated 690 Elbow Drive	Fairfax	VA	23808	Bahamas	*Carribbean Coral*	summer	June 29	April 1	Patrick
Ms. Edna Hamil	76 Rider Avenue	Redbank	NJ	07728	St. Martin	*Breathtaking Voyages*	winter	January 15	March 1	Michael

EXERCISE DIRECTIONS:

1. Create a form file and a data file from the information below.

2. Format the form file using any letter style. Use a serif 12 point font.

3. Create the data file using either a text or table file format. Use the following field names in your form and data files:

   TITLE, FIRST, LAST, ADDRESS, CITY, ST, ZIP, DATE, ITEM, COMPANY

4. Name the form file, **STOCK.FRM**; name the data file, **STOCK.DAT**.

5. Merge the form and data files to a NEW document.

6. Define the following criteria for your merge:

   Merge and print only those letters to individuals who should have received the *Model III Work Kit* and who live in *Ohio*.

7. Save the merged letters under a new document name, **STOCK.FI**.

8. Print one copy of the merged file.

9. Close the document window.

FORM FILE

```
Today's date¶Thank you for your order dated _____. ¶There are several items
on your order that we do not presently have in stock.  This includes the
_____. ¶We are arranging to have these items shipped directly to you from the
_____ in Los Angeles.¶There will be no additional delivery charges from Los
Angeles.  We will absorb the additional costs incurred.  Once again, thank
you  for your order.¶Sincerely,  John Bo Hingh  Customer Service  jbh/yo
```

DATA FILE

Mr. James G. McBride
Valley Home Furnishings
23 Home Street
Dayton, OH 45416

January 20

Model III Work Kit

Bell Company
=======================

Mr. Elliot Beverly
Beverly, Rudick and Shane, Inc.
23 Sunset Boulevard`
Los Angeles, CA 90052

June 1

Do-It-Yourself Rug

Bell Company
=======================

Mr. Jose Torres
23 Meeker Street
Ann Arbor, MI 48109

July 10

Leather Kit

P & P Industries, Inc.
=======================

Ms. Gloria Porter
3635 Boyle Avenue
Akron, OH 44315

February 2

Model III Work Kit

ABC Manufacturing Company
=======================

Ms. Ronnie Giordano, President
Coop Industries
345 West 49 Street
Cincinnati, OH 45227

July 5

Model III Work Kit

Bell Company

LESSON 12

Exercises 85-101

- Creating a Graphics Image Box
- Creating and Rotating a Text Box
- Dragging to Create a Graphics Box
- Editing a Graphics Box
- Combining a Graphics Box with Text
- Changing the Image Box Contents
- Borders and Fills
- Text Wrap Options
- Captions
- Sizing, Positioning, Scaling, Rotating and Flipping a Graphics Image
- Watermarks
- Creating and Editing Horizontal and Vertical Graphics Lines
- Paragraph and Page Borders and Fills
- Drop Caps
- Reversing Text
- TextArt
- Creating a Newsletter

EXERCISE

CREATING A GRAPHICS IMAGE

85

NOTES:

- **Graphics** are design elements, such as pictures (art), charts, and lines, used to make a visual statement. The ability to combine graphics and text enables you to create documents such as letterheads, newsletters, brochures and flyers in which pictures contribute to the effectiveness of the message.

- WordPerfect places each graphic image in a "box" without a border, which is referred to as a **graphics image box**. A graphics box can contain an image, text or an equation. *(Text boxes will be covered in Exercise 86. Equations will not be covered in this text).* Note the two graphic boxes below:

GRAPHICS IMAGE

TEXT BOX

This is an example of a text box.

- The graphics image box is commonly used to place images, diagrams, or charts. By default, an image displays without a border. You can resize and reposition the figure within your document, add or change a border, and even edit the figure itself.

- WordPerfect provides a selection of graphic image files which are often referred to as **clip art**. These files include not only pictures, but also borders and watermarks (watermarks will be covered in Exercise 95).

- By default, these files are saved in the c:\office\wpwin\template\graphics directory. WordPerfect graphics are named with a .wpg extension.

- The clip art images that are part of the WordPerfect program are illustrated in Appendix A. You can, however, purchase disks with other graphics and import them into your document.

- Graphics may be accessed by selecting Image from the Graphics main menu. You select the desired graphic file from the Insert Image dialog box. You may use the View feature to preview a graphic before selecting it.

Click to view selected graphic

Insert Image		
Filename:	c:\..\wpwin\template\graphics	OK
bord02p.wpg	QuickList:	Cancel
approved.wpg	c:\	View...
asap.wpg	c:\lngwp61	
bord01l.wpg	c:\trainbk	QuickFinder..
bord01p.wpg	c:\win6bk\wpdocs	
bord02l.wpg	c:\win6sol	File Options ▾
bord02p.wpg	Documents	QuickList ▾
bord03l.wpg	Directories:	
bord03p.wpg	c:\	Setup...
bord04l.wpg	office	
bord04p.wpg	wpwin	Help
bord05l.wpg	template	
bord05p.wpg	graphics	
bord06l.wpg		
bord06p.wpg		
Total Files: 81	Drives: 214,448 KB Free	
Total Bytes: 477,579	c:	
Sort: Filename Ascending		
List Files of Type: All Files (*.*)		
11/4/94, 6:10AM, 1,818 bytes	☐ Image on Disk	

- When a graphic is first imported, it displays with **sizing handles**. The Graphics Feature bar also appears, giving you access to the most commonly used graphics features. A Graphics Toolbar is also available which contains specialized buttons to automate many graphics features and options. *(See Lesson 14.)*

- When the graphics figure first appears, it is aligned at the left margin and presized by WordPerfect. *(Note exercise illustration.)* The default size of a graphic varies, depending on the graphic selected.

- You can reduce, enlarge, stretch, move or delete the graphic when the sizing handles are displayed. The sizing handles indicate that the graphic is selected and is in an Edit mode. You will learn to edit a graphic in the next exercise.

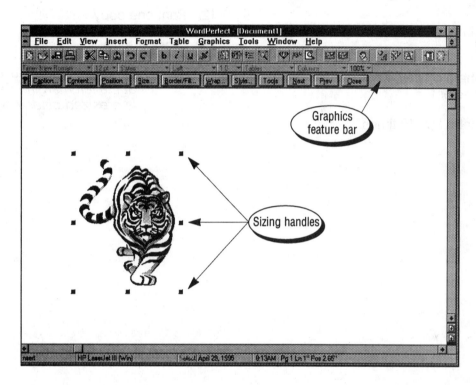

EXERCISE DIRECTIONS:

 In this exercise, you will create three graphics using the default position and size.

1. Start with a clear screen.

2. With the insertion point at the top of your screen, select CREST.WPG. Do not import it.

3. Click View to preview the image before importing it.

4. Import the image. (Double-click the graphic file.)

5. Click anywhere off the image to deselect it (remove handles).

6. Press the Enter key 10 times.

7. Import HOTAIR.WPG. (Double-click filename.)

8. Click anywhere off the image to deselect it.

9. Press the Enter key 12 times.

10. Import DRAGN.WPG.

11. Save the file; name it **IMAGES**.

12. Print one copy.

13. Close the file.

NOTE: Graphics are defaulted to align at the left margin. Each image is presized differently.

IMPORT A GRAPHIC
F11

1. Click **Image** button on Toolbar ....

   OR

   a. Click **Graphics** .... `Alt` + `G`

   b. Click **Image** .... `M`

2. Double-click desired graphic file.

NOTE: Click **View** .... `Alt` + `W`
to preview image.

3. Click **OK** .... `Enter`

EXERCISE

86

▪ CREATING A TEXT BOX ▪ ROTATING A TEXT BOX ▪ GRAPHICS FEATURE BAR

NOTES:

- The **Text Box** is typically used for setting off special text such as tables, charts, sidebars and callouts.

- WordPerfect automatically applies a thick top and bottom border to the text box.

> THIS IS A TEXT BOX. DEFAULT BORDER OPTIONS ARE "THICK" FOR TOP AND BOTTOM AND NONE FOR THE SIDES.

- To create a text box, select Text Box from the Graphics main menu. When the text box first appears, it is aligned at the right margin and presized by WordPerfect. *(Note exercise on the next page).*

- You can resize and reposition the text box within your document, and you can edit the text within the box. The Graphics Feature bar enables you to specify position, size, and wrap options for your text box as you would for an image box. You may also size and move the box on screen with the mouse.

- The text box may be rotated counterclockwise in 90-degree increments by selecting Content on the Graphics Feature Bar.

You may also want to set the size of the box to Size to Content. Sizing text to the content will size the box to the length of the text (providing that the text is not longer than the margins). To do this, select Size on the Graphics Feature Bar and Size to Content in the Box Size dialog box.

NOTE: In this and subsequent exercises, you will be directed to begin text at a particular vertical location on the page. Use the Advance feature to accomplish this. The Advance feature is used to place text at an absolute position on a page or at a position relative to the current insertion point position. For these exercises, set advance measurements from the Top of Page. Note keystrokes below.

This box is rotated 90 degrees.

CREATE A TEXT BOX
Alt+F11

1. Place insertion point where you want text box.

2. Click **Graphics**.................... `Alt` + `G`

3. Click **Text Box** .... `T`

   A text box appears with active insertion point.

4. Type text into box.

   Adjust box position, size and caption as you would an image box, if desired.

5. Click **Close** .... `C`

ROTATE TEXT BOX

1. Select text box to rotate.

OR

a. Click **Graphics**. .... `Alt` + `G`

b. Click **Edit Box** .... `E`

2. Click **Size**. .... `Alt` + `Shift` + `S`

3. Click **Width: Size to Content**............ `I`

4. Click **Height: Size to Content**........... `Z`

5. Click **OK** .... `Enter`

6. Click **Content** ...... `Alt` + `Shift` + `O`

7. Select desired degree of rotation:

   • **No Rotation** .... `N`

   • **90 Degrees**................................. `9`

   • **180 Degrees**................................ `1`

   • **270 Degrees**................................ `2`

8. Click **OK**................................. `Enter`

9. Click **Close**............. `Alt` + `Shift` + `C`

ADVANCE

   NOTE: You cannot advance text past a page break onto another page.

1. Click **Format**........................ `Alt` + `R`

2. Click **Typesetting** .... `T`

3. Click **Advance** .... `A`

4. Select a Horizontal or Vertical advance position.

5. Click horizontal or vertical text box.

6. Type desired distance.

7. Click **OK** .... `Enter`

EXERCISE DIRECTIONS:

 In this exercise, you will create four text boxes, two of which are rotated.

1. Start with a clear screen.

2. Use the default margins.

3. With your insertion point at the top of the screen, create the first text box and type the text as shown. Use a serif 14 point font. Do not click off handles.

4. Size the box to content. (Click <u>S</u>ize, Size to Content for Width and Height options.)

5. Rotate the box 90 degrees.

6. Use the Advance feature to bring the insertion point to Ln 4.15" (from top of page).

7. Create the second text box and type the text as shown in serif 12 point.

8. Use the Advance feature to bring the insertion point to Ln 6.11" (from top of page).

9. Create the third text box and type the text as shown in serif 12 point. Do not click off handles.

10. Size the box to content.

11. Rotate the box 180 degrees.

12. Use the Advance feature to bring the insertion point to Ln 7.29" (from top of page).

13. Create the fourth text box. Do not click off handles. Size the box to content.

14. Rotate the box 270 degrees.

15. Print one copy.

16. Save the file; name it **TEXTBOX**.

17. Close the document window.

90-degree rotated text box

This text box will contain entered text. You can change the font size and size while you are entering the text, or you can edit the box later and make the changes to the text at that time.

180-degree rotated text

270-degree rotated text

EXERCISE

87

▪ DRAGGING TO CREATE A GRAPHICS BOX ▪ EDITING A GRAPHICS BOX

NOTES:

▪ When a graphics box is created, it appears with sizing handles. (To remove the sizing handles, click anywhere off the graphic.) The box is aligned at the left margin and presized by WordPerfect.

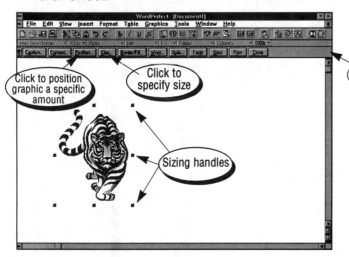

Selecting a Graphics Box

▪ The sizing handles must be displayed to edit the image or text box; that is, to delete or copy it, or to change its size or position.

▪ Displaying the handles on a graphics box is referred to as *selecting* it.

Drag to Create

▪ The **Drag to Create** option on the Graphics main menu allows you to draw the graphics box directly on your document before you select and insert the image, thus giving you control over the graphic's size and location.

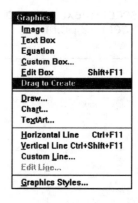

▪ When Drag to Create is selected and you select Image from the Graphics main menu, a special pointer appears 🔲. Position the pointer where you want the upper left corner of the box to begin and drag diagonally to the desired position for the lower right corner of the box. Then, release the mouse button. The Insert Image dialog box automatically appears for you to select the image you want inserted into the box.

▪ Once activated, Drag to Create remains selected until you deselect it. To deselect this feature, select Drag to Create from the Graphics main menu.

Sizing a Graphics Box

■ **To size a graphics box** using the mouse, point to one of the sizing handles. When the pointer becomes a double-headed arrow ↔, drag the side or corner of the box to the desired size. Or, you may click the Size button on the Feature bar and specify the size of the box in the Box Size dialog box. `

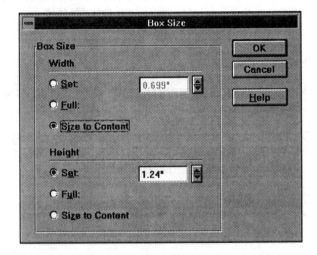

Positioning (Moving) a Graphics Box

■ **To position a graphics box** using the mouse, point, click and hold down the mouse button within the selected box. When the pointer becomes a four-headed arrow ✛, drag the box to the desired location. Or, you may click the Position button on the Feature bar and specify the desired horizontal or vertical position in the Box Position dialog box.

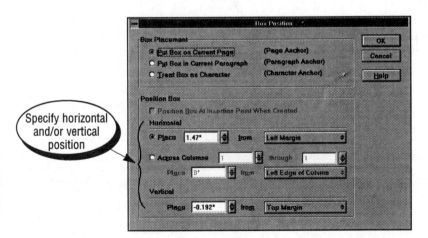

Specify horizontal and/or vertical position

Deleting a Graphics Box

■ **To delete a graphics box**, select the box (so the sizing handles appear) and press the Delete key.

Copying a Graphics Box

■ **To copy a graphics box**, select the box, and select Copy from the Edit main menu. Position the insertion point where the copied box should appear. Then, select Paste from the Edit main menu. Use this feature when you wish to make an exact duplicate of the box size and content.

EXERCISE DIRECTIONS:

 In this exercise, you will create several figure boxes and one text box. You will then align them left, right and center. You will also size, move, delete and copy them using both the mouse and the dialog boxes to do so.

To create Illustration A:

1. Start with a clear screen. The insertion point should be in the upper left corner.

2. Select the Drag to Create feature.

    NOTE: A check mark appears to the left of Drag to Create once it has been selected. Therefore, the next time you select Graphics, you will see the check mark next to Drag to Create on the pull down menu. It will remain selected until you deselect it.

3. Drag to create a graphics box and insert the image CRANE_J.WPG. Position the box horizontally 4.5" from the left edge of the page and vertically 1" from the top of the page. Size it to 1.5" wide by 1.25" high.

4. Drag to create a second graphics box and insert the image DRAGN.WPG. Position the box horizontally 2" from the left edge of the page and vertically 3" from the top of the page. Size it to 2.5" wide by 1.25" high.

5. Drag to create a third graphics box and insert the WINDMILL.WPG. Position the box horizontally 1" from the left edge of the page and vertically 5" from the top of the page. Size it to 6.5" wide by 2.25" high.

6. Create a text box below the windmill, and drag it to the width of the windmill. Enter the text as shown. Position the box horizontally 0" from the center of the paragraph and vertically 7.25" from the top of the paragraph. Size the width and height to the content.

7. Save the exercise; name it **PICTURE**. Do not close the document.

To create Illustration B:

8. Select the first graphics box (the crane) and delete it.

9. Select the third graphics box (the windmill). Using the mouse, stretch it downward so it ends just above the text box.

10. Select the second graphics box (the dragon). Move the box to the right of the windmill blades, as illustrated.

11. Select the text box. Copy it once (the copy will be directly on top of the original). Position the new text box horizontally 0" from the center of the paragraph and vertically 1.5" from the top of the paragraph.

12. Preview your document.

13. Print one copy.

14. Close the file; save the changes.

ILLUSTRATION A

The scene you see on this page is a look into someone's imagination!

ILLUSTRATION B

The scene you see on this page is a look into someone's imagination!

The scene you see on this page is a look into someone's imagination!

DRAG TO CREATE

1. Click **Graphics** .... `Alt` + `G`
2. Click **Drag to Create** .... `O`
3. Click **Graphics** .... `Alt` + `G`

   NOTE: You will see a check next to Drag to Create which means the feature is selected.

4. Click **Image** .... `M`

DESELECT DRAG TO CREATE

1. Click **Graphics** .... `Alt` + `G`
2. Click **Drag to Create** .... `O`

SELECT A GRAPHICS BOX
Shift+F11

- Click graphic.

   OR

- Click **Graphics** .... `Alt` + `G`
- Click **Edit Box** .... `E`

DELETE A GRAPHICS BOX

1. Select graphic to delete.
2. Press **Delete** key .... `Del`

POSITION A GRAPHICS BOX

- Select graphic and drag to desired position using the mouse.

OR

1. Select the graphic .... `Shift` + `F11`
2. Click Position on Graphic Feature bar.

   OR

- Click right mouse button.

- Choose **Position** .... `P`

To position horizontally:

a. Click **Horizontal Place** .... `Alt` + `L`
   text box.

b. Type desired horizontal measurement.

c. Click list box and select from where graphic placement should be measured:

- **Left Edge of Page** .... `L`
- **Left Margin** .... `M`
- **Right Margin** .... `R`
- **Center of Paragraph** .... `C`

To position vertically:

a. Click **Vertical Place** .... `Alt` + `A`
   text box.

b. Type desired vertical measurement.

3. Click **OK** .... `Enter`

SIZE A GRAPHICS BOX

1. Select the graphic.
2. Drag the sizing handle to desired box size.

OR

- Select the graphic.
- Click **Size** on Graphics Feature bar .. `S`

OR

- Click right mouse button.

- Choose **Size** .... `S`

To set height and width:

a. Click **Set Width** .... `Alt` + `S`
   text box.

b. Type desired width.

c. Click **Set Height** text box... `Alt` + `E`

d. Type desired height.

To have graphic fill page:

- Click **Full** for . `Alt` + `F`, `Alt` + `U`
  Width and
  Height

   To have WordPerfect determine optimum width and height:

- Click **Size** to .. `Alt` + `I`, `Alt` + `Z`
  Content for
  Width and **Height**

3. Click **OK** .... `Enter`

COPY A GRAPHICS BOX
Ctrl + C, Ctrl + V

1. Select the graphic.
2. Click **Edit** .... `Alt` + `E`
3. Click **Copy** .... `C`
4. Click at location on page where copied graphic should appear.
5. Click **Edit** .... `Alt` + `E`
6. Click **Paste** .... `P`

Next Exercise

EXERCISE

COMBINING A GRAPHICS BOX WITH TEXT (ANCHOR TYPES)

NOTES:

Change Graphics Box Position (Anchor Type)

▪ When a graphics box is combined with text, you must specify the way you want the graphic box to be anchored to the text. This option may be accessed by clicking the Position button on the Graphics Feature bar.

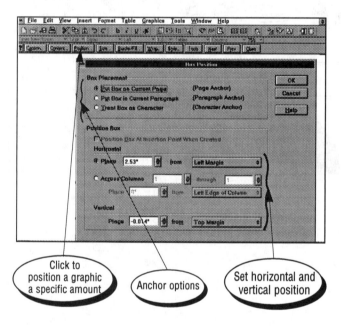

Click to position a graphic a specific amount

Anchor options

Set horizontal and vertical position

▪ In the Box Position dialog box which follows, you have three anchor options:

Put Box on Current Page *(Page Anchor)* permits the graphics box to be positioned at a fixed location on the page. The graphics box will remain in that position regardless of any changes made to the document. The graphics box can be horizontally positioned in relation to the margins, in the center of the paragraph, or the left edge of the paper. Graphic boxes can be vertically positioned at the top of page, top, bottom, or center of margins. *(Note the illustration below.)*

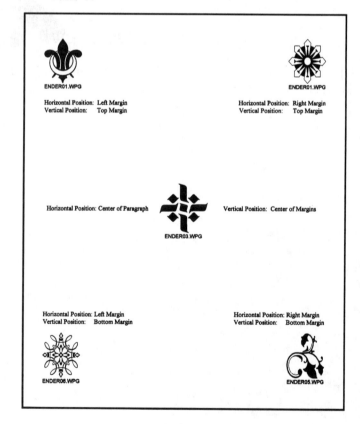

Put Box in Current Paragraph *(Paragraph Anchor)* permits the graphics box to stay with the paragraph preceding it. Then, if you add/delete material from the document or move the paragraph, the graphics box will move, too. This is the default. The box can be placed down from the top of the paragraph by specifying the desired amount of inches in the Vertical Place text box. The horizontal position is used to place the box at the left edge of the page, at the left or right margin, or in the center of a paragraph. *(Note illustration below.)*

This paragraph anchor illustration has graphics boxes placed in two locations. The image on the left is positioned at the left margin horizontally and 0.1" from the top of the paragraph vertically. The image on the right is positioned at the right margin horizontally and 0.75" from the top of the paragraph vertically. The paragraph text is full justified.

Treat Box as Character *(Character Anchor)* permits graphics boxes to stay with a character on a line. The box will move right and wrap if necessary as new text is added before the box. Since the character anchor box is automatically placed after the character to its left (at the location of the insertion point when created), the horizontal position is not used. However, the vertical position (Box Position) option allows you to align the top center or bottom of the box with the line of text the box is on. Baseline is an imaginary line upon which characters sit. The baseline option is used to align the last line of text in a box, with the baseline of the line the box is on. *(Note illustration below.)*

This vertical position is top.

This vertical position is centered.

This vertical position is bottom.

This vertical position is content baseline.

EXERCISE DIRECTIONS:

 In this exercise, you will create a letterhead using the Paragraph Anchor options to position the graphics box.

1. Start with a clear screen.

2. Use the default margins.

3. With your insertion point at the top of the screen, import WORLD.WPG.

4. Size the width of the graphic to 1.75".

5. Use the default anchor type. Horizontally place the graphic -0.205" from the Center of Paragraph; vertically place the graphic 0" from the Top of Page.

6. Type the company name in sans serif 14 point bold (use Century Gothic typeface, if available) beginning approximately on Ln 1.39". Use All justification.

7. Right-align the company name and address. Set the font to sans serif 10 point (use Arial typeface, if available).

8. Left-align the phone, fax and internet numbers. Set the font to sans serif (use same font as name and address) 10 point italics.

9. Preview your work.

10. Print one copy.

11. Save the file; name it **GLOBELET**.

ANCHOR AND POSITION A GRAPHIC

1. Select the graphic.............. Shift + F11

2. Click **Position** button Alt + Shift + P on Graphics Feature bar.

3. Click Box Placement option:

• **Put Box in Current Page** .... P (Page Anchor)

• **Put Box in Current** .... U **Paragraph** (Paragraph Anchor)

• **Treat Box as Character** .... T (Character Anchor)

4. Set horizontal and vertical placement options.

5. Click **OK** .... Enter

T H E   G L O B A L   T R A V E L   G R O U P

485 Madison Avenue
New York, NY 10034

PHONE: (212) 234-4560
FAX: (212) 345-9877
INTERNET: globetrav@vm1.Mad.Ny

EXERCISE

CHANGING THE GRAPHICS BOX CONTENTS

NOTES:

■ If you want the graphics box to remain in a certain position on the page, regardless of any changes you make to the page or document, choose the Put Box on Current Page (Page Anchor) option in the Box Position dialog box.

■ If you want the box to stay with the paragraph preceding it, choose Put Box in Current Paragraph (Paragraph Anchor Option). Then, if you add/delete material from the document or move the paragraph, the graphics box will move, too.

■ If you want the graphics box treated as a character, choose the Treat Box as Character (Character Anchor) option. Then, the box will move as text and wrap, if necessary, as new text is added before the box.

Change the Graphics Box Contents

■ The contents of a graphics box may be be changed to have the following contents:

IF YOU SELECT:	YOU WILL GET:
Empty	An empty graphics box used as a placeholder in a document.
Image	A graphics image such as CHEETAH.WPG.
Text	Regular text typed directly into the box or a text file retrieved into the box.
Equation	An equation inserted into the box through the Equation Editor (this feature will not be covered).
Image on Disk	A minimized file to save disk space when working with numerous graphics.

Document Image (This option exists if there are already one or more graphics boxes in the document.) A choice from the already used images.

■ To change the contents of a graphics box, click Content on the Feature bar. In the Box Content dialog box which follows, click the filename list box to select another image or click a content option from the Content drop-down list.

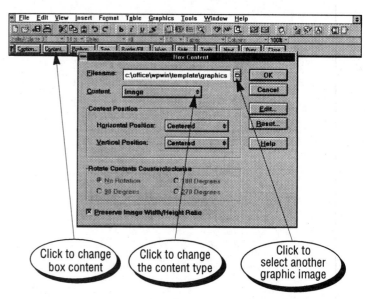

Click to change box content

Click to change the content type

Click to select another graphic image

Exercise continued

EXERCISE DIRECTIONS:

 In this exercise, you will create another letterhead using two image boxes one text box. You will size, position and copy the figure box.

1. Start with a clear screen.

2. Set the left, right, top and bottom margins to .5".

3. Create a text box and type Judy's Card Shoppe, as shown.

4. Set the text to script 48 point (use ShelleyVolante BT font, if available).

5. Size and position the text box as follows

    • Size to Content.

    • Set the anchor type as Page.

    • Set the horizontal position to 0" From Left Edge of Page.

    • Set the vertical position 0" from Center of Margin.

    • Rotate it 90 degrees.

6. Create an image box and import the image ENDERO5.WPG.

7. Size and position the first image box as follows:

    • Size the width to 1" and the height to 1.96".

    • Set the anchor type as Page.

    • Set the horizontal position to 0" from Left Edge of Page.

    • Set the vertical position to 0" from Top Margin.

8. Copy the ENDER05.WPG image. Use the Advance feature to bring the insertion point to Ln 8", and paste the image.

9. Position the second image box as follows:

    • Set the anchor type as Page.

    • Set the horizontal position to 0" from Left Edge of Page.

    • Set the vertical position to 7.93" from Top Margin.

10. Type the address text next to the top of the graphic in script 14 point and use All justification. Use the same font as the title.

11. Type the phone text next to the bottom of the graphic in script 14 point and use All justification.

12. Change both image box contents to ENDER06.WPG.

13. Print one copy.

14. Save the file; name it **CARDLET**.

15. Close the document window.

CHANGE BOX CONTENTS

1. Select the graphic.............. `Shift` + `F11`

2. Click **Content** .... `Alt` + `Shift` + `O` button on Graphics Feature bar.

3. Click **Filename** list box to. .... `Alt` + `F` select another graphic image.

4. Select a content option from the **Content** drop down list.

    To replace the image with another content type:

    • **Empty** .... `E`

    • **Image** .... `I`

    • **Text** .... `T`

    • **Equation** .... `E`

    • **Image on Disk** .... `D`

    • **Document Image** .... `D`

5. Click **OK** .... `Enter`

Judy's Card Shoppe

3456 North Michigan Avenue, Chicago, Illinois 60877

Phone: 708-555-5555 Fax: 708-666-6666

EXERCISE

BORDERS AND FILLS

NOTES:

- You may also add borders and fills (shading) to a graphics box. The default border for a graphics image is no border. The default border for a text box is a thick top and bottom line:

GRAPHICS IMAGE

TEXT BOX

Note the thick top and bottom border lines.

- Your printer determines how the printed copy will look. For example, some printers cannot produce the fine points needed for gradients (like the samples shown on page 331).

- You may select a border and/or fill while creating or editing the graphic by selecting Border/Fill on the Graphics Feature bar. You may select from 28 border styles and 30 fill styles or create a custom style.

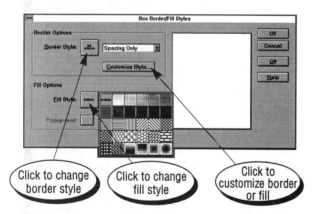

- In the Customize Border dialog box (which appears after you click Customize Style on the Box Border/Fill Styles dialog box), you may edit individual sides, change the line style, change the spacing inside and outside the border, change the corners from square to round, and add a drop shadow effect.

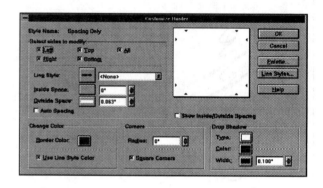

- The following samples illustrate some of the border possibilities:

Single (default)	Dashed	Thick

Dotted	Double	Shadow

Thick/ Thin 2   Button

- In the Box Border/Fill Styles dialog box, you may fill the box with shading ranging in 10 percent increments from none to 100%, with patterns or gradients displayed in the drop-down palette. If you have a color printer or if you are creating a graphic for presentation on a monitor, you may want to change the foreground and/or background colors.

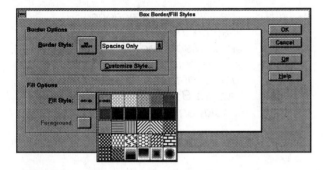

- The following samples illustrate some fill patterns:

10% Fill

40% Fill

70% Fill

100% Fill

Vertical Lines

Waves

Circular Gradient

Button Fill + Button Border

- The sample below uses rounded corners and a drop shadow selected from the Customize Border dialog box.

EXERCISE DIRECTIONS:

 In this exercise, you will create image and text boxes, and create different borders and fill styles for each.

1. Start with a clear screen.

2. Begin the exercise on Ln 1".

3. Create the image and text boxes as shown in the exercise. Use TIGER.WPG and HORSE_J.WPG as the graphic images.

4. Use the anchor, size and positions, borders and fills indicated in the exercise. Do not type these instructions.

5. Preview your exercise.

6. Print one copy.

7. Save the exercise; name it **BORDERS**.

8. Close the document window.

   NOTE: *The following directions assume the Graphics Feature bar is displayed. If not, select the graphic, click the right mouse button and select Feature Bar from the QuickMenu.*

CHANGE BORDER STYLE

1. Click the graphic box.......... `Shift` + `F11` to select it.

2. Click **B**order/Fill ...... `Alt` + `Shift` + `B`

3. Click **B**order Style button.................. `B`

   OR

   Drop-down **Border Style** list.

4. Click desired style.

5. Click **OK** to return to document ... `Enter`

CHANGE FILL STYLE

1. Click the graphic box.......... `Shift` + `F11` to select it.

2. Click **B**order/Fill ...... `Alt` + `Shift` + `B`

3. Click **F**ill Style button. .... `F`

   OR

   Drop-down **Fill Style** list.

4. Click desired style.

5. Click **OK** to return to document... `Enter`

CUSTOMIZE BORDER STYLE

1. Click the graphic box.......... `Shift` + `F11` to select it.

2. Click **B**order/Fill ...... `Alt` + `Shift` + `B`

3. Click **C**ustomize Style .... `C`

4. Make changes to desired elements.

   To create round corners, in Corners panel:

   NOTE: *This procedure works only with box with 4 identical side line styles.*

   a. Deselect S**q**uare Corners .... `Q`

   b. In Ra**d**ius box, enter.................... `D` desired radius.

To create custom drop shadow, in Drop Shadow panel:

a. Click **Ty**pe button .... `Y`

b. Click desired placement for shadow (default is No shadow).

c. Click **Width**: button, click desired width.

   OR

   Enter measurement for desired width.

5. Click **OK** .... `Enter` to return to previous dialog box.

6. Click **OK** .... `Enter` to return to document.

Tiger Image Graphic:
Begin: **Ln 1"**
Anchor: **Paragraph**
Size: **Default**
Position: **Right Margin**
Border: **Default**

Text Box:
Anchor: **Paragraph**
Size: **1.75" w x 1.75" h**
Position: **h: -0.468"**
from center of pararaph.
v: 0.149" from top of
paragraph.
Border: **Thick Shadow**
Fill: **None**

The border style on this text box has been changed to **thick shadow**. No fill has been added.

Text Box:
Anchor: **Paragraph**
Size: **3.25" w x Size to Content h**
Position: **h: 0.017" from right margin.**
               v: 0.136" from top of paragraph.
Border: **Extra Thick**
Fill: **Button**

The border style on this text box has been changed to **extra thick** with a **button fill**.

Horse Image Graphic:
Anchor: **Paragraph**
Size: **2" w x 2" h**
Position: **h: -0.033" from left margin**
               v: 0.048" from top of paragraph
Border: **Shadow**
Fill: **Chain Link**

EXERCISE

▪ TEXT WRAP OPTIONS ▪ CAPTIONS

91

NOTES:

Text Wrap Options

▪ WordPerfect provides you with several options for wrapping text around the graphic (image or text box). You can control the type and the position of the text wrap. Note the text wrap options illustrated below.

This text is designed to show you how text flows around a graphic. Wrapping Type options determine the shape of the wrapped text, and Wrap Text Around options determine its location. You choose the Contour option to remove the figure border and have text fill in any extra white space within the box. Each option creates its own effect, as well as each combination of options. Be sure to check the effects of text wrap. You may need to reposition the graphic to avoid awkward line breaks.

SQUARE LARGEST SIDE

This text is designed to show you how text flows around a graphic. Wrapping Type options determine the shape of the wrapped text, and Wrap Text Around options determine its location. You choose the Contour option to remove the figure border and have text fill in any extra white space within the box. Each option creates its own effect, as well as each combination of options. Be sure to check the effects of text wrap. You may need to reposition the graphic to avoid awkward line breaks.

SQUARE - LEFT SIDE CENTERED IMAGE

This text is designed to show you how text flows around a  graphic. Wrapping Type options determine the shape of the wrapped text and Wrap Text Around options determine its locations. You choose the Contour option to have the text fill in any extra white space. Each option, as well as each combination of options, creates its own effect. Be sure to check the effects of text wrap. You may need to reposition the graphic to avoid awkward line breaks.

**SQUARE - RIGHT SIDE CENTERED IMAGE;
VERTICAL POSITION LOWERED**

This text is how text flows Wrapping Type shape of the Wrap Text Around location. You option to remove have text fill space within the creates its own each combination to check the effects / designed to show you around a graphic. options determine the wrapped text, and options determine its choose the Contour the figure border and in any extra white box. Each option effect, as well as of options. Be sure of text wrap. You may need to reposition the graphic to avoid awkward line breaks.

SQUARE - BOTH SIDES - CENTERED IMAGE

This text is designed to show you how text flows around a graphic. Wrapping Type options determine the shape of the

wrapped text, and Wrap Text Around options determine its location. You choose the Contour option to remove the figure border and have text fill in any extra white space within the box. Each option creates its own effect, as well as each combination of options. Be sure to check the effects of text wrap. You may need to reposition the graphic to avoid awkward line breaks.

SQUARE - ON EITHER SIDE OF CENTERED IMAGE

This text is designed to show you how text flows around a graphic. Wrapping Type options determine the shape of the wrapped text, and Wrap Text Around options determine its location. You choose the Contour option to remove the figure border and have text fill inany extra white space within the box. Each option creates its own effect, as well as each combination of options. Be sure to check the effects of textwrap. You may need to reposition the graphic to avoid awkward line breaks.

CONTOUR - BOTH SIDES OF CENTERED IMAGE

This text is designed to show you how text flows around a graphic. Wrapping Type options determine the shape of the wrapped text, and Wrap Text Around options determine its location. You choose the Contour option to remove the figure border and have text fill in any extra white space within the box. Each option creates its own effect, as well as each combination of options. Be sure to check the effects of text wrap. You may need to reposition the graphic to avoid awkward line breaks.

NO WRAP

- To select text flow options, select the graphic and click Wrap on the Graphics Feature bar or click the right mouse button and choose Wrap.

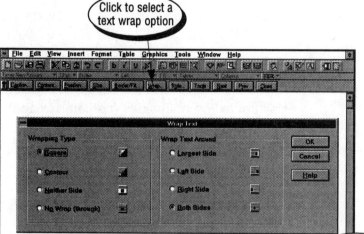

Click to select a text wrap option

- Choose one Wrapping Type option. If you choose Square or Contour, you also choose one Wrap Text Around option. You may wrap text around the Largest Side, Left Side, Right Side or Both Sides of the graphic.

- The Contour wrapping type flows text in a silhouette pattern up to/around the image.

- When using text wrap, carefully proofread the text that flows around the graphic. You may need to adjust the graphic position to avoid awkward word breaks.

Captions

- A **caption** is text that you write to appear below a graphic, usually a label or explanation.

And the winner is...

- To create a caption, click Caption on the Graphics Feature bar. The Box Caption dialog box enables you to position the caption on any side of the box, inside, outside or on the border, and at the top, bottom, or center. By default, the caption width matches the graphic width, but you may set your own width. You may rotate the caption to appear along any side of the figure. You may also control the automatic caption numbering feature.

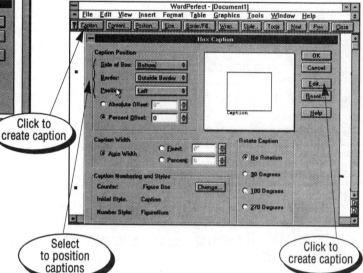

Click to create caption

Select to position captions

Click to create caption

- To create the caption, click Edit. The Caption Editor appears with the box or figure number already entered and the insertion point in place for you to type the caption. Normal editing and formatting features apply here. For instance, to delete the provided figure number, press Backspace.

EXERCISE DIRECTIONS:

 In this exercise, you will create a two-column report, import several graphic images and apply a text wrap option to each. You will also include a caption.

1. Start with a clear screen.

2. Set 1.5 left and right margins.

3. Begin the exercise on Ln 1".

4. Keyboard the heading in sans serif 24 point bold. Press the Enter key three times.

5. Create two newspaper columns.

6. Prepare the report illustrated on the right.

7. Center each subheading in sans serif 14 point bold. Use serif 12 point for paragraph text.

8. Import CHEETAH.WPG in the first column where shown.

   - Center and size the graphic to .1" wide x .5" high.

   - Include a centered caption in sans serif 10 point bold italics that reads, *The Cheetah.*

   - Wrap text on either side (of centered image).

9. Import TIGER.WPG in the first column where shown.

   - Center and size the graphic to .5" wide x .5" high.

   - Include a centered caption in sans serif 10 point italics that reads, *The Tiger.*

   - Wrap text on both sides (centered image).

   - Place a dotted border around the graphic.

10. Import CRANE_J.WPG.

    - Size it 2" wide x 1" high.

    - Use a Contour Text Wrap.

    - Using the mouse, position the graphic between the columns as shown. Adjust the graphic as necessary to avoid awkward word breaks.

11. Preview your document.

12. Print one copy.

13. Save the file; name it **EXTINCT**.

14. Close the document window.

WRAP TEXT

1. Select graphic.................... `Shift` + `F11`

2. Click **Wrap** on......... `Alt` + `Shift` + `W`
   Graphics Feature bar.

3. Select a Wrapping Type option:

   - **Square**............................ `S`

   - **Contour**.......................... `C`

   - **Neither Side**.................... `N`

   - **No Wrap (through)**............ `O`

4. For Square or Contour, click a Wrap Text Around option:

   - **Largest Side**.................... `L`

   - **Left Side**......................... `E`

   - **Right Side**....................... `I`

   - **Both Sides**....................... `B`

5. Click **OK**.................... `Enter`

ADD A CAPTION

1. Select graphic.................... `Shift` + `F11`

2. Click **Caption** on...... `Alt` + `Shift` + `A`
   Graphics Feature bar.

3. Click **Edit**................ `Alt` + `E`

4. Type and format caption text.

5. Click **Close**............. `Alt` + `Shift` + `C`

6. Click **OK**.................... `Enter`

REMOVE A CAPTION

1. Select graphic.................... `Shift` + `F11`

2. Click **Caption** on...... `Alt` + `Shift` + `A`
   Graphics feature bar.

3. Click **Reset**............ `Alt` + `R`

4. Click **OK** at warning box .... `Enter`

5. Click **OK**.................... `Enter`

ENDANGERED SPECIES

Wildlife Conservation

Many organizations are involved in efforts to preserve wild

The Cheetah

animals and plants and save them from extinction. The greatest danger to wildlife results from human activities. Wild species of animals and plants provide many substances which are valuable to the economies of different countries, both as food products and as products for trade. The existence of many species of wildlife maintains the balance of living systems on the earth. The loss of certain species will affect the existence of others that depend on it, perhaps for food.

Tigers, for example, are found only in Asia. But, until the 1800's, many lived throughout most of the southern half of the continent. While tigers still live in this area, only a few are left. This is largely a result of the fact that people have hunted tiger for years and cleared the forests in which they live. Additionally, many tiger cubs die before they reach adulthood. Thus, the tiger has become an endangered species.

The Tiger

Endangered Species of the Season:
The California Condor

The California condor, a vulture, is the largest flying land bird in North America and makes its home in Southern California. Black feathers cover most of the bird's body except for the white area on the underside of the condor's wings. The neck and head have no feathers and are a red-orange color. The condor is a unique bird because it does not build a nest, but lays its eggs in caves, holes, or among rocks. It is also a particularly strong flier; it can soar and glide in the air for long distances, flapping its wings an average of only once an hour. It is a carnivore and eats the remains of dead animals.

By the end of the 1980's, only 30 condors remained in the United States. The diminished number of condors is a result of hunting. The growth of urban areas in Southern California also poses a threat to the natural habitat of the bird. What is needed is more land for sanctuaries to help keep the condor alive.

EXERCISE

TEXT WRAP OPTIONS

92

NOTES:

▪ In Exercise 91, you used three different text wrap options. Each one wrapped text around the graphic in a different style.

▪ In this exercise, you will experiment with no wrap, in which the text overlays the graphic:

> This is an example of no text wrap in which the text overlays the graphic. It can create an interesting effect. However, if the graphic image is too dark, you will not be able to see the text. When you are using border graphics, you must use this wrap option if you want the text to appear inside the border. Otherwise, the text will print outside the border.

▪ When working with border graphics, you must use this wrap type if you want the text to appear inside the border:

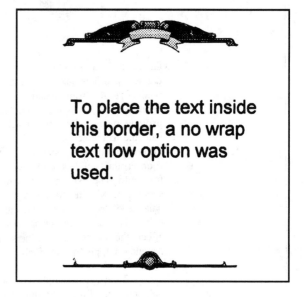

> To place the text inside this border, a no wrap text flow option was used.

EXERCISE DIRECTIONS:

In this exercise, you will use a border graphic. You will choose a no wrap option and insert a previously saved file. The document will overlay the graphic, allowing the text to appear inside the border.

1. Start with a clear screen.

2. Use the default margins.

3. Import BORD16.WPG. Size the border width and height to Full.

4. Select a "no wrap" text wrap option.

5. Insert (Insert, File) **RSVP** (a previously saved file).

6. Adjust the text as follows:

   • Press the Enter key once after EVE to break the line.

   • Press the Enter key several times to move the last two lines down on the page as shown.

   • Center the phone number information.

7. Preview the exercise.

8. Print one copy.

9. Save the file as **RSVP2**.

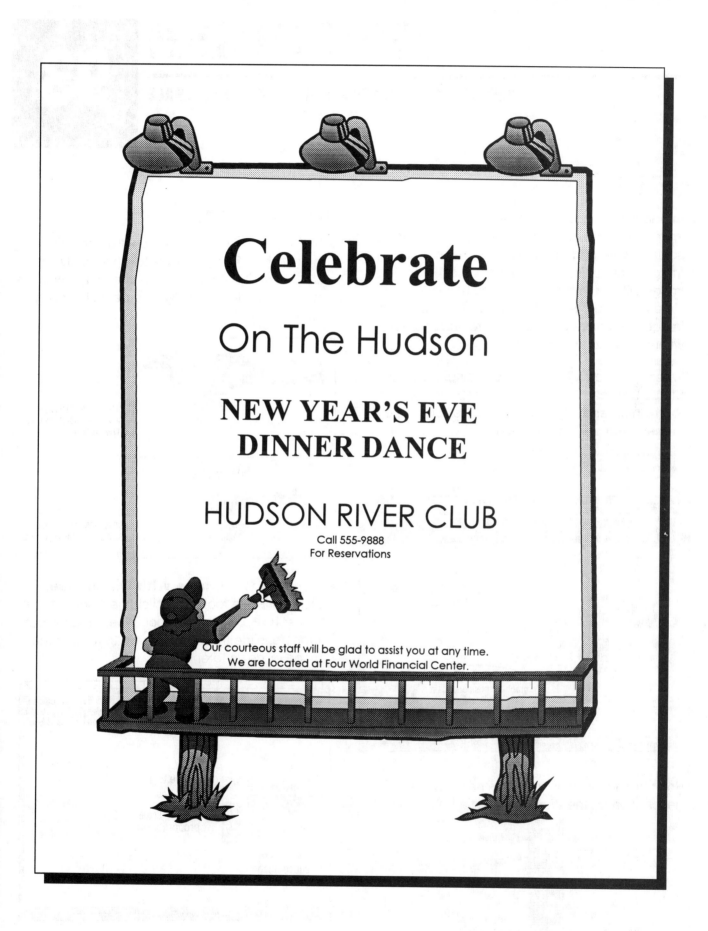

EXERCISE

SCALING, ROTATING AND FLIPPING A GRAPHICS IMAGE

93

NOTES:

- In addition to moving and resizing a graphics image, you can also edit the image. You can scale, rotate, and mirror (flip) images with the Image Tools palette. These actions affect the image within the box, but not the box itself. Note the examples on this and the next page of images that have been scaled, rotated, moved within the box, and flipped.

- When the Image Tools palette is displayed, the Status Bar reports the selected graphic's X (horizontal) and Y (vertical) axis position, scale percent and degree of rotation.

- Point to any tool icon to see its name and description on the WordPerfect title bar.

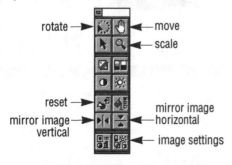

Scale an Image

- The scaling option lets you enlarge or reduce the graphics image horizontally, vertically, or proportionally. You may scale the image with the mouse or mathematically. The default scaling ratio is X:1.0, Y:1.0.

SCALE WIDTH: (X): 1.0
SCALE HEIGHT: (Y): 1.0
(The Default)

SCALE WIDTH: (X): 6
SCALE HEIGHT: (Y): 1.2

- **To scale the image with the mouse**, click the Scale tool, then click the About Image Center (up/down arrow) tool. When a scroll bar appears, slide the scroll box up to reduce the image or down to enlarge it.

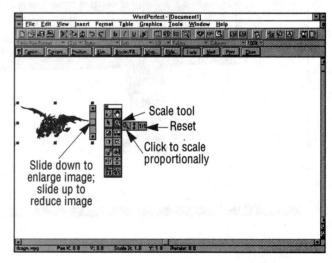

340

- **To scale an image mathematically**, click the Image Settings tool. In the Image Settings dialog box, select the Scale Image option, then enter the desired scaling ratios.

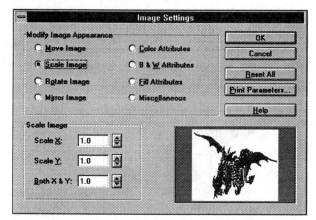

- **To scale the image but retain its original proportions**, either enter equal numbers in the Scale X and Scale Y boxes or enter the desired number in the Both X & Y box. You may increase the value up to 1000% (10.0) or reduce it as far as 1/1000 (.01).

The following graphics box illustrates a proportional image.

- **To stretch or distort the image**, enter *unequal* values in the X and Y boxes. A larger X value makes the image tall and skinny; a larger Y value makes the image short and fat.

SCALE WIDTH: (X): 1.0
SCALE HEIGHT: (Y): .5

- **To enlarge a selected portion of the image**, click the Scale tool, then click the Magnifying Glass tool. When you point to the graphics box, you see dotted lines extending from the crosshairs of the magnifying-glass pointer. Position the crosshair center at one corner of the area you want to enlarge,

click then drag to the opposite corner of the area. When the dotted box defines the area to be enlarged, click again, then click the Pointer tool on the palette to restore the normal pointer action.

- **To reset the image to its original size and proportions**, you can click the Reset tool.

Move an Image Within the Border

- **To move an image within the border or frame** with the mouse, click the Move tool. When you point to the selected graphic, the pointer becomes an open hand which you use to drag the image to the desired position. This is often referred to as *panning the image*. It allows you to display any desired part of the image.

SCALE WIDTH: (X): 2.5
SCALE HEIGHT: (Y): 2.5

- **To move an image within the border mathematically**, click the Image Settings tool to display the Image Settings dialog box. There you select the Move Image option, then enter the horizontal and vertical distance you want the image to move.

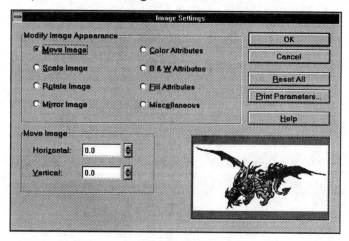

Rotate and Flip an Image

■ **To flip an image**, you can click the Mirror Vertical (switch right-to-left) tool ▐◖ or the Mirror Horizontal (switch up-to-down) tool ▤. Or you can select Mirror Image at the Image Settings dialog box, then select Flip Horizontal or Flip Vertical.

FLIP VERTICALLY

FLIP HORIZONTALLY

■ **To rotate an image with the mouse,** click the Rotate tool ▨ to activate the point-of-rotation and the corner rotation handles. By default, the point-of-rotation is in the center or the image. You can move it to a new position within the graphics box. Then drag a corner rotation handle until the figure is at the desired angle. The Status bar reports the exact rotation angle.

ROTATED -30.0 DEGREES

■ **To rotate an image mathematically**, click the Image Settings tool, then click Rotate Image and enter the desired degree of rotation (0 to +/-360 degrees).

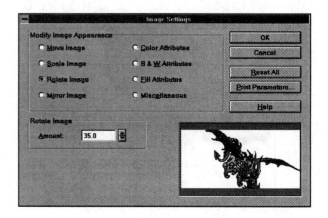

SCALE AN IMAGE

1. Select graphic to be scaled. `Shift` + `F11`

2. Click **Tools** on.......... `Alt` + `Shift` + `L`
   Graphics Feature bar.

3. Click **Scale tool** .... 🔍

4. Click **Up/Down Arrow tool.**

5. Drag scroll box up to reduce, down to enlarge image.

OR

1. Click **Image Settings tool** .... ▦

2. Click **Scale Image** .... `S`

3. Type desired scale values.

   In **Scale X** box, ... `Alt` + `X`
   type scale height.

   In **Scale Y** box, ... `Alt` + `Y`
   type scale width.

   OR

   In **Both X & Y** box, type .... `Alt` + `B`
   common scale value.

4. Click **OK** .... `Enter`

ENLARGE PORTION OF IMAGE

1. Select graphic .... `Shift` + `F11`
   to be enlarged.

2. Click **Tools** on .... `Alt` + `Shift` + `L`
   Graphics Feature bar.

3. Click **Scale tool** .... 🔍

4. Click **magnifying glass tool** .... 🔍

5. Click in one corner of area to be enlarged, drag to diagonally opposite corner, click when outline box encloses desired area.

6. Click **Pointer tool** .... ↖
   to restore normal pointer action.

MOVE IMAGE WITHIN THE BOX

1. Select graphic to be moved. `Shift` + `F11`

2. Click **Tools** on.......... `Alt` + `Shift` + `L`
   Graphics Feature bar.

3. Click **Move tool** .... ✋

4 With open hand pointer, drag image to desired position within the box.

OR

1. Click **Image Settings tool** .... ▦

2. Click **Move Image** .... `M`

3. Type measurement for.......... `Alt` + `Z`
   desired **Horizontal** distance.

4. Type measurement for.......... `Alt` + `V`
   desired **Vertical** distance.

5. Click **OK** .... `Enter`

FLIP AN IMAGE

1. Select graphic .... `Shift` + `F11`
   to be flipped.

2. Click **Tools** on.......... `Alt` + `Shift` + `L`
   Graphics Feature bar.

   • Click **Mirror Vertical tool** .... ▌▐
     to flip right-to-left.

   • Click **Mirror Horizontal tool** .... ▀▄
     to flip upside down.

OR

1. Click **Image Settings tool** .... ▦

2. Click **Mirror Image** .... `I`

3. Click **Flip Horizontal** .... `Alt` + `Z`

   AND/OR

   Click **Flip Vertical** .... `Alt` + `Y`

4. Click **OK** .... `Enter`

ROTATE AN IMAGE

1. Select graphic .... `Shift` + `F11`
   to be flipped.

2. Click **Tools** on.......... `Alt` + `Shift` + `L`
   Graphics Feature bar.

3. Click **Rotate tool** .... ▨

4. Drag corner rotation handle to desired rotation angle.

5. Click **Pointer tool** to .... ↖
   restore normal pointer action.

OR

1. Click **Image Settings tool** .... ▦

2. Click **Rotate Image** .... ▨

3. In **Amount** box, ... `Alt` + `A`
   type desired rotation angle.

4. Click **OK** .... `Enter`

RESTORE ORIGINAL SETTINGS

1. Select graphic .... `Shift` + `F11`
   to be flipped.

2. Click **Tools** on.......... `Alt` + `Shift` + `L`
   Graphics Feature bar.

3. Click **Restore tool** .... ▨

OR

1. Click **Image Settings tool** .... ▦

2. Click **Reset All** .... `Alt` + `R`

*NOTE: It is easier to rotate the image within the **Image Settings** dialog box than by using the mouse.*

EXERCISE DIRECTIONS:

 In this exercise, you will create a letterhead using scaled, rotated, flipped, and moved graphics images.

1. Start with a clear screen.

2. Use the default margins.

3. Import DRAGN.WPG. and position it 0" left margin (the default) and 0" from the top margin.

4. Edit the left graphic as follows:

   • Select the graphic.

   • Select Tools from the Graphics Feature bar.

   • Use the magnifying glass (the scale tool) to enlarge the dragon's head to fill the box.

   • Scale the height of the graphic (Y) to 2.5 degrees and the width (X) to 1.7 degrees.

   • Flip (mirror) the graphic vertically.

   • Move the image within the box so the head is visible.

   • Size the box to 1" x 1".

5. Copy the graphic and position it 0" from the right margin and 0" from the bottom margin.

6. Edit the right graphic as follows:

   • Select the graphic.

   • Select Tools from the Graphics Feature bar.

   • Flip (mirror) the graphic vertically.

   • Move the image within the box so the head is visible.

7. Right-align letterhead text using sans serif 14 point bold for the title and sans serif 10 point for the address beginning on Ln 1".

8. Left-align the phone number information in sans serif 10 point beginning on Ln 9.22".

9. Preview your document.

10. Print one copy.

11. Save the letterhead file; name it **DRAGON**.

12. Close the document window.

Drag-On Inn
8763 Wilton Road
Arlington, Virginia 22207

PHONE: 703-555-5555
FAX: 703-666-6666
PROPRIETOR: Shanna Touris

EXERCISE

SIZING, POSITIONING, ROTATING AND FLIPPING A GRAPHICS IMAGE

94

NOTES:

▪ In this exercise, you will enhance an advertisement you created earlier by importing and editing a graphic.

EXERCISE DIRECTIONS:

PART I

1. Start with a clear screen.

2. Open **PAPER**.

3. Import BORD8P.WPG. Size it to Full horizontally and vertically.

4. Set the text wrap option to No Wrap.

    NOTE: The document will then appear within the border.

5. Keyboard the additional text as shown. Use any desired special character to precede each paper type.

6. Import ENDER01.WPG. Edit the graphic as follows:

    • Size it to 1" x 1".

    • Position it so the bottom of the design rests on the left end of the bottom border as shown.

    • Copy the graphic once and position it so the bottom of the design rests on the right end of the bottom border.

    • Copy the graphic again and position it at the top left of the page.

    • Flip vertically the top left image. Then position it so the top of the graphic touches below the left end of the border as shown.

NOTE: Select the image first before you click Tools on the Graphics Feature bar.

    • Copy the flipped image and position it so the top of the graphic touches below the right end of the border.

7. Preview your document. If the document is not centered on the page, insert returns.

8. Print one copy.

9. Save the file; name it **PAPER1**.

PART II

10. Rotate the left images -25 degrees; rotate the right images 25 degrees.

11. Print one copy.

12. Save the file; name it **PAPER2**.

13. Close the document window.

PART I

COLOR PAPER

Paper is a significant part of publishing. Paper establishes a visual and tactile experience. Therefore, using anything but white gives you an important advantage over your competition.

Bright colors communicate an urgent message. Neon-colored paper can be offensive, but no one will ignore it. It is almost impossible to lose neon paper in a stack of ordinary white paper.

Serious and dignified messages demand a softer color paper. To impart the warmth of a sun-soaked vacation, you might try a paper that exhibits the warm radiance of a summer day. Our four leading papers are:

☆ENVIRONMENT
☆CLASSIC LINEN
☆CREST LINEN
☆RAINDROP

insert }

Call **Jaime's Paper House,** 1-800-555-5555 for your free *Think Color Guide*.

PART II

COLOR PAPER

Paper is a significant part of publishing. Paper establishes a visual and tactile experience. Therefore, using anything but white gives you an important advantage over your competition.

Bright colors communicate an urgent message. Neon-colored paper can be offensive, but no one will ignore it. It is almost impossible to lose neon paper in a stack of ordinary white paper.

Serious and dignified messages demand a softer color paper. To impart the warmth of a sun-soaked vacation, you might try a paper that exhibits the warm radiance of a summer day. Our four leading papers are:

☆ENVIRONMENT
☆CLASSIC LINEN
☆CREST LINEN
☆RAINDROP

Call **Jaime's Paper House,** 1-800-555-5555 for your free *Think Color Guide*.

EXERCISE

WATERMARKS

95

NOTES:

- A **watermark** is a lightened graphics image or text that prints in the background, behind the printed text. A watermark can appear on every page of your document or on selected pages. You can also create two watermarks that will appear on alternating pages.

- A watermark may be accessed by selecting Watermark from the Format main menu.

- When the watermark window appears (it is blank), you can insert a graphic image, a file, or type text. You can edit text content, apply font changes, and use most figure editing features at the watermark window. A Watermark Feature bar appears at the top of the window.

- If you choose to insert a graphics image as a watermark, the Graphics Feature bar will appear, allowing you to edit the graphic image. When the Graphics Feature bar is closed, the Watermark Feature bar will again appear.

- The shading of a watermark image or watermark text can be adjusted in the Watermark Feature bar by selecting the Shading button. This can be done before or after a graphic image is chosen, or it may be done by editing the watermark after it is in the document window.

- To discontinue a watermark at a certain point in a multiple page document, choose Watermark from the Format main menu and then select Discontinue.

- Among the graphic images provided in WordPerfect's graphics directory are graphics designed for use as page borders. These borders, along with any of the other graphic images, can be used as watermarks.

- While you can create watermarks in any view, they do not display in Draft view.

Click to insert image

Click to adjust Watermark shading

Watermark Feature bar

Exercise continued

EXERCISE DIRECTIONS:

In this exercise, you will create an invitation using a graphic image design as a watermark.

1. Start with a clear screen.

2. Use the default margins.

3. Add a graphic image, INVITATN.WPG, as watermark A.

4. Add a graphic image, BORD01P.WPG, as watermark B.

5. Create the invitation shown below. Press the Enter key approximately 10 times after the date. Use a script 16 point font for the invitation text and a 24 point bold script font for Pamela Davis.

6. Center the text hortizonally and center the page top to bottom.

7. Edit the watermark shading of the graphic images to 20%.

8. Preview your document.

9. Print one copy.

10. Save the file; name it **WISH**.

CREATE A WATERMARK

1. If in Draft view, ... `Alt` + `F5`
   click **V**iew, then **P**age.

   OR

   • Click **V**iew .... `Alt` + `V`

   • Click **Tw**o Page .... `W`

2. Click **F**ormat .... `Alt` + `R`

3. Click **W**atermark .... `W`

4. Click Watermark **A** .... `A`

   OR

   Click Watermark **B** .... `B`

5. Click **C**reate .... `C`

   Watermark Feature bar and window appear.

6. Click **Pa**ges on .... `Alt` + `Shift` + `A`
   Watermark Feature bar.

   • Make page option selection.

   • Click **OK** .... `Enter`

7. Click **I**mage on .... `Alt` + `Shift` + `M`
   Watermark Feature bar.

   • Select image to be inserted.

   • Click **OK** .... `Enter`

   To change shading:

   Click **S**hading .... `Alt` + `S`

   • Select shading amount.

   • Click **OK** .... `Enter`

8. Click **C**lose on.......... `Alt` + `Shift` + `C`
   Watermark Feature bar.

9. Type document text as desired.

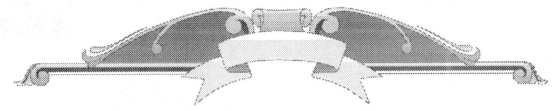

*You are cordially invited
to attend a birthday party
in honor of*

Pamela Davis

*who will be celebrating her
21st Birthday
on September 9, 1995*

INVITATION

8:00 p.m.

*234 Maple Drive
South Hampton, New York*

RSVP 515 999-9999

EXERCISE

WATERMARKS

96

NOTES:

- In the last exercise, you used two graphic images as watermarks. Text that you create may also be used as a watermark.

- When the watermark screen appears, you may type the text you desire as your watermark. If you want the watermark to appear across or down the page, you will need to use a large type size.

- You can also create interesting effects using large size Wingdings and Special Characters *(see Exercise 76)* as watermarks.

EXERCISE DIRECTIONS:

 In this exercise, you will create an advertisement containing two watermarks.

1. Start with a clear screen.

2. Set .5" top and bottom margins.

3. Create watermark A:

   - Type and center LABPRO text as shown using a sans serif 20 point font beginning at the top margin. Use any desired special character preceding and following words.

   - Shade the watermark text to 20%.

4. Create watermark B:

   - Beginning at Ln 9.76", type and center LABPRO text as shown using the same font, point size, special character and shading used in watermark A.

5. Close the watermark screen and return to the document.

6. Insert the file, **DESIGN** created in Summary Exercise 4.

7. Preview your document.

8. Print one copy.

9. Save the file; name it **DESIGN1**.

10. Close the document window.

Create a
Design with Color

4 Reasons Why

The world is a colorful place.
So, why not include color in all your
processing?

❶ *Color increases the visual impact of the*
message and makes it more memorable.
Don't you want your ads to have impact and be noticed?

❷ *Color creates a feeling and helps explain*
the subject. Greens and blues are cool, relaxing tones,
while reds and oranges scream with emphasis. Pastels
communicate a gentle tone.

❸ *Color creates a personality.* You can make your
corporate forms and brochures have their own identity
and personality with color.

❹ *Color highlights information.* An advertisement
or manual might have warnings in red, explanations in
black and instructions in blue.

◆ ◆ ◆

Our color processing labs will take care of all your color processing needs. Just call *1-800-555-6666*
for information. Our courteous staff is ready to assist you with any technical question.

L◆A◆B◆P◆R◆O
FOR
◆COLOR PROCESSING◆

◆LABPRO◆LABPRO◆LABPRO◆

EXERCISE
CREATING AND EDITING HORIZONTAL GRAPHICS LINES
97

NOTES:

- You can use the **Graphics Lines** feature to insert horizontal and vertical lines in your document, in headers, or in footers.

- In desktop publishing, lines are sometimes referred to as **rules**. Lines are used to create designs, to separate parts of a document, or to draw attention to a particular place.

- You may adjust the position, length, and thickness of the lines. You may select decorative line styles such as triple, thick-thin, and dashed. Sample line styles appear below:

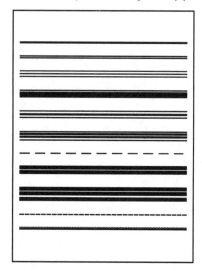

- After choosing Horizontal Line from the Graphics main menu, WordPerfect automatically inserts a full line (a single line that extends from the left to the right margin) at the insertion point position.

Custom Line/Edit Line

Using the Dialog Box

- To create a line of a particular thickness, size or style (other than the default), you may create a **custom line**.

- Or, you may select an existing horizontal line, then select Edit Line from the Graphics main menu.

  NOTE: To select a line, point to the line. When the insertion point turns to an arrow, click it and handles will appear.

The Edit Graphics Lines dialog box appears when you create a custom line or you are editing an existing line:

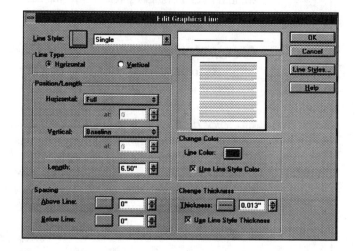

- You may specify the horizontal position and length of the line. If you select Full, the length automatically extends from the left to the right margin of the page or column. The remaining options (Left, Right, Centered, and Set) allow you to specify the line length.

- You may determine the amount of spacing to leave blank above and/or below the horizontal line.

- You may also specify the thickness of the line at the Change Thickness panel by either clicking the Thickness button and visually selecting a line or by entering the measurement in the text box. The default thickness is 0.013" — about 1 point.

- You may select a line style by sight or by name. When you click the Line Style button, a palette of defined styles pops up. When you select a style, it appears on the Line Style button; its name is listed in the drop-down list box, and its appearance displays in both preview windows.

Using the Mouse

- To move, size or change the thickness of a line with the mouse, click to select it, then drag it to a new position. Or, you may drag one of the sizing handles to enlarge or reduce its width and/or length.

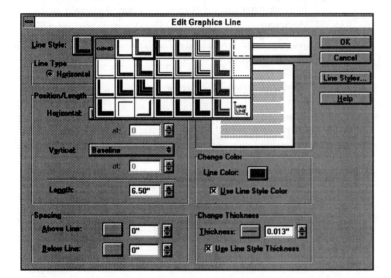

EXERCISE DIRECTIONS:

 In this exercise, you will create a letterhead using a graphic image and horizontal graphic lines.

1. Start with a clear screen.

2. Set the top and bottom margins to .5".

3. Create a horizontal line between the margins (full). Use the default thickness (.013").

4. Press Enter twice.

5. Create a left horizontal line 1" in length using the default width (.013").

6. Center text "The Seaside Inn" in serif 18 point bold. Using the letter P and a Wingding font, create a flag between each word.

7. Create a right horizontal line 1" in length using the default width (.013").

8. Press Enter once.

9. Create a left horizontal line 1" in length, setting the width to 0.03". Create a right horizontal line using the same measurements.

10. Press Enter twice.

11. Create a left horizontal line 1" in length, setting the width to .1".

12. Import and center MARSH.WPG. Size the graphic to 3" wide by .5" high.

13. Create a right horizontal line 1" in length, setting the width to .1".

14. Press Enter as many times as necessary to bring the insertion point to Ln 10".

15. Create a left horizontal line .5" in length, using the default width; center the footer text in sans serif 8 point. Use the same Wingding symbol (the flag) between each word. Create a right horizontal line using the same measurements.

16. Preview your document.

17. Print one copy.

18. Save the file; name it **INN**.

19. Close the document window.

CREATE DEFAULT HORIZONTAL LINE

Ctrl+F11

1. Place insertion point at desired horizontal position for line.

2. Click **G**raphics .... Alt + G

3. Click **H**orizontal Line .... H

CREATE CUSTOM HORIZONTAL LINE

1. Follow steps 1-2, above.

2. Click **Custom Line** L

3. Click **H**orizontal .... R in **Line Type** panel.

4. Select one or more of the following options:

   a. Click **H**orizontal pop-up .... Alt + R list, select one:

   - **Set** .... S , *number* and type position.

   - **Left** L

   - **Right** .... R

   - **Centered** C

   - **Full** .... F

   b. Click **Vertical** pop-up list... Alt + E and select one:

   - **Set** .... S , *number* and type distance from top of page.

   - **Baseline** .... B

   c. Click **Length** .... Alt + N , *number* text box and type length.

   d. Click **Spacing** .... Alt + A , *number* **Above Line** and type amount.

   e. Click **Spacing** .... Alt + B , *number* **Below Line** and type amount.

   f. Click **Thickness** button...... Alt + T and select thickness from list.

   OR

   Type desired thickness.

   g. Click **Line Style** button...... Alt + L and select style from palette.

   OR

   Click **Line Style** .... Alt + L drop-down list and double-click desired style.

5. Click **OK**.

The ✒ Seaside ✒ Inn

123 Wheel Avenue ✒ Fire Island ✒ New York ✒ 11527 ✒ 516 ✒ 555-5555

EXERCISE

98

- **CREATING AND EDITING VERTICAL GRAPHICS LINES**
- **COPYING AND DELETING LINES ▪ SHADING LINES**

NOTES:

- Vertical lines may be created using similar methods used to create horizontal lines.

- After choosing <u>V</u>ertical Line from the <u>G</u>raphics main menu, WordPerfect automatically inserts a full length vertical line at the left margin position.

Custom Line/Edit Line

Using the Dialog Box

- You may create a custom vertical line by selecting Custom <u>L</u>ine from the <u>G</u>raphics main menu. Or, you may select an existing vertical line (place mouse pointer on line and click), then select Edit <u>L</u>ine on the <u>G</u>raphics main menu. The Edit Graphics Lines dialog box appears when you create a custom line or you are editing an existing line.

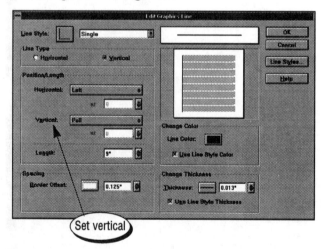

- You may specify the vertical position and length of the line. If you select Full, the length automatically extends from the top to the bottom margin. The remaining options (Top, Bottom, Centered, and Set) allow you to specify the line length.

- The default Baseline vertical position places the line at the base of the current line of text. Or, you can manually set the vertical position by choosing Set and entering the distance you want the line drawn from the top of the page.

Using the Mouse

- You may move, size or change the thickness of a vertical line with the mouse as you did with the horizontal line *(see page 356).*

Copying and Deleting Lines

- Lines, like graphics images and boxes, may be copied and deleted.

- When the graphics line is selected, handles appear and the line is in an edit mode. Once in an edit mode, the line may be copied, deleted, sized or moved.

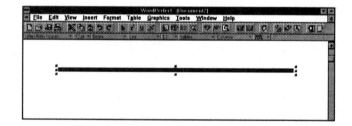

Shading Lines

■ Like fonts, lines may be tinted in shades of gray or in color. This can add interesting effects to your document. However, you must have a printer that supports color to get color output. To create a line color or shade, click the Line Color palette in the Edit Graphic Line dialog box and select colors and/or shades from the palette.

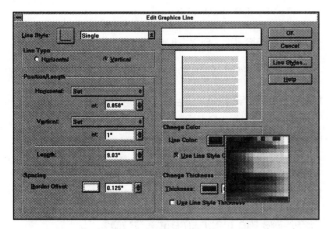

CREATE DEFAULT VERTICAL LINE
Ctrl+F11

1. Place insertion point at desired vertical line position.

2. Click **Graphics** .... +

3. Click **Vertical Line** ....

CREATE CUSTOM VERTICAL LINE

1. Follow steps 1-2, above.

2. Click **Custom Line** ....

   —IN LINE TYPE PANEL—

3. Click **Vertical** ....

4. Select one or more of the following options:

   a. Click **Horizontal** .... **Alt** + **R**
      pop-up list, select one:

   • **Set** .... **S** , *number*
      and type position.

   • **Left** .... **L**

   • **Right** .... **R**

   • **Centered** .... **C**

   • **Column Aligned** .... **A** , *number*
      and type column number.

   b. Click **Vertical** pop-up list... **Alt** + **E**
      and select one:

   • **Set** and type distance.... **S** , *number*
      from left margin.

   • **Top** .... **T**

   • **Bottom** .... **B**

   • **Centered** .... **C**

   • **Full** .... **F**

   c. Click **Length** .... **Alt** + **N** , *number*
      text box and
      type length.

   d. Enter desired spacing option:

   • **Above Line** .... *number*

   • **Below Line** .... *number*

   e. Click **Thickness** ... **Alt** + **T** **↑** **↓**
      button and
      select thickness.

   OR

   Type desired thickness.

   f. Click **Line Style** button....... **Alt** + **L**
      and select style.

   OR

   Click **Line Style** drop-down list and
   select style.

5. Click **OK** .... **Enter**

SHADE A LINE

1. Select line to be shaded (point to line and click once).

2. Click **Graphics** .... **Alt** + **G**

3. Click **Edit Line** .... **N**

4. Click **Line Color** palette.

5. Select a line color.

6. Click **OK** .... **Enter**

EXERCISE DIRECTIONS:

 In this exercise, you will enhance a menu you created earlier by adding vertical and horizontal lines.

1. Start with a clear screen.

2. Open **FOOD**.

3. Set the top and bottom margins to .5".

4. With your insertion point at the top of the screen, create a left vertical line extending the full length of the page, setting a .3" thickness.

5. Create a right vertical line extending the full length of the page, setting a .3" thickness.

6. Change the typeface, type style and type sizes of the text as follows:

   • Set "The Sherwood Forest Inn" to a serif 36 point font.

   • Set the address and phone number text to a serif 10 point font.

   • Set food item headings to a serif 14 point font.

   • Set the food items to a serif 12 point font.

7. Press Enter six times after the phone number.

8. Create a centered horizontal line below "BREAKFAST MENU." Set the length to 5" and the thickness to .02". Color the line light gray.

9. Import BUCK.WPG.

   • Set the size 1" by 1".

   • Scale the height to 1.2" and the width to 1.7".

   • Center the graphic.

10. Delete two hard returns before David Zeiss, Proprietor, so that his name remains on the page.

11. Preview your document.

12. Print one copy.

13. Save the file; name it **FOOD1**.

14. Close the document window.

The ❦ Sherwood ❦ Forest ❦ Inn

125 Pine Hill Road
Arlington, VA 22207
703-987-4443

❧BREAKFAST MENU❧

BEVERAGES

Herbal Tea...$1.00
Coffee...$2.00
Cappuccino...$2.50

●❖✦✿❖✦✿❖●

FRUITS

Berry Refresher...$3.00
Sparkling Citrus Blend...$3.00
Baked Apples...$3.50

●❖✦✿❖✦✿❖●

GRAINS

Fruity Oatmeal...$3.50
Bran Muffins...$3.00
Whole Wheat Zucchini Bread...$3.00
Four-Grain Pancakes...$5.00

●❖✦✿❖✦✿❖●

EGGS

Baked Eggs with Creamed Spinach...$6.50
Poached Eggs with Hollandaise Sauce...$6.00
Scrambled Eggs...$2.50
Sweet Pepper and Onion Frittata...$6.50

David Zeiss ✪ Proprietor

EXERCISE

▪ **PARAGRAPH/PAGE BORDERS AND FILLS**
▪ **DROP CAPITAL** ▪ **REVERSING TEXT**

NOTE:

Paragraph and Page Borders and Fills

▪ WordPerfect's **Border/Fill** feature allows you to place a border around, and add shading to, a paragraph, page, or column. This feature is similar to the Border/Fill option for graphics boxes.

▪ The Paragraph, Page, and Columns options on the Format main menu each offer the Border/Fill option *(see below)*. In each case, you may select from a list of border styles or create a custom style. You may also select or create a fill style. You may limit the border to the current page, paragraph, or column group, or have it apply to the entire document.

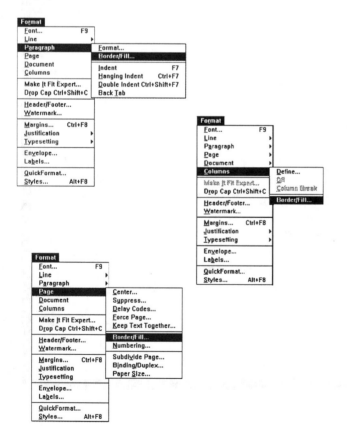

▪ To place a border around a paragraph or page, position the insertion point in the desired paragraph or page, and follow the keystrokes outlined on page 359. By default, the border applies to just that particular paragraph or page, but you may have the border appear around not only that paragraph/page, but all paragraphs/pages following. Or, you may select, for example, several paragraphs, then apply the border to that selection.

▪ To place a border around columns, position the insertion point anywhere in a column. The border will enclose all columns in the document.

Drop Capital

▪ A **drop capital** is an enlarged capital letter that drops below the first line of body text. It is usually the first letter of a paragraph. It is often used to draw the reader's attention to chapter beginnings, section headings and main body text.

> **D**rop capitals are large, decorative letters often used to mark the beginning of a document, section or chapter. Drop caps are set to a much larger font than the text, and often span the height of three or four lines.

▪ Drop caps may be created before or after typing a new paragraph. To apply a drop capital to text before it is typed, select Drop Cap from the Format main menu and type the first few words. To apply a drop capital to existing text, position the insertion point anywhere in the first paragraph and then select Drop Cap from the Format main menu.

- After selecting Drop Cap from the Format main menu, a Drop Cap Feature bar appears, giving you options to edit your drop capital. You may select a different predefined drop cap style, or you can customize the drop capital by changing the font style, height and position or adding a border around it.

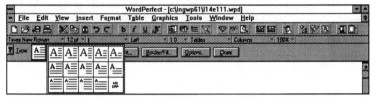

Reversing Text

- **Reverse text** is text that appears white against a dark background. Black letters on a white background are converted to white (or colored) letters on a black background.

Reverse Text

- WordPerfect provides a macro named reverse.wcm that automates the process of reversing text. After text is selected, the macro is played and stops for you to choose a Text Color and Fill Style/Color. The default is White Text Color with a 100% Black Fill Style/Color.

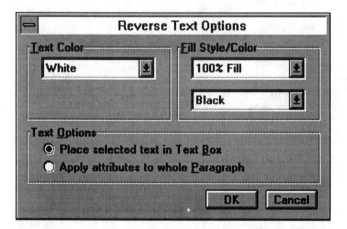

- WordPerfect places text which has been reversed in a graphics box. If you click on the reversed text, handles will appear. The graphics box may then be edited like any other graphics or text box.

 Reverse text adds an interesting effect to text. Reversing a small amount of text is an attention-getting technique. Avoid reversing a large amount of text since it is difficult to read. Use a large point size in a sans serif font face to improve type clarity. If a small point size is used, bold the font face.

EXERCISE DIRECTIONS:

In this exercise, you will enhance a document you created earlier by applying a paragraph border and fill style, a page border, drop capitals and reverse text.

1. Start with a clear screen.

2. Open **COCOA** if you completed it in Exercise 55.

   OR

   🖫 Open **COCOA.99** from the data disk as a read-only file (Open As <u>C</u>opy).

3. Create a dashed line paragraph border with a 5% fill for the paragraph shown.

4. Create drop capitals using a script font where shown. Place a shadow border around each drop capital.

5. Set the title to reverse text.

6. Create a Gray Mat page border.

7. Use the Make-it-Fit feature to keep text on one page, if necessary. You may adjust the top and bottom margins when using this feature.

8. Preview your document.

9. Print one copy.

10. Close the file; save the changes.

   OR

   🖫 Close the file; *save as* **COCOA**.

ADD PAGE OR PARAGRAPH BORDER/FILL

1. Place insertion point on desired page or paragraph.

   OR

   Select desired pages or paragraphs.

2. Click **Fo<u>r</u>mat** .... `Alt` + `R`

3. Click **<u>P</u>age** .... `P`

   OR

   Click **P<u>a</u>ragraph** .... `A`

4. Click **<u>B</u>order/Fill** .... `B`

5. Select desired **Border Style** from palette or drop-down list.

6. Select desired **Fill Style** from palette or drop-down list.

   To apply border to all paragraphs/pages from insertion point on:

   Deselect **Apply border** .... `P`
   to current page only.

   OR

   Deselect **Apply border** .... `A`
   to current paragraph only.

7. Click **OK** .... `Enter`

ADD COLUMN BORDER/FILL

1. Set insertion point anywhere in a column.

2. Click **Fo<u>r</u>mat** .... `Alt` + `R`

3. Click **<u>C</u>olumns** .... `C`

4. Click **<u>B</u>order/Fill** .... `B`

5. Select desired **Border Style** from palette or drop-down list.

   • To add only a vertical separator between columns, select **Column Between**.

   • To add a vertical separator between columns and a border on the outside edge as well, select **Column All**.

6. Select desired **Fill Style** from palette or drop-down list.

   NOTE: The following option applies only if you have more than one column group defined in the document.

7. To apply border to just the currently selected column group, select **Apply border to current column group only**.

8. Click **OK** .... `Enter`

DROP CAPITAL

1. Select text to receive drop capital.

   OR

   Begin typing a new paragraph.

2. Click **Fo<u>r</u>mat** .... `Alt` + `R`

3. Click **<u>D</u>rop Cap** .... `R`

   To select a drop cap edit option, select appropriate button on Feature bar:

   Click **Type palette** button .... `[A≡]`
   and select desired drop cap type.

   OR

   Click **Position** button .... `[Position ▾]`
   and click desired drop cap position.

   OR

   Click **Font** button .... `[Font]`
   and select a desired font.

   OR

   Click **Border/Fill** button .... `[Border/Fill]`
   and select a desired border/fill.

4. Click **Close** button .... `[Close]`

REVERSE TEXT

1. Type text to reverse, using desired font.

   OR

   Select text to reverse.

2. Click **<u>T</u>ools** .... `Alt` + `T`

3. Click **<u>M</u>acros** .... `M`

4. Click **<u>P</u>lay** .... `P`

5. Type **REVERSE.WCM**.

6. Click **<u>P</u>lay** .... `Alt` + `P`

7. Select desired color.

8. Click **OK** .... `Enter`

CHOCOLATE

Chocolate is probably the world's favorite food. You can drink it hot or cold, or eat it as a snack or as part of a meal. It is made into pies, cakes, cookies, candy, ice cream and even breakfast cereal. It is nourishing, energy-giving and satisfying.

Chocolate came to us from Mexico, by way of Europe. When the Spanish explorer Cortez arrived at the court of Montezuma, the Aztec Emperor, he found him drinking a cold, bitter drink called Chocolatl. It was made from seeds of the cacao tree, ground in water and mixed with spices. Montezuma gave Cortez the recipe and some cacao and vanilla beans. Cortez took them back to Spain, where the Spanish king and queen quickly improved the drink by adding sugar and having it served hot. For about a hundred years, chocolate was exclusively a royal Spanish treat. But once the secret leaked out, the upper classes in most of the European capitals were soon sipping hot chocolate. The Dutch settlers brought chocolate to the American colonies, and in 1765 a man named Baker started a chocolate mill near Boston.

A hundred years later a man in Switzerland found a way to make solid sweet milk chocolate, and a great candy business was born. Chocolate companies like Nestle and Hershey need a lot of cacao beans. About one-third of the supply, over 350 thousand tons, is imported each year from the African country of Ghana. Ghana is the world's largest supplier of cacao beans. For many years, chocolate was made by hand. Now, machines do most of the work.

THE CHOCOLATE FACTORY has been specializing in the finest chocolate products for over 50 years. Stop in and sample some of our outstanding chocolate delights.

EXERCISE

TEXTART

100

NOTES:

- WordPerfect's TextArt feature can create striking text effects for special uses such as flyer headings or logos. Waves, pennants, circles and crescents are among the included effects.

- To access the TextArt program, select TextArt from the Graphics main menu or click TextArt on the Toolbar ![icon]. The TextArt program enables you to create an image which will then be imported into the current document.

- At the TextArt screen, you can enter up to 58 characters on one, two, or three lines of text. You select a font, font style, justification and capitalization style. You select a TextArt shape from a palette of shapes. You may also change the text color, define an outlined character format, fills, shadow direction and width. For the image itself, you may set a rotation degree, width and height. These options may be accessed by clicking the appropriate button or selecting it from the menu.

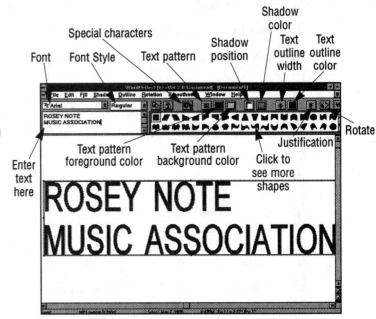

- The TextArt image is placed in a graphics box which can then be positioned and sized like any other graphics box on the page.

- If you accidentally exit the TextArt screen, double-click the text box to return.

EXERCISE DIRECTIONS:

 In this exercise, you will create a flyer using the TextArt feature.

1. Start with a clear screen.

2. With your insertion point at the top of the screen, select the TextArt button.

3. Using a sans serif bold font, type ROSEY NOTE on the first line and MUSIC ASSOCIATION on the second line of the Enter text box.

4. Select the ∧ on the third line of the palette.

5. Return to the WordPerfect document.

6. Size the box to 5" wide by 2" high.

7. Import ROSE.WPG graphic; set the size to approximately 1.5" by 1.5".

8. Insert the graphic in the middle of the heading text as shown.

9. Type the remaining text beginning below the TextArt graphics box (approximately 7.3"). Set "Presents..." to serif 30 point bold; set remaining text to serif 14 point bold.

10. Create a shadow paragraph border around the last sentence and shade it using a button fill.

11. Preview your document.

12. Print one copy.

13. Save the file; name it **MUSIC**.

14. Close the document window.

Presents...

its annual *spring music festival*
on
Friday, May 12, 1995
at
Bridgewater Auditorium
8:00 p.m.

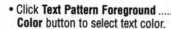 Tickets are on sale at the box office.

CREATE A TEXTART IMAGE

1. Place insertion point where you want to insert the image.

2. Click **Graphics** .... Alt + G

3. Click **TextArt** X

   OR

   Click **TextArt** button on Toolbar .... ABC

4. Click in Text box and enter desired text.

5. Click **Font** list arrow and select desired font.

6. Click **Font style** list arrow ...... Alt + N and select desired style, if applicable.

7. Click desired shape on shape palette.

To make optional changes:

- Click **Special Characters** button .... to insert special characters in text box.

- Click **Text Pattern Foreground Color** button to select text color.

- Click **Text Outline Color** .... button to select outline color.

- Click **Outline Width** button............ to select outline thickness.

- Click **Shadow Color** button .... to select desired shadow color.

To rotate text box:

Click **Rotation** button and drag on a rotation handle in desired direction.

OR

- Click **Rotation** .... Alt + R

- Click **Rotation** .... R

- Click Rotation amount.

- Click **Apply** .... Alt + A

To return to your document:

Click anywhere outside the text image.

EXERCISE

CREATING FIGURE BOXES 101

NOTES:

■ A **newsletter** is a document used by an organization to communicate information about an event, news of general interest, or information regarding new products.

■ Newsletters consist of several parts:

Nameplate — May include the name of the newsletter, the organization publishing the newsletter, the logo (a symbol or distinctive type style used to represent the organization).

Dateline — Includes the volume number, Issue number and the date.

Headline — Title preceding each article.

Body Text — The text of the article.

■ Newsletters may also be created using a template *(see Lesson 13)*.

EXERCISE DIRECTIONS:

 In this exercise, you will create a newsletter and apply many of the graphics features learned in previous exercises.

1. Start with a clear screen.
2. Use the default margins. Begin the exercise at Ln 1".
3. Using the TextArt feature and any desired design, type the nameplate (American Traveler) in a sans serif font as shown. Size the graphics box to 2" wide x 1" high and place it as shown.
4. Import WORLD.WPG; size it to 2" wide x 1" high and place it as shown.
5. Press the Enter key twice.
6. Change the font size to 10 point.
7. Create a .13" thick full horizontal line (between the margins) and place it below the nameplate. Press the Enter key once.
8. Enter the dateline information as shown; (left-align "Volume 3, Number 3," center "A Publication of Carls Travel Network," and right-align "Summer 1995". Press the Enter key three times.
9. Create three columns; insert vertical lines between each column.
10. Type the newsletter as shown; note the following:
    - Center the subheadings; set them to a sans serif 14 point bold reverse font.
    - Set all paragraph text to a serif 12 point font.
    - Create drop initial capitals for the paragraphs shown.
    - Set Greek Island text to a sans serif 10 point font.
    - Enter the following text into a text box in sans serif 10 point bold italics:
      Travel Trivia: Q: What city is said to take its name from a Huron word meaning "Meeting Place of the Waters?" A: Toronto.
      Use a triple border around the text box. Use the mouse to size it to approximately 1.75" wide x 2.5" high, and place it as shown.
    - Import HOTAIR.WPG. Use the default size; use a Neither Side text wrap, and place it as shown.
    - Shade the indicated paragraph text using the following settings:
      Border Style: None
      Fill Style: 10%
    - Create a page border in any desired style around the entire document.
11. Use the Make–it–Fit feature to keep all text on one page, if necessary. You may adjust top and bottom margins.
    NOTE: *If you use this feature to shrink the page, you may need to move the horizontal line back into position.*
12. Import ENDER05.WPG below the shaded paragraph as shown. Use the default size.
13. Spell check.
14. Preview your document.
15. Save the file; name it **JOURNEY**.

AMERICAN TRAVELER

Volume 3, Number 3   A Publication of Carls Travel Network   Summer 1995

SMOKERS MEET NEW RESTRICTIONS DURING TRAVEL

Travelers should be aware of increased constraints on the ability to smoke in public places. About five years ago, smoking was prohibited on all domestic airline flights. The Dallas-Fort Worth Airport recently declared the

---

TRAVEL TRIVIA:

Q: *What city is said to take its name from a Huron word meaning "Meeting Place of the Waters?"*

A: *Toronto.*

---

entire passenger terminal off limits to smokers. Those wishing to smoke will now have to leave the airport premises to do so. Perhaps more far reaching is the law passed in Los Angeles which makes cigarette smoking illegal in restaurants. Violators

face a $50 fine for the first offense, a $100 fine for the second offense within a year, and a $250 fine for every offense after that. Be cautious when traveling not to violate unexpected smoking laws!

CRUISING ON and BALLOONING OVER THE RHINE

Strasbourg, the capital of French Alsace, is a wonderful city to begin or end a cruise or a hot air balloon ride. Its pink sandstone Cathedral and a well-preserved old town are enchanting attractions for vacationing tourists. The cost of a three-day cruise including an afternoon hot air balloon ride, two evening meals, two breakfasts, two luncheons and coffee and cakes will be approximately $567 a person. The view from the air and/or from the middle of the river is more dramatic than the glimpses of the same scenery that a passenger sees on the train ride along the river bank from

Cologne to Frankfurt. For further information, contact your local travel agent and request the **RHINE RIVER PACKAGE.**

TRAVEL HIGHLIGHT OF THE SEASON THE GREEK ISLANDS

There are over 3,000 islands which comprise "The Greek Islands." However, only 170 of these islands are inhabited, each with its own character and terrain. This summer, *Sunshine Travel Network* is offering special fares on cruises to many of these charming islands. A four-day cruise to Rhodes, Heraklion, Santorini, and Piraeus costs $799 per person. This package is definitely the buy of the season!

EXERCISE DIRECTIONS:

 In this exercise, you will create an advertisement using two, balanced newspaper columns and graphics.

1. Start with a clear screen.

2. Use the default left and right margins. Set .5" top and bottom margins.

3. Center the page top to bottom.

4. Import CRANE_J.WPG graphic.

5. Size the graphic to approximately 2.15" wide x 1.35" tall.

6. Copy the graphic five times. Size and position each to approximately the same as those shown in the exercise.

7. Use the Advance feature to bring the insertion point to Ln. 3.99" on the page.

8. Create two balanced newspaper columns.

9. Type the exercise as shown.

10. Create a shadow paragraph border around the last paragraph as shown. Use a button fill.

11. Full justify all text.

12. Turn off the column feature.

13. Copy each of the graphics and position them below the text as shown. Flip each horizontally and rotate each -15. degrees.

14. Press enter enough times to bring the insertion point to approximately 9.99" on the page.

15. Type the bottom text in serif 10 point. Use the letter S and the Wingding font to create the symbols between words. Set the justification to All.

16. Create a full horizontal line above and below the name and address information. Use the default line thickness.

17. Create a Thick/Thin2 page border.

18. Preview the exercise.

19. Print one copy.

20. Save the file; name it **CONDOR**.

21. Close the document window.

The **CALIFORNIA CONDOR**, a vulture, is the largest flying land bird in North America and makes its home in Southern California. Black Feathers cover most of the bird's body, except for the white area on the underside of the condor's wings. The neck and head have no feathers and are red-orange color. The condor is a unique bird because it does not build a nest but lays its eggs in caves, holes or among rocks. It is also a particularly strong flier. It can soar and glide in the air for long distances.

By the end of the 1980s, only 30 condors remained in the United States. The diminished number of condors is the result of hunting. The growth of urban areas in Southern California also poses a threat to the natural habitat of the bird. Help us to **SAVE THE SPECIES**.

Write to your Congressperson and local government officials to inform them of your support of more land for sanctuaries to help keep the condor alive.

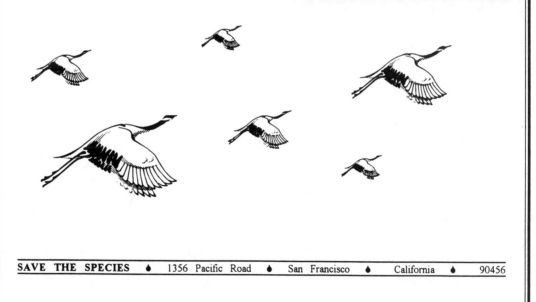

SAVE THE SPECIES ◆ 1356 Pacific Road ◆ San Francisco ◆ California ◆ 90456

LESSON 12
SUMMARY EXERCISE B

EXERCISE DIRECTIONS:

1. Create the magazine cover shown below.

2. Set top and bottom margins to .5".

3. Use any desired TextArt design to create the heading.

4. Create a full horizontal line using any desired thickness.

5. Insert the text below the horizontal line as shown in a sans serif 14 point font.

6. Import WORLD.WPG as the top graphic; and WINDMILL.WPG as the bottom graphic.

7. Size the bottom graphic to 5" wide x 2.5" tall. Scale the X and Y axis to 1.0.

8. Create the text box shown using a sans serif 14 point font.

9. Use 10% fill and a dashed border for the text box.

10. Create a button border around the bottom graphic.

11. Preview your document.

12. Print one copy.

13. Save the file; name it **MAGAZINE**.

14. Close the document window.

VACATIONING

june 1995   volume 16 number 3

In This Issue:

■ Dining in the Bahamas
■ Fishing Vacations
■ Safaris Anyone?
■ Skiing in the Alps
■ The Windmills of Holland

The Windmills of Holland

LESSON 13

Exercises 102–110

- Using a Template to Create:

  Letter

  Memo

  Fax Cover Sheet

  Calendar

  Résumé

  Newsletter

  Envelope

- Creating a Letter/Envelope Using Letter Expert Template

- Envelopes

- Labels

EXERCISE

CREATING A MEMO USING A TEMPLATE

NOTES:

- A **template** is a skeleton document that may contain formatting, graphics and/or text. It may be used to create documents that are used over and over again.

- Using WordPerfect's predesigned templates, you can create documents such as newsletters, menus, faxes, letters and résumés (as well as other documents).

- After selecting the Group you desire in the New Document dialog box, you must select the actual template. For each template, there are usually several styles from which to choose. The memo group provides four styles: Contemporary, Cosmopolitan, Traditional and Trimline. Each template style is designed to communicate a different feeling, as indicated by its name.

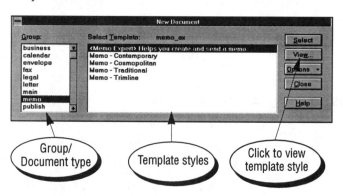

- Many groups also offer an Expert option *(note <MemoExpert> option above)*. (The Expert option will be covered in Exercise 104.)

- If you select Memo-Contemporary as your desired template, you will be prompted to supply the name of the recipient and the subject. The date is pulled from the computer's memory and automatically inserted in the proper location. After entering the prompt information, you are ready to type the body of your memo.

Note the Contemporary memo style illustrated in the exercise.

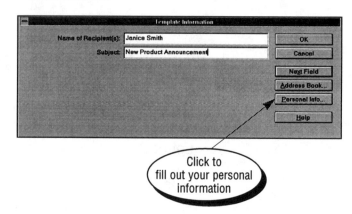

- If you use templates often, you may fill out the Personal Information dialog box which asks you to insert your name, title, company name, address, phone and fax number. When the template needs any of this information, it automatically pulls it from the personal information file it has saved for you. The Personal Information dialog box is shown below.

- The first time you open a template, you will be prompted to enter your personal information. Choose OK at the Personalize Your Templates message.

EXERCISE DIRECTIONS:

In this exercise, you will use templates to create a memorandum. Once you insert your personal information, you do not need to do it again for other templates.

1. Start with a clear screen.

2. Use the Contemporary Memo template to create the memo illustrated below.

3. Fill in the Personal Information form using the following information:

Name:	Your name
Title:	Manager
Organization:	Video Conferencing Centers
Address:	2323 Image Street
City, State ZIP:	Baldwin, NY 11543
Telephone:	(516) 555-5555
Fax:	(516) 555-0000

4. Use the following information when prompted:

Recipient's name:	Janice Smith
Subject:	New Product Announcement

5. Type the memo text as shown.

6. Print one copy.

7. Save the file; name it **ANNOUNCE**.

8. Close the document window.

Interoffice
M E M O R A N D U M

to: Janice Smith
from: Your name
subject: New Product Announcement
date: February 6, 1995

The New Product Development Committee will meet on Thursday at 10 a.m. to discuss the details of the MicroForm announcement.

We will need to prepare a press release later this month and plan for promotion. Please bring development files with you.

ACCESS TEMPLATES

1. Click **File** .... `Alt` + `F`
2. Click **New** .... `N`
3. Highlight **Group** .... `Alt` + `G`
4. Click **Template** style............. `Alt` + `T`
5. Click **Select** .... `Alt` + `S`

To fill in Personal Information:
a. Click **Personal Info** button. `Alt` + `P`
b. Type personal information.
c. Click **OK** .... `Enter`
6. Type prompted information.

7. Click **OK** .... `Enter`
8. Type document body text.

EXERCISE

▪ CREATING A LETTER USING A TEMPLATE ▪ USING THE ADDRESS BOOK

103

NOTES:

▪ Like memos, when you select a letter template from the New Document dialog box, you are provided with several template styles from which to choose. Each letter style contains a designed letterhead in the style indicated by its name. Letterhead information is automatically inserted from the Personal Information file you created earlier.

▪ If you desire a letter without a letterhead, you can select the Letter-Blank Letterhead option. (The <Letter Expert> option will be covered in Exercise 104.)

▪ The Letter Format preview window displays the style in which your document will format. Full-block letter style (the default) is noted below the preview window. WordPerfect provides three other formatting styles from which to choose: modified-block style, semi-block or simplified.

▪ After typing the recipient's name, address and the salutation in the appropriate windows in the Letter Format dialog box and clicking OK, a document window displays for you to enter the body text of your letter. The date is pulled from the computer's memory and is automatically inserted in the proper location on the letter. Note that a new Toolbar appears with buttons appropriate for the specific type of document you are creating.

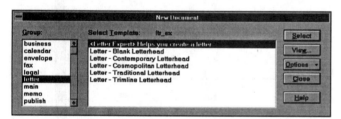

▪ After selecting the letter style you desire, a Letter dialog box appears:

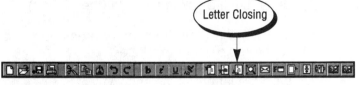

Letter Closing

- After completing the body of the letter, click the Letter Closing button on the new Toolbar ▣. In the Letter Closing dialog box which follows, select an appropriate closing and indicate if you wish to include the Writer's Initials and/or the Typist's Initials and/or an Enclosure(s) notation. You may also indicate to whom you wish copies sent in the Courtesy Copies To text box.

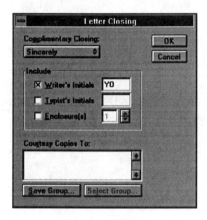

- Your name and title will be pulled from the Personal Information file you created earlier and inserted properly below the closing.

Using the Address Book

- The **address book** allows you to save names and addresses of people to whom you frequently send letters, memos and faxes. Once the name and address information has been entered, you can quickly retrieve it when you need to enter the recipient's name, address and the salutation in the Letter dialog box.

- The Address Book feature may be accessed by clicking the Address Book button in the Letter dialog box. In the Template Address Book dialog box which follows, click Add to enter one person's name and address information.

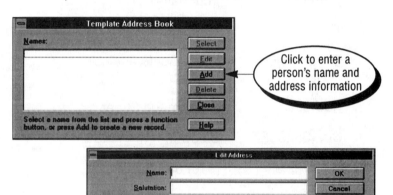

Click to enter a person's name and address information

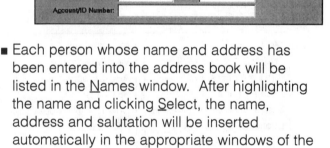

- Each person whose name and address has been entered into the address book will be listed in the Names window. After highlighting the name and clicking Select, the name, address and salutation will be inserted automatically in the appropriate windows of the Letter dialog box *(see illustration above)*.

EXERCISE DIRECTIONS:

In this exercise, you use will create two address book entries. You will then create a letter using the Traditional Letterhead template and use one of the address book entries for your inside address and salutation.

1. Start with a clear screen.

2. Use the Traditional Letterhead template to create the letter as illustrated on the right.

3. If you have not already done so in the previous exercise, fill in the Personal Information form using the following information:

Name:	Your name
Title:	Manager
Organization:	Video Conferencing Centers
Address:	2323 Image Street
City, State ZIP:	Baldwin, NY 11543
Telephone:	(516) 555-5555
Fax:	(516) 555-0000

4. Create two address book entries, inserting the information below into the appropriate spaces. Leave the Account/ID Number space blank.

Ms. Kirti Naik	Mr. Adam Roth
Director	Vice President
Kirti Enterprises, Inc.	ABC Corporation
2333 Ivy Lane	55 Oak Drive
Seacaucus, NJ 07094-3606	New York, NY 10021
phone: (201) 666-1111	phone: (212) 555-1111
fax: (201) 666-2222	fax: (212) 555-2222
Dear Ms. Naik:	Dear Mr. Roth:

5. Use the full-block letter style (the default).

6. Select Adam Roth from the address book list as the recipient of this letter.

7. Type the letter text as shown.

   NOTE: Press Enter once at the end of each paragraph. The paragraph format is set to add 1.75" spacing between paragraphs.

8. Use *Sincerely* as your letter closing (the default). Include the writer's initials (your own) and an enclosure notation.

9. Spell check.

10. Print one copy.

11. Save the file; name it **VIDEO**.

12. Close the document window.

VIDEO CONFERENCING CENTERS
2323 IMAGE STREET
BALDWIN, NY 11543
(516) 555-5555
FAX: (516) 555-0000

February 14, 1995

Mr. Adam Roth
Vice President
ABC Corporation
55 Oak Drive
New York, NY 10021

Dear Mr. Roth:

Thank you for your interest in our new video-conferencing service centers.

Now, there's a way to have a face-to-face meeting with business associates or relatives across the country without the time and expense of travel. At our video conferencing center, it is easier and more affordable than ever. You can see and talk to people thousands of miles away *without* leaving town.

The enclosed brochure will give you all the details you need to book and plan a video conference, including a cost breakdown.

If you have any further questions that the brochure cannot answer, please do not hesitate to phone me at 1-800-555-5555.

Sincerely,

Your name
Manager

YO
Enclosure

CREATE ADDRESS BOOK

1. Click **File** .... `Alt` + `F`
2. Click **New** .... `N`
3. Select **Group** .... `Alt` + `G`

   NOTE: Select a group that requires an address (such as fax or letter).

4. Select **Template** .... `Alt` + `T`
5. Click **Select** .... `Alt` + `S`
6. Click **Address Book** .... `Alt` + `A`
7. Click **Add** .... `Alt` + `A`
8. Fill out template with desired information.
9. Repeat steps 7 and 8 for each person you wish to add.
10. Click **Close** .... `Alt` + `C`

USE ADDRESS BOOK AND ACCESS LETTER TEMPLATE

1. Click **File** .... `Alt` + `F`
2. Click **New** .... `N`
3. Click document type .... `Alt` + `G`
   from **Group** list.
4. Click document style .... `Alt` + `T`
   from **Select Template** list.
5. Click **Select** .... `Alt` + `S`
6. Click **Address Book** .... `Alt` + `A`
7. Highlight desired .... `Alt` + `N`
   recipient's **Name**.
8. Click **Select** .... `Alt` + `S`

   If you desire to change letter style:

   a. Click **Full-Block** list arrow.

   b. Select desired letter style.

9. Click **OK** .... `Enter`
10. Type document body text.
11. Click **Letter closing** ....
    button on Toolbar.
12. Specify one or all of the following closing options:

    • **Complimentary Closing** ..... `Alt` + `M`

    • **Writer's Initials** .... `Alt` + `W`

    • **Typist's Initials** .... `Alt` + `T`

    • **Enclosure(s)** .... `Alt` + `E`

    • **Cou_r_tesy Copies To** .... `Alt` + `R`

13. Click **OK** .... `Enter`

EXERCISE

▪ USING THE EXPERT FEATURE ▪ PREPARING AN ENVELOPE USING EXPERT

104

NOTES:

Using the Expert Feature

▪ Some groups contain an expert option (such as <Memo Expert>, <Letter Expert>, <Fax Expert>, etc.) as one of the document styles listed in the New Document dialog box.

▪ The Expert option walks you through the steps for creating and sending a document.

▪ When you access <Letter Expert>, for example, the following dialog box appears in which you must choose the template style you desire.

▪ After clicking the Next> button, follow the prompts to complete your letter. *(See keystrokes, page 385.)*

▪ After completing the closing of your letter and clicking OK, you can have Letter Expert perform one or more of the Finish Options listed in the Letter Expert dialog box:

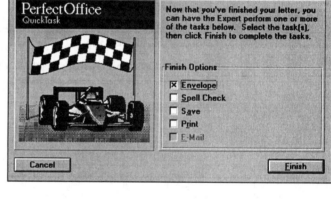

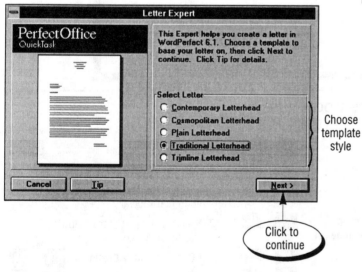

Choose template style

Click to continue

Preparing an Envelope Using Expert

- If you select Envelope as one of the Finish tasks you wish Expert to perform, an Envelope dialog box appears.

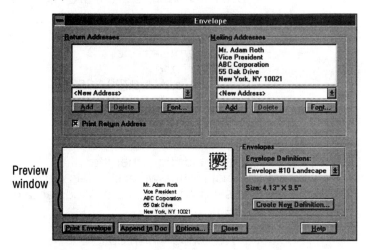

- WordPerfect automatically retrieves the mailing address into the Mailing Addresses window from the letter which is on screen.

- The preview window displays how your envelope will appear when printed.

- If you desire a return address, you may type it in the Return Addresses window. To insure that the return address is printed, click the Print Return Address check box.

- Clicking the Append to Doc button inserts the envelope file at the end of your document so you can print it at a later time (it will be saved as part of your document file).

- The Print Envelope button allows you to print your envelope without appending it to the document.

   NOTE: Envelope options will be covered in Exercise 109.

EXERCISE DIRECTIONS:

 In this exercise, you will use Letter Expert to create a full-block letter.

1. Start with a clear screen.

2. Use Letter Expert and the Cosmopolitan Letterhead. Create a letterhead from the text shown on the right.

3. If you have not already done so in the previous exercises, fill in the Personal Information form using the following information:

Name:	Your name
Title:	Manager
Organization:	Video Conferencing Centers
Address:	2323 Image Street
City, State ZIP:	Baldwin, NY 11543
Telephone:	(516) 555-5555
Fax:	(516) 555-0000

4. Select Kirti Naik from the address book list (which you created in Exercise 103) as the recipient of this letter.

NOTE: If you did not enter Ms. Naik's information into the address book, her address information is:

Ms. Kirti Niak
Director
Kirti Enterprises, Inc.
2333 Ivy Lane
Seacaucus, NJ 07094-3606

5. Type the body of the letter. When you are ready for the closing, click Continue.

6. Select a letter closing (other than the default). Include the writer's initials (your own) and send copies to Peter Wooster and Nancy Chen.

7. Select the following Finish options:

    *   Envelope — Do not include a return address; append the envelope to the document.

    *   Spell Check

    *   Save — Name the file **RESPONSE**.

    *   Print — Print one copy of the letter and envelope.

8. Close the document window.

We are in receipt of your duplicate invoice #2222.

Please accept our apology for the long delay in paying these charges. When we checked our records, we found that a check was, in fact, issued in August. We are not certain why the check did not get to you.

We have stopped payment on check #291, and we are sending you today a new check for the full amount of your invoice.

Again, we apologize for any inconvenience this has caused you.

USING EXPERT

1. Click **F**ile .... **Alt** + **F**

2. Click **N**ew .... **N**

3. Click **Letter** in **G**roup window **Alt** + **G**

4. Click **<Letter Expert>** .... **Alt** + **T** in Select **T**emplate window.

5. Click **S**elect .... **Alt** + **S**

6. Click radio button of desired style:

   • **C**ontemporary Letterhead .. **Alt** + **C**

   • C**o**smopolitan Letterhead ... **Alt** + **O**

   • P**l**ain Letterhead .... **Alt** + **L**

   • T**r**aditional Letterhead .... **Alt** + **R**

   • Tr**i**mline Letterhead .... **Alt** + **I**

7. Click **N**ext .... **Alt** + **N**

8. Type recipient's name .... **Alt** + **R** and address in **R**ecipient's **Name and Address** window.

9. Type salutation .... **Alt** + **S** in **S**alutation window.

   OR

   Select an address from the address book.

10. Click **OK** .... **Enter**

11. Click **N**ext button .... **Alt** + **N**

12. Click in document window.

13. Type the body of the letter.

14. Click **C**ontinue .... **C**

15. Select desired Closing options:

   • **C**omplimentary Closing ..... **Alt** + **M**

   • **W**riter's Initials .... **Alt** + **W**

   • **T**ypist's Initials .... **Alt** + **T**

   • **E**nclosure(s) .... **Alt** + **E**

   • **C**ourtesy Copies To .... **Alt** + **R**

16. Click **OK** .... **Enter**

17. Select desired Finish options:

   • En**v**elope .... **Alt** + **V**

   • **S**pell Check .... **Alt** + **S**

   • S**a**ve .... **Alt** + **A**

   • **P**rint .... **Alt** + **R**

18. Click **F**inish .... **Alt** + **F**

   If Env**elope was selected:**

   Click **P**rint Envelope .... **Alt** + **P**

   OR

   Click Append **t**o Doc .... **Alt** + **T**

   OR

   Click **C**lose .... **Alt** + **C**

   If Sa**ve was selected:**

   Using procedures learned previously, save document file.

EXERCISE

CREATING A FAX COVER SHEET USING A TEMPLATE

NOTES:

▪ A **fax cover sheet** is used as the first page of several to be faxed. Its purpose is to identify the recipient and the sender of the faxed pages. You can also use the fax cover sheet to type a message.

▪ Like memos and letters, when you select a fax template from the New Document dialog box, you are provided with several document styles from which to choose.

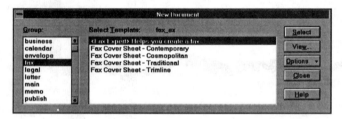

▪ After selecting a fax cover sheet template style, a Template Information dialog box follows in which you must fill in the recipient's name and

fax number. In addition, you must indicate what the fax message or information is in regard to, and the number of pages (including the cover sheet) of the faxed material.

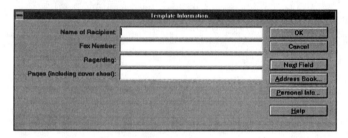

▪ If you already filled in your personal information in the Personal Information dialog box, you need not do it again. The company name and address information is pulled from the Personal Information form you created earlier and automatically inserted in the appropriate places on the fax cover sheet.

EXERCISE DIRECTIONS:

 In this exercise, you will create a fax cover sheet using the fax template.

1. Start with a clear screen.

2. Use the Traditional fax template to create the fax cover sheet illustrated below.

3. If you have not already done so in the previous exercise, fill in the Personal Information form using the following information:

Name:	Your name
Title:	Manager
Organization:	Video Conferencing Centers
Address:	2323 Image Street
City, State ZIP:	Baldwin, NY 11543
Telephone:	(516) 555-5555
Fax:	(516) 555-0000

4. Use the information shown in the exercise to fill in the recipient's name and comment information.

5. Print one copy.

6. Save the file; name it **FAX**.

FAX TRANSMISSION

VIDEO CONFERENCING CENTERS
2323 IMAGE STREET
BALDWIN, NY 11543
(516) 555-5555
Fax: (516) 555-0000

To: Brittany Williams   **Date:** May 16, 1995

Fax #: (516) 777-7777   **Pages:** 1, including this cover sheet.

From: Your Name

Subject: Cancelled June 5 Meeting

COMMENTS:

Please make note that the June 5 meeting, scheduled in my office, has been cancelled until further notice.

EXERCISE

CREATING A CALENDAR USING A TEMPLATE

NOTES:

- The **calendar template** allows you to create a monthly calendar and enter daily appointments and/or events. This is useful to distribute to staff or students, or to display as a reminder of upcoming happenings.

- When you select a calendar template from the New Document dialog box, you are provided with only two document styles (besides Calendar Expert) from which to choose: Monthly Calendar—Landscape orientation and Monthly Calendar—Portrait orientation.

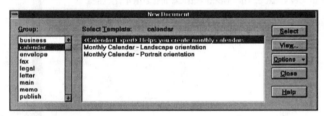

- **Orientation** refers to the way the paper is positioned. If the page is taller than it is wide (8.5" x 11"), it is said to be in **portrait orientation**; if the page is wider than it is tall (11" x 8.5"), it is said to be in **landscape orientation**.

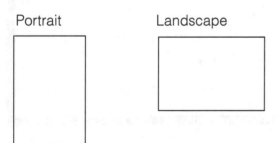

Portrait   Landscape

- Only the Calendar Expert feature provides you with Calendar Template styles like those used for memos, letters and faxes.

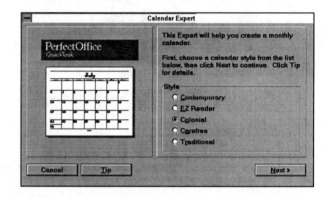

- After selecting a calendar style, you must indicate the desired month and year of your calendar in the Calendar dialog box.

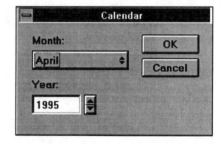

- When the calendar appears, you may click in each date (or use the Tab key to advance from day to day) and enter desired appointments or events.

December

Sunday	Monday	Tuesday	Wednesday	Thursday	Friday	Saturday
					1	2
3	4	5 Meeting: ABC Partners 3 p.m.	6	7	8 Department Meeting: Accounting 10 a.m.	9
10	11 Denver Conference Out of Office	12 Denver Conference Out of Office	13 Denver Conference Out of Office	14 Denver Conference Out of Office	15	16
17	18 Lunch: Jordan Hynes 12 noon	19 Holiday Party: Plaza Hotel 6 p.m.	20	21	22	23
24 / 31	25 Office Closed	26	27	28	29	30

1995

EXERCISE DIRECTIONS:

1. Start with a clear screen.

2. Use the Monthly Calendar—Landscape orientation template to create a calendar for the month of December 1995. Use any desired template style.

3. Enter the following appointments and events:

December 5:	Meeting: ABC Partners 3 p.m.
December 8:	Department Meeting: Accounting 10 a.m.
December 11-14:	**Denver Conference Out of Office**
December 18:	Lunch: Jordan Hynes 12 noon
December 19:	Holiday Party: Plaza Hotel 6 p.m.
December 25:	**Office Closed**

4. Print one copy.

5. Save the file; name it **CALENDAR**.

6. Close the document window.

EXERCISE

CREATING A RESUME USING A TEMPLATE
107

NOTES:

■ A **résumé** is a document which lists your experience, skills and abilities. It is used to gain employment.

■ A résumé is usually enclosed with a **letter of application** and sent to a prospective employer.

■ Résumé formats vary, depending on the extent of your education and work experience. Unless education and work experience are extensive, résumés should not exceed one page.

■ WordPerfect provides three résumé template styles: Contemporary, Cosmopolitan and Traditional.

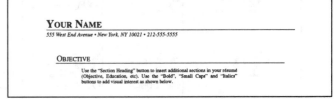

Traditional

■ Your education and work experience should be listed beginning with the most recent.

■ Résumés should contain references. A reference is someone who can attest to your academic, professional abilities and/or personal qualities.

■ If a section is not included in the template, you may insert one by clicking the Section Heading button on the new Toolbar which appears when you access résumé templates.

Contemporary

Cosmopolitan

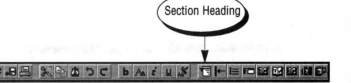

■ To insert your résumé information on the template, highlight the text you wish to replace and type the new information.

EXERCISE DIRECTIONS:

 In this exercise, you will create a résumé using the résumé template.

1. Start with a clear screen.

2. Access the Contemporary Resume template.

3. Use the information from the résumé shown on the following page to create a résumé with the template.

4. Use the Section Heading button to insert an additional section for Hobbies and References.

5. Spell check.

6. Print one copy.

7. Save the file; name it **RESUME**.

```
                                    Your Name
                                 555 West Avenue
                             Staten Island, NY  10314
                                 (718) 654-9870


OBJECTIVE: To secure a responsible management position in a leading
           hotel chain with opportunities for growth.
EDUCATION
Sept. 1990-June 1994  Cornell University, School of Hotel
                      Administration, Ithaca, NY 14850.  Received a
                      Bachelor of Science degree in Hotel Administration
                      with a 3.5 overall average.  Minor: Economics
                      . Vice President of Cornell University
                      Management Society
                      . Member of Cornell University Student
                      Senate
                      . Staff reporter for Cornell University
                      Management News


EMPLOYMENT

June 1994-August 1994  Holiday Inn, Richmond Avenue, Staten Island, NY
                       10314.  Title: Assistant to Manager Duties:
                       Assisted manager with accounting tasks.

June 1993-August 1993  Marriott Hotel, Broadway, New York, NY  10012.
                       Title: Data Entry Assistant Duties: Entered data
                       for accounting department.

SKILLS

    . Keyboarding,50 wpm

    . IBM Personal Computer, knowledge of WordPerfect for
    Windows, Lotus for Windows, Excel and PageMaker

    . Speak Spanish fluently

HOBBIES

    Horseback riding
    Skiing
    Reading

REFERENCES

    Dr. Stanley Simon, Professor of Management, Cornell University,
    Ithaca, NY 14850

    Ms. Maria Lopez, Manager, Holiday Inn, Richmond Avenue,
    Staten Island, NY  10314
```

DESIRED RESULT

Your Name
555 West End Avenue
Staten Island, NY 10314
(718) 654-9870

OBJECTIVE

To secure a responsible management position in a leading
hotel chain with opportunities for growth.

EMPLOYMENT

Assistant To Manager	**June 1994-August 1994**
HOLIDAY INN, RICHMOND AVENUE	STATEN ISLAND, NY 10314

Assisted manager with accounting tasks.

Data Entry Assistant	June 1993-August 1993
MARIOTT HOTEL, BROADWAY	NEW YORK, NY 10012

Entered data for accounting department.

EDUCATION

Bachelor of Science	**September 1990-June 1994**
CORNELL UNIVERSITY	

Major:	Hotel Administration
Minor:	Economics
Activities:	Vice President of Cornell University Management Society
	Member of Cornell University Student Senate
	Staff reporter for Cornell University *Management News*

SKILLS

• Keyboarding, 50 wpm

• IBM Personal Computer; knowledge of WordPerfect for Windows, Lotus for Windows, Excel and PageMaker.

• Speak Spanish fluently

HOBBIES

Horseback riding
Skiing
Reading

REFERENCES

Dr. Stanley Simon, Professor of Management, Cornell University, Ithaca, NY 14850

Ms. Maria Lopez, Manager, Holiday Inn, Richmond Avenue, Staten Island, NY 10314

EXERCISE

CREATING A NEWSLETTER USING A TEMPLATE

108

NOTES:

▪ Like other templates, when you select Newsletter from the publish Group of templates, you are provided with several template styles from which to choose. The Expert feature is also available to step you through procedures for creating a newsletter.

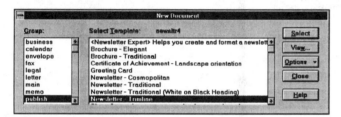

▪ After selecting the newsletter style you desire, a Template Information dialog box appears which requires you to indicate the newletter title and subtitle, the volume and issue number as well as the date.

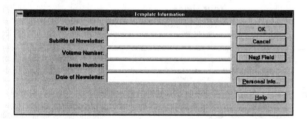

▪ After completing the information in the Template Information dialog box and clicking OK, a newsletter appears, displaying a sample headline, subhead and article text. In addition, new buttons appear on the Toolbar that relate to creating the newsletter.

▪ To create your own headline, select WordPerfect's sample headline and type your own. To create your own subheadline, select the sample and type your own. To create subsequent subheadlines, click where a new subhead will appear. Then, click the Article Heading button ⬛ on the Toolbar and type your new subhead.

▪ When all newsletter information has been entered, click the Table of Contents button ⬛ on the Toolbar. WordPerfect automatically selects each subhead you entered and creates and formats a Contents section, indicating the articles which appear inside this issue.

▪ If you wish to include a graphics image in your newsletter, click the Image button ⬛ on the Toolbar and insert a desired graphic as you learned in Lesson 12.

EXERCISE DIRECTIONS:

1. Start with a clear screen.
2. Access the Trimline Newsletter template from the publish Group to create the newsletter shown on next page.
3. Import TIGER.WPG. Size it to .75" wide by .75" tall and position it where shown.
4. Center the headline and each subhead.
5. Create a dashed border with a 5% fill for the paragraph shown.
6. Create a drop cap for the paragraphs shown using any desired style.
7. Preview your document.
8. Print one copy.
9. Save the file; name it **ALUMNI**.

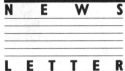

Alumni News

Vol. 27 No. 27
Winter 1995

Thomas Jefferson High School

Happy New Year from the Association!

Alumni News

---

*Published by the Alumni
Association of Jefferson High
School.*

*Alumni dues are $15.00 a year
which includes a subscription
to this quarterly newsletter.*

Alumni Scholarship Fund Established

The Alumni Association has voted to establish a scholarship fund. Each year, the Association will award a $200 savings bond to a graduating senior who demonstrates outstanding scholarship and service. Mr. Ted Johnson, class of '73, will present this year's award at the graduation awards ceremony to the held on Monday, June 3 at 7:30 p.m. We invite all alumni to contribute to the Alumni Scholarship fund so that we can build enough reserves to fund deserving seniors for years to come.

Your Dues are Needed

We wish to remind you to check your dues status for '95 on your mailing label and, if you have not paid, send your dues in now. We cannot continue mailings to those who are delinquent in their dues. Don't risk being dropped from our mailing list...Pay up now!!!

Class of '75 Reunion Planned

Mr. Robert Wascher, 1975 Class President, is organizing a reunion for the graduating class of 1975. The reunion will be held on September 29, 1995 at the Ritz Carlton Hotel in Laguna Beach, California. Those interested in attending should send a check for $75.00 per person to the Alumni Association. Tickets will be mailed to you. No tickets may be purchased on the day of the event.

In Search Of...

'34 Gladstone, Jack
"If there is anyone still around from the Class of '34, I would sure like to hear from them." Reach me at:

888 North 6th Street
Burbank, CA 91344

'52 Edwards, Phyllis
"I am searching for any alumni from the class of '48 and/or any grads who remember me. I am the administrator at the Met Society in Mt. View, California." Reach me at:

999 Horizon Avenue
Mountain View, CA 94045

'65 Rass, Peggy
"I would love to hear from anyone in my class who remembers the football season of '65 and the fun we had." Reach me at:

7658 Fourth Street
Chicago, IL 60533

Jefferson Apparel Available

Remember how you wore with pride the great white sweatshirt with the large letter "J"? Well, if you loved it, but somehow can't remember where it is, don't worry. We still have the same Jefferson apparel available. Make your checks payable to "Jefferson Alumni Association" and send it together with your order to Jefferson High School.

Jefferson white long sleeve sweatshirt (l, xl) $17.00.

Jefferson "Alumni Assn." fisherman's knit natural-color 100% cotton sweater (m, l, xl) $30.00 (full sized).

EXERCISE

ENVELOPES **109**

NOTES:

- In Exercise 104, you created an envelope as part of the Finish Options within Letter Expert.

- Envelopes can also be created using an Envelope template or completely independent of templates.

- To create an envelope independent of templates, select Envelope from the Format main menu.

- In the Envelope dialog box which follows, select an envelope size from the Envelope Definitions list box.

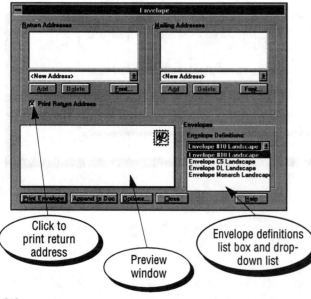

Click to print return address

Preview window

Envelope definitions list box and drop-down list

- If a document is on screen (in the current document window), WordPerfect automatically retrieves its mailing address into the Mailing Addresses window.

- You may also type a return address in the Return Addresses window. Or, if the Personal Information form was previously filled out, the return address will automatically be retrieved into the Return Addresses window. To insure that the return address is printed, the Print Return Address check box must be selected.

- To change the appearance of the return or mailing address text, you may select a desired font face and font size by selecting one of the Font buttons.

- When landscape is specified, you must insert the narrow edge of the envelope into your printer, and the information comes out of the printer rotated 90 degrees. When portrait is specified, you must insert the wide edge of the envelope into the printer, and information comes out of the printer like you normally read text.

- Depending on the capabilities of your printer, the envelope definition will specify landscape or portrait, which is the way the font prints on the envelope.

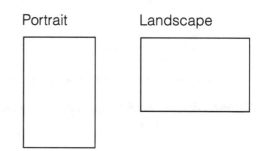

Portrait   Landscape

■ As indicated in Exercise 104, clicking the Append to Doc button inserts the envelope file at the end of your document so you can print it at a later time. The Print Envelope button allows you to print your envelope without appending it to the document.

Using the Envelope Template

■ The Envelope template formats the inside and return addresses using a template style: Contemporary, Cosmopolitan, Traditional or Trimline.

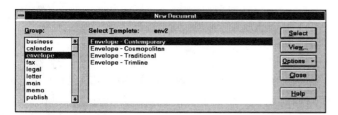

■ After selecting a template style, an Envelope Template dialog box appears, in which you must insert the Mailing Address. The mailing address may be entered by typing it in the Mailing Address window or selecting a mailing address from the address book *(see Exercise 103)*.

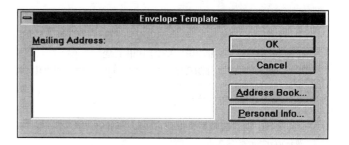

■ The return address is pulled from the Personal Information form (if the form was previously filled out) and is automatically inserted on the envelope. However, the mailing address does not automatically insert into the Mailing Address window from a document on screen.

■ Once the envelope is addressed, it may be saved and used again.

EXERCISE DIRECTIONS:

 In this exercise, you will create an envelope from a previously created letter.

1. Start with a clear screen.

2. Open **REGRETS** if you created it in Exercise 3A.

    OR

    Open **REGRETS.3AS** from the data disk as a read-only file (Open As Copy).

3. Create an envelope using the main menu procedure. Do not include an inside address. Use a 10 Landscape envelope, if available.

4. Append the envelope file to the document.

5. Print one copy of the letter and the envelope.

6. Close the file; save the changes.

    OR

    Close the file; *save as* **REGRETS**.

CREATE AN ENVELOPE

—FROM MAIN MENU—

1. Click **Format** .... `Alt` + `R`

2. Click **En̲velope** .... `V`

3. Click **En̲velope Definitions**.... `Alt` + `V`

4. Select definition from drop-down list.

5. Type mailing address in........ `Alt` + `M`
   M̲ailing Addresses window.

*NOTE: If a document containing an inside
address is on screen, the mailing
address will automatically be retrieved
into the M̲ailing Addresses window.*

6. Type return address in.......... `Alt` + `R`
   R̲eturn Addresses window.

   To print return address:

   Click **Print Return Address** check box.

7. Select printing option:

   • **Append t̲o Doc** .... `Alt` + `T`

   • **P̲rint Envelope** .... `Alt` + `P`

USING A TEMPLATE

1. Press **Ctrl + T**..................... `Ctrl` + `T`

   OR

   a. Click **F̲ile** .... `Alt` + `F`

   b. Click **N̲ew** .... `Alt` + `N`

2. Click **Envelope**.................. `Alt` + `G`
   in **Group** window.

3. Click to highlight desired....... `Alt` + `T`
   t̲emplate style.

4. Click **S̲elect** .... `Alt` + `S`

5. Type mailing address in........ `Alt` + `M`
   in **M̲ailing Addresses** window.

6. Click **OK** .... `Enter`

7. Click Print button on Toolbar ....

   OR

   a. Click **F̲ile** .... `Alt` + `F`

   b. Click **P̲rint** .... `P`

**To save a copy of the addressed
envelope:**

a. Click Save button on Toolbar ....

   OR

   i. Click **F̲ile** .... `Alt` + `F`

   ii. Click **S̲ave** .... `Alt` + `S`

b. Type envelope filename.

> To identify this as an envelope file
> easily, type the last name of the
> addressee and the extension
> .env (example: jones.env) as the
> envelope filename.

c. Click **OK** .... `Enter`

EXERCISE

LABELS

110

NOTES:

■ The **Label** feature allows you to create mailing labels, file folder labels or diskette labels.

■ Labels may be printed on label sheets or rolls.

■ Labels may be accessed by selecting Labels from the Format main menu.

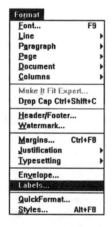

■ In the Labels dialog box which follows, you may select the type of label on which you will be working from the predefined Labels list.

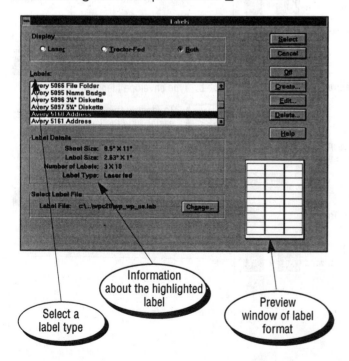

Select a label type

Information about the highlighted label

Preview window of label format

■ For each label type you highlight, information about the label and sheet size display in the Label Details area of the dialog box; an illustration of the label arrangement displays in the preview window.

■ Once the label format has been specified, the first blank label displays ready for you to start keyboarding text. Once the label is filled, a new label appears.

■ If you do not enter enough text to fill a label, press Ctrl + Enter to end the text you are keyboarding and display a new one.

■ The status bar reports each new label as a new page. WordPerfect calls these **logical pages**, as opposed to the **physical page**, or sheet, to which the labels are physically attached.

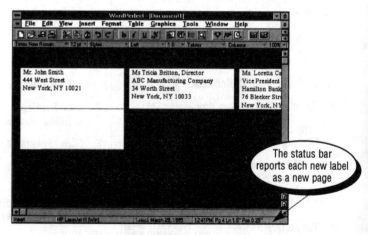

The status bar reports each new label as a new page

■ To see the labels as they will be arranged when you print, use Page view or Two Page view (View, Page or Two Page).

■ When you are ready to print, load your printer with the proper size and type of label paper you specified, and then print. When you print a single page, the entire physical page is printed.

 Smaller fonts let you type more characters per line as well as more lines on each label.

EXERCISE DIRECTIONS:

 In this exercise, you will create labels for three addresses.

1. Start with a clear screen.

2. Create three labels using the addresses below:

> Mr. Harold Dembo
> Holistic, Inc.
> 654 Sanborn Street
> Denver, CO 80202

> Ms. Jennifer Downing
> 766 Utica Avenue
> San Antonio, TX 78202

> Mr. Daniel Davis
> Acme Plumbing Supply
> 90 Plaza Z
> Milwaukee, WI 53212

3. Use 3M 7730 laser as your label type.

4. Print one copy of the page.

   NOTE: If you have the label type specified, insert a sheet of labels and print. Otherwise, print on letter size paper.

5. Save the file; name it **LABEL**.

CREATE LABELS

1. Click **Format** .... `Alt` + `R`

2. Click **Labels** .... `B`

3. Select a label type:
   - **Laser** .... `Alt` + `R`
   - **Tractor-Fed** .... `Alt` + `T`
   - **Both** .... `Alt` + `B`

4. Click **Labels** box .... `Alt` + `L`

5. Highlight label type.

6. Click **Select** .... `Alt` + `S`

7. Keyboard address for first label.

   If label text does not fill label:

   Press **Ctrl + Enter** .... `Ctrl` + `Enter`

   Use the following keystrokes when typing labels:

TO:	PRESS:
End text you are typing on current label and move to next label.	`Ctrl` + `Enter`
End a line of text within a label.	`Enter`

   Move to next label .... `Alt` + `PgDn`

   Move to previous label .... `Alt` + `PgUp`

8. Keyboard next address.

9. Repeat step 7-8 for each additional address.

10. Load labels into printer.

11. Print as a normal document.

LESSON 13
SUMMARY EXERCISE A

EXERCISE DIRECTIONS:

1. Start with a clear screen.

2. Use Letter Expert and a Trimline Letterhead template style to create the letter below.

3. Use a full-block letter style.

4. Fill in the Personal Information form using the following information:

Name:	Your name
Title:	Project Director
Organization:	Multimedia Presenter, Inc.
Address:	7677 Archer Road
City, State ZIP:	Gainesville, FL 32608
Telephone:	(904) 555-5555
Fax:	(904) 444-4444

5. Use the appropriate Finish Options to include the information shown in the letter. In addition:

- Spell check

- Create an envelope without a return address and append the envelope to the document.

6. Print one copy of the letter and envelope.

7. Save the file; name it **SHOWIT**.

Today's date

Mr. Paul Laffer
464 Brittany Drive
Gainesville, FL 32666

Dear Mr. Laffer:

Thank you for your inquiry about our MULTIMEDIA PRESENTER SYSTEM. We believe we have developed a unique product.

It is the first remote control for the PC with a built-in full color screen. You will enjoy total confidence and control of your presentation. The MULTIMEDIA PRESENTER SYSTEM allows you to privately preview your notes and your next image for perfect transitions in your presentation.

We are enclosing a brochure which provides details about this amazing new product. If you have any questions, call us at the toll free number listed in the brochure.

Cordially,

Your name
Title

yo

Enclosure

LESSON 13
SUMMARY EXERCISE B

EXERCISE DIRECTIONS:

1. Start with a clear screen.

2. Using a Traditional Resume template, create your own résumé.

3. Include a Hobbies and References section.

4. If necessary, use the Make–It–Fit feature to keep the document on one page.

5. Spell check.

6. Print one copy.

7 Save the file; name it **MYRESUME**.

LESSON 14

Exercises 111–114

- Copying, Moving, Renaming and Deleting Files

- Creating and Removing a Directory

- QuickList

- Searching

- Listing Files

- Toolbars

- Edit Toolbars

- Keyboard Preferences

EXERCISE

COPYING, MOVING RENAMING AND DELETING FILES

NOTES:

- By accessing File Options in the Open, Save As or Insert File dialog box, you can:
  - Copy a file (Copy).
  - Move a file (Move).
  - Rename a file (Rename).
  - Delete a file (Delete).
  - Change attributes (Change Attributes).
  - Print a file (Print).
  - Print a list of files in the current directory (Print File List).
  - Create a new directory (Create Directory).
  - Remove a directory (Remove Directory).
  - Rename a directory (Rename Directory).

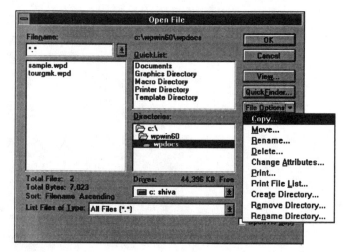

- When File, Open; File, Save As; or Insert, File is accessed, the dialog box displays all the files in the current directory. If you wish to see files in another directory, double–click a directory in the Directories window.

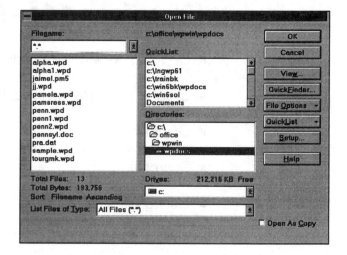

Copying Files

- To prevent loss of data, it is recommended that backup files be made. You may use the Copy feature to copy files from a hard drive or network to an external disk or from an external disk to a hard drive or network.

- After accessing Copy from the File Options drop-down list, you must indicate in the Copy dialog box the location of your source disk (where the data is coming from) and the location of your destination disk (where the data is going to).

- You may select one or several files to copy.

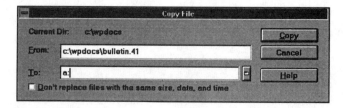

Moving Files

- The Move option allows you to move a file to another directory or subdirectory by specifying a different path, yet keeping the same filename.

Renaming Files

- Use the Rename option to give a file in the current directory a new name.

Deleting Files

- Use the Delete option to delete a file. You may select one or more files in the directory to delete. WordPerfect asks you to confirm the files you wish to delete before removing them permanently.

EXERCISE DIRECTIONS:

 In this exercise, you will use File Options to delete a single file and a group of files. You will also name several files.

1. Access File Options from the File, Open dialog box.

2. Select the files listed in the delete column, and delete them at one time.

3. Rename the files listed in the rename column as indicated.

DELETE the following files:	RENAME the following files:		
Images	Wish	→	Happy
Textbox	Wages	→	Money
ABC	Condor	→	Bird
Compare			
Receipt			

DELETE, RENAME OR COPY A FILE

1. Click **File** .... `Alt` + `F`
2. Click **Open** .... `O`
3. Click **File Options** .... `O`

   NOTE: Change drive/directory if other than default.

4. Select file to be deleted, renamed or copied.

   To select one file to be deleted, rename or copied:

   Click the desired file.

To select a group of contiguous files:

Drag the mouse to highlight the desired files.

To select a group of non-contiguous files:

Hold down the **Ctrl** key while you click the desired files.

5. Click an option:

   • **Delete** .... `D`

   Click **Delete** to confirm .... `D`

   • **Rename** .... `R`

   Type current filename .... `Alt` + `F`
   in **From** text box.

NOTE: The selected file appears in the From text box.

Type desired new filename .... `Alt` + `T`
In **To** text box.

Click **Rename** .... `Enter`

• **Copy** .... `C`

NOTE: The selected file appears in the From text box.

Type where file is to be .... `Alt` + `T`
copied to in **To** textbox.

6. Click **OK** .... `Enter`

EXERCISE 112

▪ CREATING AND REMOVING A DIRECTORY ▪ QUICKLIST

NOTES:

Creating and Removing a Directory

- A **directory** is a location on your hard drive in which your files reside. Think of a hard drive as a file cabinet; think of a drawer in the file cabinet as a directory; think of a folder in the drawer as a subdirectory.

- To create additional directories or "drawers," select Create Directory within File Options in the Open File, Save As or Insert File dialog box.

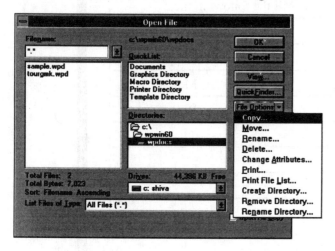

- When the Create Directory dialog box appears, you must indicate the drive and directory name of the new directory. For example, if you want to create a directory to save your personal documents, you might create a directory using your own name. In this case, you would enter, for example, c:\jane as your new directory name.

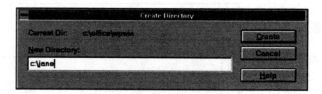

- To remove a directory, select Remove Directory within File Options. When removing a directory, the contents of that directory are also removed.

 If you do not specify a directory name to remove, the current directory will be removed. Once a directory is removed, you cannot recover the deleted files.

QuickList

- QuickList allows you to select a list of directories and/or files you use most frequently and display them in the QuickList list box which is in the Open File, Save As or Insert File dialog box. Then, when you need to access a document or a directory listed in QuickList, it is conveniently displayed in the list box.

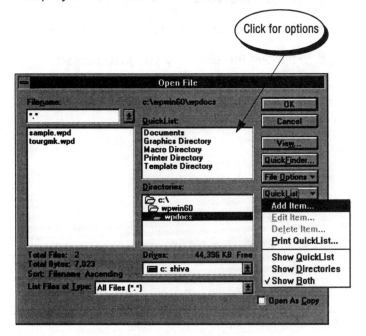

- If QuickList is not displayed when you access the Open, Save As or Insert File dialog box, select QuickList, then Show QuickList or Show Both. The Show Both option will show the QuickList and Directories. *(See keystrokes on the following page to add an item to the QuickList.)*

EXERCISE DIRECTIONS:

1. Create a new directory using your name and the current drive.

2. Start with a clear screen.

3. Horizontally and vertically center the exercise shown.

   - Use a script font (ShelleyVolante BT, if available) in 40 point for the name.

   - Use a serif 18 point italics font for the second and third lines; use a 12 point italics font for the phone number information.

- Use any desired special character to separate the first and second lines.

- Use any desired spacing between the lines.

4. Save the file in your newly created directory; name it **LUNCH**.

5. Close the document window.

6. Remove the directory you just created.

CREATE DIRECTORY

1. Click **File** .... Alt + F

2. Click **Open** .... O

   OR

   Click **Save As** .... A

3. Click **File Options** .. Alt + O , Enter

4. Click **Create Directory** .... T

5. In **New Directory** text box, type drive letter and new directory name.

   EXAMPLE: *c:\jane*

6. Click **Create** .... Enter

REMOVE A DIRECTORY

1. Click **File** .... Alt + F

2. Click **Open** .... O

   OR

   Click **Save As** .... A

3. Click **File Options** .. Alt + O , Enter

4. Click **Remove Directory** ...... Alt + E

---

5. In **Directory to Remove** text box, type drive letter and name of directory to remove.

 The current directory will automatically display in the text box. Be sure you enter the correct directory name you wish to remove. You cannot recover deleted files.

6. Click **Remove** .... R

QUICKLIST

1. Click **File** .... Alt + F

2. Click **Open** .... O

   OR

   Click **Save As** .... A

   If QuickList is not displayed:

   a. Click **QuickList** L

   b. Click **Show QuickList** .... Q

      OR

      Click **Show Both** .... B

---

3. Click **QuickList** L

4. Click **Add Item** .... A

5. In the **Directory/Filename** ..... Alt + F text box, enter the directory or document to add.

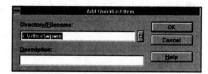

NOTE: *If adding a document, be sure to include its path.*

Example: c:\jane\lunch.

If you wish to add a description of the directory or file, enter it in the **Description** text box.

6. Click **OK** .... Enter

The Ocean Grill

is now open for

Lunch

Phone 505 345-2222
for reservations

EXERCISE

▪ SEARCHING ▪ LISTING FILES

113

NOTES:

Searching

▪ The **QuickFinder** option lets you search all files in a subdirectory for a particular word or phrase. This feature is particularly helpful if you forget the name of a file but remember some of its contents, or if you are gathering information about a particular topic and want a listing of all files containing that topic. You may also search a file by date or between dates. When the search is complete, a new screen displays with only those files which contain the particular word that was searched.

▪ QuickFinder may be accessed by clicking QuickFinder in the Open File, Save As or Insert dialog box.

▪ In the QuickFinder dialog box which follows, type the word or phrase to be searched in the Search For text box. Click the Search In list box to search a different disk drive or directory. Click the Path(s)/Pattern(s) list box to change the subdirectory to be searched.

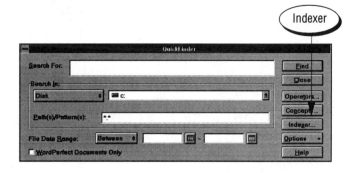

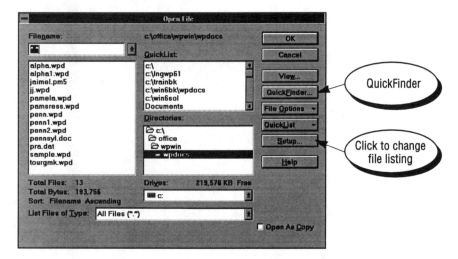

- To search a document by date or within a period of time (between dates), enter the appropriate dates in the File Date Range text box.

- Indexer lets you to search a word that was saved in a QuickFinder File Index. The QuickFinder Index is a full text, alphabetical list of every word contained in the files and directories you specify. Once you create a QuickFinder index, you can use QuickFinder to search the index for words, word patterns or phrases. *(See your software documentation to create a QuickFinder Index.)*

Listing Files

- By default, files are listed in ascending (alphabetical) order by filename and are displayed by filename in the Open File, Save As or Insert File dialog boxes. You can, however, change the way files are listed and displayed.

- You may list files by extension, file size, or date/time. You may display files by filename only, filename/size/date/time, descriptive name, or custom columns.

- To change the way files are listed and displayed, click Setup in the Open File, Save As or Insert File dialog box. In the Open/Save As Setup dialog box which follows, make the desired changes.

EXERCISE DIRECTIONS:

1. Access QuickFinder.

2. Search the current directory for all files that contain the word "computer." Make note of the filenames.

3. Search all files which contain the word "United States." Make note of the filenames.

4. Search all files for a letter addressed to Ms. Renee Brown. Make note of the filenames.

SEARCH FOR A WORD or PHRASE IN A FILE

1. Click **File** .... `Alt` + `F`

2. Click **Open** .... `O`

   OR

   Click **Save As** .... `A`

3. Click **QuickFinder** .... `Q`

   If searching in a directory other than default:

   a. Click **Search In** list box and select where word or phrase is to be searched:

   b. **Directory** .... `D`

   c. **Subtree** .... `S`

   d. **Disk** .... `I`

4. In **Search For** text box, ... `Alt` + `S` type word or phrase to be searched.

   To search by date:

   a. Click **Between** list box to indicate how to search date:
   - **After**
   - **Before**
   - **Between**
   - **On**

   b. Click first **File Date Range** text box.

   c. Type date.

   OR

   a. Click calendar button.

   b. Select date.

   c. Click second **File Date Range** text box.

   d. Type date.

   OR

   a. Click **calendar** button.

   b. Select date.

5. Click **Find** .... `Alt` + `F` or `Enter` or **Enter**.

EXERCISE

■ TOOLBARS ■ EDITING TOOLBARS ■ KEYBOARD PREFERENCES

NOTES:

Toolbars

■ There are 13 different Toolbars available in WordPerfect, each related to a particular group of tasks. Since the Toolbar is meant to access tasks quickly, changing from one Toolbar to another can actually be inconvenient and time–consuming. However, WordPerfect allows you to customize the Toolbar with commonly used tasks. You can add, delete or move buttons to make the most-often used buttons more accessible. *(See Editing Toolbars below.)*

■ Remember, only the mouse may be used to access a task from the Toolbar.

■ The default Toolbar is called 6.1 WordPerfect. To change to another predefined Toolbar, select **Preferences** from the Edit main menu, then double-click on the Toolbar icon in the Preferences dialog box.

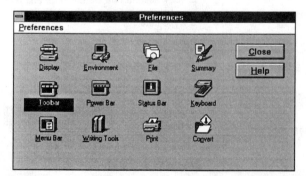

■ When the Toolbar Preferences dialog box appears, select one of the Toolbars listed.

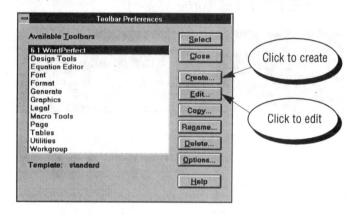

■ To view a Toolbar before actually selecting it, highlight the Toolbar option and note the new Toolbar icons which display.

■ You may also change the position of the Toolbar buttons so they appear in different locations on the screen.

Editing Toolbars

■ To create a custom Toolbar containing those tasks you use most often, you may modify an existing Toolbar by deleting or adding buttons. Or, you may create a new Toolbar and add any desired buttons for the features you need.

■ To create a new Toolbar with those features you use most often, select Create in the Toolbar Preferences dialog box. In the Toolbar Editor dialog box which follows, you will be prompted to give your new Toolbar a name. After naming your new Toolbar, select the feature category from which to choose your buttons. The feature category corresponds to each main menu item—File, Edit, View, Insert, etc. The features listed indicate all those features within the category. Select the feature you want indicated as a Toolbar button and click Add Button.

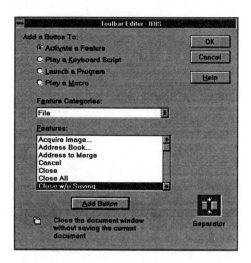

■ To modify an existing Toolbar, select Edit in the Toolbar Preferences dialog box. While in the edit mode, you can delete a Toolbar button from the existing Toolbar by dragging the button off the strip. You can add a button using the same procedure indicated when creating a new Toolbar.

■ The separator button allows you to separate items on the Toolbar.

Keyboard Preferences

■ If you were a WordPerfect DOS user and are more comfortable with the DOS keyboard commands, you can change the WPWin 6.1 keyboard to a WPDOS compatible keyboard by selecting Preferences from the Edit main menu, then double-clicking Keyboard on the Preferences dialog box. In the Keyboard Preferences dialog box which follows, select <WPDOS Compatible>.

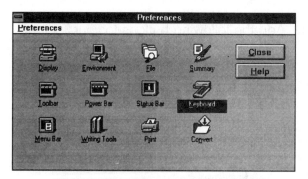

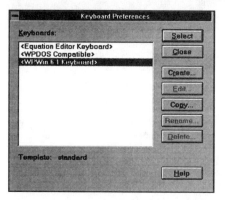

■ The keyboard definition you select remains in effect until you select another keyboard definition.

EXERCISE DIRECTIONS:

 In this exercise, you will create a new Toolbar and add buttons for a variety of features.

1. Select Toolbar from the Preferences dialog box.

2. Create a new Toolbar.

3. Use your first name as the new Toolbar name.

4. Add the following buttons to your Toolbar:

   • Close from the File category

   • Close w/o Saving from the File category

   • Case Toggle from the Edit category

   • Ruler Bar from the View category

   • Character from the Insert category

   • Drop Cap from the Format category

5. Use a separator button between categories.

6. Select your newly created Toolbar.

7. Return to the default 6.1 WordPerfect Toolbar.

CREATE A CUSTOM TOOLBAR

1. Click **Edit** .... `Alt` + `E`
2. Click **Preferences**..................... `E`
3. Double-click .... `Alt` + `T`, `Enter` **Toolbar**.
4. Click **Create**........................ `Alt` + `R`
5. In **New Toolbar Name** .... `Alt` + `N` text box, enter new Toolbar name.
6. Click **OK** .... `Enter`

NOTE: Be sure Active a Feature is selected.

7. Select a **Feature** category ..... `Alt` + `E`
8. Select a **Feature** .... `Alt` + `F`
9. Click **Add** button..... `Alt` + `A`, `Enter`
10. Repeat steps 7-9 for each new button to be added.
11. Click **OK** .... `Enter`

To add separators:

Drag a separator button to desired location on Toolbar.

To delete a button:

Drag button off Toolbar.

CHANGE KEYBOARD

1. Click **Edit** .... `Alt` + `E`
2. Click **Preferences**..................... `E`
3. Double-click .... `Alt` + `K`, `Enter` **Keyboard**.
4. Select desired keyboard.
5. Click **Select** .... `Enter`

SELECTED CLIPART GRAPHICS

approved.wpg

asap.wpg

bord01p.wpg

bord11p.wpg

bord03p.wpg

bord14.wpg

certify.wpg

confiden.wpg

bord15.wpg

bord16.wpg

bord17.wpg

buck.wpg

ender01.wpg

dontcopy.wpg

draft.wpg

duplicat.wpg

ender03.wpg

crest.wpg

ender04.wpg

ender02.wpg

dragn.wpg

horse_j.wpg

ender05.wpg

ender06.wpg

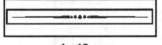

ender10.wpg

cheetah.wpg

crane.wpg

ender09.wpg

Appendix A

importnt.wpg

medical1.wpg

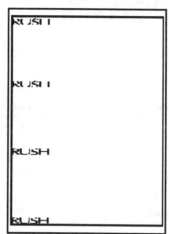

rush.wpg

rsvp.wpg

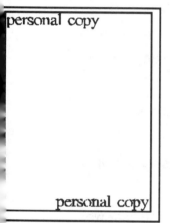

personal.wpg

past_due.wpg

winrace.wpg

silo2.wpg

windmill.wpg

tiger_j.wpg

rose.wpg

silo3.wpg

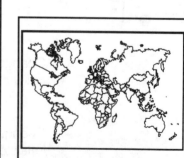

world.wpg

hotair.wpg

invitatn.wpg

thanks.wpg

417

Appendix B

PROOFREADERS' MARKS

SYMBOL	MEANING	EDITED	CORRECTED
⁓	Transpose	brochure enclosed	enclosed brochure
∧	Insert	rte (insert a)	rate
# ∧	Insert space	onthe	on the
◡	Close up	per cent	percent
ℓ	Delete	the ~~great~~ many	the many
——	Change word	We ~~carry~~ stock	We stock
Stet or	Do not delete	this service will	this service will
5 or .5	Indent number of spaces or inches shown	5 Each year we	Each year we
→ or →]	Move to the right or tab	→ it is	it is
← or [←	Move to the left	← We should	We should
/	Change capital letter to lowercase	in your Ȼompany	in your company
≡	Change lowercase letter to capital	if he comes	If he comes
≡≡≡	Change to all capitals	Business	BUSINESS

Appendix B

SYMBOL	MEANING	EDITED	CORRECTED
ss	Use single spacing	ss { I think he / will be there.	I think he will be there.
ds	Use double spacing	ds { She will not go / if you go also.	She will not go if you go also.
———	Underscore	This is <u>not</u> correct.	This is <u>not</u> correct.
═══	Double Underscore	This is <u>not</u> correct.	This is <u>not</u> correct.
∼∼∼	Use bold	This is not correct.	This is **not** correct.
◯	Spell out	Send ③ people.	Send three people.
◯⤴	Move as shown.	Try to find the (document) word in the long.	Try to find the word in the long document.
¶	New paragraph	The note was past due as of last week. ¶We know this to be true.	The note was past due as of last week. We know this to be true.
] [	Center	] Meeting Agenda [	Meeting Agenda
⟨ ⟩	Use thesaurus to replace word	The meeting was ⟨noisy.⟩	The meeting was boisterous.

Index

420

Index

Index